DATE DUE

BRODART, CO.   Cat. No. 23-221-003

Political Culture and Institutional Development in Costa Rica and Nicaragua
World Making in the Tropics

Democracy's checkered past and uncertain future in the developing world still puzzle and fascinate. In Latin America, attempts to construct resilient democracies have been as pervasive as reversals have been cruel. *Political Culture and Institutional Development in Costa Rica and Nicaragua* – based on a wealth of original historical documents and contemporary interviews with prominent political actors – analyzes five centuries of political history in these paradigmatic cases of outstanding democratic success and abysmal failure. It shows that while factors highlighted by standard explanations matter, it is political culture that configures economic development, institutional choices, and political pacts in ways that directly affect both democracy's chances and its quality. But this book argues for a fundamental revision of the concept itself. The book claims that political culture, far from being a static repository of values, is a dynamic combination of rational and normative imperatives that define actors' views of the permissible, shape their sense of realism, structure political struggles, and legitimate the resulting distribution of power.

Consuelo Cruz is Associate Professor of Political Science at Tufts University. Previously, she taught at Columbia University, where she also served for a year as director of the Institute for Latin American and Iberian Studies. Cruz received her Ph.D. from the Massachusetts Institute of Technology. She has published in *Comparative Politics*, *World Politics*, the *Journal of Democracy*, *Political Science Quarterly*, and *Latin American Research Review*, and in edited volumes.

Political Culture and Institutional Development in Costa Rica and Nicaragua

World Making in the Tropics

CONSUELO CRUZ

CAMBRIDGE
UNIVERSITY PRESS

CAMBRIDGE UNIVERSITY PRESS
Cambridge, New York, Melbourne, Madrid, Cape Town, Singapore, São Paulo

Cambridge University Press
40 West 20th Street, New York, NY 10011-4211, USA

www.cambridge.org
Information on this title: www.cambridge.org/9780521842037

First published 2005

Printed in the United States of America

A catalog record for this publication is available from the British Library.

Library of Congress Cataloging in Publication Data

Cruz, Consuelo.
Political culture and institutional development in Costa Rica and Nicaragua : world-making
in the tropics / Consuelo Cruz.
    p. cm.
Includes bibliographical references.
ISBN 0-521-84203-4 (hardback)
1. Political culture – Costa Rica – History.   2. Political culture – Nicaragua – History.
3. Costa Rica – Politics and government.   4. Nicaragua – Politics and government.   I. Title.
JL1456.C78   2005
306.2'097285–dc22   2004026762

ISBN-13   978-0-521-84203-7 hardback
ISBN-10   0-521-84203-4 hardback

For my mother,
Consuelo Sequeira Ximénez,
daughter of Julio and Adela.

Contents

Acknowledgments

A book is partly a reflection of the people in its author's life. If mine sheds light on the complexities of political development, it is thanks in good measure to the teachers and colleagues who in different ways helped me at various stages of the manuscript's preparation. I am particularly indebted to Paloma Aguilar, Sheri Berman, Nancy Bermeo, Mark Blyth, Miguel Centeno, Paola Cesarini, Douglas Chalmers, Margaret Crahan, Arturo Cruz, Jr., Frances Hagopian, Peter Hall, Katie Hite, Jeff Holzgrefe, Robert Jervis, Elizabeth Kiss, Jeffrey Legro, Daniel Levine, Anthony Marx, Uday Mehta, Ken Mills, Elizabeth Prodromou, Gideon Rose, John Ruggie, Leander Schneider, Leonardo Shinohara, Peter Smith, Jack Snyder, Alfred Stepan, Deborah Yashar, and the late Myron Weiner. To Anna Seleny, I repeat here what I have said before: Her analytical sharpness and intellectual honesty were as indispensable to the pursuit of a clear truth as her moral support was to facing the test of endurance that writing a book represents.

During the research phase of this book, I benefited from the cooperation of several institutional archives. I am especially grateful to the research staff and bibliographers at the Biblioteca Nacional in Madrid; the Banco Central of Nicaragua; the Archivo Jorge Eduardo Arellano, Managua; the Bancroft Collection at Berkeley; the Sterling Collection at Yale; and the United States Library of Congress. I also wish to thank Peter T. Johnson, bibliographer for Latin America at the Firestone Library at Princeton University, as well as the faculty and staff of the Instituto Centroamericano de Administración de Empresas (INCAE) in Managua, Nicaragua, and Alajuela, Costa Rica. The completion of this project would not have been possible without a Massachusetts Institute of Technology (MIT) MacArthur Fellowship and the assistance of the Center of International Studies at Princeton University.

In the final stages of a manuscript's preparation, when doubt assails with renewed intensity, it matters where we are. I was fortunate to be a member of the Political Science Department at Tufts University, surrounded by new colleagues who soon became like old friends. For this, I am deeply grateful. I am also indebted to the two anonymous reviewers whose incisive comments improved the manuscript greatly, and to my editor, Lewis Bateman, for his professional dedication, invaluable expertise, and life-saving humor.

Finally, as always, there is family. As with all clans, mine is both a vanishing circle of elders and a nascent garden of younger generations. Each is hidden in the pages of this book. Some I can see from start to finish: the two Arturos, the three Nydias, Olga, the two Fernandos, Alvaro, Roberto, Marcel, Christiane, Paul, Bernard, Carlos Fernando, Alejandro, and Isabella. As for my mother, she is always everywhere.

Abbreviations

Periodicals

APSR	*American Political Science Review*
ASGHG	*Anales de la Sociedad de Geografía e Historia de Guatemala* [Annals of Guatemala's Society of Geography and History]
AHRN	*Archivo Histórico de la República de Nicaragua* [Historical Archive of the Republic of Nicaragua]
HAHR	*Hispanic American Historical Review*
LARR	*Latin American Research Review*
RAGHCR	*Revista de la Academia de Geografía e Historia de Costa Rica* [Journal of Costa Rica's Academy of Geography and History]
RAGHN	*Revista de la Academia de Geografía e Historia de Nicaragua* [Journal of Nicaragua's Academy of Geography and History]
RCPC	*Revista Conservadora del Pensamiento Centroamericano* [Conservative Journal of Central American Thought]

Costa Rica: Political Institutions, Movements, and Parties

AD	Acción Democrática [Democratic Action]
CCTRN	Confederación Costarricense de Trabajadores Rerum Novarum [Confederation of Costa Rican Rerum Novarum Workers]
CGT	Confederación General de Trabajadores [General Confederation of Workers]
CTCR	Confederación de Trabajadores de Costa Rica [Confederation of Workers of Costa Rica]
INDECAFE	Instituto de Defensa del Café [Institute for the Defense of Coffee]
PLN	Partido Liberación Nacional [National Liberation Party]
PSD	Partido Social Demócrata [Social Democratic Party]
PUN	Partido Unión Nacional [National Unity Party]

Nicaragua: Political Institutions, Movements, and Parties

COSEP	Consejo Supremo de Empresa Privada [Supreme Council of Private Enterprise]
EPS	Ejército Popular Sandinista [Sandinista Popular Army]
FAO	Frente Amplio Opositor [Broad Opposition Front]
FSLN	Frente Sandinista de Liberación Nacional [Sandinista Front of National Liberation]
PLC	Partido Liberal Constitucionalista [Liberal Constitutionalist Party]
PTN	Partido Trabajador Nicaraguense [Nicaraguan Workers' Party]
UDEL	Unión Democrática de Liberación [Democratic Union of Liberation]
UNO	Unión Nacional Opositora [National Opposition Union]

Chronology

Colonial Period

1814   Ferdinand returns to Spain; abrogates the 1812 Constitution
1820   Spanish liberals force Ferdinand to restore constitutional rule
1821   Colonel Agustín de Iturbide declares Mexico's "separation" from
          Spain; Mexican Congress proclaims him emperor of Mexico;
          Emperor Iturbide pursues annexation of Central America
          (previously organized under the captain generalcy of Guatemala)

Postcolonial Period

1821   Annexation debates unleash struggles throughout most of the
          isthmus
1821   Costa Rican notables craft Interim Social Pact, popularly known
          as *Pacto de Concordia*, thus keeping isthmian turmoil at bay
1823   Collapse of the Mexican Empire
1823   Costa Rican cities of Cartago and San José wage battle over seat of
          the capital; the latter prevails but is conciliatory
1823   Establishment of the Republic of Central America, a union of
          states from Guatemala to Costa Rica
1824   Civil war erupts in Nicaragua
1825   Costa Rica institutes its first agrarian reform and begins
          state-sponsored development of the coffee economy

Costa Rica

1835–7   First term of President Braulio Carrillo
1838   Coup returns Carrillo to power
1842   Overthrow of Carrillo
1850   Coffee boom

Nicaragua

1853   Legitimist (Conservative) Fruto Chamorro elected president;
          upholds "paternal" model; Democrats (Liberals) counter with a
          "fraternal" alternative
1854   Civil war between Conservatives and Liberals
1855   Liberals contract William Walker to defeat Conservatives

Costa Rica and Nicaragua

1856   Costa Rica's president, Juan Rafael Mora Porras, declares war on
          Walker; an assortment of isthmian forces unite against the
          American
1857   Walker surrenders
1859   Domestic rivals and the military overthrow and execute Mora
          Porras

Costa Rica

1870–82	Rule of General Tomás Guardia
1882	Beginning of Costa Rica's Liberal Republic, which endures until 1948
1913	Costa Rica's landmark Electoral Law
1917	New Costa Rican Constitution enshrines a series of social guarantees
1933	INDECAFE established
1940	Think-tank Center for the Study of National Problems established
1942	President Calderón's government forges coalition with the Communist Party and the Catholic Church
1943	The political party Acción Demócratica and the Center for the Study of National Problems merge
1948	Costa Rican Civil War (also referred to as the Revolution of 1948)
1948	José Figueres Ferrer establishes revolutionary governing junta, abrogates the 1871 Constitution, closes Congress, suspends freedom of the press, and bans communists from the political arena
1951	Founding of Figueres Ferrer's political party, Partido Liberación Nacional (PLN)
1953	Figueres Ferrer elected president
1958	PLN splits; opposition candidate Mario Echendi elected president; PLN and the splinter Partido Independiente retain congressional majority
1962	PLN regains the presidency, retains control of the legislature
1966	PLN retains legislative majority but is narrowly defeated in the presidential race by Unificacion Nacional; José Joaquín Trejos elected president
1970	Figueres Ferrer elected president again; PLN increases its majority in Congress
1974	PLN loses its congressional majority; its presidential candidate, Daniel Oduber, wins the presidency; first time that PLN wins successive presidential contests
1978	PLN loses both the presidency and congressional majority
1982	PLN regains both branches of government
1983	Political elites agree to remove legal impediments previously blocking opposition parties from fusing into a single, competitive entity; marks a departure from a multiparty to a two-party system of electoral competition
1986	PLN wins the presidency and attains congressional majority
2002	Strong third contender emerges in electoral contest

Nicaragua

1893	Conservatives and Liberals combine to overthrow the Conservative Republic; General José Santos Zelaya leads subsequent Liberal Revolution to victory and sponsors a new Constitution; rules for sixteen years
1909	General Zelaya sails into exile
1912	Taft administration sends in marines
1925	United States withdraws marines
1926	Liberals launch Constitutionalist War
1927	Liberal General Agusto César Sandino begins guerrilla war against marines and former comrades
1932	Hoover administration withdraws marines after supervision of elections
1932	Liberal General Anastasio Somoza García becomes chief of the National Guard
1934	National Guard murders Sandino
1937	Somoza García assumes presidency; begins construction of *democracia ordenada*
1947	Rebellion against Somoza García
1954	Second rebellion
1956	Assassination of Somoza García; eldest son Luís Somoza Debayle inherits power
1956–67	Luís Somoza rules either directly or by proxy
1959	Frente Sandinista de Liberación Nacional (FSLN) founded
1967	Luís Somoza dies of massive heart attack; younger brother Anastasio inherits power
1967–79	Anastasio rules either directly or by proxy
1960s–1970s	Expansion of agroexport
1972	Earthquake devastates the capital city Managua
1974	Private sector, through Consejo Superior de Empresa Privada (COSEP), openly condemns regime
1978	Group of Twelve (political arm of FSLN) formed
1978	Assassination of opposition journalist Pedro Joaquín Chamorro Cardenal
1978	Broad anti-Somoza coalition, Frente Amplio Opositor (FAO), formed
1978–9	Popular insurrection; FSLN-led armed uprising
1979	Somoza Debayle is overthrown and goes into exile; FSLN seizes power
1979	Government junta (FSLN)
1982–3	Armed opposition to FSLN regime, the Resistencia Nacional (Contra), begins attracting peasants
1987	FSLN regime sponsors and codifies new Constitution

1990	Violeta Barrios de Chamorro, widow of Pedro Joaquín Chamorro Cardenal, defeats FSLN candidate Daniel Ortega in supervised elections
1990	Antonio Lacayo, Chamorro's son-in-law and chief decision maker, acknowledges the Sandinista army as the country's constitutional armed forces in a private discussion with General Humberto Ortega; transition team, with support of the cardinal, reaches Toncontín Accord with Contra military leaders. The Accord stipulates the reduction of the FSLN army and the Contras' demobilization
1994	FSLN suffers acrimonious split; "orthodox" and "renovator" camps emerge
1995	Constitutional crisis
1996	Liberal mayor of Managua, Arnoldo Alemán, defeats FSLN candidate Daniel Ortega at the polls
2002	Alemán's former vice-president defeats Ortega at the polls

Political Culture and Institutional Development in Costa Rica and Nicaragua

World Making in the Tropics

Introduction

Culture is often dismissed as no more than the exotic mask of universal rationality. Less often, but with equal certitude, culture is treated as a master force capable of subordinating even the impulse and logic of self-interest. Neither extreme is theoretically or empirically justifiable, especially when dealing with the relationship between politics and culture. This book seeks an analytically sustainable middle ground. In so doing, it heeds calls for an approach to the study of politics that integrates elements of rationalist, structural, and cultural theories.[1] Two broad arguments emerge.

The first is that because politics is about the definition, pursuit, and distribution of justifiable power, polities are at base regimes of encompassing arbitration, and as such they are crucially shaped by political culture. I define a regime of encompassing arbitration as interrelated norms, practices, and processes – formal and informal – for the airing, dismissal, and resolution of momentous public disputes among subjects/citizens and between subjects/citizens and the state. Thus, the allocation of rights to vocality, the assignation of merit and responsibility, the nature of what is public, the willingness of contenders to submit to binding decisions, the regnant standards of fairness, and the mechanisms of enforcement are all features of arbitration regimes. But the emblematic features of such regimes are also their most delicate functions, namely the legitimation of their own authority and, most obviously, the elevation and displacement of arbiters.

Legitimation and the elevation and displacement of arbiters are the emblems of regimes because they represent a judgment about what constitutes authority and who is entitled or qualified to wield it. These reflexive functions

---

[1] Doug McAdam, Sidney Tarrow, and Charles Tilly, "Toward an Integrated Perspective on Social Movements and Revolution," in Mark Irving Lichbach and Alan Zuckerman, eds., *Comparative Politics* (New York: Cambridge University Press, 1997), 159.

of arbitration regimes become absolutely critical when the need for a super-arbiter arises, as during a crisis of succession.[2]

From this perspective, the rise and fall of polities through history as well as the fray of the immediate moment entwine the pursuit of interests with visions of justice and notions of the possible. Politics, in other words, is thoroughly robust. Even "the despotism of the leaders," Robert Michels once wrote about parties, "does not arise solely from a vulgar lust of power or from uncontrolled egoism, but is often the outcome of a profound and sincere conviction of their own value and of the services which they have rendered to the common cause."[3]

Political culture influences the legitimation of regimes and the elevation and displacement of arbiters in the same way that it influences the construction and effectiveness of encompassing arbitration. In highly stylized fashion, the claim here is as follows. Political culture shapes actors' understanding of what is fair and feasible – it shapes their normative realism. Actors are realistic because in the pursuit of their agendas, they seek a reasonable grip on the possibility of things – on the causal chains that presumably hold reality together across time and space.[4] Their realism is normative because difficult though it may be to quantify normative imperatives, any seasoned actor knows that in politics, as in other domains of life, people look for compelling reasons to select one alternative over another when facing a difficult choice.[5] In the struggles and settlements over vital issues such as the assignation of responsibility and merit, the crafting of standards of fairness, and the allocation of rights to vocality, no reason can be more powerful than one that appeals simultaneously to actors' selfishness, sense of justice, and notions of the possible.

The force of this manifold appeal, in fact, helps determine how, when, and why we bargain, struggle, capitulate, or create new options and reset our limits for transformative collective action. Or stated more broadly, it is partly because of political culture that we live in the worlds that we inherit but are still capable

---

[2] Short of a crisis, consolidated regimes of encompassing arbitration settle all manner of conflicting claims more or less simultaneously. The representative model of democratic arbitration, for example, relies on the principle of election to settle differences in claims to authoritative roles, and it relies on the derivative prerogatives of elected officials to reach substantive settlements. The profound dilemmas and ambiguities that emerge from time to time are typically the concern of judicial courts, whose deliberations are the most easily recognizable form of arbitration but not its *ultima ratio*.

[3] Robert Michels, *Political Parties: A Sociological Study of the Oligarchical Tendencies of Modern Democracy*, trans. Eden and Cedar Paul, 2nd paperback ed. (New York: Free Press, 1968), 222.

[4] Actors' realism, to the extent that it implies a concern with causality and interests, resembles the theory that seeks to explain phenomena in the field of international relations. For the theory of international relations, see Alexander Wendt and Ian Shapiro, "The Misunderstood Promise," in Kristen Renwick Monroe, ed., *Contemporary Empirical Political Theory* (Berkeley, CA: University of California Press, 1997), 169–71.

[5] For the concept of compelling reasons, see Eldar Shafir, Itamar Simonson, and Amos Tversky, "Reason-Based Choice," *Cognition: International Journal of Cognitive Science* 49, nos. 1–2 (October/November 1993): 11–36.

of making the worlds that we imagine. This broad assertion brings us to the question: What precisely is political culture? Almost four decades ago, Gabriel A. Almond and Sydney Verba provided a definition of political culture which, even as it came under increasingly intense challenges, remained influential. Relying on the view that *culture* is a set of "psychological orientations toward social objects," Almond and Verba defined *political* culture as a population's "internalized cognitions, feelings, and evaluations" of the political system.[6]

Taking into account subsequent reformulations of culture in general and political culture in particular (see Chapter 1), this book's second argument, however, is that political culture is best defined as a system for normative scheming embedded in a field of imaginable possibilities. The premise here is that political actors must traffic between their interior and external worlds because they are concerned not only with practical outcomes but also with the relational feasibility of their goals and the appropriateness of their means. This crossdimensional character of actors' operations, like the compound nature of their concerns, is an extension of the imperatives they face as self-interested, rational beings who, *a fortiori*, operate in a universe of relationships.[7]

So how do actors negotiate this complex of imperatives? Thucydides gave one possible answer long ago when he observed that "the strong do what they can and the weak suffer what they must." But if he was right, how do we explain the variations in inclusiveness, efficacy, resilience, and legitimacy of particular regimes, both strong and weak? And what are we to make of the informal adaptations that in the practice of politics so often reshape formal frameworks?

The most straightforward answer to these queries is that arbitration regimes themselves provide the rules and processes for adjudicating among imperatives. This response, however, ultimately raises deeper questions.[8] For example, what accounts for different notions of appropriateness, and for the different types of arbitration regimes we find throughout history and across nations? Chiefs, sultans, kings, and emperors, after all, have proven more ubiquitous and, in the broad sweep of history, more enduring arbiters than firmly established party-states and liberal democracies.[9] Studies that are particularly concerned with democratic-capitalist development, as this book is, must contend with the

---

[6] Gabriel A. Almond and Sydney Verba, *The Civic Culture: Political Attitudes and Democracy in Five Nations* (Boston: Little Brown, 1965), 13–14.

[7] Gary Miller, "The Impact of Economics on Contemporary Political Science," *Journal of Economic Literature* 35, no. 3 (September 1997): 1178.

[8] The rule of law, for example, is generally seen as an obvious extension of effective democratic arbitration. But the rule of law itself must rely on a final arbiter; and deciding, typically in moments of crisis, who is to be this arbiter can be a contentious process even in firmly established democracies. This ambiguity helps explains why American constitutional scholars continue to probe the meaning and applicability of judicial primacy.

[9] For an excellent analysis of the democratic model, see Larry Diamond, "Three Paradoxes of Democracy," in Larry Diamond and Marc F. Plattner, eds., *The Global Resurgence of Democracy* (Baltimore, MD: Johns Hopkins University Press, 1993), 97–107.

underlying riddle of arbitration regimes. They must confront the question of how they arise, consolidate, transform, and collapse.

Redefining Political Culture

By redefining political culture as a system of normative scheming embedded in a field of imaginable possibilities, we can begin to trace and link the microfoundations and macrodynamics that hold the key to this puzzle. As with the arguments outlined previously, this one, too, is elaborated in Chapter 1. A schematic discussion, however, may be useful at this point.

Max Weber once said that a group has a "distinctiveness" all its own.[10] In this book, this distinctiveness is tantamount to a collective identity; it is the group's intersubjective understanding of its own defining virtues and practical competence. It is in the context of normative realism, grounded in a collectivity's identity, that political actors behave as normative schemers, calibrating a more or less tenable balance between their own self-seeking behavior and the collectively acceptable and relationally feasible. Through normative scheming, in other words, political actors try as best they can to conciliate the pressure of self-regard with the "distinctive" norms and capabilities that stem from their group's identity.

From this perspective, a group's understanding of its own practical competence is identity-based because political actors craft past struggles, victories, and defeats into a putatively evidentiary record of their possession and use of common moral, intellectual, military, and technological resources. It is from this ongoing relationship between identity-based narratives and politics that common visions of fate and possibility emerge.

Also from this perspective, norms are neither pure artifacts of self-interested rationalization, nor are they reducible either to individual or collective optimization.[11] If anything, because rational actors defend, manipulate, and reshape collective norms, they acquire proprietary stakes in their formation. Thus, by drawing on the "evidence" of collective competence for their individual ends, and by constantly engaging with collective norms, rational, self-seeking members of a group, as if directed by a Lockean hand, mix their creativity and labor with their group's distinctiveness. This is why even the most unabashed manipulators of norms are also cultural proprietors capable of normative outrage. Among other things, this means that while group distinctiveness is malleable, so-called cultural entrepreneurs are not themselves beyond the reach of the culture they manipulate.

The practice of normative scheming thus reunites that which can only be divorced in theory. It reunites, in Albert Hirschman's words, "the passions and

---

[10]　See Peter Breiner, "The Political Logic of Economics and the Economic Logic of Modernity in Max Weber," *Political Theory* 23, no. 1 (February 1995): 25–47.

[11]　This argument is best developed by Jon Elster, *The Cement of Society* (New York: Cambridge University Press, 1989), 125.

the interests." This reunification means taking seriously the general observation
that while parsimonious theoretical models may ignore, "greed, hatred, and
envy, as well as morality and self-sacrifice," they are not "absent in the world."[12]
And it means recognizing the simple fact that properly socialized individuals are
expected to distinguish between "honest self-interest" and "opportunism."[13]

The distinction itself between honest self-interest and opportunism, undoubtedly, can be an object of contention. In pre-Columbian Mexico, for example, the
Mexica people criticized the Pochtecas – a tribe of professional long-distance
merchants – as "greedy" and "covetous." But the Mexica political authorities
intervened in the matter, celebrating the Pochtecas as "caravans of bearers"
who "made the Mexican state great."[14]

This ancient story about selfish appetites, collective judgments, and arbitration powers repeats itself a thousand times. In pursuit of our interests, we
seek a throne, a spouse's allegiance, a plot of land. But our quests often evoke
contradictory passions because thrones, marital fidelity, and material resources
are more than the stuff of security and power. They are also collective normative statements that specify the requisite merits and duties of those who claim
or possess them. Hence Hamlet's outrage at his uncle's usurpation of kingly
authority and his anguish over his mother's incestuous transgressions. Hence
the need for socialist revolutionaries to launch moralist campaigns before seizing private banks and landed estates. And hence the careful attention paid by
capital, labor, and even politicians to the legitimating mechanisms of market
economies.

Implicit in this view of the world is not only the robustness of politics and
the centrality of arbitration to regime definition, but also the importance of
expressive articulation. The mechanics of normative scheming, for instance,
lead even seemingly "unreasonable" leaders to justify to themselves and to
others their quest for power, as well as its possession and uses. Moreover,
in order to lead, leaders must externalize and amplify – they must broadly
communicate and defend – their own compelling reasons. This is especially
true at points when reason-based choice making involves alternative political
and developmental paths.

The communication and defense of compelling reasons, as I show in this
book, take place with close reference to actors' collective field of imaginable
possibilities. This field, it must be clarified at once, is not necessarily the turf
of "reasonable" interlocutors as conceived by liberal theorists.[15] It is simply

---

[12] Robert Jervis, "Realism, Game Theory, and Cooperation," *World Politics* 40, no. 3 (April 1998): 344.

[13] Elster, *The Cement of Society*, 263–4.

[14] Hugh Thomas, *Conquest: Montezuma, Cortés, and the Fall of Old Mexico* (New York: Simon & Schuster, 1993), 8.

[15] For John Stuart Mill, for example, the *absence* of communication among even the most opin-
ionated contenders impoverishes all the parties involved. See Diana C. Mutz, "Crosscutting
Social Networks: Testing Democratic Theory in Practice," *American Political Science Review*
(henceforth *APSR*) 96, no. 1 (March 2002): 111.

the intersubjective domain for rhetorically organized assertions and contestations of the doable and the desirable. It is here that political vocality and normative realism meet; and so it is here that arbitration regimes find their primary grounding.

Rhetorical Politics: Revelation and Observation

The book's central arguments about political culture and its impact on regimes of encompassing arbitration flow directly from the integrative approach mentioned at the start. As in rational choice, normative scheming entails strategic action by goal-oriented, self-seeking actors.[16] But in accordance with key insights from structuralism, strategic action in both cooperation and conflict is embedded in a normative structure that is held together by actors' "moral grammar."[17] Finally, the concept of a collective field of imaginable possibilities builds on culturalists' concern with the construction, communication, and transformation of intersubjective meaning.

To gain analytical purchase on these moving parts, the book focuses on the observable strategies and practices of political actors as normative schemers, and on their equally observable influence on formal and informal arbitration. Thus, the book pays special attention to the rhetorical plays that make the "motives of competing parties intelligible, audiences available, expressions reciprocal, norms translatable, and silences noticeable."[18]

This emphasis on rhetorical politics enriches our analytical capacity on several counts. Most notably, because rhetoric is both about conflict and the search for commonly justifiable action,[19] it highlights not only the key points of contention and consensus that arise within a polity, but also the sources of contestation, the grounding of authority, and the nature of entitlements. Understanding

---

[16] Some rational choice theorists in political science have discarded the assumption of self-interest while retaining the element of consistency. Perhaps it ought to be the reverse. Self-interest, as Kristen Renwick Monroe points out, *is* a "good starting place for theories about how people act." See her essay "Human Nature, Identity, and the Search for a General Theory of Politics," in Kristen Renwick Monroe, ed., *Contemporary Empirical Political Theory* (Berkeley, CA: University of California Press, 1997), 282. The same cannot be said for consistency. As Amos Tversky and Daniel Kahneman have shown, "people systematically violate the [rationality] requirements of consistency and coherence" when faced with decision problems. More interestingly still, these violations are closely related to the "decision frames" that actors adopt, which in turn are "controlled partially by the formulation of the problem and partly by the norms, habits, and personal characteristics of the decision-maker." Amos Tversky and Daniel Kahneman, "The Framing of Decisions and the Psychology of Choice," *Science* 211, no. 4481 (January 1981): 453–8.

[17] This concept belongs to Axel Honneth. See Joel Anderson, translator's introduction to Honneth's *The Struggle for Recognition: The Moral Grammar of Social Conflicts* (Polity Press, Cambridge, UK: 1995), xix.

[18] Thomas Farrell, *Norms of Rhetorical Culture* (New Haven, CT: Yale University Press, 1993), 1, 9.

[19] For a discussion on this dual aspect of rhetoric, see Arabella Lyon's commentary on Eugene Garver's *Rhetoric: An Art of Character* in Lyon's *Intentions: Negotiated, Contested, and Ignored* (University Park, PA: Pennsylvania State University, 1998), 14.

these sources better prepares us to investigate the more obvious particulars of arbitration. Who, for example, is in a position to render enforceable judgments, and why is that the case? And what are the requisites for vocality? In effect, who has access to the politics of contestation and accommodation, and why?

Beyond yielding these analytical advantages, a focus on rhetorical politics also provides us with interpretative insights about the intrinsically significant role of rhetorical politics. First and foremost, rhetorical politics tell us a great deal about the construction of actors' normative realism. Realist narratives, for example, make a strong claim to neutrality, and derive their authority from rendering history "as it really occurred" and the world "as it is."[20] A common understanding of political reality – the essential stuff of rhetorical strategies – is typically embedded in this kind of narrative. Rhetorical strategies, in turn, contain clues about the identity-based normative judgments that impinge on self-seeking agendas, precisely because they frequently hinge on the construction, manipulation, and reformulation of internally consistent arguments along the following line of reasoning: If this is who *we* are, then this is what we stand for, and this is what we are capable of; if this is who *they* are, then this is what they stand for, and this is what they are capable of.

In the most dramatic contestations of normative realism, sufficient upheaval may ensue to give rise to new arbiters – formal and informal. Disruption, however, can also entrench existing arbiters and can force novel combinations of old and new. In any event, close examination of rhetorical politics enables us to decipher the nature and distribution of responsibility and merit, and the calculations and preoccupations behind the formal and informal rulings that ultimately settle disputes and ratify agreements.[21]

In all of this, finally, the analyst need not be concerned with the sincerity of the actor(s), but rather with the blunt question: Are their actions consistent with their words? In the crudest terms, do they adhere, do they deliver? Other actors, of course, may be concerned with sincerity. Indeed, the politics of trust and mistrust hinge on the degree to which sincerity is an issue. And this second issue is also a matter of concern for the analyst. But the two – actual sincerity and perceived sincerity – are analytically distinguishable. This distinction, as we shall see, makes all the difference for our focus on rhetorical politics.

---

[20] See Patricia Seed, "Failing to Marvel: Atahualpa's Encounter with the Word," in *Latin American Research Review* (henceforth *LARR*) 26, no. 1 (1991): 10–11.

[21] For example, political explanations or accounts that aim either to justify or excuse the behavior of public officials – that is, accounts that aim to influence attribution of responsibility – have been shown to affect strongly American citizens' judgments of those officials. See Kathleen M. McGraw, "Managing Blame: An Experimental Test of the Effects of Political Accounts," *APSR* 85, no.4 (December 1991): 1133–57. Similarly, the "framing" of sociopolitical issues, ranging from poverty to racial inequality, by television newscasts affects the viewing public's attribution of responsibility. See S. Iyengar, *Is Anyone Responsible? How Television Frames Political Issues* (Chicago: University of Chicago Press, 1991).

By maintaining this focus on rhetorical politics across long stretches of history, as well as on rhetorical politics at points of rupture, this book aims to accomplish three interrelated theoretical/explanatory goals. The first is to establish the endogenous sources of political-cultural continuity and transformation. The second is to identify the ways in which political-cultural dynamics shape the effectiveness, legitimacy, and changing stability of arbitration regimes. The third is to gain a more precise understanding of why some countries succeed at building both democratic regimes of arbitration and effective engines of socioeconomic progress while others fail at these major tasks. In sum, the book aims to explain how systems of normative scheming and attendant fields of imaginable possibilities help shape the development of nations.

Two Archetypical Cases

Culturalist approaches to democratic and economic development often turn on the distinction between Western and non-Western values and institutions. Civil democracy, in particular, is often seen from this perspective as determined either by countries' inheritance of such values and institutions, or by their (unlikely) capacity to Westernize their societies.[22] Eschewing this regional/civilizational dichotomization, this book tests its arguments against the radically divergent developmental experiences of two neighboring countries, Costa Rica and Nicaragua. Both are small, peripheral economies, and both are former possessions of the Spanish Crown, and as such, both are Catholic, Spanish-speaking societies.

Each case is intriguing in its own way. Each case, in fact, is a developmental archetype. At the start of this new millennium, Costa Rica is the oldest democracy in Latin America, the brilliant success in whose light the failures of others can only appear more dismal. Its old regional competitors for high democratic distinction – Uruguay, Chile, Colombia, and Venezuela – no longer pose a credible challenge. Between 1973 and 1984, a military dictatorship shattered Uruguay's strong democratic record; the same is true for Chile (1973–89); and for decades now, the Colombian and Venezuelan democracies have teetered on the brink of ruin.

Costa Rica also remains *the* Central American exception. While most of the isthmus plunged into political violence in the 1980s, Costa Rica's citizens not only held fast to their self-perception as an "inherently" civic people, but also held earnest discussions about how best to perfect and defend their democracy. (These discussions are all the more remarkable if we consider, for example, that voter abstention declined in Costa Rica from 32.8 percent in 1953 to 18.2 percent in 1990, while Latin America as a whole witnessed a noticeable erosion

---

[22] Robert W. Hefner, "On the History and Cross-Cultural Possibility of a Democratic Ideal," in Robert W. Hefner, ed., *Democratic Civility: The History and Cross-Cultural Possibility of a Modern Political Ideal* (New Brunswick, NJ: Transaction Publishers, 1998), 10–11.

in citizens' confidence in political institutions and/or an increase in voter absenteeism.[23])

Nicaragua, on the other hand, offers a sobering example of serial regime variation, having experienced in straight sequence a dynastic regime under the increasingly capricious rule of the Somoza family, a revolutionary regime under the FSLN, and since 1990, an electoral democracy which, afflicted by extreme venality and polarization, can barely begin to face its representational functions.[24]

The available explanations for these countries' sharply contrasting outcomes generally replicate the positions that have dominated broader social scientific debates about the sequencing of political and economic development. For some analysts, socioeconomic structures determine the modes of political struggle and organization – the battles, processes, and institutions that organize the pursuit of power and its distribution. For others, politics is a prior and autonomous realm in which socioeconomic structures are contested and configured. But careful exploration of the political and economic histories of Costa Rica and Nicaragua shows that there is no fixed rule as to which must come first. Rather, the sequencing of political and economic development is contingent on the establishment and efficacy of particular institutional ensembles of arbitration.

Examining the political-cultural development of the two countries from the colonial period to the present allows us to explore not only the formation of regimes of encompassing arbitration but also their relationship to political and economic development, including the issues of sequencing or timing. Once again, close examination of rhetorical politics is revealing. For example, scrutiny of political debates and associated struggles among political elites uncovers an explosive admixture of traditional and novel patterns of legitimation in postcolonial Nicaragua. First, postcolonial elites overwhelmingly agreed that the arbitration of competing claims to positions of authority ought to be organized around the principle of election. Second, their guiding vision was liberal republican, in the sense that the royal sovereign – the supreme colonial arbiter – was to be replaced by the popular sovereign. Third, however, elites'

---

[23] See Frances Hagopian, "Democracy and Political Representation in Latin America in the 1990s: Pause, Reorganization, or Decline?" in Felipe Aguero and Jeffrey Stark, eds., *Fault Lines of Democracy in Post-Transition Latin America* (Coral Gables, FL: North-South Center Press, University of Miami, 1998), 117, 119.

[24] The Somoza dynasty has been typically categorized as a Sultanistic regime. We will see that this categorization is only partially accurate. Sultanism is best described by Juan J. Linz and Alfred Stepan: In Sultanism, there is a high fusion by the ruler of the private and public. The Sultanistic polity becomes the personal domain of the sultan. In this domain, there is no rule of law and there is low institutionalization. In Sultanism, there may be extensive social and economic pluralism, but almost never political pluralism, because political power is so directly related to the ruler's person. However, the essential reality in a Sultanistic regime is that all individuals, groups, and institutions are permanently subject to the unpredictable and despotic intervention of the sultan, and thus pluralism is precarious. See Juan J. Linz and Alfred Stepan, *Problems of Democratic Transition and Consolidation: Southern Europe, South America, and Post-Communist Europe* (Baltimore, MD: Johns Hopkins University Press, 1996), 52–3.

strict preference for electoral procedures took hold in an internal Manichean context shaped by the country's colonial experience. Fourth and finally, this blend of elections and Manicheanism yielded a system of normative scheming that ultimately diminished the value of "the people," polarized elite competition, stunted state building, and blocked economic development for almost four decades after independence. In short, an emphatic attempt to create a "pure" electoral, representative regime ushered in a dysfunctional postcolonial hybrid.

In postcolonial Costa Rica, by way of contrast, analysis of rhetorical politics shows that political elites paid no more than lip service to the principle of election. Instead, they organized their normative scheming and arbitration institutions around the criterion of substantive performance. Most notably, the legitimacy of rulers hinged not on an electoral mandate but on their demonstrable ability to deliver socioeconomic prosperity to the "inherently good" Costa Rican people while simultaneously refraining from displays of excessive ambition. Here, the faint emphasis on electoral, representative processes ushered in a functional hybrid regime.

The rhetorical politics of these countries in the twentieth century, moreover, point to a difficult but unmistakable transformation of these older patterns of legitimation. In Costa Rica, the increasing valorization of electoral politics began to catch up in the mid-1940s with the traditionally high valorization of substantive performance (measured by advances in socioeconomic development). In the late 1940s and early 1950s, a functional and inextricable coexistence between the substantive criterion and the electoral principle was finally established by the interim revolutionary junta that governed the country in the wake of the 1948 Civil War. In Nicaragua, on the other hand, the electoral principle was drained of legitimating power as the Somoza and Sandinista regimes, each in its own way, sought substantive legitimation by touting economic transformation *and* political order as their justificatory logic. Both of these regimes ultimately failed, for reasons to be explored later in this book.

We can anticipate part of the answer to the question of the two countries' divergence, however, by referencing critical points of rupture in their political-cultural development. The Civil War of 1948 and subsequent junta rule in "law abiding and peaceful" Costa Rica is the most obvious example of discontinuity in that country. Less obvious but just as important is the so-called Thirty-Years Regime in "anarchic" Nicaragua (1857–93). Under this regime, an oligarchic democracy headed by the Conservative Party ruled in cooperation with Liberals, and was able to promote state building and infrastructural and economic development from a platform of relative political stability. This book is concerned with the origins and consequence of these uncharacteristic yet crucial episodes. In both instances, endogenous changes within the existing political cultures generated new imaginable possibilities.

The origins of Nicaragua's Thirty Years, also known as the Conservative Republic, can be clearly traced to elite regulation of political vocality, which in combination with a new set of supportive institutional rules provided the political-cultural foundation for identity transformation and the enhancement of possibilities for making alliances. In a brief period of time, Nicaraguans managed the seemingly impossible: bipartisan cooperation in the arbitration of power disputes. Similarly, the Costa Rican Civil War of 1948 can be traced back to a struggle among different interpretations of commonly cherished traditions associated with the country's "exceptional" identity. Most notably, a new group of modernizers deployed Costa Rican exceptionalism – in the face of perceived foreign threats – against domestic opponents. In so doing, these modernizers crafted a "realistic" research and policy-making agenda based on "dispassionate" exploration of the country's "true" strengths and weaknesses, and devised a series of general prescriptions to enhance the former and ameliorate the latter. The modernizers' agenda, however, also represented a confrontational challenge to the ruling coalition, and triggered a war that put at risk the country's tradition – a tradition that all contenders described as one of harmony and civility.

In Costa Rica, this critical juncture ushered in an era of social democratic reformism that set the pace for the national political economy. In Nicaragua, the outcome was the Conservative Republic, during which, for almost three and a half decades, an oligarchic democratic regime of arbitration presided over a successful institutional-developmental program. The regime's ultimate collapse led to many more decades of oscillation between war and dictatorial arbitration. The long-term ramifications of these divergent outcomes in the two countries would prove especially significant to their economic development.

Economic Institutions and Policies

Mancur Olson cogently argued that large inequalities in the wealth of nations cannot be explained by theories that rely exclusively on the rationality of individual agents to eliminate macrodisequilibria, or by theories that look for the answer in countries' "access to the world's stock of productive knowledge or to its capital markets, differences in the ratio of population to land or natural resources, or differences in the quality of marketable human capital or personal culture." Instead, Olson concluded, it is the quality of policies and institutions that determines outcomes, in large measure because it is policies and institutions that shape incentive structures.[25] This book, however, demonstrates that policies, institutions, and incentive structures, while crucial, are embedded in the relationships between underlying systems of normative scheming and regimes of arbitration.

Normative scheming draws on individual rationality and affects "personal culture," but is reducible to neither. Personal culture, for example, is likely to change when the individual agent is transplanted, for example, from Japan to

---

[25] Mancur Olson, Jr., "Big Bills Left on the Sidewalk: Why Some Nations Are Rich, and Others Poor," *Journal of Economic Perspectives* 10, no. 2 (Spring 1996): 3–7, 19, 22.

Argentina, precisely because individual rationality dictates that for his or her labor to be efficacious and investment to be productive, the agent must accommodate to the group norms of his or her new environment. But for as long as the individual agent remains within his or her group of origin, he or she is likely to operate in accordance with its established practices and to calculate within the bounds of the corresponding field of imaginable possibilities. Otherwise, probabilities are that the agent will be deemed irrational at best and a deviant at worst. This is why successful innovators often break with tradition not through transgression but through alteration. And this is why revolutionaries, to be recognized as such, declare themselves system outsiders and, by extension, assume a position of radical defiance.

Political-cultural development in Costa Rica has engendered a regime of arbitration whose cumulative effect has been the formation of an encompassing incentive structure that rewards innovative reformism. Such reformism generates great benefits for the citizenry while simultaneously setting limits on permissible contestation. Expert observers of the Costa Rican political economy, for example, have been impressed by the system's capacity to reduce both absolute poverty *and* income inequality. Part of this success stems from economic growth. Between 1960 and 1974, to take a recent period, Costa Rican GDP per capita grew at an annual rate of between 3 and 3.5 percent. But growth performance is not everything. After all, Nicaragua was the fastest growing economy in Latin America between the 1950s and 1960s; indeed, its per capita income rose impressively, surpassing even Costa Rica's in the 1960s, before falling to second place in the 1970s.[26] (Nicaragua's GDP per capita growth rate was 3.9 percent from 1950 to 1959, and 4.3 percent from 1960 to 1969.[27])

If growth is not everything, neither are structural conditions. After World War II, for example, Costa Rica and Nicaragua were the least socially polarized countries on the isthmus, thanks in part to the existence in both countries of a small rural bourgeoisie. As late as the 1970s, the percentage of all farms in small and medium-sized holdings was far greater in Costa Rica than in El Salvador, but the difference was not nearly as dramatic with respect to Nicaragua (7 percent in El Salvador, 37 percent in Nicaragua, and 48 percent in Costa Rica).[28]

The key factor, to repeat, is the way in which systems of normative scheming shape the imaginable and, ultimately, encompassing arbitration. This point is vividly underscored by the case of Costa Rica, where in the early nineteenth century, political and economic elites presciently recognized the stabilizing properties of titled land. As one political document explained in 1831, only "good titles" could establish a "spirit of good faith among citizens," and only in this

[26] Frederick Stirton Weaver, *Inside the Volcano: The History and Political Economy of Central America* (Boulder, CO: Westview Press, 1994), 163, 203, 211.

[27] John Booth, "Socioeconomic and Political Roots of National Revolts in Central America," *LARR* 26, no. 1(1991): 39.

[28] Stirton Weaver, *Inside the Volcano*, 163, 203, 211.

way could Costa Ricans avoid "fights" over "what belongs to whom, and who owes what."[29]

Costa Rica's emerging national state, in a word, sought to adjudicate *pre-emptively* among potential competing claimants to land. And it did so because as early as 1825, political and economic elites saw agrarian reform as part of a resolute effort – based on the promotion of coffee production – to achieve by economic means what they could not do militarily: safeguard Costa Rica's identity and all its virtues from the violent upheavals of neighboring countries. The upshot of all this is that while Costa Rica's land distribution was not egalitarian, it was broad and, perhaps more importantly, it came to be firmly rooted in property rights granted and guaranteed by the state.

Displaying similar prescience in the 1950s, Costa Rican elites constructed an increasingly broad welfare state that ameliorated the social dislocations of economic modernization. And more recently still, during the economically trying times of the 1980s, when GDP per capita declined by 2.3 percent during the first four years of the decade, it became patently clear that state institutions, coupled with pressure groups' willingness to work with the state, have enhanced decision makers' capacity to cope with and even transcend economic crisis. This capacity, we will see, is a direct extension of the state's role as arbiter of competing interests and of institutions' role as arenas for mediation and conciliation. The adjustment programs of the 1980s and economic policy making in the 1990s, for example, were deliberately embedded in intense consensus-building processes among government, business, labor, and community groups.[30] The result was restored output growth and price stability, but no significant increase in inequality.[31]

Dissent, of course, has not been entirely absent from Costa Rican politics. Key trade union leaders, for example, vowed in the late 1990s to prevent the "Central-Americanization" of their country.[32] That trade unions would oppose a low-wage export competitive strategy is not surprising. But that they would encapsulate all that is repugnant to them in the term "Central-Americanization" is quite significant because, as we will see, it hints at a distinctive sense of exceptionalism among workers and peasants, who themselves generally embrace "civil" means and support reformist means.

The legitimacy of the Costa Rican polity, as well as the reformist and civil bent of its key actors, stand in sharp contrast to that of Nicaragua. Consider the

[29] "Dictámen de la Comisión para recabar arbitrios" (Cartago), 15 August 1831, in Carlos Meléndez Chaverri, ed., *Documentos Fundamentales del Siglo XIX* (San José: Editorial Costa Rica, 1978), 481–5.

[30] Marc Lindenberg, "Recent Central American Transitions: Conclusions and Policy Implications," in Jorge Domínguez and Marc Lindeberg, eds., *Democratic Transitions in Central America* (Gainsville, FL: University Press of Florida, 1997).

[31] Albert Berry, "The Income Distribution Threat in Latin America," *LARR* 32, no. 2 (1997): 29–30.

[32] Trade union leader Albino Vargas, quoted in "Singapore, Central America," *Economist*, 11 January 1997, 42–3.

dynastic Somoza regime (1936–79). In the regime's early stages, its founder was able to garner acquiescence if not approbation among significant portions of powerful economic groups, as well as the middle class and popular sectors. The regime achieved this acquiescence through a blend of promises and injunctions: political order, populist redress, and a clear boundary between the private and public sectors.

The fulfillment of these substantive claims naturally required the exercise of arbitration power. Yet it is precisely this power that everywhere presents arbiters with both the opportunity to legitimate their regimes and the temptation to reshape them. To the extent that arbiters succumb to the latter, and to the extent that this is widely perceived as a transgression against the former, arbiters become vulnerable to charges of injustice.

The potential for this sort of slippage is particularly acute in dynastic regimes, as each ascending heir must contend not only with changed conditions but also with his own particular impulses. In the case of the Somoza dynasty, the arbiters' transgressions, by commission and omission, led to widening repudiation by the citizenry. One illustration may suffice here. Nicaragua's dynasts fomented the cotton boom – a boom that further modernized agriculture – but failed to compensate for, much less prevent, the displacement of peasants from their (often untitled) plots.[33] In contrast to Costa Rica, where elites began to address property rights as an arbitration challenge preceding modernization, in Nicaragua, the regime increasingly left small de facto holders at the mercy of the dislocations the regime itself helped unleash.

Over time, the displacement of peasants led to high demographic concentration in the urban centers. Indeed, by the 1970s, large segments of the rural population had gravitated toward the capital city, where they morphed into an expanding informal sector. This meant, in essence, that internal migrants flowed in unstructured fashion into the very places where the regime's other transgressions elicited a cacophony of normative outrage. The regime's violation of the dividing line which the regime itself had established between the public and private sectors, for example, drew criticism from aggrieved business groups, and the regime's curtailment of political rights prompted attacks from the independent press.

Modernizing business groups, traditional elites, the middle classes, students, workers, *informales* (informal workers), the Church – these were all actors who, increasingly concentrated in space, seized for themselves the right to vocality. And it is there, in that cacophonous city, that internal Manicheanism – which the Republic had managed to suppress but which reemerged newly articulated from its ruins at the end of the nineteenth century – was used by disparate groups to impose order on vocality and, by extension, on normative scheming.

---

[33] As in the earlier displacements associated with the introduction of coffee at the end of the nineteenth century, in the 1950s, peasants moved on to uncultivated lands, much of which had been traditionally "owned" by the state, either de facto or by constitutional fiat.

By the mid-1970s, Manicheanism reached a high pitch, and the polity was ripe to be organized into a categorical dichotomy, with the regime on one side and nearly everyone else on the other.

The Sandinista Revolution that overthrew the last of the dynasts arose out of this history and replicated many of its essential features. This is partly why the new "fratricidal" confrontations that plagued the country in the 1980s came as no great surprise to the participants, since "history" told both young and old, regardless of partisan or ideological affiliation, to expect the worst from their compatriots.

But intersubjective perceptions and expectations about a group's normative integrity and its practical competence are not immutable. The 1990 transition to democracy was for a moment a heady experience precisely because it seemed to confound Nicaraguans' bleak predictions. Beginning with the historic elections of that year, political actors from across the ideological spectrum bowed, with varying degrees of enthusiasm, to the political democracy that appeared to embody the spirit of the age. Hope, however, faded as democratization itself became a bitterly conflictive process in which adversaries tried simultaneously to preserve the principle of election *and* refashion constitutional rules to rig the electoral game in their favor. Today, the reflexive function of the democratic model of arbitration – the electoral selection and replacement of arbiters – is technically operative but is also a source of simmering dissatisfaction.

Nor is the substantive criterion of legitimacy binding. The governments that have ruled since the FSLN's defeat at the polls in 1990 – the first of three consecutive defeats – have to varying degrees used their electoral victories to turn state institutions into personalistic instruments for self-dealing and punitive exclusion. Under these conditions, the perceptions and expectations of citizens in general and elites in particular tend to revert to the mean. By the mid-1990s, Nicaraguans' genuine expressions of democratic aspiration were overwhelmed by an equally heartfelt lament that echoed the central theme of their nation's traditional historiography and political lore: Their land, they said, is haunted by an antidemocratic past.

The national historian who in 1927 believed he had captured Nicaragua's past and future in the title of his book – *Country of Irredeemables* – would have concurred with this assessment.[34] But this pervasive view of the nation as doomed does not survive in a vacuum. The publication of *Country of Irredeemables* itself contributed to the historiographic limitations that constrict actors' field of imaginative possibilities. And of course, so do the practices of contemporary elites. In the last decade and a half, one government after another, unable to govern without some minimal compliance from the very opposition

---

[34] For a discussion of Gustavo Alemán-Bolaños' *El País de los Irredentos*, see Arturo J. Cruz, Jr., *Nicaragua's Conservative Republic, 1858–93* (New York: Palgrave/Saint Antony's Oxford, 2002), 3.

groups that it demonized and excluded, has eventually been forced to enter into narrow, tactical pacts with those same groups. The result is that these pacts offend the sense of justice of everyone not included in the deal. At such moments, a fatalistic recognition of the past as prelude offers the path of least resistance. For if you read closely the labyrinthine tomes of Nicaragua's leading historians, and listen carefully to the folksy accounts of its most obscure story-tellers, a persistent warning rises loud and clear: Sooner or later, leaders shall betray their followers, and allies will abandon allies for a "pactist" embrace with the enemy.[35]

It is in this context of normative realism that, as rational agents, Nicaraguans organize their strategies. They scheme to prevail for their own sake while making the Manichean claim, to themselves and to others, that they struggle against "evil" forces in order to make possible a better future for the nation. The "ungovernability" that typically flows from this dynamic, and the pacts that foes must craft to survive politically, have a profound impact on the actual function of democratic elections. This function is to produce governments whose defining role is that of chief negotiator of ad hoc deals. Not surprisingly, legitimate encompassing arbitration is rendered neither viable nor imaginable.

Manicheanism, of course, can be found anywhere in the world. But it is also important to note that successful, pluralist democracies tend to externalize its logic, relegating it to the domain of world politics. Partly for this reason, the international plane is often described as anarchic, that is, as devoid of an effective governmental structure. Winston Churchill spoke of "evil-doers" when confronting England's foes in the titanic struggle of the Second World War; Ronald Reagan saw an "evil" force in the Soviet empire; and at the opening of the twenty-first century, the second Bush administration warned the world about an "axis of evil."

This is not to say that strong nationalism and other categorical oppositions that pit the domestic "us" against the foreign "them" guarantee the development of internal tolerance, or facilitate the development of a legitimate regime of arbitration. A group's intersubjective understanding of itself is also crucial. Costa Ricans' construction of a virtuous national identity began prior to its repudiation of external corruption. Moreover, Costa Ricans actually spelled out the virtues they claimed and valorized, most notably civility and harmony. Lastly, Costa Ricans specified the practical implications of these virtues: in economic affairs, for example, a constant dedication to hard work; and in politics, a commitment to compromise for the sake of the collective welfare.

Political-cultural classification, then, does more than describe the world. It entails discernment, and it shapes expectations and behavior. Commenting on

---

[35] In the 1960s, Nicaraguan political lore even integrated the Miskito term *Kupia Kumi* – the union of two hearts – to denigrate understandings between the Somoza regime and segments of the traditional opposition.

the wave of democratic transitions that swept the region in the 1980s, Jorge Domínguez wrote in 1997:

A persistent fear haunts the region: what the economist Albert Hirschman once called *fracasomanía* or an obsession with failure. Many still believe that ... democracy's worst enemies are the politicians who speak in its name.[36]

If this astute observation regarding perceptions and expectations in posttransition Latin America fits the Nicaraguan case exceedingly well, it also underscores Costa Rica's uniqueness. While Costa Ricans have concentrated optimistically on perfecting their democracy, Nicaraguans seem to concentrate on perfecting their pessimism.

I take seriously both the Nicaraguans' lamentations and the Costa Ricans' perfecting debates, though not because there is anything inherently Nicaraguan or Costa Rican about the entwinement of national historiography, political lore, and collective outlook. After all, beliefs in American exceptionalism, for as long as they persisted, could no more be delinked from Louis Hartz's *The Liberal Tradition in America* than his own work could be detached from what he called the "storybook truth about American history."[37] Rather, I take them seriously because a people's political expectations help shape the polity itself, and individuals' behavior as members of a collectivity is partly dependent on what they think is viable and legitimate given their own descriptions of the system in which they operate.[38]

The Costa Ricans' unselfconscious optimism and the Nicaraguans' striking fatalism, then, represent more than emotive responses to the socioeconomic facts of life. They are themselves constructions of different brands of normative realism. And they are concrete expressions of collective identities captured in the act of creating, through the practice of normative scheming, their own fields of imaginable possibilities. At its briefest, this is the story of Nicaragua and Costa Rica as told in this book.

The book, however, also engages one of the most enduring enigmas of social science – the complex relationship among history, structure, and agency[39] – in an effort to advance both a macro- and microlevel approach to the study of political culture. The macro-institutional conclusions yielded by this approach can contribute to a better understanding of other countries in the region. From Mexico to Argentina, encompassing arbitration in general and arbiter elevation and displacement in particular have been extremely problematic. Indeed, they have been implicated in virtually every major political crisis of the last two centuries. At this writing, the hopes that came on the crest of the Third Wave

---

[36] Jorge Domínguez, "Latin America's Crisis of Representation," *Foreign Affairs* 76, no. 1 (January/February 1997): 101.

[37] Louis Hartz, *The Liberal Tradition in America* (New York: Harcourt Brace Jovanovich, 1955, 1983), 3.

[38] Ross Harrison, *Democracy* (New York: Routledge, 1993), 1–2.

[39] Michel-Rolph Trouillot, *Silencing the Past: Power and the Production of History* (Boston: Beacon Press, 1995), 6.

of democratization have begun to dissipate: Surveys indicate that less than half of Latin American citizens consider democracy the best form of government.[40]

Similarly, the microdynamics highlighted by the book can provide insights into severe polarization and the categorical dichotomies in which it is often rooted. For Latin Americans, the need to understand the endogenous sources and mechanisms of polarization has never been more urgent. Two decades ago, the international environment exerted pro-democratic pressures on their nations. These pressures are now eclipsed by the lethal enmities that have been let loose upon the world since the end of the Cold War. Less than ever, then, can the solution to the region's dilemmas be expected to come from abroad.

[40] Eduardo Lora and Ugo Panizza, "Latin America's Lost Illusions: The Future of Structural Reform," *Journal of Democracy*, 14, no. 2 (April 2003): 124

I

Theoretical Framework

> Democracy thrives in social patterns that display certain characteristics and it might well be doubted whether there is any sense in asking how it would fare in others that lack those characteristics – or how the people in those patterns would fare with it.[1]
>
> –Joseph A. Schumpeter

There are polities in which even the keenest competitors agree on a basic understanding of politics as both the play of divergent interests and the forging of shared norms. And then there are polities in which even allies come to see politics as the machinations of master players and the power grabs of hostile rivals for whom legitimacy is no more than a cloak for plots and scrambles. Intuition tells us that while the former view may be conducive to a democratic regime of arbitration, the latter is surely detrimental.

But intuition notwithstanding, at the end of the Cold War, an old debate about democracy's universal reach became new again. In this debate, some argued that democracy was now the "exclusive claimant to set the standard for legitimate political authority." Others countered that democracy's victory might turn out to be more fleeting than conclusive, and that the equivalence of democracy and modernity might turn out to be no more than an alarmingly "flimsy" notion.[2]

We had been there before. This was not the first time we had heard proclamations of democracy's superior strength. Nor was it the first time we had heard prudential reminders of the flimsiness of our faith in democracy's sway over others. We had, in fact, heard both in the same breath. In the early 1940s,

---

[1] Joseph A. Schumpeter, *Capitalism, Socialism and Democracy* (New York: Harper Torchbooks, 1950), 290.

[2] John Dunn, "Conclusion," in John Dunn, ed., *Democracy: The Unfinished Journey* (New York: Oxford University Press, 1992), 239; Alain Touraine, *What Is Democracy?* (Boulder, CO: Westview Press, 1997), 7.

Joseph Schumpeter offered us democracy as a "political method" for leadership selection; a method, that is, for the orderly production and expulsion of governments, or in the terminology of this work, for the arbitration of competing claims to positions of high authority.

Simplified in this way, democracy assumed an aura of universality in the eyes of many. But we ought not to forget that Schumpeter also set down a series of crucial preconditions for the proper functioning of the democratic method. He presupposed a well-established social stratum whose members were "fit" to govern because, as carriers of "tradition," they were endowed with "a professional code and a common fund of views." He further presupposed electorates and parliaments which, capable of exercising "democratic self-control," were resistant to "the offerings of the crook and the crank." And he presupposed, of course, a society tolerant enough to absorb differences of opinion.[3] Qualified in so many ways, then as now, democracy appeared less suitable for transplantation to the divided societies that traditionally have resisted its allure.

Yet at the dawn of this new millennium it is precisely in these divided societies that democracy is called upon to meet its defining challenge: "to reconcile unity and diversity, liberty and integration."[4] From Africa to the Middle East, the results thus far have been sobering. Indeed, disparate opinions about democracy's sway in the world hold more than academic import because if there is one indisputable empirical fact, it is this: Robust democratic development consistently eludes most countries, while for some, successful democratic consolidation – improbable in theory but resounding in practice – becomes the very emblem of national identity.

The cases at the heart of this book represent these two archetypical opposites: Costa Rica, whose mere mention summons the idea of democracy triumphant; and Nicaragua, a country that has, at critical junctures, transited from petty despotism to authoritarianism, from revolt to civil war, and most recently, from this bleak progression to what is at best a troubled formal democracy. The book's central empirical claim is that in each case, political culture crucially affected democracy's chances and the way that democracy actually works.

Neither Slow-Moving nor Rigid

Many prominent scholars of democracy and democratization have acknowledged that culture plays a role in these processes. But typically, these scholars also attach to culture either glacial or architectonic attributes that make it unwieldy for analysts and an unpromising project for politicians and policy makers. From a glacial perspective, political culture takes a very long time to develop and perhaps just as long to change. As Guillermo O'Donnell sees it, for example, reshaping a nondemocratic culture into a democratic mold means "educating" citizens to be "democrats" – a long-term task that cannot

---

[3] Schumpeter, *Capitalism, Socialism and Democracy*, 290–5.
[4] Touraine, *What Is Democracy?* 16.

be given priority by decision makers facing the acute short-term challenges of democratic transition and consolidation. The better option, for O'Donnell, is to turn analytical and political attention to the socioeconomic foundations of democratizing polities, in the hopes of strengthening the underlying conditions necessary for the proper functioning of democratic institutions.[5]

Even students of democracy who give culture pride of place, such as Francis Fukuyama, tend to treat culture as untreatable – that is, as the most obdurate layer in the multilayered architecture of political order. Descending into these architectonic depths, Fukuyama encounters at the surface level the most pliable layer, ideology. Just beneath ideology, he finds institutions. Deeper still he locates civil society, already more stubborn than the previous two. And on the deepest, most resistant layer, he situates culture, firmly embedded in the structures of family and religion.[6]

Glacial and architectonic renditions of political culture strike us as eminently plausible in no small measure because such renditions accord with the views of the great modern theorists of democracy. Schumpeter, as we saw at the outset, posited a propitious political culture as an indispensable condition for the success of the democratic method. But he also understood political culture as a sturdy tradition sustained by elites and citizenries who, by dint of their values, habits, and skills, are themselves the living executors of the polity's cultural endowment. Similarly, Robert Dahl explicitly states that polyarchy's "chances" are affected by political culture, but he too defines political culture as a slowly evolving ensemble of "beliefs, attitudes, and predispositions" that changes in "lagged" fashion.[7]

This book shows that political culture is indeed historically shaped, but also argues that political culture endogenously generates critical junctures. At these key points, political culture itself can change at a surprisingly rapid pace, sometimes ahead of institutional and even socioeconomic restructuring. This is so partly because political learning, as Nancy Bermeo has demonstrated, can occur in a compressed time period; and, as O'Donnell observed in some of his earlier work, influential actors' experiences with particular types of regimes – dysfunctional dictatorships come most quickly to mind – can lead to shifts in the prestige of associated discourses.[8] A political education, in other words, need not take a conventionally didactic form, and it need not be about teaching individuals to be democrats either.

When discursive formations fall into disrepute, they can cause accelerated political-cultural change. But since the ideological change that presumably underlies such disrepute is not verifiable because it is ultimately internal to actors,

---

[5] Guillermo O'Donnell, "Do Economists Know Best?" *Journal of Democracy* 6, no. 1 (January 1995): 23–8.

[6] Francis Fukuyama, "The Primacy of Culture," ibid., 7–9.

[7] Robert Dahl, *Democracy and Its Critics* (New Haven, CT: Yale University Press, 1989), 262–3.

[8] For both O'Donnell and Bermeo's insights, see Nancy Bermeo, "Democracy and the Lessons of Dictatorship," *Comparative Politics* 24, no. 3 (April 1992): 275, 281.

rhetorical adaptations are a further requisite for accelerated transformation. Specifically, rhetorical adaptations can help actors reframe both their difficult choices and the compelling reasons they craft in order finally to make a choice. Typically, actors simplify complex scenarios in the keen immediacy of a political moment by crafting a clear binary opposition that takes its inspiration from long and hard experience. This means that the dangers associated with entrenched mistrust are implicit in rhetorical politics. But implicit too is the possibility for a constructive departure from fatalistic visions and destructive practices.

One vivid example of such a constructive departure in the late 1970s was Spain's transition to democracy. Widely regarded as the epitome of successful democratization, the Spanish case is most often explained as the result of interest convergence through pact making. Simply stated, a transitional pact conciliates the strategic interests of key elite groups.[9] Closer inspection of this model transition, however, shows that the transition hinged on a reconfiguration of normative realism based on memory and political learning. This cognitive process took as its central referent the Spanish Civil War, which had put an end to the Second Republic (1931–6), the country's only historical example of democracy. The process also recognized living actors as the ideological heirs of the Civil War, and *a priori* valorized the goal of dialogue between them. Finally, in order to render this goal a "possible" one, all relevant actors agreed not to contest the past. This meant that adversaries shared in an "implicit recognition of collective culpability for crimes during the war and the unanimous desire that a similar drama should never be repeated."[10]

One key consequence of this cognitive shift, then, was that the transition proceeded *pari passu* with the collective arbitration of a historical dispute. Rhetorical patterns, however, also show that adaptations in normative scheming were crucial. This was so on two counts. First, successful pact making entailed key actors' redefinition of their "interests," such that democracy became a goal and violence an unacceptable instrument for both the government and the opposition.[11] Second, although plagued by a history of political conflict and authoritarianism, transitional Spain was able to create a "consensual" political framework through the rhetorical elevation of a historically given binary opposition of symbols. In other words, the relevant actors reconfigured their common field of imaginable possibilities by pitting the promise of a "new beginning" – based on "national reconciliation" and democracy – against the specter of a return to "civil war."[12]

Finally, political-cultural shifts may occur swiftly because actors can learn to recognize the broader, unintended consequences of their rhetorical politics and

---

[9] For a review of the strategic interests argument, see Laura Desfor Edles, *Symbol and Ritual in the New Spain* (New York: Cambridge University Press, 1998), 14–15.

[10] Paloma Aguilar, "The Memory of the Civil War in the Transition to Democracy: The Peculiarity of the Basque Case," *Journal of West European Politics* 21, no. 4 (October 1998): 5–6.

[11] Desfor Edles, *Symbol and Ritual*, 14–15.

[12] For the symbolic content of this binary opposition, see ibid., 8–9.

amend them accordingly. This delicate process, as we will see, can take the form of tinkering – merely altering the old in order to create new rhetorical frames. I refer to this tinkering as *tailored communicative regulation*: the informal institutionalization of a mutually reinforcing set of prescriptions and proscriptions. Though informal, if these institutions take hold, they can alter actors' vulnerabilities, resources, and incentives; and for this reason, they may prompt actors to create *formal* rules to assuage the fears and control the ambitions that the new rhetorical regulations may incite or heighten.

Developing the Theoretical Argument

In schematic form, the argument is elaborated as follows. First, since I posit that identity shapes politics, I explore how identities are formed and changed. Second, since I argue that identity shapes politics by forcing actors to engage in normative scheming, I outline the ways that actors negotiate their particularist agendas with the imperatives of collective identity. Third, because I further argue that different systems of normative scheming give rise to different fields of imaginable possibilities, I trace the historical formation of such fields. Finally, I show how these constitutive elements of political culture shape arbitration regimes.

In approaching the two empirical cases at hand, I begin by assuming that individual actors are indeed rational. But I also assume with Amartya Sen that rationality cannot be viewed simply as internal consistency of choice or as the maximization of self-interest. Pure internal consistency, in fact, may be no more than a chimera because our attempts to be consistent in the face of "a set of observed choices" are tightly connected to our "interpretation" of those choices. Self-interest maximization – the second common approach to rationality – is problematic in its own way. Sen asks, "Why should it be uniquely rational to pursue one's own self-interest to the exclusion of everything else?"[13]

So how do political actors interpret and make choices? Like the self-interested rational agent who is often the protagonist of modern political economy, actors train their sight on practical goals in pursuit of which they employ the best means at their disposal.[14] But as previously mentioned, the more difficult the selection, the more likely actors are to reach for compelling reasons. They begin to do this by making an assessment of reality – an assessment that at the most fundamental level is anchored in a structure of binary oppositions. Here I borrow Zdravko Radman's argument that "even in the most sophisticated forms of rationality, we never quite succeed in escaping simplifications which

---

[13] Amartya Sen, *On Ethics and Economics* (New York: Basil Blackwell, 1987), 12–15.
[14] For an excellent discussion on the rational actor and methodological individualism in political-economic analysis, see Jeffry A. Frieden, *Debt, Development, and Democracy: Modern Political Economy and Latin America, 1965–1985* (Princeton, NJ: Princeton University Press, 1991), 17–22.

help classify objects and concepts, no matter how imprecisely, in a global binary way: positive, negative, true, false."[15]

Recall, for example, how Weber himself relied on a stark opposition between rationality and emotion to arrive at an idealized description of the modern bureaucracy. As in a mirror reflecting Prussia's official face, for Weber, this abstract ideal of bureaucracy took the concrete form of a meritocracy composed of salaried, career functionaries. Operating in what he called the "sphere of official business," such functionaries were technically superior; performed highly specialized functions in a precise, frictionless manner; faithfully adhered to firm administrative rules; enveloped the execution of their duties in a veil of secrecy; and at their most advanced level of development, successfully banished from their ranks "love, hatred, and all purely personal, irrational, and emotional elements which escape calculation."[16]

Three interrelated propositions are worth noting here. First, these seemingly robotic functionaries operate under a canonical idea known as *raison d'etat*. Second, the more strictly they conform to their prescribed roles, the greater the social esteem they derive. Finally, their "dehumanized" careerism is inextricably entwined with the "specific nature of bureaucracy," which in turn is "appraised as its special *virtue*."[17] In other words, neither the substance of Weber's vision nor the binary premise of his analytical approach manage to escape the normative component of systematic simplification.

This is crucial for our purposes because, as in Weberian analytics and Weber's view of modern bureaucracy, every polity has its own defining system of simplification: a historically shaped *lingua franca* that enables political actors to communicate with each other – be it in agreement or dissent – as members of a particular collectivity. A collectivity's *lingua franca*, more specifically, is the binary opposition that simplifies a group's sociopolitical reality to the point where no further reduction seems possible. Deciphering a polity's *lingua franca* helps us understand how actors use rhetorical strategies to organize or structure difficult choices, as well as how they craft "compelling reasons" to select between alternatives.

A *lingua franca* shapes actors' interpretative actions in more subtle ways as well. Political actors must make sense of an array of changing "circumstances," and they do this, as Kenneth Burke once noted, through a "grammar" that defines those circumstances. Such a grammar, in this book, specifies for actors the virtues and vices that elevate or degrade them as members of a distinctive group with clear notions of the noble and the repugnant – the "oughts" and "ought nots" that attach to rational behavior according to the conditions at hand. This is the grammar of the *lingua franca* that actors use to construct their

---

[15] Zdravko Radman, *Metaphors: Figures of the Mind* (Netherlands: Kulwer Academic Publishers, 1997), 157.
[16] Max Weber, "Bureaucracy," in H. H. Gerth and C. Wright Mills, eds., *From Max Weber: Essays in Sociology* (New York: Oxford University Press, 1946), 116–216, 220
[17] Ibid., 216, 220.

claims to material resources and social prestige, and to articulate their bids for power. Because of this normative grammar, actors may not rise in the morning to ponder their group's distinctiveness, but they do bring to bear its essential injunctions, as if by second nature, on their transactions and conflicts.

Burke also tells us that actors approach reality rhetorically – that is, with an intent to persuade.[18] In making these efforts at persuasion, rivals appeal to their group's sense of practical competence (its sense of mastery over the world) and to its convictions about "the possible" (what the group can or cannot do, and normatively, what it must or must not do). In brief, rivals seek a political "grip" on the constitutive elements of collective identity.[19] But they cannot achieve this grip without restraint. They must advance their competing visions and agendas within a dominant rhetorical frame: a discursive formation that articulates in accessible ways the fundamental notions a group holds intersubjectively about itself in the world, and allows or disallows specific persuasion strategies on the basis of their presumptive realism and normative sway. Such strategies come into play most vigorously at points when rival leaders and entrepreneurs seek to convince themselves and others that things must either remain as they are or that they must be changed in significant ways.[20]

Macro- and Microdynamics

Political actors situate their practical struggles within a dominant rhetorical frame. And, whether in unity or in conflict, they engender a collective field of imaginable possibilities, which can be defined as an intersubjective domain in which actors contest, within a restricted array of plausible scenarios, the ways in which their world can or cannot be changed and how the future ought to look. This field's boundaries are established at historical junctures, along with new sets of power relations and the rhetorical settlements that accompany their construction. Within such boundaries, actors routinely make claims to vocality, manipulate the positive and negative values assigned to past defining experiences, generalize from these claims and experiences to craft "simply is" assertions about reality, and drawing on such generalizations, identify viable routes – be they conservative or transformative – to a "better" future.

---

[18] J. Gusfield, *Kenneth Burke: On Symbol and Reality* (Chicago: University of Chicago Press, 1989), 13, 29.

[19] This claim is congruent with the notion that national identity formation is inseparable from the interplay of actors' other political identities and agendas. See Prasenjit Duara, "Historicizing National Identity, or Who Imagines What and When," in Geoff Eley and Ronald Grigor Suny, eds., *Becoming National* (New York: Oxford University Press, 1996).

[20] The starkness of binary opposition may be blurred (although not easily) through a discursive strategy of complexification. American liberal discourse engenders complexity by rejecting the possibility of any one individual or group possessing "the truth." For an exemplary deployment of compexification, see Michael Walzer's defense of immigrant groups – outsiders and others – as a revitalizing force in American democracy. Michael Walzer, *What It Means To Be an American* (New York: Marsilio, 1992), especially 11–24.

This is how, to borrow from Michel Trouillot, some memories and not others become "powerful enough to pass as accepted history, if not historicity itself."[21] In this respect, the communitarians' proposition that we derive our identity and sense of belonging from our narratives of communal tradition and aspiration remains valid. Alasdair MacIntyre is thrice correct when he speaks, first, of the "narrative phenomenon of embedding"; when, second, he characterizes tradition as a "context" for rationality; and finally, when he posits that tradition is either "sustained" or "corrupted" by the "exercise or lack of exercise of the relevant virtues."[22]

But this view, which is at base the benign rendition of Michel Foucault's interpretation of discourse as a system of control, exclusion, and punishment,[23] is only half the story. After all, tradition is more than a source of cohesion, and discourse is more than a restrictive force. Tradition and discourse can also be sources of conflict, precisely because calculating political actors employ shared narratives against rival claimants to virtuous identity. The rhetorical employment of narratives, in fact, may disrupt the field of imaginable possibilities. This is so because such a field is both a system of meanings (attached to vocality, past experiences, reality, and the future) *and* an arena for the play of rhetorical practices, and so it is also internally vulnerable to endogenous shifts.[24] Actors' rhetorical struggles may even at times challenge the dominance of a particular rhetorical frame.[25] In short, field disruptions may occur at moments of deep ambiguity when collective identity itself is open to revision, and actors' choices and power relations may be reconfigured.

At the micro level, the dynamic plays out as follows. The rational self, as Charles Taylor posits, is also endowed with "temporal depth," so that by necessity "self-understanding incorporates narrative."[26] The faculty of self-understanding and individuals' ability to weave it into an intersubjective narrative make possible rhetorical clarity, which is in turn essential to rhetorical potency. But competing political leaders and entrepreneurs also intuit Edmund Burke's dictum that "It is one thing to make an idea clear and another to make it

---

[21] Michel-Rolph Trouillot, *Silencing the Past: Power and the Production of History* (Boston: Beacon Press, 1995), 6.

[22] Alasdair MacIntyre, *After Virtue*, excerpted in Michael Sandel, ed., *Liberalism and Its Critics* (New York: New York University Press, 1984), 125–47.

[23] This view was articulated by Michel Foucault in *The Archeology of Knowledge and the Discourse on Language* (New York: Pantheon Books, 1972).

[24] This conceptualization of fields of imaginable possibilities accords with William Sewell's argument against the dichotomization of culture as practice and culture as system. See William H. Sewell, "The Concept(s) of Culture," in Victoria Bonnell and Lynn Hunt, eds., *Beyond the Cultural Turn* (Berkeley, CA: University of California Press, 1999), 47.

[25] Effective challenges to a dominant frame engender fundamental doubt among adherents. Even in the natural sciences, individuals live with such doubt, to which they respond in a variety of ways, ranging from isolated tinkering to heated debate and paradigmatic discovery. See Thomas S. Kuhn, *The Structure of Scientific Revolutions* (Chicago: University of Chicago Press, 1970).

[26] Charles Taylor, *Sources of the Self* (Cambridge, MA: Harvard University Press, 1989), 50.

affecting to the imagination."[27] Thus, if political actors aim to convince others either to keep things as they are or to change them in significant ways, they must simultaneously seize the authority of "realism" and awaken visionary appetites. This, however, they cannot do at will. They must fashion a rhetorical strategy that achieves one of two goals: either recast a self-regarding agenda as "appropriate" to a given collective "reality," or recast reality by establishing a newly credible balance between the known and the unknown. In the former, the objective is to establish the "facts" and weave them into a whole that is likely to be accepted as both "realistic" and "just." In the latter, the objective is to shake the premises of the "rational" stories that the group tells itself about the world and its place in it.

What actors understand to be feasible and appropriate – the normative realism that conditions rational behavior – is at the root of stable expectations. This is no small matter. Stable expectations, after all, enable us to strive for new accomplishments in our waking moments while resting in the knowledge that our gains will not be lost in slumber. Put more generally, our sense of mastery over the world and, conversely, our retreats into docility are influenced by our interpretations of what is possible and what is inevitable. With stable expectations, the notion that things might have been otherwise appears remote or even unthinkable. Because of this remote, unthinkable character of alternatives to historic settlements, identity declares, "we are as we are because the world has made us this way." This is why identity is contingent on a "realistic" description of the world. For this same reason, too, identity also says, "because we are who we are, we can change our world only so much without changing ourselves." Identity thus requires some strict understanding of the permissible and the forbidden, the possible and the inconceivable. The upshot is that, both in the immediate fray of politics and in the long sweep of history, we are who we are in large part because we exact certain kinds of behavior from ourselves and from others through the injunctions of our norms and the power of our methods.

Building on the Masters

The study of political culture once dealt primarily with intangibles such as civic values and political orientations.[28] This approach has been amended by analysts like Ronald Inglehart, who views culture as a shared system of "attitudes, values, and knowledge" that can be slowly transformed as the "formative experiences" of a younger generation diverge from the experiences of older generations.[29] In a similar adaptation, Robert Putnam argues that a society's degree

[27] Cited in Virginia Sapiro, *A Vindication of Political Virtue* (Chicago: University of Chicago Press, 1992), 190–1.

[28] Gabriel Almond and Sidney Verba, *The Civic Culture: Political Attitudes and Democracy in Five Nations* (Princeton, NJ: Princeton University Press, 1963).

[29] Ronald Inglehart, *Culture Shift in Advanced Industrial Society* (Princeton, NJ: Princeton University Press, 1990), 3–6, 18.

of "civicness" – the density of its social capital – crucially shapes the context in which a democratic government operates and, by extension, the trust that a government receives from citizens and the effectiveness with which it designs and executes policies.[30]

Our understanding of culture itself has shifted significantly. Many now regard culture as a "symbolic, expressive, and behavioral phenomenon" that is observable in "language, ritual, and systems of classification."[31] Phenomenology, anthropology, and neostructuralism have each contributed to this new understanding. For Peter Berger, human beings create institutions out of shared symbols in an effort to establish a stable order of meaning, regulation, and control. For Mary Douglas, moral boundaries demarcate identity and permissible behavior, while rituals enable people to "make" social reality. For Foucault, generations and social systems are immersed in the language – the "code of knowledge" – of their epoch.[32] For Clifford Geertz, we are suspended in "webs of meaning" that we ourselves weave, so that our actions are "texts" with a symbolic content to be interpreted.[33]

These approaches take us a long way toward explaining not only how sociopolitical order is possible at all, but also differences in regime types. Geertz, for example, interprets the Balinese Negara as a theater state bent on approximating the imagined ideal of a divine ranking order.[34] Conversely, Pierre Clastres has found that the interplay between discourse and role playing in so-called primitive societies suffocates hierarchical impulses and thus precludes the emergence of states.[35] But these accounts of power relations contain a critical flaw that stems from their strength: So persuasive are these accounts in the hands of masterful exponents that while in their thrall we tend to forget that social life is as much about discontinuity as it is about stable order.

Symbolic power and symbolic violence, as Pierre Bourdieu has demonstrated, are crucial to the maintenance of bonds of domination and to the breaking and remaking of these bonds. Symbolic strategies, in brief, are deployed on behalf of clashing identities and interests.[36] This makes culture the stuff of strategic action, which means that individuals are not simple creatures of obedience.[37] The rules of the body politic, the dictates of tradition, and even identities are

---

[30] Robert Putnam, *Making Democracy Work* (Princeton, NJ: Princeton University Press, 1993).

[31] Robert Wuthnow, James Davidson Hunter, Albert Bergesen, and Edith Kurzweil, *Cultural Analysis: The Work of Peter L. Berger, Mary Douglas, Michel Foucault and Junger Habermas* (New York: Routledge, 1987), 3–15.

[32] Ibid., 15–20.

[33] Lynn Hunt, ed., *The New Cultural History* (Berkeley, CA: University of California Press, 1989), 12–13, 72–7.

[34] Clifford Geertz, *Negara: The Theatre State in Nineteenth-Century Bali* (Princeton, NJ: Princeton University Press, 1980).

[35] Pierre Clastres, *Society against the State* (New York: Zone Books, 1989).

[36] Pierre Bourdieu, *Language and Symbolic Power* (Cambridge, UK: Polity Press, 1991), 23. See also Bourdieu's *Outline of a Theory of Practice* (New York: Cambridge University Press, 1991).

[37] Pierre Bourdieu, *In Other Words: Essays towards a Reflexive Sociology* (Stanford, CA: Stanford University Press, 1990), 130–5.

subject to change. Primordialists, to be sure, take identity as fixed by inherited linguistic, racial, ethnic, and/or territorial commonalities. But constructivists see identity as tied not to a marker but to the civic and political commonalities that bind together a national group. Moreover, not even these commonalities are fixed, since national tradition is a political invention. Indeed, for constructivists, identity can be contingent on choices that individuals make within shifting sociopolitical and historical environments, especially in response to the bids of "entrepreneurs" who trade in the business of identity politics.[38]

Primordial markers can matter in cases where linguistic, religious, and racial groups are in conflict, or where exclusivist claims to a particular territory are at play.[39] But such markers are less useful in getting at the core of collective identity in relatively homogeneous settings where they are not used by the actors themselves, or where these markers have been either marginalized in the public arena or subsumed under a broader worldview. Constructivist accounts have flaws of their own. The civic and political variant often treats identity as a functional extension of modernization and nation building.[40] The invention-of-tradition variant, in turn, risks voluntarism by stressing the will and capacity of nation builders in the invention and sacralization of collective identity.[41]

This book, therefore, builds selectively on constructivist scholarship. It stresses the intersubjective, constructed properties of identity. But it tries to avoid functionalism and voluntarism in several ways. First, it starts from the premise that political invention is a constrained activity because its product must be credible; it must "ring true." This is why at critical moments political rivals draw on the same rhetorical frame – the same fundamental, easily grasp-able "truths" – to advance their contending views of past and future. Indeed, this tendency to turn to easily grasped truths is partly why, as Radman reminds us, "invention is little more than a new combination of those images which have been previously gathered and deposited in the memory."[42]

Second, political invention can take place inadvertently. The underlying claim here is that rhetorical politics can destabilize actors' purposeful aims. Contending arguments, for example, need not always remain a linear projection of shared premises, since they interact in unpredictable ways with the behaviors and events they promote. In addition, the changing demands of competition prompt rivals to make rhetorical refinements, elaborations, and connections,

---

[38] Clifford Geertz, *The Interpretation of Cultures* (New York: Basic Books, 1973).

[39] See Walker Connor's *Ethnonationalism: The Quest for Understanding* (Princeton, NJ: Princeton University Press, 1994), for an example of the argument that ethnicity is the core determinant of national identity. See also Anthony Smith's *National Identity* (London: Penguin Books, 1991), for the claim that the ethnic factor is always present to some degree in the making of national identity.

[40] Ernest Gellner, for one, treats national identity as necessary to modernization and nation build-ing. See his *Nations and Nationalism* (Oxford, UK: Basil Blackwell, 1983).

[41] See Eric Hobsbawm and Terence Ranger, eds., *The Invention of Tradition* (Cambridge: Cambridge University Press, 1983).

[42] Cited in Radman, *Metaphors: Figures of the Mind*, 63–5.

which in turn may cause shifts in the collective field of imaginable possibilities. Part of a field of imaginable possibilities is a people's "way of life." For analysts such as Richard Ellis and Aaron Wildavsky, a way of life *is* political culture.[43] By contrast, in this book, a "way of life" is simply a group's short-hand emotive description of the established "truths" that its members must observe and employ, sometimes in self-startling ways, in their rational pursuit of prestige, wealth, loyalties, and power.[44] The way-of-life concept, broad as it may sound, cannot encompass the concept of political culture.

Third, and lastly, the book assumes that both cultural entrepreneurs and their potential "clients" are embedded in the same collective field of imaginable possibilities. As in Ann Swidler's "tool kit" approach to culture, all actors draw on the same "repertoire" of symbols, stories, and worldviews to craft and execute their strategies. If actors persist in their political-cultural practices, it is not because they are "cultural dopes." If they quit, it is not because they are without culture. In both cases, rather, actors behave as competent "users of culture."[45] This key assumption helps us get both at the "naturalness" and "plasticity" of identity without falling prey to the problems that plague instrumentalist approaches, such as the tipping model of identity formation.

David Laitin's rendition of the tipping model, on the other hand, treats "cultural entrepreneurs" as if they were invulnerable to the "equilibrium" conditions under which other members of a linguistic, racial, ethnic, and/or national group experience their beliefs and practices as "natural." That is, cultural and political elites "give meaning to the equilibrium" by providing the group with a set of "beliefs, principles, and constraints," but elites themselves appear unencumbered by meaning as they respond strategically to changing incentives.[46] The agency, of followers and clients, on the other hand, is split. Laitin proclaims political actors to be sovereign decision makers when facing a "dilemma." For example, when members of a peripheral culture must choose between their mother tongue and a newly legislated national language,[47] they weigh the costs and benefits of "switching" according to instrumental criteria, disregarding the judgment that others might make about their choices. And yet, once the tipping logic is introduced, what matters most to these presumably sovereign decision makers is what others are doing, because that is how individuals evaluate future costs and benefits. This, in fact, is the reason that

---

[43] Ellis and Wildavsky argue that societies do not perform functions, but have "constituent ways of life," and it is these ways of life that must prove functional to us if they are to survive. See M. Thompson, R. Ellis, and A. Wildavsky, *Cultural Theory* (San Francisco, CA: Westview Press, 1990), 3.

[44] For a discussion on the uses and surprises of truths, see Trevor Barnes, *Logics of Dislocation: Models, Metaphors, and Meanings of Economic Space* (New York: Guilford Press, 1996), 154–5.

[45] Ann Swidler, "Culture in Action: Symbols and Strategies," *American Sociological Review* 51, no. 2 (April 1986): 273–86.

[46] David Laitin, *Identity in Formation: The Russian-Speaking Populations in the Near Abroad* (Ithaca, NY: Cornell University Press, 1998), 22.

[47] Ibid., 25–7.

a "cascade" can occur at all. The result of all this is that the importance of meaning – acknowledged by Laitin as key to identity's sense of "naturalness" – is lost in the thick of actors' instrumentalism.

Swidler's approach does not divide actors in this manner, but it does presume two models of cultural causality: one that obtains during "settled" periods, and another during "unsettled" times. In settled times, culture influences behavior because it provides the resources with which agents put together "lines of action." In unsettled periods, "explicit ideologies" rule over action, but structural opportunities for action determine the fate of competing ideologies.[48] This duality, however, begs the question of transition from settled to unsettled times and its causes. In contrast, this book specifies the endogenous sources of transitions. Contestation is present when political actors construct rhetorical frames in an attempt to organize "realistic" strategies. But contestation is also present once a particular frame has been imposed, precisely because that same frame generates internal interpretative conflicts that may eventually lead to critical historical junctures. At such points, a dominant frame becomes one among competing frames, and its fate becomes indeterminate. This is partly why times become unsettled in the first place, and shifts occur in a collective field of imaginable possibilities.

In further contradistinction to Laitin and Swidler, this book is concerned solely with what political actors make discursively explicit. This restriction is grounded in three related considerations. First, it is virtually impossible to know actors' interior worlds. As Joseph Schull argues, even individuals who belong to the same ideological group can hold divergent interpretations of the relevant ideological claims. This divergence is possible because an ideology is located in people's minds.[49] Ideological treatises and platforms are objectively "out there," but their content is processed and transformed internally. For this very reason, the authenticity of political agents' ideological pronouncements can be called into question, both by other actors and by detached observers.

Second, because ideological tenets may diverge from actors' internal interpretations, it is analytically prudent to concentrate on actors' discursive productions and manipulations. James Scott, for one, argues that in power relations between oppressors and subordinates, the latter can and do feign ideological conviction – put on masks – and keep false faith with a dominant ideology.[50] Conversely, as Timur Kuran points out, subordinates may well loathe an oppressor and still fail to develop "cognitive autonomy" – fail to craft an alternative ideology – "precisely because of the social conditions created by the oppressor."[51]

---

[48] Swidler, "Culture in Action," 280–2.

[49] Joseph Schull, "What Is Ideology? Theoretical Problems and Lessons from Soviet-Type Societies," *Political Studies* 40, no. 4 (December 1992): 731.

[50] James C. Scott, *Domination and the Arts of Resistance: Hidden Transcripts* (New Haven, CT: Yale University Press, 1990), 110.

[51] Timur Kuran, *Private Truths, Public Lies: The Social Consequences of Preference Falsification* (Cambridge, MA: Harvard University Press, 1995), 175.

The claim that subordinates possess an indomitable capacity to manipulate and feign is as plausible as the claim that oppression devastates their ideological imagination. Yet neither claim can be asserted without empirical investigation. In both cases, the advantage of concentrating on rhetorical frames and fields of imaginable possibilities is clear. Because discourse is an intersubjective event, as Schull argues, discourse and its individual agents are relatively autonomous from each other. Discourse is relatively autonomous since its viability does not require the "faith" of its agents; discourse merely requires agents "to respect certain conventions for meaningful communication." Agents, in turn, are relatively autonomous because to be "taken seriously" they need *not* demonstrate ideological exactitude and depth; they need *only* demonstrate a significant degree of consistency between their "respect" for discursive conventions and their own actions.[52] And since discursive conventions and actors' actual respect for those conventions are both observable phenomena, neither one requires the empirical investigator to "know" agents' internal processes in order to arrive at plausible findings.[53]

Thirdly, the book focuses on rhetorical politics because the "observable" properties of discourse are even more pronounced in rhetorical productions. Rhetorical strategies, for example, are closely aimed at persuasion, and thus generate recognizable patterns of argumentation. In fact, the more distinct a particular pattern, the greater its potential effectiveness, but also the more exposed its vulnerable points become, and therefore the greater the ability of contending actors to organize and focus their attacks.[54] This competitive dynamic can lead either to entrenchment of a dominant rhetorical frame or to varying degrees of disarray within the collective field of imaginable possibilities – and perhaps to the emergence of a new dominant frame. Regardless of the outcome, however, the relevant meanings, practices, and structures remain analytically discernable.

The Connection to Democracy and the Cases

Like the mechanisms of normative scheming, the link between normative scheming and democratic development is best captured by rhetorical institutions and practices. Democracy, after all, depends partially but crucially on "rituals of participation and forms of dialogue between ruler and ruled."[55] Indeed, if these rituals and forms function properly, then people have a fair chance to create a community of citizens who live by the dual notion that "speech"

---

[52] Schull, "What Is Ideology?" 732.

[53] Ibid., 731.

[54] See, for example, "contrasting pairs" of arguments in Albert O. Hirschman, *The Rhetoric of Reaction: Perversity. Futility. Jeopardy* (Cambridge, MA: Belknap Press of Harvard University Press, 1991), 166–7.

[55] George Reid Andrews and Herrick Chapman, eds., *The Social Construction of Democracy, 1870–1990* (New York: New York University Press, 1995), 6.

should "take the place of blood" and that "acts of decision" are meant to take the place of vengeance."[56]

Thus the quest for justifiable power and justice more generally – if it is to proceed within the bounds of a democratic regime of arbitration – requires "communicatively competent individuals."[57] But as the empirical cases in this book make plain, this quest also requires the construction of a collective identity that extols the virtues of "the people" not as an abstract notion of republican ideology, but as a factually verifiable article of faith. This seemingly oxymoronic combination is precisely what the Costa Ricans successfully assembled during the transition from colony to nation, while the Nicaraguans quickly became mired in the establishment of an electoral system for the selection and replacement of arbiters – a system that in interaction with the logic of Manicheanism led to intractable violence and petty despotism throughout the first half of the nineteenth century.

So how do we account for the Costa Rican difference at the nation's foundational moment? One type of explanation – call it the *national character thesis*[58] – emphasizes the countries' colonial peculiarities. Exponents of this type of explanation tend to accept *prima facie* the "conciliatory" nature of Costa Rica's conquest,[59] and regard postcolonial elites as carriers of the traits and habits first exhibited by the country's "exceptional" conquerors.[60] One renowned historian, for example, looking back on the achievements of Costa Rica's first postcolonial elites, concluded that as descendants of a small "Spanish population," these notables were endowed with superior "attributes," which in turn enabled them to organize the country's political economy with an "acumen" that was "missing in the other Central American nationalities."[61]

---

[56] J. G. A. Pocock, "The Ideal of Citizenship since Classical Times," in Gerson Shafir, ed., *The Citizenship Debates* (Minneapolis, MN: University of Minnesota Press, 1998), 32.

[57] John S. Dryzek, *Discursive Democracy* (New York: Cambridge University Press, 1990), 41.

[58] These explanations, it should be noted, bear scant analytical relation to sophisticated national character arguments. Alex Inkeles, for example, posits that national character refers to "the mode or modes of distribution of personality variants within a given society." The national-character explanations articulated by Costa Rican and Nicaraguan scholars, in contrast, merely echo and reinforce dominant mythologies that are part and parcel of intersubjective "realisms" established through long-forgotten contestations. And yet, analytically unrelated as they are, both Inkeles' reductionist argument and the home-grown national character explanations eclipse intersubjective dynamics and contestation processes. Alex Inkeles, *National Character: A Psycho-Social Perspective* (New Brunswick, NJ: Transaction, 1997).

[59] Jorge Lines, "Integración de la Provincia de Costa Rica Bajo el Reinado de Carlos V," in Academia Costarricense de la Historia, ed., *IV Centenario de la Entrada de Cavallón a Costa Rica, 1561–1961* (San José: Imprenta Nacional, 1961), 21, 25–31; Carlos Melendez, "Los Poderes Conferidos al Alcalde Mayor Licenciado Juan de Cavallón," in ibid., 41; Eugenio Rodríguez Vega, *Biografía de Costa Rica* (San José: Editorial Costa Rica, 1981), 19.

[60] Hernán Peralta, *Don José María Peralta* (San José: Editorial Hermanos Trejos, 1956), 21. See also Juan Rafael Quesada, "Educación y Democracia en Costa Rica," in Jorge Mario Salazar, ed., *Democracia y Cultura Política en Costa Rica* (San José: Ministerio de Cultura, Universidad de Costa Rica, 1990), 60–85.

[61] Peralta, *Don José María*, 21.

Conversely, Nicaraguan traditional historiography tends to accept uncritically the especially brutal character of the country's conquest,[62] attributing the country's postcolonial instability and petty despotism to the dark legacy of ruthless conquering clans. One highly influential historian, for example, saw the early national period as a time of resurgence, when "the proclamation of independence summoned the fury and greed of [Nicaragua's conqueror], and the anarchic violence of his grandsons."[63] Once vested with the authority of "history," the national-character thesis entrenches the very mythologies that help set the parameters on these two countries' field of imaginable possibilities.

Another type of explanation casts aside the national-character thesis in favor of socioeconomic or ideology-based accounts of the countries' developmental trajectories. And yet, in the end, these explanations unwittingly reinforce the countries' mythological legacies and render the countries' histories as chronicles of success and failure foretold. Accounts that stress divergent socioeconomic conditions at the start of the postcolonial period, for example, often share a logic that runs as follows. The Spanish metropole consistently overlooked the province of Costa Rica because it was poor in Indians. This neglect caused the province's politico-administrative marginalization and widening poverty. And both these conditions in turn accustomed Costa Rica's colonial elites and their postcolonial successors to de facto politico-administrative autonomy and to the more egalitarian relations associated with labor-scarce colonies.[64] Indian-abundant Nicaragua, conversely, grew accustomed to the exploitative relations that characterized better-endowed colonies.[65]

But in fact, the countries' endowments of indigenous labor were not radically unequal. In Costa Rica, it is true, the conquerors' failure to subjugate and exploit the Indian population[66] plunged the province into abject poverty because "there was simply never enough Indian labor or external demand to permit substantial or sustained export activities of any kind."[67] But here it is essential to note that the successful subjugation and exploitation of Nicaragua's natives also led to acute labor scarcity in that province: By the late sixteenth century, the majority of Nicaragua's Indians had been worked to death, succumbed to

[62] See, for example, Gustavo Alemán Bolaños, *El País de los Irredentos* [Country of irredeemables]; (Guatemala: 1927); Ernesto Cardenal, *El Estrecho Dudoso* (Mexico/Buenos Aires: Ediciones Carlos Lohlé, 1972); José Coronel Urtecho, *Reflexiones sobre la historia de Nicaragua*, vol. 1 (León: Editorial Hospicio, 1962).

[63] Ibid., 165.

[64] The most important exponent of this view is Carlos Monge Alfaro. See *Historia de Costa Rica* (San José: Hermanos Trejos, 1980).

[65] Edelberto Torres Rivas, *History and Society in Central America* (Austin, TX: University of Texas Press, 1993).

[66] For the causes of colonial Costa Rica's labor scarcity, see Carlos Meléndez, "Bosquejo Para una Historia Social Costarricense Antes de la Independencia," in Carmen Lila Gómez et al., eds., *Las Instituciones Costarricenses del Siglo XIX* (San José: Editorial Costa Rica, 1985), 35–48. See also Yamileth González García, "Estructura Agraria en el Período Colonial," in ibid., 53–81.

[67] Lowell Gudmundson, *Costa Rica before Coffee: Society and Economy on the Eve of the Export Boom* (Baton Rouge, LA: Louisiana State University Press, 1986), 1.

disease, or perished on slave ships en route to Perú. Because of this savage dev-astation of the indigenous population, by the early decades of the nineteenth century land abundance merely reinforced the economy's labor shortage.

Furthermore, both provinces suffered from insufficient capital accumulation. In eighteenth-century Nicaragua, cocoa production failed to lift the province out of its virtual autarchy. In Costa Rica, meanwhile, the "nobles" who con-trolled the production of cocoa managed to turn a profit in good times, but failed to amass substantial fortunes. By the late eighteenth century, with cocoa on the decline and the nation facing perennial labor scarcity, both the Costa Rican "nobles" and the Nicaraguan *señores* turned to cattle ranching.[68] This development brings us back again to land.

In both provinces, land was by far the most abundant factor of production, with plenty of communal tracts and "vast expanses" of unclaimed territories be-longing to the Crown.[69] Land ownership, in fact, was *not* the "key to wealth." Instead, the key to wealth was the ability to "acquire and organize" *all* factors of production – capital, land, and labor, plus entrepreneurial skills.[70] And here again the two provinces had much in common. Already reined in by capital and labor shortages, they were both stifled commercially – especially prior to the Bourbon reforms of 1774 – by Spain's impositions, which ranged from custom duties and the *alcabala* tax, to the strict regulation of inter-American trade.[71] (Contraband, of course, went on as most everywhere else; but even after the implementation of the reforms, the share of exports in overall pro-duction remained small.) The upshot of all this was that by the beginning of the nineteenth century, commercial agriculture was severely limited in both provinces. This meant, first, that both populations were dedicated mainly to subsistence agriculture; and second, while coercive labor recruitment thrived in Guatemala and El Salvador, in Nicaragua and Costa Rica it stagnated *pari passu* with commercial agriculture.[72]

If the provinces' initial factor endowments cannot explain divergent pat-terns of political and economic development, neither can their distributional structures. The argument is often made that Costa Rica's widespread poverty, in combination with conditions of labor scarcity, gave rise to forced egali-tarianism, which in turn set the stage for a yeoman democracy. But Costa Rica's generalized poverty and labor scarcity did not translate ipso facto into

---

[68] Rodríguez Vega, *Biografía de Costa Rica*, 24–31.

[69] This situation lent itself to abuses. In Costa Rica, for example, cocoa farmers sold and be-queathed Crown lands as if they were private property, even though the lands had never been purchased from the Crown, and the farmers held no titles. See González García, "Estructura Agraria en el Período Colonial," 53–81.

[70] Lowell Gudmundson and Héctor Lindo-Fuentes, *Central America, 1821–1871: Liberalism be-fore Liberal Reform* (Tuscaloosa, AL: University of Alabama Press, 1995), 14–15.

[71] The Bourbon reforms briefly changed this bleak picture for Costa Rica. In 1776, the Crown awarded that province a monopoly on the cultivation, processing, and export of tobacco. But in 1792, the Royal authorities in Guatemala revoked the privilege.

[72] Gudmundson and Lindo-Fuentes, *Central America*, 22–4.

an egalitarian society. In an early nineteenth century document, the governor of Costa Rica noted that in Villa Vieja, "there [were] some Spanish [families], reputed as nobles; the rest [were] mestizos and mulattos, and considered plebeians."[73]

The premium placed on racial and hierarchical distinction was by no means peculiar to Costa Rica.[74] But the separation of the races and the elites' social and political exclusionary practices were arguably the strictest on the isthmus. As William Roseberry has argued so convincingly, "small holders produced and sold their coffee – and secured labor for their coffee plots – within hierarchical social fields." Hence his caution against the "temptation" to treat "smallholder regimes" as the foundation for "rural democracy."[75] Costa Rica's labor scarcity certainly did not readily translate into an egalitarian society.[76]

Indeed, in the first postcolonial decades, Costa Rica's elite family networks used their sociopolitical dominance to secure control of the best lands.[77] Moreover, while coercive labor recruitment was not an established practice, elite dominance assumed other forms – most notably, exclusionary control of credit and information, which in turn translated into an equally skewed control of coffee processing and export marketing.[78] Elite control of these key resources came together with the state's progressive developmental measures to create a pyramidlike production structure, with a small number of large producers at the apex, and a broad band of small producers at the base. Postcolonial Costa Rica's initial structure, then, was neither remarkably egalitarian nor extraordinarily polarized, which is to say that it was not substantially different from the structure that obtained spontaneously in land-abundant Nicaragua.

Analyses that focus on socioeconomic interests as determinants of postcolonial ideologies are similarly flawed.[79] Costa Rican exceptionalism, for example, has been explained as the felicitous outcome of an ideological struggle between the "republican" disposition of an aborning bourgeoisie and the "retrograde" impulses of the colonial aristocracy.[80] In contrast, ideological backwardness in postcolonial Nicaragua – characterized by weak or nonexistent modern ideologies – has been treated as merely the superficial expression of

---

[73] Meléndez, "Bosquejo," 35–48.

[74] Coronel Urtecho, *Reflexiones*.

[75] William Roseberry et al., eds., *Coffee, Society, and Power in Latin America* (Baltimore, MD: Johns Hopkins University Press, 1995), 20; Samuel Stone, *La Dinastía de los Conquistadores: La Crísis del Poder en la Costa Rica Contemporánea* (San José: EDUCA, 1975), 75–96. See also Gudmundson and Lindo-Fuentes, *Central America*, 46–7.

[76] Carlos Meléndez, "Bosquejo," 35–48.

[77] Stone, *La Dinastía*, 75–96.

[78] Gudmundson and Lindo-Fuentes, *Central America*, 46–7.

[79] For a prominent exponent, see Rodolfo Cerda Cruz, *Formación del Estado en Costa Rica* (San José: Editorial Universidad de Costa Rica, 1967), 96–9, 156–9.

[80] This account also overlooks the fact that Costa Rica's aristocracy (located in the "closed" city of Cartago) *and* the progressive elites (located in "bourgeois" San José) were one and the same, both in terms of social origins and access to national power. See Stone, *La Dinastía*, for the shared genealogy of power holders.

socioeconomic undifferentiation.[81] But this ideological variant of the socio-economistic account is contradicted by scholarship demonstrating that Costa Rican elites, like all the other regional elites, "lacked clear socioeconomic or ideological lines of party affiliation."[82] If anything, we will see that already during the transition to independence, Costa Rica's elites showed a remarkable inclination to construct ideological and institutional alloys – a hybrid constitution, a hybrid government – in their efforts to minimize internal conflict and to promote economic progress.

Finally, all of these explanations, like most other available approaches to Latin American political and economic history, tend to overlook the dynamics that link rhetorical practices, identity formation, and political-economic development.[83] Fortunately, a few scholars have recently taken important steps in this direction. Jeffery Paige, for instance, argues that divergent developmental paths can be traced to the patterns of elite dominance that emerged in the export coffee economies of the nineteenth century and to elites' relations to the rural masses. But the Costa Rican pattern, Paige also shows, can be properly understood only with close analytical reference to elite "narratives" and "stories" – most notably the "White Legend" that shaped relations of production in a coffee economy in which aristocratic producers became symbiotically entwined with medium-size and small producers in mid-nineteenth century.[84] Paige, however, does not theorize the broader theme of exceptionalism, nor does he link the White Legend's viability – either structurally or semiotically – to this theme or to the colonial antecedents of national identity formation.

Another remarkable account is provided by Deborah Yashar, who cogently argues that democratic development is determined by institutional legacies, political coalitions, and the ideological context of reform legacies.[85] These are undoubtedly crucial factors. But they can be most revealing when placed in a full historical context – a task that calls for scrutiny of the formative political-cultural struggles that took place *prior* to the mid- and late nineteenth century (the starting point for Yashar's in-depth analysis of Guatemalan and Costa Rican development).

---

[81] Jaime Wheelock, *Imperialismo y Dictadura: Crisis de Una Formación social* (Mexico, DF: 1975).

[82] Gudmundson, *Costa Rica before Coffee*, 4.

[83] Ralph Lee Woodward, for example, astutely concentrates on familial and localist struggles but does not connect them to actors' rhetorical strategies. See his superb essay, "The Aftermath of Independence, 1821–1870," in Leslie Bethell, ed., *Central America since Independence* (New York: Cambridge University Press, 1991), 1–36. Similarly, Victor Bulmer-Thomas treats the emergence of "national identity" in Latin America as dependent on the success or failure of economic development. Bulmer-Thomas is certainly correct that the two are related. But I will argue that the causality runs in the other direction: National identity shapes developmental outcomes. See Bulmer-Thomas' excellent *Economic History of Latin America since Independence* (New York: Cambridge University Press, 1994), 19–45.

[84] Jeffery Paige, *Coffee and Power: Revolution and the Rise of Democracy in Central America* (Cambridge, MA: Harvard University Press, 1997), 47.

[85] Deborah Yashar, *Demanding Democracy: Reform and Reaction in Costa Rica and Guatemala, 1870's–1950's* (Stanford, CA: Stanford University Press, 1997).

Accordingly, this book delves deeper into the countries' colonial and early postcolonial politics and emphasizes *multiple* critical junctures. (See the next section "Overview of the Book"). This approach stands in contrast to studies that stress a single determinative period, such as the decades of nineteenth century liberal reform. The advantage of a fuller political-historical exploration is clear: It allows us to identify the various openings and closings of opportunities for democratic development and state building, and to obtain a better grasp on how political actors employ legacies and create new ones. One benefit of this multijunctural approach is that the historical record as written by the winners does not distort our understanding of path dependence winners. Indeed, this book demonstrates that the defeats of once-viable actors and alternatives, as well as the impact of their subsequent obscurity on the winners' future options, are key to path dependence. In the second half of the nineteenth century, for example, we find that in Nicaragua it was not the Liberals but the Conservatives who launched the first serious effort at state building and economic modernization. More importantly, we also find that the labels "Conservative" and "Liberal" not only overdraw the ideological differences and policy preferences of actors, but are secondary in importance to more profound processes of identity formation.[86] Finally, we find that the virtual oblivion of the Conservatives' oligarchic Republic after its collapse diminished the victorious Liberals' chances of successful institution building.

Overview of the Book: Relevant Historical Junctures and Puzzles

The key junctures in this book are those in which a regime of arbitration is established, or in which an established regime becomes unstable, collapses, or is overthrown. The establishment and transformation of the colonial regime are the first junctures to explore. Thus, the book's chronological starting point

---

[86] James Mahoney, for example, acknowledges the importance of liberal reforms undertaken by the Conservative Republic preceding the Liberal Zelaya regime, but overstates the distinction between the two regimes' modernization policies and state-building accomplishments, hardly mentioning the crucial, large-scale infrastructural works initiated by the Conservative Republic. Moreover, although Mahoney portrays the Conservatives as key agents in the promotion of coffee, he misses the central fact that large coffee-growers, including Zelaya himself, emerged on the scene as a social product of the pro-coffee policies implemented by the Conservatives. In Mahoney's account, Conservatives appeared ready to "transform" themselves into Liberals only after Zelaya's ascent, when in fact the Republic generated a marked tendency toward "fusión" – the term Liberals themselves used to describe the political unity they felt should reflect an already-existing reality: ideological and identity boundaries so blurred by the Republic's policies that Conservatives and Liberals could hardly be distinguished from one another. Finally, in Mahoney's account of Costa Rican development, Liberal reformism carries forward the tasks of modernization and state building. But in fact, it was postcolonial Costa Rican elites – known for their pragmatic ideological blends – who first acted on the notion that political stability, land reform, and a well-defined property rights regime were indispensable to the nation's development. See James Mahoney, *The Legacies of Liberalism: Path Dependence and Political Regimes in Central America* (Baltimore, MD: Johns Hopkins University Press, 2001), 11–16, 29–49, 180–93.

is the conquest and colonization of the Indies, a moment when Spain had just emerged triumphant from the *Reconquista* and was poised to become a great world power.

All that the conquest and colonization entailed – from practices of war and administrative institutions to racial classifications and systems of wealth formation – shaped in significant ways the behavior of postcolonial Latin America and the development of its nations. Of course, the idea that colonial legacies exercise remarkable power over founding national moments is not new. Douglas North once argued that the United States and Latin America turned out so differently because the former inherited from England a parliamentary, decentralized approach to governance while the latter inherited from Spain a centralist tradition.[87]

North was not alone. Claudio Veliz attributed Latin America's inability to construct stable, liberal democracies to this same centralist tradition.[88] Similarly, Howard Wiarda pointed to corporatist, oligarchic, and authoritarian modes of organization and rule as the signal legacy of Latin America's colonial history.[89] Samuel Huntington, for his part, was so struck by Latin America's propensity to oscillate between openly authoritarian rule and substandard democratic regimes that he pronounced cyclicality to be the hallmark of Latin American political development. Echoes of these older arguments are now heard in claims about the "illiberal" character of several new democracies in Latin America.[90]

Individually and together these claims capture undeniable features of Latin American political development. But they underestimate the dynamism of the colonial regime and its internal transformations, while overemphasizing its uniformity across the region. These two flaws leave proponents of the centralist thesis unable to differentiate between countries' postcolonial paths. Fortunately, we can remedy both these flaws if we bear in mind that "significant change may occur due to a minor intervention in the structure of old knowledge," so long as this intervention is of the "kind that opens new cognitive horizons."[91]

Minor interventions in the structure of old knowledge occurred at various points and places under the colonial regime, in the process causing significant reconfigurations of power relations. Chapter 2 shows that more than once the much touted centralist tradition was actually the primary casualty of these reconfigurations, as local *cabildos* and American-born creoles enhanced their power at the expense of the center's local representatives. Indeed, the Crown

[87] Douglas C. North, *Institutions, Institutional Change, and Economic Performance* (New York: Cambridge University Press, 1990), 101–17.
[88] Claudio Veliz, *The Centralist Tradition of Latin America* (Princeton, NJ: Princeton University Press, 1980).
[89] Howard J. Wiarda, *The Soul of Latin America: The Cultural and Political Tradition* (New Haven, CT: Yale University Press, 2001), 4–5, 25, 119, 197, 263.
[90] Fareed Zakaria, "The Rise of Illiberal Democracy," in *The New Shape of World Politics* (New York: Foreign Affairs, 1999).
[91] Radman, *Metaphors: Figures of the Mind*, 67.

itself contributed to these subtle transformative processes by centralizing with one hand and devolving power with the other.

Moreover, minor interventions of the kind that open "new cognitive horizons" did take place, albeit in a variety of forms across the region. Clues pointing to differences in the countries' cognitive horizons can be found in each country's rhetorical politics. Not surprisingly, the clues are easiest to find at moments of transition. Consider the following. In 1825, scarcely four years after independence from Spain, Costa Rica's State Assembly prophesied that if Costa Ricans guarded against the "corruption of their mores," they would enjoy "eternal and exemplary tranquility."[92] That same year, the first head of state in Nicaragua deployed what was to become the dominant rhetoric of electoral politics. Dark, evil forces, he argued, had gained control of the country, by which he meant that elected local officials were mostly ignorant men who, led by the wicked, supported disorder and gave free rein to insults.[93]

Why the difference? Why so early? And what does this difference tell us? Locating the origins of the articulations themselves is the first analytical step toward an answer. Chapter 2 traces these articulations back to the colonial regime's pervasive freedom of expression and its crucial relationship to the colonial regime of arbitration. This freedom was actually fomented by a Crown that, preoccupied with the impact of conquest and colonization on its own legitimacy, was avid for "intelligence." Conquerors and colonials, in turn, proved to be contentious scribblers who pursued their self-seeking agendas through a system of Manichean normative scheming.

In this system, subjects owed compliance to their wise and just sovereign, and the sovereign in turn owed his subjects justice and protection from "wicked" rivals. Not surprisingly, then, colonial society was infused with mistrust and plagued by conflicts that, at the end of the day, could only be contained by the frequent intervention of the royal arbiter. But as Chapter 2 finally shows, Costa Rica proved that this was not an unavoidable outcome. Not only did Costa Rica's conquerors and their creole descendants manage to forge a virtuous collective identity, but while their Nicaraguan counterparts rhetorically deployed the Manichean logic against one another, the Costa Ricans deployed it exclusively against outsiders, by which they meant peninsular Spaniards.

The story, however, cannot end with the colonial past. The interaction between legacies and political agency is also crucial, as was obvious in the transition to independence. Chapter 3 begins to contend with this turbulent juncture by focusing on the salient rhetorical patterns that emerged at the end of the eighteenth century and beginning of the nineteenth. On the side of legacies, these patterns show that the Manichean system of normative scheming engendered

---

[92] "Manifiesto de la Asamblea del Estado" (San José), 19 April 1825, in Carlos Meléndez Chaverri, ed., *Documentos Fundamentales del Siglo XIX* (San José: Editorial Costa Rica, 1978), 135–6.

[93] Manuel Antonio de la Cerda, "A Ciudadanos Secretarios de la Asamblea Constituyente" (León), 10 May 1825, *Revista de la Academia de Geografía e Historia de Nicaragua* (henceforth *RAGHN*) 1 (1936–7): 255.

a field of imaginable possibilities which, except in Costa Rica, made creole solidarity nearly inconceivable. On the side of agency, rhetorical patterns show that, in the postcolonial processes of identity formation and political competition, it was the Nicaraguan creoles, not their Costa Rican counterparts, who proved to be radical, albeit mimetic, modernizers. The Nicaraguans, to put it simply, became fixated on the idea that electoral mechanisms and popular sovereignty could replace the royal arbiter and the norm of obedience. And they did in fact channel their localist, clannish, and personalist rivalries into electoral competition. They even appealed to the "people" repeatedly. But they appealed for acclamation and obedience, and as becomes clear in Chapter 4, while they embraced a new formal regime of arbitration and its legitimating electoral principle, they remained immersed in the colonial system of normative scheming. The interaction between the two proved at once paradoxical and destructive. Nicaraguans could not live with the results of elections, even when they won. By 1824, different *caudillos*, localities, and clans had established an array of autonomous juntas that unleashed civil wars as confusing as they were barbaric.[94]

Postcolonial Costa Ricans, too, debated, competed, and struggled over preeminence, predominance, and modes of arbitration. The outcome, however, was radically different. Costa Ricans set out to protect their "virtuous" people from external contamination by other Central Americans – a goal they maintained was realistic only if Costa Rica, traditionally poor and militarily weak, grew socioeconomically strong. Chapter 4 argues that the result of all this was that as Nicaraguan elites became embroiled in violent struggles over electoral results, Costa Ricans legitimated and expelled their rulers not through electoral procedures but through reference to a substantive standard. That is, Costa Ricans judged a ruler by the balance of his performance as an agent of developmental progress *and* his capacity to pursue personal ambitions within permissible bounds.[95] In this way, which they considered to be autochthonous, they not only managed to avoid the "fratricidal butchery" that drenched Nicaragua in blood, but attained significant success in preserving their "tradition" of domestic "peace" and "civility."[96]

Time and again, legacy and agency combined in different ways to reshape the countries' systems of normative scheming, as well as regnant visions of

---

94 For localist disputes, see "Acta, Se Acuerda Auxiliar a Granada" (León), 10 July 1824, *RAGHN* 1 (1936–7). For clannish and personalist rivalries, see José Coronel Urtecho, "Paradojas de las Intervenciones de Valle y Arce en Nicaragua," *Revista Conservadora del Pensamiento Centroamericano* (henceforth *RCPC*) 28, no. 140 (May 1972): 45; idom., *Reflexiones*; José Dolores Gámez, *Historia de Nicaragua* (Managua: Fondo de Promoción Cultural, Banco de América, 1975).

95 Despite ideological, class, and interest commonalities among elites, most of the individual states of the Central American Federation were either buffeted by internal political turmoil, oppressed by dictatorial "saviors," or prone to external clashes. See Gudmundson and Lindo-Fuentes, *Central America*, 30; Woodward, "The Aftermath of Independence," 12.

96 *RAGHN* 6, no. 1 (April 1944): 181–5.

possibility and fate. In Costa Rica, an exceptionalist field of imaginable possibilities emerged, which in turn sustained the elites' relentless developmental thrust. In Nicaragua, aspirants to office and incumbents alike increasingly
found themselves waging Manichean campaigns which, though lethally serious,
rapidly became devoid of specific programmatic value.

Costa Rica's exceptionalist system, however, was neither perfect nor invulnerable to disruption. Chapter 5 explores the makings and resolution of that
country's most important juncture in the twentieth century: the Revolution
of 1948. The chapter argues that this juncture was the result of political-cultural
change that was fast in pace, minor in its alteration of actors' normative realism,
and profound in its political-institutional ramifications. Specifically, we will see
that a modernizing, scientifically oriented elite group – by deploying rhetorical
arguments for modernization based on fear of "extreme, foreign ideologies" –
nearly destroyed the nation's self-image as a cradle of temperance and a haven
for civility.

But as the chapter also shows, it was from this crisis that Costa Rica's polity
at last emerged as a supple arbitration regime formalized in the institutions of
a social democracy. Prior to this turning point, electoral processes had been
deeply flawed and the electoral principle had been subordinated to the goal of
developmental progress, which had been traditionally seen as the "logical" line
of defense for a nation populated by nonviolent, hard-working citizens.[97] After
the juncture of 1948, Costa Rica's regime came to depend on both principles
of legitimation, a dual dependence that has actually endowed the polity with a
remarkable capacity to meet and transcend socioeconomic challenges.

The Nicaraguan case is explored more fully in Chapters 6, 7, and 8, each dealing with attempts at institutionalization of encompassing arbitration. Chapter 6
details how, by the mid-nineteenth century, Manichean normative scheming
had engendered a field of imaginable possibilities in which rivals perceived the
reality of "anarchy" and the possibility of "order" as *the* inescapable binary
opposition. They organized accordingly. *Caudillos* from rivaling localities and
clans formed keenly antagonistic camps that waged mutually exhausting wars,
and in fits of desperation, did not hesitate to seek external arbitration.

The national humiliations and catastrophes that flowed from this set of conditions merely deepened political mistrust, which in turn blocked the quest
for peace and just order. Yet out of this impasse, as Chapter 6 demonstrates,

---

[97] In this very specific sense, Costa Rica's political development is strikingly similar to that of the
United States, where the democratic theme became part of rhetorical institutions only in the
1830s, as pluralism grew and mass parties began to emerge on the scene. Prior to that critical
juncture, American leaders were almost exclusively preoccupied with the task of making their
new nation viable and strong. This common goal was deemed possible because, the differences
between federalists and republicans notwithstanding, the leadership repudiated "excesses" and
honed closely to the rhetoric of a reasoned path to basic principles and rights.

For the U.S. case, see Tadahisa Kuroda and Erwin Levine, "The United States: Creating the
Republic," in Mary Ellen Fischer, ed., *Establishing Democracies* (Boulder, CO: Westview Press,
1996), 63–5, 71–5.

Nicaraguan elites finally managed to build a successful arbitration hybrid of their own. This breakthrough was possible because the elites' early inclination to embrace foreign models wholesale now gave way to improvisation and adaptation on the basis of historical experience and political learning. More specifically, the breakthrough was possible because the emerging regime simultaneously addressed rivals' power and normative concerns. Its builders put in place a blend of informal rhetorical regulations and formal supportive institutions that provided both a controlling norm for rulers – moderation – and institutional protection for those called upon to assume the initial risks that new practices typically entail.

This regime, alternatively known as the Conservative Republic and the Regime of the Thirty Years, was formalized in an oligarchic democracy that for three decades expanded its capacity to arbitrate struggles over power, status, and resources among rival leaders, clans, and localities. Moreover, although headed by Conservatives, this regime became increasingly bipartisan in spirit and outlook. Indeed, the Republic sponsored a liberal program of socioeconomic modernization and state building, which in turn brought the nation an unprecedented degree of prosperity and peace. Finally, and most importantly, this regime shifted the field of imaginable possibilities: As cooperative alliances among previously irreconcilable foes became permissible in principle and viable in practice, a political mainstream capable of articulating a vision for a brighter national future began to emerge.

The Republic, however, also endogenously generated the pressures that brought it down. The proven feasibility of bipartisan cooperation and the growing ideational similarities between leading Conservatives and Liberals, for example, did create a mainstream, but the latter in turn gave rise to "authentic" forces, thus producing severe identity-based friction within the camps themselves. In addition, the regime engendered new economic elites whose rising material fortunes made them all the more resentful of the traditional notables who were slow to grant them corresponding political vocality and influence. Against the background of these and other pressures, it took only one errant incumbent to upset the regime's delicate balancing act of arbitration among *caudillos*, notables, clans, and localities.

Chapter 7 examines the long-term consequences of the Republic's collapse. The chapter, for example, uncovers the link between the Manichean historiography incipient in the closing days of the Republic and the Manichean arbitration adopted by the successor regime. For a brief illustration, consider the contention of the preeminent Liberal historian writing in Nicaragua in the late nineteenth century and the early years of the twentieth. A good historian, this politically influential scholar argued,

...is *never impartial* in the strict sense of the word. He puts himself in the place of the society for which he writes, and feels and loves with that society. He is not indifferent to the personae he brings to the stage; he becomes enamored of some while abhorring others to the death. *He conveys his affections and hatreds to his reader.* In his hands, history becomes more than a teacher of life and an oracle to be consulted. *History also becomes a sharpened knife and avenging torch against the wicked; and it becomes the glorious crown and recompense for the virtuous* [emphasis added].[98]

By the 1930s, even Conservative historians agreed wholeheartedly with this point of view. For them, too, historiography was a Manichean enterprise. They disagreed only with the Liberal historian's capacity to discern correctly the "wicked" from the "virtuous."[99]

Chapter 7 also contends that after the collapse of the Republic, four different regimes of arbitration emerged, each a product of continuities and contradictions engendered by its predecessor. The chapter examines in detail the first three – beginning with the Liberal regimes of José Santos Zelaya and the Somoza dynasty, and ending with the revolutionary regime of the Frente Sandinista de Liberación Nacional (FSLN). The fourth regime, formally established in internationally supervised elections that were widely recognized as fair and transparent (1990), is analyzed in Chapter 8.

Chapters 7 and 8 jointly demonstrate that from one regime to the next, the central points of contention have been the meaning of justifiable power, the distribution of rights to vocality, and the establishment of just claims to material rewards and authority. In all this, two different principles of legitimation were also at stake. One was the substantive criterion, which as previously mentioned sustained the Costa Rican regime of arbitration until the late 1940s. The other was the electoral principle of legitimation, which the Costa Ricans managed to conciliate with the substantive principle only *after* the Revolution of 1948. Chapter 7 shows that in Nicaragua, the electoral principle, so avidly pursued by leaders throughout much of the nineteenth century, was subordinated in the twentieth to the substantive alternative by the Zelaya, Somoza, and FSLN regimes. The supremacy of the substantive criterion led to political violence and economic ruin because of the more profound dynamics of Manichean normative scheming.

In Chapter 8, we will see that the electoral principle props up a regime whose attempts at encompassing adjudication thus far have led to severe crises that are solved by special and/or external arbitration. Government itself functions as a pact-making machine because incumbents, unable to govern without the consent of the opponents that they vilify and seek to exclude, are ultimately forced to enter into "stabilizing" understandings with those same opponents.

This kind of pact might be mistaken for a truce, if not a peace treaty of sorts. But like the long string of pacts that punctuate Nicaraguan history, it should not be seen as an indication of reconciliation between foes, or even as a glimmer of a minimally shared vision of the common good. Rather, this kind of pact is a means for achieving a relatively stable division of spoils between two mutually recognizable antagonists. Or to mix market and military analogies, the pact

---

[98] Quoted in Pedro Joaquín Chamorro, *Máximo Jerez y sus Contemporáneos: Estudio Histórico-crítico* (Managua: Editorial La Prensa, 1937), 7.
[99] Ibid., 8.

raises barriers to entry for new political warriors in order to secure exclusive dominion of the battleground for well-established combatants.

Costa Ricans, for their part, are able to continue "perfecting" their democracy in large measure because they are the heirs to an enabling historiography that integrates leaders and people alike into the nation's exceptional identity. In this historiography, even Costa Rican "dictators" are an exception to the rule. As one of the country's venerable historians once put it:

> The historian must ponder the past with an open mind and a serene spirit. We hate ignorant and cruel dictators. But Costa Rica's dictators – Carrillo, Guardia, and Yglesias – were the pioneers of our progress and established our deepest republican and democratic foundations. This is perhaps because they were moved by patriotic love and a desire to make the *patria* great and prosperous.[100]

Thirty years after this scholar rendered his judgment concerning the exceptional character of the country's dictators, an editorial board of Costa Rica's brightest intellectual lights reached the same conclusion.[101] The country's scholars are not alone in their appreciation of their nation's exceptionalism. Political leaders still try to outdo one other by exalting the nation's pre-1948 past while at the same time according special glory to the legacies of 1948.[102]

The promises and limitations of Costa Rica's political culture, like those of its Nicaraguan counterpart, are explored in the concluding chapter. More broadly, the last chapter also highlights the key links between the study of institutional development and the approach to political culture advanced throughout the book. But first we turn to a time of conquest and colonization; to the making of a distant world whose stark language and elaborate practices hold part of the key to a better understanding of our two developmental archetypes.

---

[100] Emmanuel Thompson, *Defensa de Carrillo: Un Dictador al Servicio de América* (San José: Inprenta Borrase, 1945), 22, 37.

[101] Academia de Geografía e Historia de Costa Rica, *Gobernantes de Costa Rica* (San José: Academia de Geografía e Historia de Costa Rica, 1978).

[102] Daniel Oduber, "De Dónde Venimos," in Carlos José Gutiérrez, *El Pensamiento Político Costarricense: La Social Democracia*, vol. 2 (San José: Libro Libre, 1986).

Manichean Identities and Normative Scheming

Origins

> ... language serves to declare what is advantageous and what is the reverse, and
> it is the peculiarity of man that he alone ... possesses a perception of good and
> evil, of the just and the unjust ... and it is association in [a common perception
> of] these things which makes a family and a polis.[1]
>
> –Aristotle

In part because Aristotle was right, polities are at base regimes for the arbitration of contending claims to a wide range of valuable resources, from authority
and prestige to access and control of capital and labor. An intuitively appealing
view of arbitration regimes posits that their legitimacy ultimately rests on the
contenders' conviction that the judges are not self-interested and that the rules
are fair.[2] But in fact, these particular strictures need not encumber a legitimate
arbitration regime. People may well widely perceive a self-interested arbiter,
so long as he or she stands for a greater righteousness, as their rightful judge.
Moreover, rules that are just may be repudiated on the basis of their unfair
application; and conversely, unjust rules may be accepted if they are perceived
to be fairly applied.

In sixteenth century Spanish America, arbitration hinged on the authority of
the royal sovereign. The king unabashedly protected the interests of the Crown.
But the Crown belonged to the king only because as sovereign he possessed
specific, emblematic attributes, such as benevolence, wisdom, and Christian
zeal. This admixture of grand self-interest and selfless virtue rendered the
sovereign an unimpeachable arbiter in the eyes of Spanish Americans. And yet
the sovereign's colonial subjects constructed a sprawling and contentious system of normative scheming – a system that colonials manipulated rhetorically

---

[1] Aristotle, *The Politics*, trans. Ernest Baker (New York: Oxford University Press, 1958), 6.

[2] John F. Padgett and Christopher K. Ansell, "Robust Action and the Rise of the Medici, 1400–
1434," *American Journal of Sociology* 98, no. 6 (May 1993): 1259–1319.

to extract regal favors, circumvent royal mandates, undermine local rivals, and even question particular rulings by the Crown.

The Iberian past helped account for this state of affairs. By wavering between absolutist and contractual logics, traditional Castilian theories of legitimate rule simultaneously secured the exemplary status of the royal arbiter *and* endowed colonials with the sense of entitlement that animated their contentiousness. Kings were responsible directly to God, and thus stood above the people and, at least in principle, even the laws. But the monarch also "placed himself at the head of his court for the purpose of shielding the people from harm," and the people, in turn, agreed that "as the head does not injure the body so must the body protect the head."[3]

The upshot of this duality was a normatively grounded space for subaltern vocality and, ultimately, for the contestation of particular acts of monarchical legitimation. Moreover, all this was reinforced in practice by the peculiarities of Iberian politics during the protracted *Reconquista*. In medieval Castile, for example, it was nearly impossible to find the prestigious bloodlines that in France and England allowed royal succession to proceed according to the hereditary principle alone, and as a result, a Castilian contender's "appeal to inheritance" was simply not enough to claim the throne. "Election and acclamation of the nobility and people" were also crucial.[4]

If the politics of royal succession reinforced subaltern vocality and contested legitimation throughout the *Reconquista*, so too did the production of archetypical identities and institutional arrangements. At the level of identity, monarchs, particularly in Asturias and León, were expected to conform to the exigent profile of the "good king." A good king served "justice" in order to "contain" the "wicked." He demonstrated "fortitude" in resisting "tyrants." He was "benevolent" in dealing with the "people." He was "authoritative" toward all. And he showed "true wisdom," of which the first principle was recognition of the "equality of men's nature."[5]

At the level of institutions, the *Reconquista* produced in twelfth century León something unprecedented in Europe: Alfonse IX decreed that elected citizens from each city would participate in Political Assembly, along with bishops and magnates. The king even committed himself not to reach "agreement" without the consent of the "three arms" of the kingdom.[6] In Aragón, meanwhile, the institutions of confederation and local government through viceroyalties became so deeply entrenched that King Ferdinand himself swore before the *Córtes* (the

---

[3] Colin MacLachlan, *Spain's Empire in the New World: The Role of Ideas in Institutional and Social Change* (Berkeley, CA: University of California Press, 1988), 9.

[4] Teófilo Ruiz, "Unsacred Monarchy: The Kings of Castile in the Late Middle Ages," in Sean Wilentz, ed., *Rites of Power* (Philadelphia, PA: University of Pennsylvania Press, 1985), 110, 121–2; I. A. A. Thompson, *Crown and Córtes* (Brookefield, VT: Variorum, 1993).

[5] José Antonio Maravall, *Estudios de Historia del Pensamiento Español* (Madrid: Ediciones Cultura Hispánica, 1983), 59.

[6] Ibid., 59–60.

assembly of town representatives) to "observe and respect their privileges and laws."[7]

Of course, the past did not determine everything, either in Iberia or the Indies. Most notably, the consolidation of monarchical authority under Ferdinand and Isabella was undeniable, especially after the reconquest of Granada in 1492 brought the *Reconquista* to a triumphant conclusion. On that occasion, the Pope pronounced Ferdinand of Aragón and Isabelle of Castile "Catholic Monarchs" and "athletes of Christ," then granted them "dominion of all the lands which they discovered 300 miles to the west of the Azores, on condition that they converted to Christianity the peoples whom they found."[8] The monarchs' prestige soared. Machiavelli acclaimed Ferdinand as a "new prince, because from being a weak king he [had risen] to being, for fame and glory, the first king of Christendom."[9]

More importantly still, the Crown's approach to colonial vocality contained a distinct element of novelty. In an absolutist departure from Iberian institutional tradition, the Crown decided against establishing elective bodies in the Indies. This meant that colonials would have no formal representation in the metropole.[10] Instead, colonials were granted the right to correspond directly with their sovereign. Early on, Ferdinand announced that he would not tolerate a governor's interference with the mail because:

All who want to write to us should be free to do so, and any information received we will inquire about and we shall make our decisions on the basis of the whole truth; and truth once known we shall decide.[11]

The Crown, in fact, ordered that "no official should prevent anyone from sending to the monarch or anyone else letters and other information which concern the welfare of the Indies."[12] This was a momentous choice. The decision not to establish elective representative bodies *(córtes)* in the Indies spared the Crown the troublesome pressures that such institutional channels might have gathered from below. But the Crown also lost the advantages that those same institutional channels might have brought, such as the structured aggregation of divergent opinions and grievances.

Moreover, by declaring itself *the* final arbiter of colonial disputes, the Crown unleashed a remonstrative variant of "freedom of speech." Friars, conquerors, colonists, Indians, judges, and a multitude of royal administrative officials

---

[7] Richard Bonney, *The European Dynastic States, 1494–1660* (New York: Oxford University Press, 1991), 92.

[8] This papal bull took as its precedent the *Dum Diversas* of 1452. Hugh Thomas, *Conquest: Montezuma, Cortés, and the Fall of Old Mexico* (New York: Simon & Schuster, 1993), 58–9.

[9] Bonney, *The European Dynastic States*, 90.

[10] Edwin Williamson, *The Penguin History of Latin America* (New York: Penguin, 1992), 93.

[11] Ursula Lamb, "Cristobal de Tapia v. Nicolás de Ovando, Residencia Fragment of 1509," in *Hispanic American Historical Review* (henceforth *HAHR*) 33, no. 3 (August 1953): 427–41.

[12] Lewis Hanke, "Free Speech in Sixteenth Century Spanish America," *HAHR* 26, no. 2 (May 1946): 135–43.

composed personal messages to their king, "explaining what and who was wrong, and describing the measures needed to remedy the situation."[13]

The extreme multivocality[14] of the colonial regime – replete with contradictory claims that were rendered intelligible only by the polarizing clarity of a Manichean *lingua franca* – shaped every aspect of the conquest, from its martial rituals and economic institutions, to the legitimacy of the Crown and the theological and juridical debates regarding its claims to dominion over the Indies.

This chapter has two goals. First, to demonstrate through historical reconstruction the emergence of a Manichean system of normative scheming in which competing actors conciliated their particularist interests with the pursuit of virtuous identity while simultaneously identifying their rivals' endeavors with the forces of "vice." Rulers and subjects, in brief, created an uncivil society dependent for arbitration upon a Crown whose legitimacy remained intact even as its own loyal subjects compromised its actual capacity to govern. The chapter's second goal is to explain in comparative perspective the historical fact that the same system of normative scheming endogenously shaped in radically different ways the collective identities and power relations of colonial Nicaragua and Costa Rica.

Subaltern Vocality and Rule Legitimation

In 1511, a friar on the island of Hispaniola went to his pulpit and voiced indignation at the "cruel and horrible servitude" that Spaniards imposed on the natives. He thundered at his congregation that they were living in mortal sin, and referred to Indians as "men" endowed with a "rational soul." The incident was so explosive that it led to a polemic at Burgos, conducted in the presence of King Ferdinand. On one side stood those who argued that a Christian prince could wage war on "infidels" only if necessary to spread the faith. On the other stood those who claimed that the papal "donation" of the Indies to the Catholic monarchs authorized the conquest and, resorting to Aristotle, that there were certain peoples – such as the savages of the Indies – who were slaves by nature.[15]

Out of this debate came the Laws of Burgos of 1512, which in essence decreed the Christianization of the natives while simultaneously fashioning a system of labor exploitation. Most notably, the Laws codified a modified version of the *Encomienda* – an institution of trusts developed in Iberia during the *Reconquista*. Under the *Encomienda* system, Indians remained free subjects of the

---

[13] Ibid.

[14] In this book, multivocality and univocality refer to the range of legitimate vocal actors, whereas for Padgett and Ansell these terms refer to plausible interpretations, so that multivocality, for example, is about being able to make coherent sense to different audiences simultaneously. Moreover, for Padgett and Ansell, an actor's ability to deploy multivocality depends on his or her sociopolitical position. In this book, on the other hand, a rhetorical strategist can transcend his or her position.

[15] Thomas, *Conquest*, 71–2.

Crown, but the Crown "commended" them to "worthy" conquerors. These *encomenderos* became the Indians' Christian tutors and protectors, and received in return tributary labor from their spiritual charges.[16]

After Burgos, another meeting was held at Valladolid in 1513. This one led to the conclusion that if Indians refused to accept the full implications of the papal donation, then the conquerors could be said to possess "just" cause for war.[17] All that remained, it seemed at that point, was Spain's obligation to prosecute the conquest in compliance with this principle, which helps explain why Spain was alone among European powers in creating a "fully ritualized protocol for declaring war against indigenous peoples."[18]

This protocol, known as the *Requerimiento*, or Requirement, was rooted in the *Reconquista*'s "elaborate code of rules about the 'just war,' and in the rights of the victors over the vanquished population, including the right to enslave it."[19] But the *Requerimiento* also accorded central importance to the papal grant. Consider the protocol that a typical conqueror read to the "heathen":

On behalf of His Majesty...I...his servant...make known as best I can that God...gave charge [of all peoples] to one man named Saint Peter, so that he was lord and superior of all the men of the world...and gave him all the world for his lordship and jurisdiction....One of these Pontiffs...made a donation of these islands and mainland of the Ocean Sea to the Catholic kings of Spain....Therefore I beg and require you as best I can...[that] you recognize the church and lord and superior of the universal world, and the most elevated pope...and His Majesty and I in his name will receive you...and leave your women and children free...and we will not compel you to turn Christians. But if you do not do it...I will enter forcefully against you, and I will make war everywhere...and I will subject you to the yoke and obedience of the Church and His Majesty, and I will take your wives and children, and will make them slaves....[20]

The *Requerimiento*, according to the scholar who drafted it, was designed to "calm the conscience of Christians." But the Friar Las Casas, the preeminent defender of Indians, did not know whether "to laugh or weep."[21] The *Requerimiento* so blatantly served the prefabrication of just wars against the natives (who could not even understand Spanish) that contentious reports soon began to arrive in Spain from across the ocean. Friars, chroniclers, and even

---

[16] The *Encomienda* was different from the system of compulsory labor known as the *Repartimiento*, first used by Christopher Columbus to "distribute" Indians among members of his expedition. Lesley Byrd Simpson, *Studies in the Administration of the Indians in New Spain: The Repartimiento System of Native Labor* (Berkeley, CA: University of California Press, 1938), 4–5.

[17] Anthony Pagden, *Spanish Imperialism and the Political Imagination* (New Haven, CT: Yale University Press, 1990), 15.

[18] Patricia Seed, *Ceremonies of Possession in Europe's Conquest of the New World, 1492–1640* (New York: Cambridge University Press, 1995), 70.

[19] J. H. Elliot, *Imperial Spain* (New York: Saint Martin's, 1967), 58.

[20] Seed, *Ceremonies*, 69.

[21] Thomas, *Conquest*, 72.

conquerors themselves noted abuses of the protocol committed by rivals, and informed the Crown accordingly.[22]

Because of this deluge of reports, in fact, we know that in the most egregious cases of abuse,

...captains muttered [the *Requerimiento's*] theological phrases into their beards on the edge of sleeping Indian settlements, or even a league away before starting the formal attack.... Ship captains would sometimes have the document read from the deck as they approached the island, and at night would send out enslaving expeditions.[23]

Such reports fed the controversy raging in Spain, where the Catholic Monarchs' grandson Charles, heir to the Spanish kingdoms, was forced to rely ever more for legitimation of the conquest on the papal grant at the core of the *Requerimiento*. In 1519, Charles proclaimed that, "Through the donation of the Holy Apostolic See and other legitimate titles, we are the Lord of the West Indies, isles and Main of Ocean Sea...incorporated in our Crown of Castile."[24]

The Crown's persistent interpretation of the papal grant as a donation of such lands, however, failed to thwart the juridical and theological critiques of the conquest that arose in Spain.[25] And as if this were not enough, in Castile, Charles' election as King of the Romans provoked xenophobic sentiments, aristocratic apprehension, and localist suspicion.[26]

To be sure, the notion that a universal monarchy under Charles' leadership might serve as the bulwark for Christianity exerted a powerful appeal.[27] But the equivalence of monarchy and empire remained a point of keen contention in Spanish political thought.[28] Still, Charles continued to stake claims to jurisdiction and property rights over the Indies. To bolster the emperor's case, official "image makers" made a series of bold assertions. Some argued that Charles V had been placed "on earth by God to fulfill the work begun in the ninth century by Charles I"; others posited that the Spaniards' singular devotion to Christianity made them the obvious heirs to the *imperium romanum*.[29]

[22] Gonzálo Fernández de Oviedo, *Historia General y Natural de las Indias*, in Eduardo Pérez Valle, ed., *Nicaragua en los Cronistas de Indias: Oviedo* (Managua: Fondo de Promoción Cultural, Banco de América, Editorial y Litografía San José, 1976), 167–8.

[23] Lewis Hanke, *The Spanish Struggle for Justice in the Conquest of America* (Boston: Little, Brown, 1965), 34.

[24] D. A. Brading, *The First America* (New York: Cambridge University Press, 1991), 214.

[25] For a discussion of the debates, see Reinhard Bendix, *Kings or People: Power and the Mandate to Rule* (Berkeley, CA: University of California Press, 1978), 142–3; Bonney, *The European Dynastic States*, 93–4.

[26] Ibid., 110.

[27] The *comuneros*, who took their name from *comunidad* (the municipal council established early on in Toledo by town rebels), demanded a new governmental framework based on a confederation of free towns, with the *Córtes*, or assembly of town representatives, as the key state institution. Ibid., 110.

[28] As the contradictory impulses behind the revolt of the *comuneros* illustrated, the equivalence of monarchy and empire also remained a source of political confusion. Ibid., 111, 114.

[29] Pagden, *Spanish Imperialism*, 43.

Potent counterarguments soon proliferated; two were particularly bother-some. First, because "civil power could only be transferred by society acting as a single body," the legitimate enhancement of the universal empire to include the Indies required, quite literally, a world electoral assembly. Second, "the Castilian monarchy might claim sovereignty and property rights in America" only with the natives' permission, a stipulation as implausible as the other was impractical.[30]

Normative Scheming: Obedient or Roguish Interests?

Dependent on the Church for moral endorsement of conquest activities, the Crown could ill afford to ignore the pleas of pro-Indian religious orders, or the arguments of theologians and jurists stirred by those pleas. At the same time, however, the Crown remained acutely vulnerable to the conquerors' self-seeking appeals, for two reasons. The most obvious reason was that monarchs and conquerors routinely entered into contracts that made conquest a joint enterprise. Conquerors financed and staffed expeditions; monarchs licensed the expeditions, and used the power of the state to protect colonial settlements, structure them politically, and envelop them in the hallowed grandeur of an evangelical empire. The second, more profound reason involved the essence of the social compact: As subjects of the Crown, conquerors were expected to submit to royal authority, but they were also entitled to a "fair" hearing from the sovereign.

A fair hearing, however, was no longer a simple matter, precisely because of the Crown's freedom of expression policy. Faced with the dual challenge of recognizing the conquerors' rightful claims while simultaneously preventing the rise of local potentates, the Crown established early on a system of incentives. It rewarded meritorious conquerors with such prizes as Indian labor power *(encomienda)*, local political office, and titles of distinction and rank.[31] But competition over these prizes generated constant strife and mistrust. Already in 1516, an anonymous memorial warned that informants on the affairs of the Indies should not be believed implicitly, for each one had his own particular agenda. The great chronicler Gonzálo Fernández de Oviedo even claimed that "inventors of fiction" – that is, the conquerors whose exploits he witnessed and recorded – deceived the sovereign by means of "exorbitant accounts."[32] And as late as 1563, Martín Cortés, heir to the legendary conquistador, echoed

---

[30] Ibid., 47, 50–2.

[31] The Crown expanded the traditional concept of *hidalguía* so that the title of *hidalgo* – "son of something or someone" – could be used to reward specific meritorious deeds at various ranks. See Samuel Stone, *La Dinastía de los Conquistadores* (San José: Editorial EDUCA, 1975), 52. For the different local offices given out in recompense, see Robert Himmerich Y Valencia, *The Encomenderos of New Spain, 1521–1555* (Austin, TX: University of Texas Press, 1991), 4–5.

[32] Oviedo, *Historia General*, 376.

the sentiment. In a letter dispatched from Mexico, he warned the Crown as follows:

Your Majesty and your Royal Council of the Indies should understand clearly that there is no story so improbable concerning events here that witnesses may not be found to swear to its truth, for exaggeration flowers in this land.[33]

And indeed, Spaniards in the Indies exhibited a "story-making predilection." Cortés, among others, wrote reports that were "splendid fictions," full of "politic elisions, omissions, inventions, and a transparent desire to impress [the king] with his own indispensability."[34] Even legal documents served as autobiographical affirmations of self-worth, to the point that such documents became instruments of identity formation.[35] As one literary theoretician puts it, "to write was a form of enfranchisement."[36]

The Spaniards' story-making predilection was a rational response to the Crown's declared hunger for the "truth" and its equally open admission that only on the basis of the "truth" would the sovereign render final decisions. The widespread practice of "exaggeration" and the attendant erosion of credibility, in turn, were the practical consequences of the Manichean rhetorical strategy invariably found at the core of the Spaniards' "stories."

This deep Manicheanism is hardly surprising. Past and present alike inculcated this *lingua franca* in Spaniards. The *Reconquista*, in its most elemental simplification, represented an existential struggle between Christian and infidel. The conquest of the Indies itself relied for legitimation on a papal bull that inextricably tied the pursuit of worldly goods to Christianity's spiritual mission. And then there was the role of the Crown. Determined to stunt the emergence of a powerful nobility in the Indies while simultaneously compelled by contractual obligation to reward meritorious conquerors and to safeguard the welfare of its overseas subjects, the Crown came to understand "merit" as more than sheer exploits of conquest. Merit was even more than service to God and monarchy. Merit was, above all, faithful obedience to the sovereign.

Taken together, these factors obligated all vocal actors to vindicate their particular agendas through Manichean argumentation. Persuading the sovereign of one's own meritorious deeds did not suffice; it required exposing the vile

---

[33] Hanke, "Free Speech," 147.

[34] Inga Clendinnen, "'Fierce and Unnatural Cruelty': Cortés and the Conquest of Mexico," in Stephen Greenblatt, ed., *New World Encounters* (Berkeley, CA: University of California Press, 1993), 15.

[35] Robert Chamberlain, "Probanza de Méritos y Servicios of Blas González, Conquistador of Yucatán," *HAHR* vol. 28, No. 4 (November 1948): 526–36; Henry Wagner, "Three Studies on the Same Subject: Bernal Díaz del Castillo; The Family of Bernal Díaz del Castillo; Notes on Writings by and about Bernal Díaz del Castillo," *HAHR*, Vol. 25, No. 2 (May 1945): 155–99.

[36] Roberto González-Echevarría, *Myth and Archive: A Theory of Latin American Narrative* (New York: Cambridge University Press, 1990), 44–6.

comportment of others as well. After all, any conqueror who gained physical control of a territory and baptized its Indian inhabitants could claim to have rendered great "services" to God and monarchy. But this still left open the question of which conqueror would be granted political-administrative authority over the conquered space and, by extension, the capacity to distribute *encomiendas*.

The question came up repeatedly. In the typical scenario, a successful conqueror would establish a colony and, as swiftly as humanly possible, dispatch an expeditionary captain to conquer new territory. This captain would then develop ambitions of his own and enter into a dispute with his former superior. In a less common scenario, disputes would arise when two or more conquerors either converged on the same spot or sought to enhance their respective turfs by eliminating conquering leaders already established in neighboring areas. Thus, the first step in any rhetorical approach to the king was to convey the uniqueness of one's service. The conqueror Vasco Núñez de Balboa fulfilled this minimal requirement by informing the king that previous governors had

... performed their duties very badly ... were the cause of their own perdition ... [and] imagined that they could rule the land and do all that was necessary from their beds.[37]

Next, Balboa drew a sharp contrast between his own devotion to the Crown and the dissoluteness of his predecessor. "I assure your most Royal Highness," he wrote:

I have not remained in my bed while my people were exploring the country. No party has gone into any part of this land unless I was in front as a guide, opening the road with my own hands.[38]

When dealing with a direct competitor, Balboa went even further. This is what he had to say to the Crown about his archrival, Pedrarias Dávila, conqueror and governor of Nicaragua:

He is a person who is delighted to see discord between people, and if there is [no discord] he creates it.... this vice he has to a very great extent. He is a man ... absorbed in his profit-getting and greed.

This, in turn, is what Pedrarias wrote the king about Balboa:

It is public and notorious that [Balboa] does not know how to speak the truth ... is most excessively avaricious ... is very cruel ... has no self control ... is very mercenary ... is very determined to procure, by fair means or foul, to be superior ... even if it be contrary to all loyalty and service owed to God and their Highnesses.[39]

---

[37] Irwin Blacker and Harry Rosen, *The Golden Conquistadores* (Indianapolis, IN: Bobbs-Merrill, 1960), 44.

[38] Ibid., 49.

[39] Ibid., 61–2.

Persuading the sovereign that one was in the right became a key goal. Here, once again, is Balboa:

Your Highness should receive [reports] from me as your loyal servant, and should give [them] *credence*. . . . I do not desire to make towers of wind like the governors whom your Highness sent out . . . this is the *truth* [emphasis added].[40]

Persuasion obviously posed a challenge in an atmosphere of growing mistrust:

Your Highness must know that formerly there were certain disagreements here, because the [district officers] and [aldermen] of this town, filled with *envy* and *treachery*, attempted to seize me . . . they made false charges against me with *false witnesses* and in secret . . . and because the administrators and the aldermen sent an accusation against me . . . I appointed two gentlemen as my *judges*, that they might draw up a report of my life and of the great and loyal services which I have done for your Highness. . . . I send this that you may see the *malice* of these people. . . . I beseech that favor may be shown me in proportion to my services. I also send a report of what passed with respect to those who invented these *calumnies* [emphasis added].[41]

Rival conquerors were not the only contributors to this atmosphere of "false witnesses" and "malice." Lawyers also added to the contentiousness of colonial society if only because disputants invariably turned to "judges" who, after investigating the squabble at hand and assessing the comportment of the parties involved, conveyed their reports to the metropole. Employed by all, lawyers were trusted by none. Balboa himself argued that by reducing their numbers, the Crown would rid political competition of "devils" who "not only are they themselves evil but give rise to a thousand lawsuits and quarrels."[42]

In addition, professional chroniclers played an especially significant role, superimposing Manichean clarity on the rhetorical maze that their own chronicles helped create. The famous chronicler Oviedo, for one, set out both to expose "vile" conquerors who placed their interests above those of the royal sovereign and to teach the moral that "diabolical" men would be ultimately "unmasked," if not by the temporal sovereign, then by "the Eternal and Celestial, who cannot forget the culpability of sinners, nor can He be deceived by astute or bad judges."[43]

Even the Crown complicated this expanding maze with its own fears and suspicions. The Crown, for example, considered it

. . . the special duty of the ecclesiastical authorities and the members of the [the High Court] to "watch the governors, take care of each other, and give an account to the King of what they observed and considered worthy of his knowledge". Other observers or examiners with high sounding titles, such as royal investigators (*pesquisadores*),

[40] Ibid., 52
[41] Ibid., 53.
[42] Blacker and Rosen, *The Golden Conquistadores*, 53.
[43] See Oviedo, *Historia General*, 139, 158, 206, 230–1, 376. See also Pascual de Andagoya "Relación Que da el Adelantado," in Adrián Blazquez, ed., *Relación y Documentos* (Madrid: Historia 16, 1986), 83–146.

visitors (*visitadores*), and seers (*veedores*) were sent out by the King from time to time in order to make personal reports to him as to what was going wrong and who was to blame . . . and when the viceroy or governor retired from office he was subjected to a public hearing before a lawyer appointed by the King, who acted as a sort of one-man court before whom all who had grievances could air them.[44]

The first Judicial Review of an outgoing official held in the New World prompted Friar Bartolomé de Las Casas to comment that "it was a marvel to see people outdo each other to accuse and to turn upon him who had been the most generous of governors."[45] Indeed, power transfers rapidly turned into treacherous affairs that often culminated in disgrace and dispossession for the outgoing official. This commonplace outcome was due to the ways in which royal officials conciliated practical exigencies with the controlling norm of obedience to the Crown. By relying on the old Iberian practice of "I obey but do not comply" – *(Obedezco pero no cumplo)* – officials found a compromise solution to what was in effect a principal-agent problem:

When a royal statute considered contrary to the colonial interests arrived, the viceroy or the president of the supreme court would read it solemnly, and placing it over his head as a token of submission and humbleness, would say in a loud voice *"Se acata pero no se cumple"* – it shall be respected but not enforced. This act satisfied both the principle of submission to the king, and the necessity of realism in colonial government. The common people referred to such royal statutes as "unconsecrated hosts".[46]

This practice, a sort of dramaturgical obedience, proved functional to monarch and subjects alike in the short term. From the monarch's perspective, the practitioner of "I obey but do not comply" reaffirmed both the primacy of royal authority and its centrality to the formation of the virtuous colonial identity. From the perspective of the practitioner, dramaturgical obedience enhanced his degree of freedom at the local level without ipso facto incurring the punitive costs associated with open disobedience. In *obedezco pero no cumplo*, there was no desecration, only devout pragmatism.

By paying formal homage to the norm in the very act of violating it, the practice of dramaturgical obedience afforded administrators the kind of discretionary authority they needed to execute their duty more efficiently. The compromise was highly functional at the moment of execution. But ultimately, it contributed to the colonies' broadening propensity for strife, since officials who engaged in the practice were almost doomed to have it dredged up in the Judicial Review at the end of their term, and might even prompt a general investigation.

Despite its long-term risks to the practitioner, however, the practice of dramaturgical obedience endured because, in the final analysis, the legitimation of

---

[44] John Crow, *The Epic of Latin America* (Berkeley, CA: University of California Press, 1992), 167.
[45] Lamb, "Cristobal de Tapia v. Nicolás de Ovando," 427–41.
[46] Crow, *The Epic*, 175.

interests – those of the Crown and those of its colonial subjects – had to be conciliated. The imperative of conciliation was in evidence everywhere. The Crown accommodated the interests of its colonial subjects by responding as best it could to their appeals. Colonials, for their part, promoted their own particular interests with those of the Crown by recasting the latter's perception of how its interests would best be served. To this end, colonials played on the Crown's fondest hopes and darkest fears. Where persuasion failed, furtive disobedience – practiced with the Crown's complicity – served as a functional equivalent. Where neither persuasion nor furtive disobedience proved effective, violent confrontation became unavoidable. This occurred only twice, in Perú and Nicaragua. In the vast majority of cases, accommodation prevailed. And in one instance – Costa Rica – it actually produced the image of a Manichean ideal: a seemingly harmonious community of Spaniards who, obedient to the Crown and dedicated to Christian labor, managed to "persuade" the heathen into the virtuous fold.

Manichean Accommodation

In 1530, the Crown issued an antislavery decree. Guatemala's *cabildo* (municipal government) responded as follows:

> ...it is most insufferable that [war] slaves are not permitted, for the people here are indomitable and obstinate; an in order to subject them to Your Majesty's service, it is necessary that [Indians] think that their sacrifices and many other excesses which they commit daily shall not be tolerated. As for the slaves who the Indian themselves hold, giving such slaves to Spaniards saves them from being sacrificed to their idols, and from being eaten, as it is their custom. In addition, the great majority of these slaves, by moving among Spaniards, are converted to the Catholic faith and shall become good Christians. Above all, however, the king will lose a considerable sum in gold pesos for the Spaniards have only begun to enjoy the fruits given them by Indians who hand them some slaves for labor and for the extraction of gold, which now shall cease because of Your Majesty's order.[47]

The depiction touched a nerve with the Crown, which now amended its antislavery decree by allowing conquerors in Guatemala to take "rescue slaves" – Indian servants who passed from the hands of their Indian masters into those of Spaniards. Moreover, this partial revocation was soon followed by another edict allowing for the taking of war slaves. With these concessions, however, the Crown opened itself up to appeals from yet another set of actors: the Indians' defenders. Consider now the protestations addressed by the Franciscans of Mexico to the king:

> We cannot grasp the spirit that moved the man who gave the account to your Council which in turn led [the Council] to grant such cruelty. Nor can we imagine how

---

[47] Silvio Zavala, *Contribucíon a la Historia de las Instituciones Coloniales en Guatemala* (Guatemala: Editorial Universitaria, Universidad de San Carlos, 1986), 15.

peremptory were the reasons of that man who was able to persuade such wise and lucid men as those who are members of your Council to grant such a thing.[48]

This remonstration stopped short of a challenge to monarchical authority, suggesting instead that could dupe the insidious eloquence of wicked men even the wise and benevolent sovereign. In a letter dispatched from the city of Granada in Nicaragua, Las Casas expressed his astonishment: "How can such malice in those who inform the [Council] deceive such an eminent and admirably wise [body]?"[49]

As the Crown's vacillation became more pronounced, it reversed itself by allowing war slaves while prohibiting rescue slaves. Soon thereafter, the Crown reversed itself further in a decree sent to Honduras forbidding Christians to remove Indian slaves from the province, except for one or two in their personal service. But the Crown was about to face a broader rhetorical attack from pro-Indian activists, who went on the offensive when the Pope declared Indians "rational" and thus capable of receiving the faith (1537). The first move came from the humanist Francisco de Vitoria, who argued in 1539 that "the gospel fulfilled and perfected the natural virtue of pagan philosophy and politics" – a claim that subverted the presumably insuperable opposition between "pagan evil" and "Christian grace."[50]

The papal pronouncement, Vitoria's reasoning, and the arguments and evangelical work of pro-native religious orders in the Indies all combined to render plausible the moral equality between Spaniard and Indian. And once the Indians' moral development became more than conceivable – once it became a realistic objective – the Friar Las Casas was free to proceed with a more explicitly "political" line of attack against the conquerors. In his "Very Brief Account of the Destruction of the Indies," he astutely deployed terms fraught with significance, such as "tyrant-governor," when referring to royal officials who were also *encomenderos*. More importantly, he brought to the attention of the Crown the likelihood that its colonial regime was becoming "morally and politically illegitimate." This deplorable state of affairs, the friar concluded, could be remedied only if "our Emperor Charles V will harken to and comprehend the evils and betrayals against the will of God and His Majesty."[51]

Given the Crown's ongoing preoccupation with the legitimation of the conquest, Las Casas' argument was disturbing. The emperor listened and acted swiftly. The New Laws, promulgated in 1542,

... prohibited the use of the "just war" concept as an excuse for enslavement, and declared that those illegally enslaved must be free. The Crown also ordered royal officials to release Indians held ... in any form of personal bondage and, in direct attack on

[48] Ibid., 21.
[49] Bartolomé de Las Casas cited in Silvio Zavala, *Aportaciones Históricas* (Mexico, DF: Editorial Nueva Imagen, 1985), 225.
[50] Brading, *The First America*, 82.
[51] MacLachlan, *Spain's Empire*, 57.

the *Encomienda*, prohibited future grants of tributary Indians. The most unpalatable restriction provided that on the death of the incumbent holder of an *encomienda* the grant reverted to the Crown.[52]

The New Laws of 1542 were an unusual demonstration of monarchical will, especially because by targeting the *Encomienda* the Laws also took aim at the vital colonial interests wrapped up with the institution. But the New Laws also brought the Crown and conquerors to a head on the critical issue of justice. In theory, sovereign and subjects, bound together in a relationship of mutual obligation, were in a position to cause each other "unjust" harm. This theoretical possibility now seemed a reality. The Crown was persuaded by Las Casas' arguments that the conquerors' abuse of the *Encomienda* further eroded the legitimacy of the conquest and thus injured the Crown's fundamental interests. The conquerors, for their part, believed that the New Laws were the handiwork of evil friars and a violation of their own rights.

The Crown stood its ground to the extent that it continued to phase out private *encomiendas*. Over the next sixty years, royal officers managed gradually to reduce the number of such *encomiendas* so that the institution's formal abolition in 1720 simply delivered a coup de grace.[53] But the Crown also accommodated the conquerors' interests as best it could. In some colonies, it temporarily suspended its attack on the *Encomienda*. The Crown also legalized a modified variant of the *Repartimiento* (labor draft).[54] Finally, and most importantly, the Crown proved receptive to appeals for exemptions, thus deepening the conquerors' belief that benevolence and wisdom were inextricably entwined in the royal arbiter, so that a worthy supplicant could expect to find justice in the sovereign if the latter were "properly" informed.

And in fact, the Crown responded to the conquerors' self-serving appeals precisely because these appeals were also effective rhetorical vehicles for normative outrage. In Guatemala, for example, the conquerors wrote the king, "We are scandalized, as we have been told to cut off our heads." Blaming the "scandalous" ordinances on Las Casas, they demanded, "Pay us Your Majesty what you owe us, and grant us great favors."[55] The use of the words "pay" and "owe" in conjunction with "favors" harkened back to the contractual relationship between sovereign and subjects, while the indignant tone of the demand reflected the Guatemalans' awareness of the difference between legitimate and arbitrary exercise of royal power.

Similarly, Guatemala City's *regidores* (administrators of Indians) wrote the Crown's new governor and president of the *Audiencia* (high court) that the

---

[52] Ibid., 58.

[53] Murdo MacCleod, *Spanish Central America* (Berkeley, CA: University of California Press, 1973), 161.

[54] The legalized variant of the *Repartimiento* was meant to preclude the abuses that in the early stages of the conquest had made the practice so destructive to the Indian populations.

[55] Claudio Veliz, *The Centralist Tradition of Latin America* (Princeton, NJ: Princeton University Press, 1980). See also Zavala, *Contribución*, 29.

New Laws were merely the result of the Dominicans' "zeal" – a "zeal" that might "appear to be holy and good" but was in truth destructive to the "Republic of Christians" and detrimental to the "loyal vassals" of the Crown.[56] But Guatemala's governor, who understood the Crown's interest in collecting tribute from the freed slaves as well as the complex juridical and theological challenges facing the king in Spain, proceeded with the emancipation of war slaves. The *cabildo* again wrote the king, asking him to consider that slaves had been taken in the first place with his permission. More importantly, the *cabildo*'s members complained about the manner in which the governor enforced the ordinances, and they reiterated the duties of the monarch, the evils committed by his new official representative, and the merits of their own deeds.

The Crown responded, yet again, by granting exemptions to conquerors, something it was able to do because while the freedom of Indians was established as a general principle, this principle did not protect those natives who tried to repel Spanish aggression. The conquerors also launched a new wave of Manichean appeals, demanding protection from "arbitrary" officials. In typical fashion, they emphasized that failures of justice originated not with the Crown but with clever friars and avaricious, power-hungry officials who, endowed with remarkable powers of persuasion, "duped" the sovereign and his council.[57]

The strategy worked. A voluminous stack of royal decrees indicates that the Crown responded quickly and forcefully when informed of "anomalies" in the conduct of its officials and religious orders. The king, in fact, often recapitulated the charges and countercharges lodged in the narratives to which he was responding, and wrote as if tracing contradictory story lines that, by means of a corrective decree from the royal pen, might converge into a fair and peaceful outcome.[58] Also indicative of the Crown's responsiveness were the frequent arrivals of official "visitors" in the various provinces of the Kingdom of Guatemala (Central America) – visitors who came for the express purpose of investigating charges that local elites leveled against royal officials in a stream of contentious correspondence.[59]

[56] Byrd Simpson, *Studies in the Administration of the Indians*, 6–7.

[57] James Lockhart and Enrique Otte, eds., *Letters and People of the Spanish Indies: Sixteenth Century* (New York: Cambridge University Press, 1989), 73–7.

[58] For original texts, see Federico Arguello Solórzano and Carlos Molina Arguello, eds., *Monumenta Centroamericae Histórica: Colección de Documentos y Materiales Para el Estudio de la Historia y de la Vida de los Pueblos de la América Central* (Managua: Instituto Centroamericano de Historia, Universidad Centroamericana, 1965), 321–5, 358–61, 364–8, 388–94, 432, 460–5, 468–9, 487–91, 532–5, 641–4, 835–43, 916–17.

[59] See also Javier Ortiz de la Tabla et al., eds., *Cartas de Cabildos Hispanoamericanos: Audiencia de Guatemala* (Sevilla: Publicaciones de la Diputación Provincial de Sevilla; Publicaciones de la Escuela de Estudios Hispano-Americanos, 1984).

Manichean Confrontation

The New Laws of 1542, as previously noted, prohibited officers of the Crown from holding *encomiendas*. The first reaction on the part of Nicaragua's governor – who was also the province's most powerful *encomendero* – was furtive disobedience, a tradition by then well established in the Indies and finely honed by Nicaragua's administrators. The governor simply transferred his *encomienda* Indians to his wife and sons. Given this particular governor's highly concentrated power, the subterfuge might have worked. But the High Court in Guatemala ruled that the governor's maneuver had been illegal, and so the official had to travel to Spain to make his case at court.[60]

The governor's troubles were the result of an astute rhetorical campaign that the bishop of Nicaragua, a defender of royal prerogative and a strict enforcer of the New Laws, had been waging for some time. Soon after his arrival in Nicaragua in 1544, the bishop drafted his first report to the king, accusing the governor and his family of comporting themselves as if they were "lords of everything." The bishop's subsequent letters went on to express concern over the horrendous maltreatment of Indians. On the latter point, the bishop reminded Charles V that one day he – the king – "would have to account to God."

Eventually, the bishop combined forces with Las Casas, coauthoring a report to the Council of Indies in which they argued that the "tyranny" and "violence" of Nicaragua's dominant clan imbued Indians with hatred and disdain for Christianity. This doubly authoritative document was followed by another, describing the retaliatory attacks that the bishop and Las Casas suffered at the hands of the local tyrants. The bishop then resumed his own letter-writing campaign, independently of Las Casas, conveying in each missive the disturbing claim that despite the New Laws, the conditions of Indians continued to deteriorate in Nicaragua.[61]

These authoritative condemnations triggered a series of familiar rhetorical countermoves. First, Nicaragua's leading *encomenderos* argued that the Laws violated their contract with the Crown. Second, they insisted that "wicked" friars had "inspired" the Laws. Third, they bolstered their grievances by referencing the general view that although the king was above reproach, his officers (and even friars and ecclesiastical hierarchs) were moved by evil intentions.

With the justification for rebellion finally in place, and in the absence of the governor, the governor's own sons could now take action. They stabbed the bishop to death. From the conquerors' perspective, this rebellion was simply a frontal, unmediated encounter between good and evil. From the perspective

---

[60] For egregious examples of furtive disobedience and the export of Indians in Nicaragua prior to 1542, see MacLeod, *Spanish Central America*, 51.

[61] Frances Kinloch Tijerino, "La Cruz Frente a la Espada," *Revista de Historia* 5–6 (1995): 11–14.

of the Crown, however, the rebels had done much worse than break the rules: They had jeopardized the entire game of conquest. After all, Las Casas' most disturbing argument against the *encomienda* hinged on the claim, now supported by the Nicaraguan bishop's reports, that the colonial regime, controlled by tyrannical governors and abusive *encomenderos*, was sliding into moral and political illegitimacy.

The New Laws had been introduced precisely to stop that insidious trend. So the conquerors' open repudiation of these particular laws called attention to the shaky foundation of the conquest's justification and rendered the enterprise still more vulnerable to the political, theological, and juridical attacks that were by now recurrent in Europe. In Spain itself, ongoing debates on the Indian question generated another scheme to rival Manicheanism. On this alternative view, the world was divided between morally "backward" and more "advanced" peoples, but redemption was a universal possibility. Put another way, while the Manichean scheme placed the two races in immutable categories, its rival scheme held out the promise of moral development for both.

Spanish society was also divided on the Indian question between those who believed hierarchy was the "natural state of human society" and those who saw equality as its inherent condition.[62] But the emergence of a new vision in the field of imaginable possibilities was never more palpable than during the famous polemic between the humanist Juan Ginés de Sepúlveda and the friar Las Casas (1550 – 1). The humanist argued that Indians were born to be slaves – an argument that, as D. A. Brading notes, ignored Vitoria's view of the pagan and Christian souls as located along a developmental continuum. Thus, Sepúlveda now made the odious claim that Indians – "wild, cruel and grossly intemperate" – and Spaniards – "merciful," "continent," and temperate" – were as different as "men and monkeys." Las Casas contended that Indians, as much as Spaniards, were children of God, thus rejecting with Vitoria the notion of an insuperable moral gap between the races. Finally, following Vitoria yet again, Las Casas made the case that the kingdom formed a "mystical body" over which the king presided with the free consent of his subjects – an argument that allowed ample space for Indian self-government and even defiance in the face of an unjust conquest.[63]

The ancient notion of the *corpus mysticum*, however, lent itself to contradictory interpretations of jurisdiction and dominion, which were in turn crucially tied to the nature and scope of the Pope's authority.[64] The *corpus mysticum* assigned to each "member" a unique role, complete with anatomical similes such as, "in our mortal body, a finger does not wish to be an eye." Thus, advocates of papal primacy could always reason by analogy that the Church hierarchy was as immutably vertical as the body itself. But also by analogy, opponents

---

[62] Tzvetan Todorov, *The Conquest of America* (New York: Harper Perennial, 1982), 149–53.

[63] Brading, *The First America*, 82–100.

[64] See F. Vitoria, in A. Pagden, ed., *Political Writings* (New York: Cambridge University Press, 1991), 31.

could well claim that the Church was "dispersed among all who share in the faith of Christ and the sacraments."[65]

These rhetorical struggles over the Indian question took place in a context of growing geopolitical uncertainty for Spain. In 1556, Charles V abdicated as Holy Roman Emperor, thus formalizing the separation of the *Imperium* and the *Monarchia*. Philip II became in name "the most powerful ruler in Christendom," but was in fact highly constrained by geopolitical challenges. Worse yet, these challenges arose simultaneously with reassertions of Aragonese prerogatives, which in turn were rooted in Spanish contractualism: " . . . the community was not created for the prince, but rather the prince was created for the sake of the community."[66]

In this context of unresolved debates and geopolitical challenges, the Crown made yet another pragmatic decision. Assailed by a multiplicity of colonial voices, all articulating their contradictory claims in the rigid language of Manicheanism, the Crown commissioned the Americas' first official story from the state's senior cosmographer and chronicler. The purpose of this metanarrative of conquest was to confirm "the justice and right of the Spanish claim to dominion" – a task that entailed a series of rhetorical maneuvers. The first move was to admit "the abuses" of the conquerors while emphasizing the Crown's efforts "to protect its native subjects." The second was to praise Las Casas' labor on behalf of Indians, so as to valorize the monarchy's support of the good friar. The third move was to depict those same Indians as "great liars, drunkards, thieves, and in some cases sodomites," so as to underscore the urgent need for the "good government" that only Catholic Spain could provide.[67]

The final product was a Manichean rhetorical synthesis in which the Crown figured as the ultimate guarantor of good. Commissioned in the 1560s, the state's metanarrative was only published in 1601, at which point the Indian question began to lose salience in the rhetorical culture, and the formation of provincial collective memories and identities reached a stable point in the Indies. During the sixty-year period encompassing the promulgation of the New Laws in 1542 and the publication of the Crown's own account of imperial conquest at the beginning of the seventeenth century, Nicaragua's collective memory was shaped by two key events. One was the rebellion itself, which disgraced the province. The other was the punishment that followed the rebellion: The Crown eliminated the provinces's governorship and placed it instead under the direct rule of the *Audiencia* of Guatemala for over twenty years.

This was a fateful decision. First, the depletion of the Indian population at the hands of the province's founding clan now combined with the province's political subjugation to render it thoroughly unappealing to potential settlers. Spaniards came and went, disillusioned by the grim prospects for personal enrichment. Consequently, Nicaragua was quite slow to develop a creole elite.

[65] Maravall, *Estudios*, 196.
[66] Bonney, *The European Dynastic States*, 124, 144–8.
[67] Brading, *The First America*, 209–10, 295.

Second, the absence of such an elite meant that for a long time Nicaragua had no significant political actors with any durable interest in displacing or modifying the memories of anarchy and tyranny associated with the conquest of the province. Third, by the time Nicaragua was released from the *Audiencia's* tutelage, the Crown was close to publishing its official story, and by the time a local creole elite began to form, the state's formal process of incorporating and excluding memories from recorded history had come to an end.

The result was that the Nicaraguan colonists of the seventeenth century had little incentive to engage in major rhetorical campaigns aimed at the metropole. Consequently, no important record was made of postrebellion Nicaragua, and no high-level account given of its growing immersion in the normality of a poor and marginal colony. All that was left were the old documents and stories detailing the horrors perpetrated by Nicaragua's conquerors against local Indians, the conquerors' sacrilegious murder of the bishop, and the province's fall from royal grace. From whichever angle one examined the province's recorded past, then, the forces at play seemed to be the same: ambition, despotism, and violence, all combining and recombining to render Nicaraguans as either tyrants or anarchists, or both.

Manichean Exceptionalism

The same system of normative scheming that shaped Nicaragua's ignoble image produced a different outcome in Costa Rica, where the New Laws had a fortuitous effect on the process of memory preservation and exclusion. When the Laws were issued in 1542, Costa Rica's conquest was suspended between two seemingly discontinuous phases. The first phase had peaked around 1539, when conquerors managed to penetrate the territory's interior. This phase, however, came to an abrupt end because the savage persecution of Indians provoked a native uprising, which beat the conquerors into retreat. The second phase began only in 1561, almost two decades after the New Laws had been promulgated and upheld in the face of rebellions in Perú and Nicaragua. Moreover, by now the Crown was quite explicit in its disapproval of the conquerors' quarrelsome politics throughout the Indies.

Accordingly, the Crown issued explicit instructions that conquerors were to "govern [themselves] in peace and quiet" and to deal "peacefully" with the Indians, who were to be "attracted" to the faith.[68] The instructions were bolstered by the cautionary tales of Nicaragua and Perú, which in essence told the second-phase conquerors of Costa Rica that they could expect to pay dearly were they openly to disregard the Crown. The career of the conqueror Juan de Cavallón, who in 1561 initially led the second phase, illustrates the initial impact of this warning. Prior to his arrival in Costa Rica, Cavallón had been

---

[68] Carlos Meléndez, "Los Poderes Conferidos al Alcalde Mayor Licenciado Juan de Cavallón," in Academia Costarricense de la Historia, ed., *IV Centenario de la Entrada de Cavallón a Costa Rica, 1561–1961* (San José: Imprenta Nacional, 1961), 41–9.

stationed in Nicaragua, where he had personally prevented "shady individuals" and would-be "libertines" from infecting Costa Rica with the "same kind of disorder" that had reigned in Perú and Nicaragua.[69] Now that he was engaged in conquest activities, the Crown forbade him from distributing Indian laborers among the members of his expedition. He acquiesced – a decision that not only limited his powers of command at the outset but destroyed all hope of personal enrichment. He soon departed, leaving the seemingly unrewarding enterprise of conquest to his successor, Juan Vázquez de Coronado.

This conqueror founded the province's capital city and became governor. But above all, he shaped Costa Rica's early collective memory through his narrative reports to the Crown. Both the singular authority commanded by the governor's reports and the image they conveyed of Costa Rica's conquest as exceptional are of crucial interest here. Why was Coronado so persuasive? Why did his version of events gain such wide credibility? And what made this conquest appear so different from others? One important factor was the governor's rhetorical adaptation to the Crown's express wishes. In keeping with the new royal guidelines instructing conquerors to live in mutual harmony and to "attract" Indians to the faith, for example, the governor actually downplayed intra-Spanish conflict.[70] Further, the reports themselves contained no vitriol. Instead, the governor invariably wove subtle criticism of other Spaniards with stark descriptions of the "great love and benevolence" with which *he* treated Indians. Indeed, the tone of the reports was almost technocratic, as when the governor pointed out that his benign method of colonization proved

... so efficacious that it was publicized throughout the land, and [one chief]... came to render obedience and to recognize his serfdom.[71]

Here at last the Crown had not only admirable exercises in reportage, but also documented accounts of the "ideal" conquest – that is, a conquest relatively free of jealousies among conquerors, and above all a conquest apparently accomplished without recourse to willful deceit or wanton violence against the natives. In short, here at last the Crown had before it a case of exemplary obedience.

But just as importantly, for the first time, there was an unchallenged rendition of conquest activities. This was so for two reasons. First, Coronado brought no professional chroniclers to Costa Rica,[72] so that the conqueror was free of the rhetorical contentiousness that these professionals had introduced during prior conquests. Second, Costa Rica had no articulate defenders of Indians in the mold of Las Casas and the bishop of Nicaragua. That is, there was no authoritative voice to raise controversy when the conqueror

[69] Ibid.
[70] José Francisco Trejos, ed., *Progenitores de los Costarricenses: Los Conquistadores* (San José: Imprenta Lehmann, 1940), 34.
[71] For the original texts, see *Cartas de Relación Sobre la Conquista de Costa Rica* (San José: Academia de Geografía e Historia de Costa Rica, 1964).
[72] Trejos, ed., *Progenitores*, 34.

deviated in practice from the letter of his reports and disregarded the Crown's directives.[73]

The hegemonic status of the governor's accounts produced two novelties in the Indies. First, because their content was never in dispute, the accounts managed to create a favorable image for the entire collectivity. The narrator elevated himself, but not at someone else's expense, and so his narratives conveyed an impression of general harmony. And since there were no competing reports, the impression seemed more than plausible; it seemed unquestionable. Hence the motto *"Fide et Pace,"* emblazoned on the coat of arms granted by the Crown to Cartago, the capital city.

The second novelty was that the accounts' collective scope left the conquerors of Costa Rica well positioned, as a group, to cope with the Crown's formal recasting of its own rhetorical strategy of conquest. In 1573, for example, the Royal Ordinances shifted emphasis away from the *Requerimiento* and the just war principle and toward the power of the word:

The preachers, together with the Spaniards and friendly Indians, should be hidden ... [and] at the opportune moment they should disclose themselves and begin teaching the faith with the aid of interpreters.[74]

This shift in emphasis might have complicated matters for conquerors anywhere else. But given the already existing reputation of Costa Rica's founding "nobles"[75] as men of peace, the shift actually bolstered their exemplary status. They kept up appearances by "observing" the Crown's increasingly sharp admonitions against the persecution and exploitation of natives (while in fact disregarding royal wishes). They even strengthened their identity by seeking sympathy and exemptions from the metropole on the grounds that their peaceful habits left them exposed to the Indians' savagery. (This was the nobles' cry when Indian chiefs dared retaliate against abusive missionaries. And this was the cry that persuaded a reluctant Crown to recognize as necessary the allotment of Indian laborers among conquerors.[76]) Thus, in the very act of extracting favors from the royal sovereign, Costa Rica's conquerors accomplished something that had eluded their quarreling predecessors elsewhere in the region: They staked a credible collective claim to Manichean righteousness. With no one to dispute the Costa Ricans' narrative, they were who they claimed to be: good "Christians" doing battle against the Indians' "diabolical errors."[77]

[73] Arnoldo Mora Rodríguez, *Historia del Pensamiento Costarricense* (San José: Editorial Universidad Estatal a Distancia, 1992), 64.

[74] "Royal Ordinances of Pacification," 1573, in Lewis Hanke, ed., *History of Latin American Civilization: Sources and Interpretations,* vol. 1, *The Colonial Experience* (Boston: Little, Brown, 1973), 113.

[75] The Crown seldom granted titles of nobility, but this did not diminish the nobiliary pretensions of Costa Rica's conquerors.

[76] Francisco Montero Barrantes, *Elementos de Historia de Costa Rica* (San José: Tipoqrafía Nacional, 1892), 44.

[77] "El Obispo de Nicaragua al Consejo Supremo de las Indias Sobre la Reducción de Talamanca por los Misioneros Fray Melchor López y Fray Antonio Margi" (León de Nicaragua), 24 December 1692.

The nobles' ability to stake a credible claim to a morally privileged ancestral identity had important implications for power relations between them and the metropole's officials. As descendants of exceptionally dutiful and peaceful conquerors, for example, the local "nobles" were able to maintain a united front when dealing with "Spaniards" – officials whose birth in Spain convinced them of their own innate superiority and often led them into antagonistic relations with creole elites throughout Spanish America.

Further, a colonial regime embedded in a Manichean culture could not deny such a virtuous nobility a say in the selection of their Spanish governors. Local nobles informally set the quality standards to be used in the appointment of their governors, giving preference to conquerors who were "experienced" in dealing with "Spaniards" and adept at "attracting Indians to the Catholic faith and His Majesty's dominion." As early as the 1570s, the local nobles managed to install one such expert as their governor. The nobles subsequently manipulated the colonial bureaucratic machinery in order to discipline their new governor, whom they soon judged insufficiently sensitive to their prerogatives. And once they were rid of him, the nobles were even able to extract a dramatic public act of "restitution" from the monarchy.[78]

Costa Rican nobles continued throughout the remainder of the sixteenth century and the length of the seventeenth to undermine their governors, whom they found either too young and "scandalous," or too old and "stubborn"; too "stern," or too "lax"; too "haughty" in manner, or too "humble" in origin. As in the comic's complaint, governors "got no respect." Local priests threatened them with excommunication, the nobles routinely sued them and occasionally assaulted them physically, the nobles' wives mounted gossip campaigns against them, and the city's *cabildo* constantly sabotaged their authority.[79]

Collectively emboldened by Manichean righteousness, the nobles eventually reduced their governors to veritable subalterns. At the beginning of the eighteenth century, the *cabildo* actually declared the governor's successor "inept" and deposed him from his post. In mid-eighteenth century, another harassed governor was forced to flee the province disguised as a woman. Soon thereafter, yet another had to quit the province (only to go literally insane, perhaps haunted into madness by the memory of the indignities he had suffered at the hands of the local nobility).[80]

And yet, above this ongoing revolt against "Spaniards" hovered the image of a people living in internal harmony and always loyal to the Crown. Costa Ricans had constructed – if only as a figment of the collective imagination – the ideal corporeal state, with the head and extremities of the body politic acting in perfect concert. To evoke a repugnant alternative – discord and rebellion – one had only to think of neighboring Nicaragua.

[78] Ricardo Fernández Guardia, *Crónicas Coloniales* (San José: Imprenta Hermanos Trejos, 1921), 5–17.
[79] For a detailed account based on original documents, see ibid.
[80] Rodolfo Cerda Cruz, *Formación del Estado en Costa Rica* (San José: Editorial Universidad de Costa Rica, 1967), 85.

Conclusion

The political organization of sixteenth century Spanish America was initially based on a practical blend of absolutist and contractual logics of rule legitimation. Colonials, for example, were denied elective representative bodies but were granted the right to address the sovereign directly. As a result, a wide range of actors burdened the royal arbiter with incessant, contradictory claims, all of which were articulated in a compelling Manichean *lingua franca*. Moreover, since even sovereign rulings were vulnerable to the de facto amendment process that flowed from the Crown's policy of free expression and its openness to "truth-telling" accounts, the emerging system of normative scheming locked indisputably legitimate monarchs into a pattern of enervating oscillation. One moment the king dictated laws in response to theological and juridical criticism, the next he addressed colonials' appeals by partially revoking prior decrees, or granting favors in the form of exemptions.

In this way, colonial society grew accustomed to a protoconstitutional regime of arbitration that responded to the play of subaltern multivocality and was keenly focused on the delivery of justice. But there were other serious contradictions. On the one hand, obedience to the Crown became the controlling norm for competition and arbitration. On the other hand, the practice of dramaturgical obedience and Manichean argumentation and persuasion polarized colonial actors while sapping the Crown's capacity to rule in a sustainable, coherent fashion. As we will see next, colonial society came to be pervaded by suspicion and strife; while state–society relations came to be characterized both by piecemeal appropriation of de facto autonomy from below and vital dependence on the arbiter above.

In Costa Rica, however, the same system of normative scheming endogenously produced a radically different outcome. The most obvious reason for this divergence was timing: The province's conquest began in earnest only in 1561, almost two decades after the New Laws had been promulgated and upheld in the face of rebellion. Yet, fortuitous accidents, to the extent that they constitute an opportunity, can be ineffectively exploited, or even missed entirely. Similarly, legacies can be squandered or distorted. The uses that actors make of resources are thus of great import. Through rhetorical and strategic adaptation, Costa Rica's conquerors and early creole elites forged a credible collective claim to Manichean righteousness, which they then used systematically to gain the upper hand in their power relations with the metropole's local officials.

The two colonies' divergent experiences helped shape their respective fields of imaginable possibilities, both during the mature colonial period of the seventeenth and eighteenth centuries and through the turbulent postcolonial decades (1821–50). To these we now turn.

3

Orphans of Empire

Constructing National Identities

> As in the ship of fools, we are embarked, without the possibility of an aerial view or any sort of totalization.[1]
>
> –Michel de Certeau

Historical ruptures are most often understood as outward manifestations of underlying conflicts between irreconcilable forces, from antagonistic economic groups to rival technological paradigms, from contending ideologies to clashing identities. Spanish America's break with Spain is no exception. Benedict Anderson, for example, explains it as a result of the sense of "nation-ness" that Spanish American "creole communities" had developed by the dawn of the nineteenth century.[2] Similarly, Michael Doyle argues that Spain's "surrender" of its empire to Napoleon in 1808 was a betrayal of Spanish America and broke the "links of legitimacy" between metropole and periphery.[3]

But the forces underlying the rupture were not so stark, either in the consciousness of protagonists or in the events that flowed from their actions. Then, as now, political actors may not be embarked on a ship of fools, but they are still likely to lack an aerial view of their changing world. Early nineteenth century creoles, to be sure, made one sharp distinction: They distinguished between the Crown and Spaniards. But they remained faithful to the former even as they moved, in most cases hesitatingly, toward independence from the latter.[4] Indeed, contrary to Doyle's claim, the Napoleonic crisis in Spain actually fortified the ties between creoles and the Crown. The failure of analysts to

---

[1] Michel de Certeau, *The Practice of Everyday Life* (Berkeley, CA: University of California Press, 1988), 11.

[2] Benedict Anderson, *Imagined Communities: Reflections on the Origin and Spread of Nationalism* (New York: Verso, 1991), 50, 60.

[3] Michael W. Doyle, *Empires* (Ithaca, NY: Cornell University Press, 1986), 121.

[4] Because Spanish Americans were juridical subjects of the king alone, independence implied a break with the Crown. But in practical terms, independence came to mean a rupture with peninsular Spaniards.

distinguish between "king" and "nation" – a distinction that was key for the Spanish Americans of the time – lies at the heart of their error.

The rhetorical strategies that creoles deployed to exploit to advantage the Napoleonic crisis indicate that creoles manipulated the tempo of political action in order to achieve two objectives: first, to highlight their loyalty to the Crown while undermining the authority of Spanish officials; and second, having accomplished the first goal, to elevate their own localities and clans in the colonial hierarchy at the expense of other creoles. The use of political tempo typically takes one of two forms, each associated with particular practical aims. Acceleration may enable political actors to take their opponents by surprise; a slowdown, conversely, may enable them either to postpone measures best taken later or, given sufficient time, to find a superior alternative.[5]

Beyond their practical aims, the deployment of these strategies also points us in the direction of the regime's central conflict and its root source. The Crown held the creole political imagination firmly in its grip because of the royal arbiter's universal legitimacy in a society increasingly rife with mistrust. Both the sovereign's legitimacy and societal mistrust, moreover, interacted along the same axis: Manichean normative scheming. For if we think of trust as "a device for coping with the freedom of other persons,"[6] then we can say that in Spanish America, the Crown sanctioned colonials' "freedoms," but colonials themselves often perceived these freedoms, when exercised by others, as ill-gotten.

One striking result of this conflict within the regnant arbitration regime was that well into the late colonial period, creoles lacked any positive sense of collective unity and were able to act in concert only when motivated by shared resentment of Spanish-born officials and fear of the *castas* (mestizos and mulattoes). Once independence either coopted or removed those officials, and once the creoles themselves effectively controlled the *castas*, the absence of positive unity among creoles became glaringly obvious.

The creoles' prolonged attachment to the Crown combined with Manichean normative scheming to stunt the emergence of creole solidarity and to turn constitutional liberalism – the ideology that creoles embraced even prior to the colonial collapse – into an instrument of political intolerance. The upshot of all this was that early electoral experiments conducted during the late colonial period intensified the conflicts they were meant to resolve. And yet, among Central Americans, Costa Ricans were able to construct a sense of positive unity by drawing on the collective memories, self-image, and power relations they forged throughout their colonial experience. Although this unity was not easily accomplished, much less foreordained, it ultimately allowed Costa Rican elites to fashion an effective regime of arbitration – a regime, interestingly enough, that hardly took note of the electoral and liberal principles that obsessed their neighbors.

---

[5] See Andreas Schedler and Javier Santino, "Democracy and Time: An Invitation," *International Political Science Review* 19, no. 1 (January 1998): 10.

[6] N. Luhmann, cited in John Dunn, "Trust and Political Agency," in Diego Gambetta, ed., *Trust: Making and Breaking Cooperative Relations* (Cambridge, MA: Basil Blackwell, 1988), 80.

Fidelity and Opportunism: Strange Complementarities

The seventeenth century and much of the eighteenth witnessed a marked decline in the Spanish state's coercive-administrative capacity. In Spain, royal ministers not only failed to reassert the Crown's effective leadership, but managed to make it less and less clear "who was ruling the country and whose voice the command of the king represented."[7] In the Indies, this state of affairs was no cause for alarm because while the Crown stood immutably for "justice" and merited "reverence," *cabildos* (municipal councils) reaffirmed a range of local corporate "privileges, freedoms, and preeminences," which kings had "sanctioned since the conquest."[8] In short, colonials enjoyed "self-rule at the king's command."[9]

Conditioned self-rule was possible in part because severe fiscal troubles led the Hapsburg monarchy in the seventeenth century to wish merely that its American dominions be governed "without expense."[10] But even when the Bourbon monarchy began in the eighteenth century to destabilize this arrangement of colonial self-rule, the colonials did not turn on the king. Instead, modernizing shifts in royal outlook and policy making actually intensified the creoles' efforts to seek final arbitration from the head of the body politic. Even as creoles began to discover their love of *patria* – by which they meant various things, including love of town or city, just as peninsular Spaniards cherished the *patria chica* – they looked to the king for justice, especially when seeking protection from arbitrary harm.

By the mid-eighteenth century, innovative ministers and political thinkers in Bourbon Spain had modified the monarchy's position in the grand scheme of things. Bourbon monarchs now staked absolutist claims to power derived from the divine rights of kings. Moreover, a king's principal responsibility was redefined along economistic lines. A fair and competent king was one who created the necessary conditions for general prosperity, and collective "happiness" was now understood as "that state of abundance and comfort which a good government ought to procure for its subjects."[11]

This modified understanding of just rule paved the way in the late eighteenth century for reformist attempts to recentralize the administrative colonial apparatus and liberalize trade between Spain and the Indies. In short order, droves of peninsular officials and merchants began arriving in the colonies to implement the new governmental designs and to exploit the profit-making opportunities opened up by commercial liberalization. This new invasion of Spaniards, which the historian John Lynch has characterized as a "second conquest," engendered

---

[7] I. A. A. Thompson, *Crown and Córtes* (Brookefield, VT: Variorum, 1993), 87–9.

[8] Colin MacLachlan, *Spain's Empire in the New World* (Berkeley, CA: University of California Press, 1988), 22.

[9] J. H. Elliot, in Leslie Bethell, ed., *Cambridge History of Latin America*, vol. 1 (Cambridge, UK: Cambridge University Press, 1984–92), 338.

[10] John Lynch, *The Spanish American Revolutions, 1808–1826* (New York: W. W. Norton, 1986), 7.

[11] MacLachlan, *Spain's Empire*, 69.

a series of political and economic conflicts between peninsular *parvenus* and creole elites who had for a while enjoyed Spain's benign neglect. But the regnant rhetorical frame in the colonies indicates that the most fundamental tensions centered on the Spaniards' view of creoles as a "contaminated" class of racial and intellectual "degenerates."

In fact, the Spaniards' prejudicial view managed, like a magnet, to concentrate the creoles' political energies. But as this same regnant rhetorical frame also shows, the creoles' energies took a royalist form. The remedy creole elites often proposed for the "evil situation" in which they now found themselves is telling. As one Peruvian creole saw it, this remedy was simple: Have the royal arbiter personally govern his American possessions, or at least send a member of the royal house to rule.[12] Although no prince was ever dispatched, the creoles' monarchical orientation remained intact. This was evident throughout the system of normative scheming, both at the level of spontaneous competitive practices and at the level of self-conscious political argumentation.

On the first level, *cabildos* strove to obtain from the king titles of distinction like "Excellency" and "Very Noble and Loyal."[13] Creoles in general sought royal certificates of untainted blood in a bid to rise above the growing *castas*.[14] And notables in particular strove earnestly to show their affection for the king. In the late eighteenth century, for example, Nicaraguan *cabildo* members and notable clans were willing to endure "fatigue, tribulations, expenses, and exertions" in an effort to signal their loyalty to the Crown. They were even prone to embroil themselves in internal quarrels as each tried with "the best of intentions" to put on the most brilliant displays of fidelity.[15]

At the level of political argumentation, the crucial role of the Crown was even more obvious. Here, the key issue, once again, was justice. On one side, peninsular officials took the stance that creoles were by birth inferior and unfit to hold high political office. On the other, creoles not only resented their exclusion from high office, but also nursed a deeper injury: an injury exposed by Mexican creoles' bitter complaint to the Crown about how the royal inspector of troops, in a "despotic action," drafted militia forces without making distinction between "nobles" and "commoners," as if in Mexico "there [were] no nobility, lineage, or worth."[16]

Caught in the middle as always, the Crown resorted to a ploy. Rather than decree the outright exclusion of creoles from high office, the Crown made attendance at a Castilian university a prerequisite for officialdom. The requirement was patently unrealistic, and left creoles confused and hurt. How could the king – their wise and benevolent arbiter – be capable of such an

---

[12] D. A. Brading, *The First America* (New York: Cambridge University Press, 1991), 316–17.
[13] MacLachlan, *Spain's Empire*, 34.
[14] Jorge Eduardo Arellano, *Historia de la Universidad de León: Epoca Colonial*, vol. 1 (León: Universidad Editorial, UNAN, 1973).
[15] See Anónimo, "Relación de 1794," *Revista Conservadora* 1, no. 1 (August 1960): 11.
[16] Brading, *The First America*, 468.

"unjust" act? "In what, Sire, have we erred that we should be marked in this way?"

One scholar likens the creoles' grievances to those of "their contemporaries in British North America," because

...like [the North Americans] the *criollos* insisted that it was the crown, not they, who had transgressed what they saw as the ancient laws and privileges of the realm....For all these colonists their monarch had transformed himself into a tyrant and by so doing had freed his subjects from any further obligation to obey his laws.[17]

But there was also a critical difference between the patriots in the North and the creoles to the South. First, the Spanish American creoles took pains to exempt their king of blame, which they assigned instead to his advisers and ministers. Second, while North American colonials articulated an alternative view of just government to supplant their traditional contract with the British monarchy, their counterparts to the South sounded like conquerors speaking in tongues: cobbling together aristocratic reassertions of "natural" rights; serviceable doctrinal selections from the Enlightenment's political philosophies; and ringing declarations carefully selected from the rhetorical arsenals of the American and French revolutions. At the first serious test of consistency, this amalgam began to disintegrate.

Such a test came in 1808, when a palace coup forced Charles IV to abdicate in favor of his son, Ferdinand VII. The royal family's inner turmoil broke out at a most inopportune time. Napoleon Bonaparte forced them to abdicate in his favor, then handed the Spanish crown to his brother, Joseph. This provoked a popular revolution that broke out in Madrid and spread to the rest of Spain:

The first impulse...was centrifugal – that is, regional juntas were formed to govern individual provinces. In the absence of the king, political theorists argued, sovereignty reverted to the people, and each provincial junta acted as though it were an independent nation. Finally, the need for a unified defense led to the organization of a national governing committee, the Junta Suprema Central, which first met on September 25, 1808.[18]

In an effort to exploit the centrifugal ramifications of the king's absence, Napoleon offered American creoles two mighty incentives for defection: participation in government, and a share in the benefits of free trade. Yet throughout Spanish America, creoles rebuffed the offer. They declared that if Napoleon established his rule definitively, they would seek independence from Spain, accepting Ferdinand VII alone as their sovereign. Allegiance to the monarchy also prevailed on the Spanish peninsula, where "not even the most radical sectors dared suggest the establishment of a republican government." For as was plain

[17] Anthony Pagden, *The Uncertainties of Empire* (Brookefield, VT: Variorum, 1994), 62.
[18] Colin MacLachlan and Jaime Rodríguez, *The Forging of the Cosmic Race* (Berkeley, CA: University of California Press, 1990), 297–8.

to all concerned, "the king, prisoner of the French, symbolized the invaded patria and was the sole bond uniting Spaniards and Americans."[19]

As long as Spain defended the Crown's integrity, most creoles identified with the metropole. The South American Simón Bolívar, who as leader of a vibrant independist movement faced the unenviable task of "detaching the masses from the loyalist cause,"[20] had this to say in retrospect:

The habit of obedience, a community of interests, of understandings, of religion; mutual goodwill; a tender regard for the birthplace and good name of our forefathers; ultimately, all that fulfilled our expectations came from Spain. From there arose a principle of fidelity that seemed eternal.[21]

More importantly still, the embodiment of the monarchy – the king – was captive but not dead, which meant that the central referent of traditional normative scheming remained viable, and the pale of the imaginable remained in place. Thus creoles could seek to gain selfish advantage from the Napoleonic crisis in Spain, but they would have to do so in a very particular way. That is, they could discuss the idea of self-government and even try to implement it, since self-government was a necessary condition for effective resistance to French subjugation and/or illegitimate Spanish rule, by which they meant continued peninsular control without the king. But they could not and would not question the legitimacy of the royal arbiter.

This last point was clear from the colonials' response to the king's abdication. In Guatemala, the leading province of Central America (the isthmian colonies were collectively known as the Kingdom of Guatemala, and later as the captain generalcy of Guatemala), news of the abdication prompted an unabashedly pathetic demonstration of sorrow among creole elites:

The bitter spectacle of that afternoon will eternally enshrine Guatemala's fine emotions.... The tribulation reflected on our faces...the agitated beating of our hearts....

The Guatemalans, in fact, were for once in harmony with their Spanish captain general, whose "tearful oration" they fully endorsed:

[The assembly's] unanimous and glorious agreement stands as a perpetual monument to the honor of Guatemala, whose unquestionable loyalty has now crowned years of fidelity and chained its vassalage to the fate of the beloved king.[22]

---

[19] Jorge Sáenz Carbonell, *El Despertar Constitucional de Costa Rica* (San José: Libro Libre, 1985), 63–73, 81.

[20] David Bushnell and Neill Macaulay, *The Emergence of Latin America in the Nineteenth Century* (New York: Oxford University Press, 1994), 15–17.

[21] Cited in Jaime Rodríguez, *The Independence of Spanish America* (New York: Cambridge University Press, 1998), 52.

[22] Narrative by the *cabildo* of Guatemala of City, *Guatemala por Fernando Séptimo* (12 December 1808), 4–5.

The sentiment, though likely sincere, also turned out to be a first step toward the deliberate slowdown of political tempo. Drawing on colonial tradition, Guatemalans dutifully prepared the elaborate and prolonged pageantry that surrounded the oath of loyalty to the king's son, Ferdinand VII, also known as "the Beloved." Indeed, Guatemala City pledged its fealty to the king amid a splendor unprecedented in the history of Central America, thus demonstrating, in the creoles' own estimation, the unwavering character of American fidelity.[23]

Just as every detail of the pageant was meant to render indisputable the colonials' "love and dedication," the display was also expected to earn colonials due respect from Spaniards. As the *cabildo* put it, Guatemala would be upheld in Spain as a "paragon of loyalty," and the Spanish government, representing the king, would have to show "greater appreciation" for the "hopes" and "wishes" of Guatemalans.[24] Moreover, the display – intricate in structure and laboriously spread across several days – was meant to avoid creoles' subordination to royal officials and to place in its stead a legitimate claim to equality with peninsulars. The Guatemalan *cabildo* thus argued to the Supreme Junta in Spain that Guatemala – as "one of the elders of the Monarchy" and by "its many titles" – deserved direct representation in Spanish governmental institutions.[25]

The captive Ferdinand, for his part, sent his overseas subjects an emotional text[26] ratifying what in 1809 the Supreme Central Junta had already decreed in his name: As integral parts of the monarchy, the provinces of the Kingdom of Guatemala were invited to "choose their deputy to reside at court as member of the Supreme Governing Junta."[27]

The king's "benevolence" stirred Central Americans. After dissolving "in tears" of gratitude, and after burning the "perverse" Napoleon in effigy, Costa Rican colonials expressed their jubilation with "solemnity, pomp, order, decorum, and tranquility."[28] Because Costa Rica was poor, its feast was much humbler than that of wealthy Guatemala. Yet it was the ostentatiously loyal Guatemalans, not the humble Costa Ricans, who mixed their expressions of fidelity with statements of indignation at the traditional mistreatment of Spanish Americans:

America has been defamed since its discovery. . . . Our parents, as if they had become denaturalized the moment they set foot on these Kingdoms, have suffered disdain for generations, and have been excluded from government.[29]

---

[23] Luis Marina Otero, *Las Constituciones de Guatemala* (Madrid: Instituto de Estudios Políticos, 1958), 4–5, 26.

[24] Ibid., 18.

[25] *Cabildo* of Guatemala City, *Guatemala por Fernando Séptimo*, 49.

[26] See Máximo Soto Hall, "Capítulos de un Libro Inédito," *Revista de Costa Rica en el Siglo XIX* 1, no. 32 (San José: Letras Patrias, n.d.): 87–8.

[27] Hubert Howe Bancroft, *The Works of Hubert Howe Bancroft*, vol. 8, *History of Central America* (San Francisco, CA: History Company Publishers, 1887), 4.

[28] Ermenegildo Bonilla, "Fiestas Reales," in *Revista de Costa Rica en el Siglo XIX*: 87–93.

[29] Laudelino Moreno, "Guatemala y ca Invasión Napoleónica en España," *ASGHG* 7, No. 1 (September 1930), 14–15.

According to the Guatemalan *cabildo*, peninsular mistrust of Spanish America had led to a generalized belief in the need to rule the Americas with an iron hand. Such mistrust, the Guatemalans added, was unjustifiable because "loyalty" and "affection" were the only ties that bound the Americas to the Crown. The Guatemalans, however, were now encouraged by the shift in official policy, and expressed the hope that Ferdinand's "Paternal and Just Government" would "correct" traditional misrepresentations of Spanish America and thus inaugurate an era of inexorable and rapid progress for the entire region.[30] The royal arbiter, in a word, would restore justice to the relationship between creoles and peninsular Spaniards.

The Guatemalans' affirmation of hope and fidelity was backed by tangible proof of Central American solidarity with their king. Creoles and Indians alike contributed generously to the war chest for the struggle against the French – a sum equivalent to one half of the region's annual exports.[31]

Guatemala's *cabildo* also heartily endorsed the project of a constitutional monarchy, which in Spain was at that time championed by liberal monarchists. In the instructions they gave their representative to the constitutional assembly of 1810, the Guatemalans wrote that

...the *monarchy is to be affirmed constantly*, recognizing the *señor* don Fernando VII (may God keep him) as king and sovereign, and in his absence, his legitimate heirs. That in order to prevent despotism from disgracing our Majesty and from oppressing the [various provinces of the nation] a formal constitution be...instituted so that the rights of the peoples are reestablished. That...the Americas shall be considered an essential part of the monarchy, safeguarding [America's] rights and civil liberties as much as those of the peninsula *without any distinction whatsoever* [emphasis added].[32]

The Guatemalans' bid for equality under a monarchical regime, however, clearly applied only to relations between Spaniards and Americans. Within America, the traditional fixation with hierarchical rank persisted. The *cabildo* of Guatemala City, for example, when dealing with the lesser provinces of Central America, took great care to speak and act in ways befitting its traditional identity as the region's "senior." In an official letter dated November 1811, the *cabildo* cautioned urban centers throughout the isthmus that Guatemalans, so frequently at odds with the Spanish-born captain general, were now his allies. They insistently claimed to share the captain general's "patriotic zeal," and supported his resolute efforts to defend the Kingdom's integrity not only against Napoleonic encroachment but also against the "greatest of dangers": anarchy in the other provinces.[33]

---

[30] Ibid., 15.

[31] Arturo J. Cruz, Jr., unpublished early draft for "Overcoming Mistrust: The Quest for Order in Nicaragua's Conservative Republic, 1858–1893" (Ph.D. diss., Oxford University, Michaelmas 1997), 75.

[32] César Branas, *Antonio Larrazabal: Un Guatemalteco en la Historia* (Guatemala: Editorial Universitaria, 1969), 42–3.

[33] Academia de Geografía e Historia de Costa Rica, ed., *Centro América en las Vísperas de la Independencia* (San José: Imprenta Hermanos Trejos, 1971), 290.

The Guatemalans' allusion to anarchy reflected the fact that while creoles in the other Central American provinces welcomed direct political representation in Spain, they also seized the crisis to strike at local peninsular officials. Between 1811 and 1814, there were disturbances in the cities of San Salvador, León, and Granada. By focusing more closely on these events and the rhetorical strategies of the protagonists, we can uncover the workings of Manichean normative scheming in its early nineteenth century variant. One recurrent strategy hinged on the acceleration of tempo through dramas of what I call inexorable collective ire: mutinies that "forced" local elites to strike compromises with an "intractable" mass surreptitiously mobilized by the creole notables themselves.

In San Salvador, the notables began by convening an open *cabildo* – a step they justified by resorting to an old principle dictating that municipal authorities, when faced with a momentous decision, were to consult with "honest" and "reputable" citizens about the matter. The notables then used the meeting to stir up a seemingly spontaneous drama in which "decent" elements were overwhelmed by the voices of the "rabble," that "frightful" and "volatile" force that left the notables no option but to take action against royal officials.[34]

Soon thereafter, in the Nicaraguan city of Granada, a liberal creole mobilized "outraged" citizens against peninsular-born officials who led "scandalous" private lives.[35] The bid paid off. The High Court in Guatemala condemned the Spaniards' conduct. Emboldened by the Court's ruling, local creoles then convened the *vecinos* (citizens) to an open *cabildo*, where they demanded the resignation of all Spanish officials. Increasingly isolated, the officials escaped to a neighboring villa, from where they sent word of their predicament to the captain general in Guatemala City.[36] In the Nicaraguan city of León, meanwhile, a Manichean drama led to a radical outcome: the establishment of a local governing junta. According to the junta's ex post narrative of events, the disturbances began when the "plebs," deluded by "false rumors," turned against honest individuals who, half-defeated from the start, were in the end unable to dissuade the crowd from engaging in violence.[37]

The narrative itself, however, hints at a more intricate subtext. The creole-dominated *cabildo*, to begin with, extended a general pardon to the authors of subversive broadsheets. The *cabildo*, moreover, allowed the barrios to elect deputies to the Governing Junta that was to replace Nicaragua's governor intendant. The elections, in turn, produced a miraculous result: Every deputy-elect turned out to be a notable known for his "good character" and "probity."

---

[34] For more on the *cabildo abierto*, see Gabriel Ureña-Morales, "Estructura Política del Reino de Guatemala," in ibid., 18–27.

[35] Pío Bolaño, "La ciudad Trágica," *Revista Conservadora* 2, no. 13 (October 1961), 14–15.

[36] José D. Gámez, *Historia de Nicaragua* (Managua: Fondo de Promoción Cultural, Banco de América, Papelera Industrial de Nicaragua), 308.

[37] Don Fray Nicolás García Jerez, Obispo de Nicaragua y Costa Rica, Presidente de la Junta, "Testimonios del Acta de la Primera Sesión de la Junta Provincial Gubernativa Que se Instaló el 14 de Diciembre de 1811 en León de Nicaragua," *RAGHN* 10, no. 1 (April 1948): 1–8.

Moreover, once the peninsular officials were dismissed, it was the local notables who proceeded to distribute the vacant offices among themselves.[38] Next, amid the "great jubilation" caused by the election of such a "virtuous" set of delegates, the new Governing Junta named the bishop, who was peninsular-born, as its president. The junta then swore fidelity and subordination to the authorities in Spain. The "plebs" (the rabble, or the commoners) swore this too, three times, and swore obedience to the junta as well. Finally, the junta and the "people" – no longer referred to as the plebs – proceeded to the church, where they swore fidelity yet again.

The junta's account, signed by the bishop, had been deftly crafted. It emphasized three factors: the prelate's impotence to control the disturbance; the *cabildo*'s repeated oaths of loyalty; and the barrios' nomination of reputable deputies. Together, these factors were then used to construct the argument that the notables of León presented to the captain general in Guatemala: Their city, they claimed, would not cause further trouble, nor would it try to extract additional advantage from any extraneous volatility.

The captain general had no choice but to "accept" that the plebs had indeed taken the "principals" of León by "surprise."[39] However, he did make the point that he was no dupe, and obliquely challenged the veracity of the bishop's account. "It is not credible," the captain general stated, "that if the people were allowed to hear freely the voice of their pastor, that they would ignore it." That said, the captain general appointed the bishop as governor intendant of Nicaragua.[40]

The colonial authorities ultimately resolved the problematic situation in Nicaragua as follows: Granada, ready to obey the bishop but unwilling to dissolve its own junta, was subjugated by force, while faithful *cabildos* were awarded such titles as "Very Illustrious."[41] León, of course, received additional rewards: Its bishopric was ultimately given the authority to dispose of its tithe without supervision from Guatemala City, and its seminary was finally promoted to the status of university.[42] These rewards were no empty symbols. Wherever one looked, Central Americans were actively seeking titles of distinction and the attendant prerogatives from the Crown. *Cabildos* reached for higher honors. Cities asked to be recognized as "Very Noble and Loyal," villas strove for the rank of "city," and pueblos, in turn, hoped for elevation to the rank of villa.

---

[38] "Informe del Capitán General de Guatemala al Secretario de Gracia y Justicia, Reservada, no. 19" (Guatemala), 30 January 1812, ibid.: 9–13.

[39] "Sr. José de Bustamante – Iltmo. Sr. Obispo D. Fr. Nicolás García, Gobernador Intendente de Nicaragua" (Guatemala), 3 February 1812, ibid.: 15–18.

[40] "Exmo. So. B. L. M. de V. E. su Mas Obligado y Reconocido Capellán, Fr. Nicolás Obispo de Nicaragua – Exmo. Sr. D. José de Bustamante, Presidente Gobernador y Capitán General del Reyno [sic] de Guatemala" (León), 20 February 1812, ibid.: 18–20.

[41] See ibid.: 13–15, 23–5. See also "José de Bustamante – Iltmo. Sr. Obispo, Gobernador de Nicaragua" (Guatemala), 3 March 1812, ibid.: 25–6.

[42] Rodríguez, *Independence of Spanish America*, 72.

Through all this, creole solidarity was fragile at best, nonexistent at worst. This was due in good measure to the vertical links between loyalty and rewards.[43] The Guatemalans' "pacification" of the Salvadoran creoles earned the *cabildo* in Guatemala City the cherished title of "Excellency."[44] Costa Rica's "perpetual fidelity," and the lobbying efforts of its representative in Spain, obtained for the capital City of Cartago the title of "Very Noble and Very Loyal," the rank of "city" for San José, and the rank of villa for various pueblos.[45] (The Costa Rican capital, the citizens, and their governor had responded to the disturbances in León by renewing their pledge of allegiance to the king, and cutting off all communication with the Nicaraguan city.[46]) Similarly, the Salvadoran villas and pueblos that had repudiated San Salvador's rebellion as a "sacrilege" subsequently received the "favors" they had sought for so long. In the name of the king, the Spanish government awarded San Miguel the title of "Very Noble and Very Loyal," recognized San Vicente as a "city," and elevated Santa Ana to the rank of villa.[47]

The Virtue of Elections: It All Depends

Even at its weakest point, then, the monarchy emerged once again as final arbiter and sole symbol of integrity and fairness. But mistrust also poisoned anew creole – peninsular relations, stunted creole solidarity, deformed constitutional liberalism, and corrupted the electoral principle. The evidence was everywhere. The alliance between the Guatemalan *cabildo* and the captain general fell apart once the Constitution was adopted in 1812, and the Ordinary Parliament was inaugurated in Spain.[48] From the *cabildo*'s perspective, the captive monarch was benevolent and just, but his captain general was "hard, inflexible, suspicious, absolute, vigilant and reserved: his government a perfect reflection of his character."[49] Accordingly, in 1813, the *cabildo's* delegate to Ordinary Parliament vowed as he departed for his post in Spain to obtain "remedy" for "the evils" they suffered at the hands of the official.[50]

Creole elites themselves were radically at odds among themselves, especially when elections were involved. The Constitution of 1812 stipulated that *cabildos* – the traditional locus of creole influence – were to assume a wide

---

[43] J. C. Pinto Soria, *Centroamérica: de la Colonia al Estado Nacional, 1800–1849* (Guatemala: Editorial Universitaria, Colección textos, 1986); Academia de Geografía e Historia de Costa Rica, ed., *Vísperas de la Independencia*, 294–5.

[44] Rodríguez, *Independence of Spanish America*, 70.

[45] Bancroft, *History of Central America*, 70.

[46] Francisco Montero Barrantes, *Elementos de Historia* (San José: Tipografía Nacional, 1892), 155.

[47] Bancroft, *History of Central America*, 13.

[48] Ibid., 20.

[49] Miles Wortman, *Government and Society in Central America: 1680–1840* (New York: Columbia Press, 1982), 201.

[50] Rodríguez, *Independence of Spanish America*, 113–16.

range of responsibilities, including internal finances and policing. Moreover, *cabildo* offices, theretofore either bequeathed or sold, were now contestable in elections: Holders were to be chosen by electors, who in turn were delegated by popular vote.[51] Electoral outcomes, however, immediately became subject to normative-strategic judgments typical of Manichean identities. The governor intendant of El Salvador – a Guatemalan creole – complained in 1814 that in the elections of San Salvador for *alcaldes de barrio*, the winners turned out to be of "dubious" and "corrupt" character. For this reason, the governor explained to the captain general, he had been compelled to call for new elections whose results did not fully please him but were less pernicious than the previous ones.[52] We also know from the Guatemalan's confidential missive that, given the less than optimal electoral outcome, he felt obliged to redouble his vigilance, feigning "trust" and "negligence" in order to encourage the "brazenness" of the Salvadorans. In the end, he was able to "unmask" them:

I pointed out to them that I was aware of their *evil* deeds and maneuvers; warned them...that they should know in advance that if there were to be an insurrection, they would find me terrifying and resolute...[the *alcaldes*] assured me nothing was afoot...and begged me not to be influenced by *gossip and envy* [emphasis added].[53]

If the Guatemalan official, though a creole himself, could not trust his Salvadoran fellows, the Spanish captain general could trust neither Guatemalans nor Salvadorans. The "recurrence of wickedness" in San Salvador, the Spaniard noted, was something he himself was battling in Guatemala City. That "loyal" city, according to the captain general, was in actuality a hotbed of rebelliousness and a frightening place where morality was engaged in an existential battle with the "willpower of evil."[54] Reflecting on the recent disturbances, the captain general even derided the Central Americans' donations to the embattled Crown as signs of "hypocrisy." Duplicitous, too, were those provinces that had pronounced themselves *fidelísimas* (most loyal). Such pronouncements, the official now argued vehemently, were meant to "lull" the king's government and to "conceal" the true objectives of "the restless and vile."[55]

   In this context, the captain general deployed a traditional rhetorical strategy to attack electoral mechanisms as the instrument of "evil" forces bent on "electing suspect [individuals] to office while excluding Europeans and Creoles whose fidelity is real."[56] But he was unable to propose an innovative solution

---

[51] Academia de Geografía e Historia de Costa Rica, ed., *Vísperas de la Independencia*, 288.
[52] José María Peinado, "Comunicación Dirigida al Capitán General del Reino, en el Que da Cuenta de la Insurrección Efectuada en la Ciudad de San Salvador el 24 de Enero de 1814," *RAGHN* 3, no. 3 (December 1940): 215–29.
[53] Pinto Soria, *Centroamérica*, 101.
[54] "Informe del Capitán General de Guatemala, *Don José de Bustamante* Sobre la Insurrección Efectuada en la Ciudad de San Salvador el Día 24 de Enero de 1814," *RAGHN* 3, no. 3 (December 1940), 245–6.
[55] Ibid., 245–6.
[56] Ibid., 251.

tó this endemic problem. Instead, he simply recommended the encouragement of "truly" loyal cities whose valor in the "battle against perfidy" earned them the title of "Very Noble."[57]

In this, the official neglected to give Costa Rica due recognition, but it was precisely this province that went beyond the call of duty:

The Costa Rican people not only deplored...the anarchic events in Nicaragua, but served as a loyal helper under such critical circumstances: two hundred of her best sons marched to the sister province to reestablish peace, ready to spill their blood in defense of the order that had been profoundly disturbed.[58]

Costa Rica seemed to levitate above the political turbulence because – well in advance of the Napoleonic invasion of Spain in 1808 – the local "nobility" had deployed its prestigious collective identity against the peninsular-born officials and merchants who elsewhere in Spanish America gave free expression to their prejudicial view of creoles.[59] Indeed, by the time the Napoleonic crisis hit the isthmus, Costa Rican nobles had learned to tame their governors. The latter, in turn, had learned that it paid to play the role of trustworthy allies, since Costa Rican elites were both highly adept at image making and influential with the Crown. Costa Rica's relations with its governors were so solid, in fact, that in 1809 the nobles of Cartago actually petitioned the *Audiencia* in Guatemala for an extended tenure for their governor, citing among his many accomplishments "the tranquility" of Costa Rica and the "progressive" intent of his administration.[60] Other Central Americans seized the crisis as an opportunity to strike against Spanish officials, but the Costa Ricans simply had no incentive to follow suit.

Liberals, Serviles, and a King of Hearts

In 1814, Ferdinand returned to Spain, where he promptly abrogated the 1812 Constitution he had sworn to uphold. Just as promptly, the age-old dynamic of colonial appeals and royal responsiveness was reestablished. The king, for example, extended a general pardon to Central American political prisoners. Creoles, in turn, exalted the king's magnanimity, then beseeched His Majesty to correct the captain general's arbitrary measures.[61] Ferdinand responded by replacing the unpopular captain general with a more acceptable successor.[62] Moreover, even after liberals in Spain began to press for the restoration of the 1812 Constitution, royal statecraft solidified relations between the king and Central Americans by fomenting the link between "loyalty" and hierarchical

---

[57] Ibid., 253–4. See also Pinto Soria, *Centroamérica*, 106.
[58] Francisco María Iglesias, "15 de Septiembre," *Revista de Costa Rica en el Siglo XIX*: 57.
[59] Rodolfo Cerda Cruz, *Formación del Estado en Costa Rica* (San José: Editorial Universidad de Costa Rica, 1967), 85.
[60] Montero Barrantes, *Elementos de Historia*, 153.
[61] "Solicitud de Aplicación de Indulto," *Revista Conservadora* 1, no. 2 (September 1960): 20–1.
[62] Lynch, *Spanish American Revolutions*, 336.

ascent. Hence the king bestowed the title of "Loyal Villa" on the faithful pueblo of Managua in 1819, in recognition of its "inalterable fidelity."

From the point of view of the pueblo receiving it, such a title of distinction signified the triumph of the pueblo's biographical narrative, which asserted its collective virtue. From the point of view of the sovereign, who publicized and exalted that biography, the title obligated him and all future monarchs to protect the recipient's newly won "graces and privileges."[63]

No less keen than the competition among pueblos, villas, and cities was the competition among family clans, whose paterfamilias wrote the king with suggestions and grievances. In 1820, Guatemalan notables dispatched a formal complaint to the secretary of state regarding the high number of government and ecclesiastical posts held by the "family" – meaning the dominant faction of the local "oligarchy"; at the same time, the notables contended that "other families and parties of [the] capital city" were also "worthy." These "worthy" Guatemalans expressly hoped that the secretary might persuade the king to distribute positions more evenly among the various elite clans so as to avoid the "resentment caused by the concentration of so many posts in a single family and a single place."[64]

While Central Americans jockeyed for the attention and favors of the king, a military mutiny in Spain and continued pressure from Spanish liberals forced Ferdinand to restore constitutional rule in January 1820. In Central America, political debate flourished on the pages of Guatemala City's newspapers. The terms of this debate are quite revealing. Two opposing creole blocs – labeled by each other *Bacos*, or drunkards, and *Cacos*, or thieves – controlled the two leading publications: *El Editor Constitucional* and *El Amigo de la Patria*.[65] Both papers repeatedly expressed the shared conviction that, if the Crown were in possession of "the truth," it would "fulminate" against the "wicked" who tormented and humiliated honorable and virtuous men. And across both political blocs the *fievres*, or "hotheads," who supported a constitutional monarchy, and *serviles*, who favored unconstrained monarchical rule, kept faith with the king.

Despite their sobriquet, when it came to the king, the hotheads were anything but radical. Central America's leading liberal – the Guatemalan *fievre* Pedro Molina – envisioned an ideal social "pact" whereby citizens agreed "not to offend" one another, and a "just prince" exercised governmental authority according to this principle of non-offensiveness.[66] More significantly still, the *fievre* believed that the people ought to look upon constitutional rule as a reward

---

[63] "Don Fernando Séptimo Concede el Título de Leal Villa a Managua," *RAGHN* 7, no. 3 (April 1945): 29–30.

[64] "Relación de los Cargos Públicos y Eclesiásticos Desempeñados por la Familia Aycinena y Larrazabal, Guatemala, 3 de Octubre de 1820," *Anales de la Sociedad de Geografía e Historia de Guatemala* (henceforth *ASGHG*) 26, nos. 3–4 (September/December 1952): 445–51.

[65] Ibid., 544–66.

[66] Pedro Molina, "Instrucción Pública," *El Editor Constitucional*, 24 July 1820, in *Escritos del Doctor Molina*, vol. 1 (Guatemala: Editorial José de Pineda Ibarra, 1969), 12–13.

for their constant fidelity to the "innocent monarch," whose rule, until then, had been distorted by the "monsters" hovering around the throne.[67]

This view of the "innocent monarch" as both dupe and energetic judge allowed creole leaders to organize and mobilize followers through a rhetorical strategy whose premise and logic were clear and powerful. Because the monarch could be deceived, foes could always blame disagreeable royal decisions on the "liars" and "impostors" who misinformed the Crown. Because such liars and impostors existed and represented a mortal danger to the king and his subjects, it was crucial to identify them through "unmasking." This task, however, could be entrusted only to the truly virtuous. Following this reasoning, Guatemalan liberals claimed to have discovered that a typical "servile" (the epithet attached to opponents of a constitutionalist monarchy) was an individual who

...loves slavery, for...he was either born under tyrannical institutions which tied his soul to error, or he enjoys, under the shadow of a despot, the sad advantage of oppressing others. Or dispossessed of all the qualities of man – lacking valor and talent – he has no other capacity than to be a slave.[68]

A liberal, in contrast,

...never adulates.... If he craves for power it is only to make men free...and is moved by an unmistakable ardor for the general welfare.[69]

By its very logic, however, this strategy of unmasking also lent itself to inwardly directed mistrust. Liberals, for example, lived in fear of "servile" impostors, who, "posing" as "liberals," "confabulated" with the power of "egoism,"[70] and found clever ways to defy the authority of the "beloved monarch" with impunity.[71] This fear, furthermore, was compounded by the widespread belief that the "innocent monarch" could not protect his obedient subjects from the "calumny"[72] and "fictions" crafted by manipulators of the truth.[73] The editor of the liberal journal himself was on the defensive against those who implied

...maliciously...that I speak [critically] of the king. I am grateful to a monarch who has always protected Guatemala, and has spoiled the plans of servility – the servility against which [the monarch] has fulminated with thunderbolts of justice.[74]

[67] "Variedades," *El Editor Constitucional*, 7 August 1820, in ibid., 42–3.
[68] "Variedades," *El Editor Constitucional*, 24 July 1820, in ibid., 13–16.
[69] "Variedades," *El Editor Constitucional*, 2 August 1820, in ibid., 31.
[70] "Variedades," *El Editor Constitucional*, 24 July 1820, in ibid., 13–16.
[71] "Variedades," *El Editor Constitucional*, 2 August 1820, in ibid., 32–3.
[72] *El Editor Constitucional*, 16 October 1820, in ibid., 225.
[73] ibid., 228–9.
[74] ibid., 225.

Orphans of Empire

Such was the state of political debate and practice in Central America when news of the mutiny in Spain persuaded the Mexican creole Colonel Agustín de Iturbide that the monarchy's supremacy had been irrevocably compromised.[75] In 1821, Iturbide declared Mexico's "separation" from the motherland. The terms of the declaration, like the political debates in Guatemala, are telling. Iturbide not only extolled Spain as "the most Catholic, pious, heroic and magnanimous nation," but made it explicit that Mexico would be ruled by a "monarchical government, moderated by a constitution appropriate for the country." Known as the *Plan de Iguala*, Iturbide's declaration even specified that

... since [Mexicans and Central Americans] already have a monarch, and in order to prevent the negative effects of ambition, Fernando VII or his dynastic heirs shall be emperors [of Mexico].[76]

Ferdinand turned down the Mexican throne, at which point Mexico's congress called for a serious "search among the royal houses of Europe for a suitable prince." But as president of the Mexican junta, Iturbide eventually managed to "intimidate" congress into proclaiming him emperor.[77] In the meantime, his Plan de Iguala tantalized Central American creoles precisely because it proposed to save the king while liberating the isthmus from his officials. Central America no longer would have to serve as the Spaniards' "dependent employee." This appealing offer – the king, yes, but not his wicked representatives – left the king's captain general in Guatemala only one option: Rather than attack the plan on substantive grounds, he would have to assail the sincerity of the man proclaiming it. The "perfidious" Iturbide, the official cautioned Central Americans, feigned "respect for a religion which he affronts, love to a king whom he demeans."[78]

Guatemala City ultimately chose "absolute independence from Mexico and from any other nation,"[79] then communicated the decision to the other provinces by express mail.[80] But as the news reached the many *cabildos* of the isthmus, it unleashed crisscrossing struggles for predominance among rival localities and clans – struggles that protagonists characterized as clashes between the "healthy" and "unhealthy" members of the collapsing body politic.[81] This was in fact the logic that was used to attack local leaders who tried to temporize. In the "Decree of the Cloudy Days," a text of studied ambivalence, the same

---

75 Edwin Williamson, *The Penguin History of Latin America* (New York: Penguin Press, 1992), 225.

76 "Plan de Iguala" (Iguala), 24 February 1821, in J. D. Gámez, ed., *Archivo Histórico de la República de Nicaragua, 1821–1826*, vol. 1 (Managua: Tipografía Nacional, 1896), 1–5.

77 Bushnell and Macaulay, *Emergence of Latin America*, 15–17.

78 Gabino Gainza, "Manifiesto," 10 April 1821, in Gámez, ed., *Archivo Histórico*, vol. 1, 11–14.

79 See Alejandro Marure, "Bosquejo Histórico," in ibid.

80 *El Genio de la Libertad*, 17 September 1821, in *Escritos del Doctor Pedro Molina*, 766.

81 "La Diputación Provincial de Nicaragua y Costa Rica Manifiesta su Lealtad, 1821," *RAGHN* 9, no. 1 (April 1947): 31–2.

notables who not so long ago had actually dared establish their own governing junta in the Nicaraguan city of León, now declared

... independence from the Spanish government, but only *until* the clouds of the day are dispelled and this Province can proceed according to its religious ends and true interests [emphasis added].[82]

León's tentative declaration of independence led Guatemalans, including *fievres*, to distinguish between León's "vile" governor intendant and the city's people, whom they invited to "enter into a fraternal pact" with Guatemala.[83] Unmoved, the notables of León "asked" their counterparts in Guatemala to desist from their independist plan, arguing that if Spanish Americans split into "small, sovereign governments," they would be exposed to "invasions by foreign powers," might even become "the toys of pirates and adventurers," and worse, could succumb to "continuous debates and clashes amongst themselves."[84]

The argument, rendered plausible by intense localist jockeying,[85] was also seized by Iturbide.[86] To avoid "calamity," Iturbide, now emperor of Mexico, called on Central Americans to ignore all "slanderous" attempts to discredit Mexican goodwill; and heeding the maxim that it is better to prevent than to lament, he informed Central Americans that he was sending a Mexican "protector army" their way.[87]

But as with Guatemala's decision in favor of absolute independence, Iturbide's move prompted a series of struggles that further accentuated the Central Americans' growing sense of disorientation and loss.[88] In this respect, the most frequent lamentation of the day is quite revealing. Everywhere, creoles decried the "orphaned" condition of Spanish America, and everywhere allusions were made to the "orphans" of Central America.[89] Central Americans might be "fraternal" peoples,[90] but no individual could replace the king, and no *cabildo* could replace the Crown.

In addressing this crisis of authority, a renowned Guatemalan political orator proposed the establishment of a federal system. Federalism, on this view, would promote "familial cohesion" by assuring the various Central American

[82] "Acta de los Nublados, 28 de Setiembre (sic), 1821," *RAGHN* 1 (1936–7): 235.
[83] *El Genio de la Libertad*, 22 October 1821, in *Escritos del Doctor Pedro Molina*, 816–20.
[84] See Tomás Ayón, *Apuntes Sobre Algunos De Los Acontecimientos Políticos de Nicaragua: De Los Años De 1811 A 1824* (León: Imprenta del Istmo, 1875), 11–28.
[85] "Orden General" (Granada), 3 October 1821, in ibid., 32. See also "Acta del 12 de Octubre 1821," *RAGHN* 1 (1936–7): 236.
[86] Agustín de Iturbide, "Manifiesto" (Palacio Imperial de Mexico), 19 October 1821, in Gámez, ed., *Archivo Histórico*, vol. 1, 38–43.
[87] Ibid., 38–43.
[88] See Marure, *Bosquejo Histórico*. See also, "El Capitán General de Guatemala a la Diputación Provincial de Nicaragua y Costa Rica. Explica el Verdadero Sentido del Acta de 15 de Septiembre de 1821," *ASGHG* 18, no. 2 (December 1942): 133–4.
[89] "Acta, Se Organiza en León un Gobierno Provisional, 1821," *RAGHN* 1 (1936–7): 43–5.
[90] "Comunicado de Gabino Gainza," (Guatemala), 22 December 1821, in Gámez, ed., *Archivo Histórico*, 43–4.

provinces that Guatemala harbored only "fraternal" – that is, *horizontal* – intentions.[91] The proposal, however, was rebuffed. From the perspective of the provincial elites, Guatemala's intentions were in fact "paternal" – a *vertical* line of authority reserved for the king alone.[92]

Ultimately, both the debate regarding independence under Guatemala's leadership and the debate regarding annexation to Mexico became pointless. Faced with the reality of an invading Mexican army, the junta in Guatemala finally "decided" in favor of annexation. Only through annexation, the junta reasoned, could it hope to preserve the "traditional unity" of Central American "brothers" and stave off dangerous forces.[93] Such forces operated on two levels. The first and more obvious one was localism, as the different provinces and cities assumed positions – against or in favor of annexation – in direct contradiction to their most immediate rival's choice.[94] At a more subtle level, historical memory itself sowed the seeds of discord. Indeed, intuiting the destructive power of historical memory, political thinkers, orators, and pamphleteers proposed "amnesia" – that is, a *tabula rasa* on which to reconstruct the national "family."[95]

But in searching for a new beginning, these opinion makers themselves drew on the traditional understanding of politics as a Manichean play of wills. They warned, for example, against the hazards of rhetorical potency, which they saw as essential to the art of deceit.[96] More importantly, they began to develop a highly restrictive view of opposition politics. On this view, making opposition to a representative government – presumed to be composed of "true" champions of law, liberty, and order – was a "scandal" that revealed the opposition's "perversity," or at the very least, "the delirium of their minds."[97] Finally, combining these two claims, they disqualified opposition activities from the realm of legitimate politics. Opposition was stigmatized as the work of artful factions, and the view of politics as a constant battle between "honest" men and "depraved souls" was reinforced.[98]

Emperor Iturbide himself offered to play the role of arbiter in this struggle between good and evil, exploiting in the process creoles' memory of the "wicked"

[91] Speech by José Francisco de Córdova, in *Genio de la Libertad*, 19 November 1821. See *Escritos del Doctor Pedro Molina*, vol. 3, 853–9.

[92] "Comunicación de las Autoridades de León Prohibiendo la Organización de la Junta Gubernativa de Granada," in Gámez, ed., *Archivo Histórico*, vol. 1, 37–8.

[93] "Acta de Anexión a Mexico, Palacio Nacional de Guatemala," 5 January 1822, in Gámez, ed., *Archivo Histórico*, 48–51.

[94] See Andrés Townsend Ezcurra, *Las Provincias Unidas de Centroamérica: Fundación de la República* (San José: Editorial Costa Rica, 1973), 44–5.

[95] José Cecilio del Valle, *Ensayos y Documentos* (San José: Clásicos Centroamericanos, 1988), 104–6, 169–73.

[96] Miguel Larreynaga, "Discurso," in *Boletín Nicaraguense de Bibliografía y Documentación*, no. 55 (November 1987–September 1988). See also Del Valle, *Ensayos y Documentos*, 109–11, 222.

[97] Ibid., 245–6.

[98] "Cartas de González Saravia, 1822," *RAGHN* 4, no. 2 (August 1942): 6–14. See also Townsend Ezcurra, *Las Provincias Unidas*, 32–3.

royal officials who had once made a habit of "intercepting" and "distorting" their communications with the king. Indeed, Iturbide proposed to reform the colonial rhetorical culture by promising Central American elites easy access to his ear. As Iturbide's new chief in Guatemala put it:

> ...the father of the *pueblos* is no longer two thousand leagues away from you, with a vast ocean in between; recourse to His Imperial Majesty is now easy and expeditious, no longer subject to interception by an absolute [local] chief.[99]

This leveling of the rhetorical playing field, Iturbide's representative believed, would eradicate ancient rivalries, once recalcitrant Spanish officials were removed from the scene.[100] But in truth, the Mexican Empire offered a second-best solution for the provinces' "orphaned condition" at the imperial level, while simultaneously intensifying rivalries among localities that were in fact incipient city-states.[101]

Survival of the Weakest

The choice between absolute independence, as proposed by Guatemala, or tentative independence, as proposed by León (Nicaragua), brought Costa Ricans face to face with their own conviction that, given their province's generalized poverty and weakness, they ought to find an outside protector until they were ready to stand on their own.

In 1821, the governor of Nicaragua tried to persuade the Costa Rican notables that their province was a fragile political infant, and as such should follow Nicaragua's lead.[102] After a brief period of ambivalence – between the Nicaraguan and Guatemalan plans – the Costa Ricans made a startling choice: They proceeded to "detach" themselves from both centers of power. Moreover, in October 1821, Costa Rican *cabildos* averted the danger of turning into veritable city-states, as representatives from the different *cabildos* resolved in common to create a government junta (October 1821). Then came the most remarkable step: As León chose annexation to Mexico, Costa Ricans, who had been initially tempted to make the same choice,[103] produced the Interim Social Pact, better known as *Pacto de Concordia*, or Pact of Harmony, in 1821.[104]

---

[99] "Manifiesto del General don Vicente Filísola," 10 August 1822, in Gámez, ed., *Archivo Histórico*, vol. 1, 73–9.

[100] "El Capitán General de Guatemala, Brigadier Don Vicente Filísola, Explica al Secretario de Guerra y Marina del Imperio Mejicano por Qué Debe ser Relevado el Gobernador Intendente de la Provincia de León," August 1822, *RAGHN* 1 (1936–7): 249–51.

[101] Bancroft, *History of Central America*, 64; "El Jefe Interino del Estado Mayor de la Provincia de León de Nicaragua, don Antonio del Villar, dá Parte al Comandante General de la Provincia Sobre la Asonada del 4 de Junio de 1822," *RAGHN* 1 (1936–7): 237–41; Gordon Kenyon, "Mexican Influence in Central America, 1821–1823," *The Hispanic American Historical Review* XLI:2 (May 1961): 175–205; Wortman, *Government and Society in Central America*, 232.

[102] "Carta de Brigadier Don Miguel González Saravia, Jefe Político de León," 9 December 1821, in Sáenz Carbonell, *Despertar Constitucional*, 299.

[103] Montero Barrantes, *Elementos de Historia*, 183–4.

[104] Saenz Carbonell, *Despertar Constitucional*, 139–40, 150.

Unlike Central Americans in general and Nicaraguans in particular, Costa Rican elites were able both to imagine and justify the practice of bargaining and compromise. The Costa Ricans, to be sure, briefly explored alternative options, one moment jockeying for localist preeminence as best they could, the next proposing that all localities band together behind one locality to keep at bay the "fratricidal" wars convulsing the rest of the isthmus. But in the process of exploration, they also discovered a two-tiered imperative imposed on them by "reality." First, they recognized the urgent need to preserve their "unique" tradition of internal harmony from external influences – a recognition that in turn pushed them to seek the conciliation of two opposing objectives: collective insulation from external disruption and vindication of internal localist claims.

By operating within the parameters of what they thought was "realistic," political leaders further reconfigured their collective field of imaginable possibilities. This process of reconfiguration began with the foundational compromise at the center of the Pact of Harmony. One of the Pact's crucial provisions was the institutionalization of an itinerant national government: High officials were obligated to reside part of every year in each of the country's four major cities. The arrangement was undoubtedly peculiar, if only because it did something never seen before in the colonies: It split in equal parts the prestige and power attached to the seat of government. The argument in favor of this peculiar arrangement, ironically, rested partially on Costa Ricans' understanding of their "unique" colonial experience: That is, political leaders concluded that they could preserve Costa Rica's "tradition" of internal harmony from external threat only if they satisfied all domestic localist claims in some equitable fashion.

In the discussions leading up to the Pact, and in the Pact itself, the Costa Ricans' lack of a contentious rhetorical tradition was very much in evidence. Indeed, where the Nicaraguans used images of "treachery" and "evil" to advance their narrow interests at each other's expense, the Costa Ricans employed a give-and-take terminology known as *transacción*, or bargaining, to arbitrate conflicts among competing claimants. The notables, for example, entertained the possibility of splitting the difference between pro-annexation "imperialists" and anti-annexation "republicans," actually considering the establishment of a "hybrid" government – half imperialist, half republican. Nothing came of the idea, but the Pact of Harmony, as its very name denotes, satisfied the widespread preference for avoiding conflict.[105]

The junta of representatives responsible for the Pact sought, above all, to prevent war among the province's major cities: Cartago, the old colonial capital; its economically ascendant rival, San José; and their respective satellites, Heredia and Alajuela. As already mentioned, the Pact stipulated an "itinerant" capital, thus affording all four cities an opportunity to host the national government. Further, the Pact combined in pragmatic fashion aristocratic presumptions,

---

[105] Chester Zelaya Goodman, "Repercusiones Inmediatas de la Independencia en Centroamérica," in Academia de Geografía e Historia de Costa Rica, ed., *Vísperas de la Independencia*, 334–8.

liberal tenets, and localist preoccupations. In the same breath, the Pact affirmed citizens' rights to civil liberty and property as well as a series of "antiquated" aristocratic conventions. The Pact also formalized the localities' agreement to use the Constitution of 1812 as a blueprint for matters of political principle. And in Article 4, it called for the creation of a provisional government junta.[106]

Costa Ricans subordinated themselves to the authority of their government junta, which in turn articulated both its own sense of mission and an incipient vision of national identity:

[This government's objective] has been to conserve our ancestors' sacred religion: total independence from the metropole, as well as the unity and peace that have *always* characterized [Costa Rica]. . . . Countrymen, if you remain united in your opinions, you shall observe from the tranquility of your homes the disastrous picture of anarchy that unfortunately becomes visible in many provinces of this continent. . . . remain attentive to the cruel circumstances of other countries so that you may *perfect* the political wisdom that brings you honor [emphasis added].[107]

The junta was not alone in using the country's colonial past in constructive ways. Other major players also resorted to a compelling vision of Costa Rica's "unique" past as guide to a "brilliant" future. The localist elites of Cartago and San José, for example, finally did go to battle over the seat of the capital city (1823). But hostilities lasted only a few hours. Moreover, once hostilities subsided, the antagonists quickly returned to the politics of exceptionalism. This was in no small measure due to the fact that the militarily victorious city of San José endorsed the notion that the new constitutional assembly should draft only laws that were compatible with the "customs" of the "beautiful" state of Costa Rica. This position had one significant practical implication: The Constitution of 1823, while naming San José as capital city, hardly deviated from the Pact of Harmony in other respects.[108] The limited scope of constitutional change, in turn, contained the spread of destructive rivalries by circumscribing the issues at stake – a feat all the more impressive now that the Mexican Empire was collapsing, and the rest of Central America began to slide into chaos and war.

Conclusion

Central American creole elites demonstrated robust self-regard and impressive tactical sagacity vis-á-vis Spain and royal officials throughout the colonial period, as well as during the Napoleonic crisis of 1808–14. But while they embraced novelties such as constitutional liberalism and the democratic electoral principle, they failed to articulate clear ideological arguments either for

---

[106] Wilburg Jiménez Castro, *Génesis del Gobierno de Costa Rica: 1821–1981*, vol. 1 (San José: Editorial Alma Mater, 1986), 32.

[107] "Proclama de la Primera Junta Superior Gubernativa" (Alajuela), 9 November 1822, in Carlos Meléndez Chaverri, ed., *Documentos Fundamentales* (San José: Editorial Costa Rica, 1978), 93–4.

[108] Jiménez Castro, *Génesis*, 35–7.

"separation" from Spain or for the loss of the royal arbiter, on whom they had so vitally depended until the very last for justice and fairness. More fundamentally still, they failed to develop an explicit and coherent defense of individual rights and freedoms. Instead, they renovated the Manichean practice of archetypical identity formation, and entrenched the old notion of the local polity as an organism whose "healthy" parts must constantly struggle to dominate and exclude "unhealthy" elements from power.

While Costa Ricans also failed to formulate alternative principles to Manichean politics, they did begin to forge a national identity that declared such virtues as civility and peacefulness to be constitutive of their "character." These virtues, they claimed, made them who they were, and consequently any "realistic" strategy had to take this "fact" into account. Costa Ricans' consistent manipulation of this identity as "factual" tempered their internal competitive practices.[109] Indeed, this political-cultural construct provided a practical solution to Jean-Jacques Rousseau's dilemma: Good laws require a good people, but a good people can emerge only as a result of good laws.[110] The Costa Ricans had merely to refer to their own "historical" record to prove their own goodness and to specify the manifestations of that goodness: a natural predilection for internal harmony, an undeniable competence in the art and science of lawmaking, as demonstrated by the founding Pact, and a habit of obedience, evident in the country's relations with the Crown and, later in the people's adherence to the Pact.

Yet Costa Rica's postcolonial path remained uncertain. In the rest of Central America, the Enlightenment project of individual rights and freedoms was overwhelmed by rampant mistrust. In addition, a Manichean system of normative scheming absorbed the institutions of electoral democracy, ultimately producing a field of imaginable possibilities in which the forces of anarchy and despotism seemed to doom the search for just order. To the extent that geographical location is destiny, Costa Rica would have to operate in this unenviable context. Moreover, as we are about to see, Costa Rica would develop a hybrid system of normative scheming that would engender its own peculiar challenges. Agency and legacy would meet again.

---

[109] "Proclama," Meléndez Chaverri, ed., *Documentos Fundamentales*, 93–4.

[110] Bonnie Honig, *Democracy and the Foreigner* (Princeton, NJ: Princeton University Press, 2001), 20.

4

Postcolonial Paths

Rhetorical Strategies and Frames

> Thrones may be out of fashion and pageantry too, but political authority still
> requires a cultural frame in which to define itself, and so does opposition to it.
>
> –Clifford Geertz[1]

When the cultural frame for political authority vanishes, the establishment of
trustworthy government structures becomes the ultimate political success. Such
an outcome, however, is not foreordained. Success or failure will depend on a
society's "inheritance" and on the "agency" of its political actors.[2] After the
disappearance of the royal arbiter in 1821 and the collapse of the Mexican
Empire in 1823, Central Americans seemed to succeed on this score, if only for
a moment.

To begin with, they adopted a foreign model of government without excessive controversy. In a mimetic exercise focused on the U.S. experience, they
created a Central American Republic constitutionally grounded in the principle
of election and the self-regulating principle of the checks-and-balances mechanism. Moreover, the constituent assembly managed to resolve the main points
of contention by ratifying the keenly federalist project championed by liberals
and opposed by conservatives.[3]

In accordance with the federalist project (1824), the member states of the
republic retained a high degree of autonomy; each would raise its own army,
and each would reproduce in miniature the union's broader institutional framework. That is, each state would have its own tripartite government and electoral

---

[1] Clifford Geertz, "Centers, Kings, and Charisma: Reflections on the Symbolics of Power," in Sean
Wilentz, ed., *Rites of Power: Symbolism, Ritual, and Politics Since the Middle Ages* (Philadelphia,
PA: University of Pennsylvania Press, 1985), 30.
[2] John Dunn, "Trust and Political Agency," in Diego Gambetta, ed., *Trust: Making and Breaking
Cooperative Relations* (Cambridge, MA: Basil Blackwell, 1990), 80–1.
[3] Conservatives accepted the liberals' victory and the establishment of a federalist union because
they were persuaded that they could gain control of the Central American legislature (the strongest
of the three branches).

processes. The formula, impeccable on paper, proved disastrous in practice. The Central American union and its republican governmental institutions became connecting vessels for the transmission of strife and jealousies from one state to another. Nicaragua was by far the most violent and unstable of all the states, while Costa Rica stood out as a relatively calm and increasingly prosperous society.

Structural and ideology-based explanations for this radical difference, as we saw in Chapter 1, are empirically and theoretically unsatisfying. Nor can identical institutional frameworks account for a divergent outcome. This chapter argues that Nicaragua's bloody debacle came about because local political actors, by taking seriously the principles of election and popular sovereignty, turned the new formal institutions of arbitration into focal points for a renovated variant of Manichean normative scheming. In this context, politics became a dangerous affair not for the faint of heart; by the early 1840s, civil men perceived high public office more as a magnet for lethal attacks than a position of influence and prestige. One director of state – selected for the job by the assembly after an electoral deadlock – immediately tendered his resignation. When it was not accepted, the director surrendered to his fate: He prepared his testament and, beseeching heaven for "divine assistance, ascended to the [office] as if he were going to the gallows."[4]

Costa Rican leaders, in contrast, gradually consolidated their nation's "exemplary" identity and closed off domestic politics to Manicheanism, which they consigned instead to the field of external relations. Again, this was no predetermined outcome. To be sure, Costa Ricans enjoyed a key advantage: They had managed to impose limits on destructive competition during the transition to independence by solving what may be called "Rousseau's dilemma." But these limits, as the previous chapter demonstrated, were rooted in the idea that Costa Rica's legacy entailed "peculiar" exigencies and "special" advantages – an idea that, as we are about to see, also exerted great pressure on political leaders to produce tangible developmental achievements and thus intensified competition at a time when localist and personalistic rivalries wreaked havoc in the rest of the region. In fact, the vaunted singularity of Costa Rica's postcolonial path generated its own obstacles before ushering in an exceptionalist system of normative scheming that was stable enough to sustain and shape a corresponding regime of arbitration.

Fears and Hopes: Preserving the Nation's Prestige

Costa Rica's transitional governing junta (1821–3), we already saw, was able to control the divisive effects of political rivalries by anchoring the transition process in a set of controlling exceptionalist claims about the colonial past. Once the junta completed its term in 1823, and Costa Ricans were integrated into the

---

[4] Anselmo Rivas, *Nicaragua: Su Pasado, Ojeada Retrospectíva* (Managua: Ediciones La Prensa, 1936), 15–17.

Central American union, they were able to elect their own chief of state (1824), as well as their own State Assembly. Almost from the start, both branches of government borrowed heavily from the transitional junta's rhetorical approach to competition. In selling their programmatic visions – and in their competing efforts to outshine one another – both the executive and the legislature repeatedly highlighted their country's distinctiveness.[5] The legislature articulated and defended the view that while the people of Costa Rica were "poor," riches were in store for them because they were "industrious," "calm," and "patriotic."[6] And in an assertion that reflected deep concern over Nicaragua's relentless upheaval, the Assembly also proclaimed in 1825 that if Costa Ricans guarded against the "corruption of their mores," they would enjoy "eternal and exemplary tranquility."[7] Similarly, the chief executive, Juan Mora Fernández, vowed to "draw" on the "virtues, morality, and good sense" of his compatriots when crafting state policy. Only distance, he told them, would allow their small and weak country to maintain "public peace." Only peace, he added, could afford them "the time" to devote themselves to "business." And only in distant peace, he concluded, could they enjoy the "fruits of their labor and investments."[8]

The first "agrarian reform" (1825) was meant to provide this virtuous people – or to put it in the language of microeconomics, this superb human capital – with another crucial factor of production: titled land. This was all part of a concentrated effort to foment coffee production, an effort that would gather momentum in the late 1830s. But just as importantly, the 1825 reform was also meant to demonstrate, yet again, Costa Rica's capacity to defy expectations and single-handedly preserve its reputation and integrity. In 1827, the Costa Rican government reassured the citizenry by referencing their proven strengths. First, however, the government had to sound the alarm:

Costa Rica, which at every point has given unequivocal proof of its love for peace, order, and law . . . now contemplates in open horror the rapid degradation of the [Central American] Republic. . . .

From there, the government moved on to issue a rallying cry that it disguised as a dispassionate self-assessment:

. . . the virtuous people of Costa Rica, notwithstanding their territory's small scale and the obscurity in which they have lived, and in spite of the erroneous and disdainful opinion about them held by others, have proved *capable* at the most critical points of

---

[5] Astrid Fishel Volio, "La Educación en el Proceso de Formación y Consolidación del Estado Costarricense," in Carmen Lila Gómez et al., *Las Instituciones Costarricenses del Siglo XIX* (San José: Editorial Costa Rica, 1985), 129–52.

[6] "Manifiesto de la Asamblea del Estado" (San José), 19 April 1825, in Meléndez Chaverri, ed., *Documentos Fundamentales*, 135–6.

[7] Ibid.

[8] Mora Fernández was elected chief of state in 1824, reelected in 1828, and governed until 1833.

surviving and retaining a *sense of self* without subsidy or assistance from their [Central American] siblings [emphasis added].[9]

This assessment proved correct, in no small measure because the strategy of matching factors of production paid off. By 1829, the country had managed to make steady progress in commerce, agriculture, and mining, while "enterprises, profits, and consumer goods" multiplied.[10]

There were, however, some ominous signs. Most notably, by 1831 the administration had accumulated a budget deficit that, in the eyes of the Cartago opposition (localist opponents of the government from Cartago, which was San José's rival city), imposed an unbearable "burden" on all the people. This harsh indictment, in combination with intense localist pressures, would have been sufficient reason anywhere else in Central America for immediate confrontation. But the Costa Rican opposition pushed instead for the creation of a special commission to investigate the state's fiscal "problem."

Once formed, the commission had at least two options: It could press for a straightforward fiscal-austerity plan and/or recommend a deepening of the state's extractive capacity. But the commission argued instead that the best way to increase the state's resources was to make citizens "rich," and that the state's fiscal soundness was inextricably tied to society's "general prosperity."

The reasoning behind this position is instructive. First, the commission deemed fiscal "impositions" problematic because they "exasperated" a people who had long sacrificed to their country's domestic "tranquility." This was crucial, since the commission considered tranquility to be the "sole support" of Costa Rica's "political viability." The commission elaborated on this last point by noting that in Costa Rica, "discontent and upheaval" were an "uncharacteristic" state of affairs, whereas peace and industry represented the country's very essence.

On this view, if discontent and upheaval displaced peace and industry, there could be no true Costa Rican nation. And because a belligerent defense of "peaceful" Costa Rica was simply inconceivable in the local field of imaginable possibilities, the developmental option took on an aura of inevitability. Inevitability, however, was not synonymous with despair. In crafting its developmental plan, the commission produced a statement that was as much a chart for the future as it was a declaration of faith in the Costa Rican people. Costa Ricans, the commission noted, were eager to contribute to the nation's welfare. Land was useless without credit, the commission added, and the Costa Ricans' "good disposition" was "wasted" in the absence of employment opportunities. Nor could the nation move forward if its leaders' hopeful utterances lacked credibility with the people. "Without wealth or credit, we cannot make

[9] Joaquín Bernardo Calvo, "Nota del Ministro General del Estado de Costa Rica al Ministro de Relaciones Interiores y Exteriores de la Federación" (San José), 8 October 1827, in Meléndez Chaverri, ed., *Documentos Fundamentales*, 147–50.

[10] Juan Mora [Fernández], "Mensaje del Jefe de Estado a la Asamblea" (San José), 11 March 1829, in ibid., 150–7.

credible promises of happiness and political viability," the commission stated, before going on to dispense one key piece of advice: Grant titled plots of land to the poor, especially in the coastal zones.

On the commission's logic, only "good titles" could establish a "spirit of good faith among citizens," and only in this way could Costa Ricans avoid "fights" over "what belongs to whom, and who owes what." No entity other than the state was able to provide this essential public good; or, put another way, no entity other than the state, by dint of its distributive capacity, could preemptively arbitrate conflicting claims. But there was more for the state to do. The commission also argued that "the state ought resolutely to force citizens to cultivate those crops that are most in demand in Europe, such as coffee, sugar, cocoa; this is the way to lift ourselves out of misery and to enrich our Costa Ricans."[11]

Through all of this, the loss of Costa Rica's status as a regional exemplar was an unbearable prospect for government and opponents alike. As one notable put it:

> It is neither reasonable nor just that Costa Rica should now lose the *beautiful prestige* that it has earned through its constant vigilance in the protection of harmony, its exact adherence to the law, and its continuous repudiation of the partisan rows and personalist ideas that have been in abundant evidence in the other [Central American] states. [emphasis added].[12]

The fear of contamination implicit in this 1830 statement was by 1835 very much out in the open. As one pamphleteer wrote, Costa Rica deserved "great happiness [given the nature of its people]," but instead was "thrown into despondence." The pamphleteer identified three culprits for this anomalous state of affairs. One was plain maladministration of governmental affairs. Another was "a gang of Nicaraguans who, after making their own country miserable, infested [Costa Rica]." The third culprit was "a few [Costa Ricans] who learned from the Nicaraguans and followed their example."[13]

Fear of contamination had two crucial effects. First, it heightened the elites' tendency to compete for positions of command on the basis of substantive programmatic visions and their effective implementation. Insulation from regional conflicts, after all, hinged on rapid economic development. Second, it deepened elite valorization of domestic peace because political leaders persistently relied on rhetorical campaigns that connected the twin imperatives of national insulation and economic development to Costa Rica's "peculiarities" – namely, its inhabitants' "innate" preference for civility and their "inclination" to hard work, neither of which could be satisfied if elites gave free rein to personalistic and localist passions.

---

[11] "Dictámen de la Comisión para Recabar Arbitrios" (Cartago), 15 August 1831, in ibid., 481–5.

[12] José María Esquivel, "Sobre la Disolución de las Costumbres" (San José), 15 May 1830, in ibid., 474–5.

[13] "Manojito de Flores," *El Josefino* (San José), 11 August 1835, in ibid., 485–8.

This dual tendency – to compete over how best to forge, in image and fact, a strong and independent nation, and to draw back from the perils of atomizing conflict – was most visible in the disputes over the so-called *ambulancia* arrangement (1834). The arrangement basically reestablished in modified form the itinerant government first stipulated by the 1821 Pact of Harmony. Intended to temper localism by "flattering" the localities equally,[14] the *ambulancia* denied San José the political-administrative preeminence to which it felt entitled.

The San José elites set out, yet again, to correct this situation. That persuasion was their first recourse – even though their city was by far the most powerful – is telling. Also revealing are their arguments. According to the San José elites, the *ambulancia* incited "distrust and jealousies" that could destroy Costa Rica's advances in industry, commerce, and the arts – advances that were "already the envy of other peoples." The *ambulancia*, they further contended, fed this destructive dynamic in two ways. First, by turning the government into a traveling body, the *ambulancia* exposed the nation to foreign ridicule.[15] Secondly, since San José's leadership had been crucial in securing the peace and prosperity that Costa Rica had enjoyed since 1823, and which now made the nation an object of "admiration" among foreigners, chaining San José to the *ambulancia* arrangement was tantamount to depriving the country of its one proven leader.

Having put forth this argument, the San José elites turned around and did something that in other Central American countries would have been simply unimaginable: They opened the way for a compromise solution whereby San José would accept the *ambulancia* in exchange for the chief of state's resignation. The reasoning underlying the compromise proposal went as follows. On the one hand, the "disappearance" of the government – meaning the resignation of the incumbent chief – would pose no threat to the nation's tranquil prosperity because the people of Costa Rica, being prudent property owners and endowed with the proper "moral habits," were unlikely to engage in the kind of disorder that might require a coercive response from the government. On the other hand, the San José elites argued, the incumbent's continuation in power generated "bad faith," which in turn put at risk the citizens' capacity to forge stable, credible contracts. Thus, in 1835, after the resignation of Chief José Rafael de Gallegos, the San José elites accepted the *ambulancia*, even though they still found it "ludicrous" and "harmful" to Costa Rica's external image.[16]

The *ambulancia*, however, remained vulnerable to the contradictory pressures of intra-elite competition. To be sure, Costa Rica's intensely competitive political leaders still showed a preference for internal conciliation, and they worked for it in the face of impending conflict. Toward the end of Juan Mora Fernández increasingly turbulent administration (1824–33), for example,

[14] *La Tertulia*, 14 March 1834.
[15] *La Tertulia*, 21 March 1834.
[16] *La Tertulia*, 30 May, 11 July, 26 September 1834, and 12 March 1835.

Congress recognized the chief's "virtues" in an effort to ease personalistic resentments. The *ambulancia* itself, as previously noted, was an attempt to refashion a *modus vivendi*, however fragile, among rival localities. But the same guiding image of a peaceful and vulnerable Costa Rica that led elites to avoid conflict also made them an impatient lot, constantly demanding resolute developmental initiatives from their heads of state. Indeed, the election of the assertive Braulio Carrillo (1835–7) signaled elites' determination to transcend the "timidity" of his predecessor (Gallegos, 1833–5). It also signaled the calculus of the San José elites in particular: Carrillo's election, they knew, would mean the end of the *ambulancia*, if only because his would be an energetic and progressive administration that could not possibly tolerate the demeaning "spectacle" of an itinerant national government.

The *ambulancia* was eventually overturned. But as in 1823, the 1835 conflict was quickly resolved. The same two interrelated sources once again pushed for conflict resolution. First, elites' own deepening belief in Costa Rica's "exemplary civility" stigmatized conflict as a "national disgrace."[17] This made even victorious San José – with its clear preponderance of force – inclined to compromise with weaker rivals.[18] Second, and most important, in the decades prior to the outbreak of hostilities, competing elites had outlined a common developmental vision rooted in widely held beliefs about the Costa Rican "character" and in equally generalized expectations about what their future could and should look like. In so doing, politicians generated powerful incentives for victors and vanquished alike to resume the business of growing the economy and protecting their national "tradition."

These incentives, in fact, further accentuated elite pressures on chief executives for quick and effective developmental action. Hence the "inadequate" Manuel Aguilar administration was overthrown, and Carrillo returned to power via a coup d'etat (1838), and hence the feverish pace and extensive scope of Carrillo's initiatives. In addition to building roads and ports to support large-scale coffee production and trade, Carrillo established civil and penal codes, a postal service, and a national defense apparatus – measures that culminated in the self-confident decision to "separate" Costa Rica from the Central American Federation.[19] Indeed, Carrillo not only managed to foment broad-based

[17] José Anselmo Sancho, Ministro General, "Comunicación al Ministro de Relaciones Interiores de la Federación," 20 October 1835; José Anselmo Sancho, "Al Ministro de Relaciones Interiores de la Federación," 20 February 1836, both in Meléndez Chaverri, ed., *Documentos Fundamentales*, 183–4, 186.

[18] The leaders of the so-called League – the anti-San José alliance – certainly did not escape unscathed. Carrillo meted out fines and even banishment. But he also made crucial concessions. For example, he gave up his initial plan to abolish the tithe, which he had intended to replace with a rural property tax. See Ricardo Fernández Guardia, *Cartilla Histórica de Costa Rica* (San José: Imprenta de Avelio Alsina, 1909), 86–7. See also Comisión Nacional de Conmemoraciones Históricas, *La Tertulia, 1834–35,* (San José: Imprenta Nacional, 1977), x–xi; Francisco Montero Barrantes, *Elementos de Historia de Costa Rica,* vol. 2 (San José: Tipografía Nacional, 1892), 235–6.

[19] Fernández Guardia, *Cartilla,* 91; Montero Barrantes, *Elementos de Historia.*

agrarian development, but was also able to entrench the elites' socioeconomic dominance. With Carrillo, national governments began systematically to pursue a policy of free land distribution for the crop's cultivation while maintaining a pyramidlike distributional structure.[20] (By 1850, when the coffee boom was in full swing, "three quarters of all major coffee growers were descended from just two Spanish colonial families, one of them that of the conquistador Juan Vázquez de Coronado himself").[21]

Under Carrillo's rule, and for decades to come, the procedural aspects of power contestation were subordinated to the actual uses of power. These uses were considered legitimate when applied to the pursuit of collective wealth creation and the preservation of national integrity. And in fact, it was precisely on this normative basis that Carrillo's self-regarding scheme aimed to expand the limits of executive authority. Pointing to his own record of effective leadership, he declared himself ruler for life – an ambitious bid that prompted a tactical alliance between the Cartago opposition and the unionist *caudillo* from Honduras, Francisco Morazán. The former, disgruntled by the *ambulancia*'s dissolution, set out to remove Carrillo and to wrest from San José the seat of the capital. The latter, disgruntled by Costa Rica's separation from the Central American Federation, proposed to bring this country and other drifters back into the fold.

To undermine the emerging ties between the Cartago elites and Morazán, Carrillo presented each with a presumably compelling reason to break the alliance. To his fellow Costa Ricans, he argued that only his leadership could keep at bay the chaos and destruction that afflicted the rest of Central America. To Morazán himself and to all Central Americans, he offered an open invitation to settle in Costa Rica, where they would be given land and a chance to emulate the Costa Ricans; that is, to learn how to become industrious, peaceful, and useful to the state.[22]

But performance-based legitimacy, unlike procedural legitimacy, is not self-reproducing: If the ruler fails to keep his programmatic promises, then he is simply not needed. And even if does keep his promises, he may not be needed any longer. Given additional time in office, Carrillo might well have attained new impressive goals. But having accomplished so many so quickly – under his rule, Costa Rica became an independent state, the coffee boom entered in full swing, and traditional elites reinforced their privileged position[23] – he made himself dispensable. He was forced out of power in 1842 by Cartago leaders (in alliance with Morazán).

---

[20] Edelberto Torres Rivas, *History and Society of Central America* (Austin, TX: University of Texas Press, 1993), 17.

[21] Jeffery Paige, *Coffee and Power: Revolution and the Rise of Democracy in Central America* (Cambridge, MA: Harvard University Press, 1997), 15.

[22] Emanuel Thompson, *Defensa de Carrillo: Un Dictador al Servicio de América* (San José: Imprenta Barrase, 1945), 183.

[23] "Three quarters of all major coffee growers were descended from just *two* Spanish colonial families, one of them that of the conquistador Juan Vázquez de Coronado himself." Paige, *Coffee and Power*, 15.

And yet the early post-Carrillo years witnessed two remarkable developments. First, Costa Rican elites transcended internal cleavages in order to close ranks against Morazán. (Dreading the likelihood that the Honduran *caudillo* would now "drag" Costa Rica into the Central American quagmire, they quickly sent him to the firing squad.) Second, and most importantly, Costa Ricans began to vindicate Carrillo as a historical figure, finally embedding his reputation into the larger theme of Costa Rica's collective virtuousness. Specifically, while Carrillo was explicitly labeled a dictator, he was also depicted as a special kind of authoritarian: a firm yet patriotic ruler under whose wise leadership Costa Rica "grew accustomed" to "self-government" and "complete independence." The dictator, in fact, became an "esteemed" figure. In a word, he became an icon of Costa Rican exceptionalism, deserving of respect because under his leadership the country had completed its journey to full independence without doing violence to its national "character."[24]

The dictator's dual accomplishment, in fact, became a crowning point in the Costa Ricans' view of their postcolonial history. On this view, that history was made up of a series of character tests that Costa Rica passed with flying colors, in spite of the hurdles thrown its way by neighboring Nicaragua. The sequence went as follows. First, after "detaching itself" from the "mother country" in 1821, Costa Ricans proved their "essential peacefulness" so vividly that they inspired the inhabitants of Nicoya and Guanacaste to seek – "spontaneously" – separation from "turbulent" Nicaragua and union with Costa Rica. Second, after Costa Rica and Nicaragua joined the Central American Federation in 1824, the latter remained in the "most complete anarchy" while the former "promptly" established a constitutional government with "utmost tranquility." And third, while Nicaraguans "waged a vicious war" against the federal government, Costa Ricans claimed that they remained true to themselves – a "hardworking, pacific people, dedicated to agriculture and devoted to commerce."

When all was said and done, then, history was about character. And this particular history established a "stark contrast" between Costa Ricans and Nicaraguans. It demonstrated that the former adhered to the belief that "men must not live to engage in bloody wars, but rather to ensure their own welfare through work." And it demonstrated that the latter, "although possessed of many good and brilliant qualities," were "generally indolent; accustomed to internal strife; and inclined to fight with neighboring states." Thus, history explained why, in its territorial disputes with Nicaragua, Costa Rica remained "patient," "sacrificing," and "conciliatory."[25] And most importantly,

---

[24] See Thompson's *Defensa de Carrillo* for the clearest articulation.

[25] See narrative by Costa Rica's minister plenipotentiary to Europe and Latin America, Felipe Molina, first published in Spanish in 1850, *Memoria Sobre las Cuestiones de Límites Que se Versan entre la República de Costa Rica y el Estado de Nicaragua* (Madrid: Imprenta de la Viuda de Calero, 1850). Also refer to Pedro Pérez Zeledón, minister plenipontenciary to the United States, *Informe Sobre la Cuestión de Límites de Costa Rica y Nicaragua y Puntos Accesorios Sometidos al Arbitraje del Señor Presidente de los Estados Unidos* (Washington, DC: Gibson Bros., 1887), especially 42–4.

it explained why Carrillo's strong rule had been "necessary." Thanks to him, Costa Rica had become sufficiently self-reliant to declare itself a sovereign nation in the face of ongoing Central American strife.

For Costa Ricans, sovereignty stood for a very specific kind of autonomy: the freedom to be peaceful and industrious. Put another way, barring an attack on the nation, sovereignty stood for the freedom to remain at the margin of regional wars. Of course, transgressions against this substantiated sovereignty still called for the severest punishment. Hence Morazán's fate after he tried to use Costa Rica as a base for the military campaign that he hoped would culminate in the political reunification of Central America. Profoundly "disappointed" by his "violent measures" – most notably, rasing a local army to march on the member states of the defunct Central American Republic – the Costa Rican people "rebelled as one and killed him."[26]

The sovereignty theme capped an increasingly dominant understanding of the past that by 1850 had acquired clear descriptive and prescriptive lines – an understanding which, in fact, had become a collective field of imaginable possibilities. For out of a series of rhetorical campaigns, concomitant policies, and individual leaders' self-seeking objectives, Costa Ricans created an exceptionalist system of normative scheming and, by extension, a new overarching view of life both as it "really" was and as it "ought to be."

At the base of this system of normative scheming and its collective field of imaginable possibilities lay a *lingua franca* that enabled actors to communicate, without complications, the binary opposition between Costa Rica's unique character and the dangerous forces of the outside world, forces that Nicaragua typified. In their more explicit practices of argumentation, actors elaborated and manipulated the virtuous national identity inherent in this binary opposition. They did this, in fact, within a rhetorical frame now sufficiently pervasive to make exceptionalism the hallmark of normative scheming. This system, in turn, engendered a set of substantive legitimacy criteria tailored to fit the nation's presumably special needs and advantages.[27] The entire system hinged on a controlling norm that, like the old norm of obedience to the Crown, was clearly recognizable to all. This was the norm of national preservation and development. This was, indeed, the norm that self-seeking actors would have to exalt and manipulate if they were simultaneously to explain and justify their particularist designs and actions. In brief, this was the norm that delineated a zone of permissible behavior for competing actors. The contours of this zone were established by a tripartite plan aimed at economic prosperity, political harmony, and insulation from external corruption.

---

[26] Molina, *Memoria*, 25–6.

[27] State-led reforms were seen as a vehicle for "revolution without war;" as a transformative means "different from the Hispanic-American revolutions." See, for example, Juan Rafael Mora, "El Presidente de la República: A La Nación" (San José: Imprenta de la República, 6 June 1850). Just as importantly, a ruler could be forgiven flaws and errors if his government brought tangible benefits to the nation. For an explicit illustration, see Unos Costaricenses, "Al Público" (San José: Imprenta de la Libertad, 24 July 1850).

In domestic politics, the upshot of all this was that political rivalry did not automatically translate into a Manichean clash, as it almost always did in Nicaragua. Leaders who, like Carrillo, preserved and strengthened the constitutive attributes of Costa Rica's exemplary identity could be said to operate within the strictures of legitimate governance. And even when, as with Carrillo, leaders engaged in excesses that led to their own ruin, their positive accomplishments could still be salvaged for integration into the national biography. In external politics, by way of contrast, the Manichean logic remained dominant among imaginable possibilities: Costa Ricans were destined to stand in vigilance, constantly guarding against the corruption of their virtuous nation by "foreign ideologies" and "practices."

Institutionalizing Confrontational Manicheanism

Conditions could not have been more different for elites in Nicaragua, where the collapse of the Mexican Empire led to a civil war so intractable and atrocious that the federal government of Central America characterized it as a horrifying display of fratricidal butchery. The barbaric practices and engulfing scope of the conflict are intriguing. Also puzzling is that even though neighboring Costa Ricans had begun to show that divisive jealousies could be controlled, Nicaraguans seemed bent on spoiling possible solutions to their destructive power struggles. Indeed, the first major civil war (1824) was just that: the first of several violent conflicts to break out in virtual succession. It was also the first to be halted by outside intervention (by the provisional government of Central America, located in Guatemala); and it was the first to lead to elections that in turn would lead to new eruptions of violence. By 1825, Nicaraguans were once again about to descend into a cycle of rivalries, betrayals, revolts, assassinations, and war, all the while insisting on elections.[28]

The Nicaraguans, like the Costa Ricans, faced the pressing challenge of creating and organizing legitimate power, by which they meant the authority to settle contentious issues. The challenge, of course, was doubly taxing in the absence of a commonly – recognized arbiter. Costa Rican leaders shifted attention away from elections per se and toward the creation of a developmental plan for national preservation – in other words, they concentrated first and foremost on the practical exigencies and potential advantages they associated

---

[28] For the atrocities and devastation of the wars of 1824, 1825, and 1827, see Emilio Alvarez Lejarza, "La Historia es Tribunal de Ultima Instancia," *RAGH* 6, no. 2 (August 1944): 125–30; Tomás Ayón, *Apuntes Sobre Algunos de los Acontecimientos Políticos de Nicaragua: De Los Años De 1811 A 1824* (León: Imprenta del Istmo, 1875); Alejandro Marure, *Bosquejo Histórico de las Revoluciones de Centroamérica, desde 1811 hasta 1834* (Guatemala: 1837). For an impression of Nicaragua's localist, clannish and personalistic imbroglios, see Ayón, *Apuntes Sobre Algunos*; José Coronel Urtecho, "Paradojas de las Intervenciones de Valle y Arce en Nicaragua," *RCPC* 28, no. 140 (May 1972): 33–53; idem, *Reflexiones sobre la Historia de Nicaragua: De Gainza a Somoza*, vol. 1 (León: Editorial Hospicio, 1962); José Dolores Gámez, *Historia de Nicaragua* (Managua: Fondo de Promoción Cultural, Banco de América, 1975).

with their collective identity. In this context, a *primus inter pares* could arise on the basis of demonstrable competence and an appropriate degree of personal ambition.

Nicaraguans, in contrast, concentrated on electoral competition, bringing to bear on the process the rhetoric and expectations of Manichean normative scheming, minus the controlling factor of the Crown's authority. This unmediated approach to institutional experimentation had profoundly negative consequences. To begin with, precisely because electoral mechanisms were seen as utterly adaptable to local practices, rivals perceived one another as "wicked men" who tainted electoral processes and sought to control electoral outcomes. Indeed, in the face of domestic rivals' "perverse" motivations, prominent leaders typically concluded that elimination of the foe was a prerequisite for electoral fairness. And when elections – secured by outside mediation – finally did take place, even top winners tried to modify adverse results at the local level. Moreover, rivals understood only too well that persuading followers either to go to war prior to elections or to risk the turmoil associated with ex post interference with electoral outcomes required a rhetorical strategy that would drive home the point that these measures were unavoidable given the harsh realities of their world.

To this end, rival leaders began to craft compelling reasons with reference to the old colonial belief that the "wicked" possessed the power to daze the ignorant. Nicaragua's first chief of state, for example, made two related claims. One was that the local officials recently elected were not free actors but rather the "ignorant" instruments of "evil" forces bent on creating an atmosphere of "disorder" and "affront." The second claim was that since local electoral results were the handiwork of "untrustworthy" men, they would have to be disregarded.[29] For their part, the chief's opponents responded by unabashedly returning to the colonial practice of oblique disobedience, paying homage to the institutional sanctity of the executive office even as they set out to depose its occupant. To manage these seemingly contradictory tasks, the Assembly ordered the chief to resign, but only after he was accused of "criminality" by his own relative and vice-chief.

Both camps converged on another typical move. They shifted the focus of rhetorical campaigns away from (a now irrelevant) royal sovereign to *El Público* (the public). The objective of this last move was to convince the new "sovereign" either to support one's cause or to remain passive altogether. Elites in the camp of the deposed chief set out to dissuade *El Público* from paying heed to the "falsities" manufactured by the acting chief – a "bloodthirsty monster" – in his effort to cause peoples to "hallucinate" into "disobeying the Assembly."[30]

[29] Manuel Antonio de la Cerda, "Ciudadanos Secretarios de la Asamblea Constituyente" (León), 10 May 1825, *RAGHN* 1 (1936–7): 255.
[30] Un Nicaraguense, "Relación del Origen y Progreso de la Revolución," 10 May 1827, *RAGHN* 2, no. 1 (September 1937): 43–7, especially 46.

The acting chief, in turn, cast himself as a self-abnegating, protective leader willing to stand up against "the spirit of evil."[31] He also warned Nicaraguans against "the malice of denaturalized men" – men, he further cautioned, who could "daze" the public with the power of their words.[32]

By describing the world in such stark terms, political actors also put in place an equally stark rationale. Cleansing the government of internal suspects, for example, was justified on the following grounds. First, a legitimate election is invalidated when, ex post, an elected official engages in "diabolical plots." Second, such plots reveal a "depraved spirit." And third, once revealed, the truth empowers the "valiant sons" of the *patria* to rescue the nation from a "perfidious" incumbent.[33]

This was the case that rivaling leaders made at various points to the Nicaraguan public. But the public, unorganized and underrepresented, could not possibly play the role of arbiter once played by the royal sovereign. Consequently, intra-elite conflict escalated, as reputational attacks bred counterattacks *ad infinitum*. Moreover, in the absence of a well-articulated understanding of just government, "liberals" and "conservatives" alike fragmented internally. In Nicaragua, the liberal acting chief broke with his key ally, the popular *caudillo* Cleto Ordoñez, whom he now deemed "disobedient," "treacherous," and, above all, a "dangerous" orator, capable of "hallucinating" people into submission. Similarly, the acting chief's own supporters began to turn against him, while a faction of the conservative camp actually delivered their own leader, the former chief, to his executioner.[34]

Nicaraguans could now agree on two things. First, they all described themselves as political "orphans" bereft of legitimate leadership.[35] Rivaling Nicaraguan camps accepted the dictates of the Honduran Francisco Morazán – the liberal unionist who would in time find his way to Costa Rica – only because, after he prevailed militarily in the capital of Guatemala (1829), he was strong enough to impose his will on the region. But even when Nicaraguans followed Morazán's "instructions" to recognize the acting chief as chief of state, they did so conditionally. Citing yet again "the horrible, orphaned

---

[31] Juan Arguello, "Proclama" (León), 1825, *RAGHN* 1 (1936–7): 61.

[32] "Proclama de Juan Arguello Sobre los Sucesos de Guatemala en 1826, Libro de Actas Municipales de León," ibid., 69–70.

[33] "Nota F" through "Nota I," and "Manifiesto a los Pueblos," *RAGHN* 6, no. 2 (August 1944): 154–6.

[34] See "Acta del 16 de Setiembre (sic) 1827, Libro de Actas Municipales de León"; "Manifiesto del Jefe de Estado de Nicaragua, Don M.A. de la Cerda, 1827"; "Cerda Trata de Reunir la Asamblea, 1827"; "Acta del 13 de noviembre de 1827, Libro de Actas Municipales de León"; and "Acta, 13 de Diciembre 1828, Libro de Actas Municipales de León." All in *RAGHN* 1 (1936–7): 84–6, 91–2, 104–5. See also Francisco Ortega, *Nicaragua en los Primeros Años de su Emancipación Política* (Paris: Librería de Garnier Hermanos, 1894), 43–56.

[35] "Acta del Barrio de San Juan de Dios," 1828; "El barrio de Saragoza reconecerá a Arguello para que convoque a elecciones," 12 December 1828; and "El Barrio de Guadalupe Opina lo Mismo," 12 December 1828. All three in *RAGHN* 1(1936–7): 108–9.

condition of the "pueblos,"[36] the city of León, for example, submitted to the chief's authority temporarily, so as to allow for the convocation of elections, which certain "evil men" had tried to block.[37] Second, Nicaraguans agreed that at the base of their struggles over positions of command lay a more fundamental battle between good and evil. Accordingly, "virtuous" Nicaraguan liberals – backed by Morazán – cleared the way for the 1830 elections by waging a punitive campaign against "factious" elements.[38] And with an eye toward establishing an effective government, they purged governmental posts of suspectious officials, quickly replacing them with "trustworthy" elements.[39]

This logic of purification, which led liberals throughout the region to remove "impostors" from government positions on grounds that they duped the "simple" and "gullible" people,[40] proved counterproductive on several counts. First, it turned against the liberal leadership.[41] Second, it failed to dispel the widespread view of Guatemala[42] as the "despot" of the Central American Republic.[43] Third, it actually fed dissent. By 1833, the states of the Republic were internally split between those clamoring for reform of the federal constitution and the liberal defenders of the status quo. Fourth, and finally, growing dissent engendered the liberal view that opinions on the constitutional issue ought to be rendered "uniform." Uniformity, they claimed, would deny "harbor" to the "wicked" and deprive them of "the opportunity to express their passions and satisfy their vengeance."[44] This view, in turn, entrenched opponents' distrust

---

[36] José Milla, "Don Antonio José de Ibarri," *ASGHG* 12, no. 1 (September 1935): 85–96. See also "Acta," 5 August 1829, *Revista Conservadora* 2, no. 10 (July 1961): 141; "Discurso," 15 September 1881, ibid., 137.

[37] "Acta" (León), 24 August 1829, ibid.: 144–5.

[38] José Barrundia, "El Presidente de la República Federal de Centro América, Nombra a Don Dionisio Herrera Conciliador, Mediador y Jefe Provisional de Nicaragua, 1830," *RAGHN* 11, no. 1 (April 1951): 193. See also "Dionisio Herrera, Jefe Electo y Pacificador del Estado de Nicaragua, Nombrado por el Supremo Gobierno Federal" (Chinandega) 7 April 1830, *RAGHN* 10, no. 3 (December 1950): 258–62.

[39] Francisco Morazán, "Manifiesto del Presidente de la República Federal" (Jalpatagua), 28 (?) January 1832.

[40] "Decreto de 10 de Febrero de 1832, por lo Que se Declara Que el Estado de Nicaragua No Reconoce por Legítimas i (sic) Constitucionales a las Autoridades Que Actualmente Rigen en El Salvador"; "El Jefe de Estado D. Dionisio de Herrera Decreta Contribuciones" (Granada) January 1832. Both in *RAGHN* 1 (1936–7): 263–4, 265–6.

[41] Los Ciudadanos Angel Vidal y Gabino Sousa, "Al Público" (Guatemala: Imprenta de la Unión, 6 May 1832).

[42] "Exposición de la Asamblea Guatemalteca al Congreso Federal," (Guatemala: Boletín Oficial, 1832), in J. C. Pinto Soria, *Centroamérica: De la Colonia al Estado Nacional, 1800–1849* (Guatemala: Editorial Universitaria, Colección Textos, 1986), 177.

[43] Un Hijo del Salvador y Ciudadano de Centroamérica, *Escrito Que Demuestra y Persuade* (San Salvador: Imprenta del Estado, 10 November 1845), 2.

[44] "Decreto de 26 de Febrero de 1833, Que Dispone Que se Nombre Una Comisión Que Pase al Salvador, Honduras i [sic] Guatemala con el Objeto de Uniformar la Opinión Sobre Reformas," *RAGHN* 1 (1936–7): 273–4.

of incumbents[45] – a distrust that they blamed on the "evil" forces that incited violence and channeled it against men of "virtue."[46]

Through the 1830s, rivals imposed and deposed rulers by violent means. But winners and losers alike continued the search for legitimate authority. Three rhetorical moves remained crucial to this quest. One was the central proposition that in politics, the forces of "light" and "dark" do battle. The second was the assertion that the forces of light fomented "perpetual forgetfulness" – literally meaning political amnesia – while the forces of dark insisted on "remembrance of old rivalries." Finally, to save familial harmony from the "wicked," de facto rulers proposed to assume the role of protective "fathers." Only as a "frank and humane" national *paterfamilias* could a ruler punish those who engaged in "scandalous" disobedience.[47] Only through punitive paternalism could a ruler begin to contend with the astute and stubborn malice of opponents.[48] And only though their own eloquence could rulers compete for the public's credence.

This last emphasis on rhetorical campaigns led to a proliferation of official newspapers. The first such paper to be founded in Nicaragua announced in 1835 that "virtuous, meritorious men of probity" (liberals) had finally prevailed over the "Servile camp."[49] On this official view, with the virtuous now in power, so-cial and political life would naturally reach a point of perfect harmony. But to reach this point, the "enthusiasts" of liberty would first have to silence the "raucous."[50] Two factors, both rooted in pre-independence normative schem-ing, complicated this task. One was leaders' use of the "mob" as camouflage for their own violent actions – a practice that allowed liberals and conserva-tives alike to engage surreptitiously in the kind of "disorderly behavior" they so loudly deplored.[51] In other words, leaders simultaneously stigmatized and promoted "disorder." The second complication had to do with the nature of rhetorical competition. Rhetorical competition requires a judge or arbiter – an audience who renders a decision regarding the merits of the arguments. In postcolonial Central America, as we have seen, the role of judge was assigned to El Público. But it was precisely this "naive" and "gullible" judge whom

45 "Manifiesto, De las Autoridades de la Villa de Nicaragua" (San José), June 1833. See also "El Departamento de Nicaragua [Rivas] Manifiesta al Público su Conducta en las Agitaciones Que ha Padecido el Estado," RAGHN 1 (1936–7): 277–80.

46 "El Gefe [sic] Político Accidental del Departamento de [Rivas] al Gefe [sic] Político, Munici-palidad y Comandante de Granada" (Rivas), 12 May 1833. See also "Al Ciudadano Jefe del Estado Dionisio Herrera, Villa de Rivas 24 de Mayo 1833." First published in Boletín Oficial de Guatemala, no. 36, 22 June 1833. Cited in Pinto Soria, Centroamérica, 264.

47 José Nuñez, "Mensaje Que el Presidente del Consejo Presenta a la Asamblea Legislativa, 1834," RAGHN 1 (1936–7): 293–9.

48 Mariano Gálvez, "Mensaje del Jefe del Estado de Guatemala, 2 de Febrero de 1834," ASGHG 2, no. 1 (September 1925): 7–17.

49 Telégrafo Nicaraguense, August 1835.

50 Ibid.

51 For an example, see "Circular Que Relata la Sublevación contra el Jefe Zepeda y su Asesinato, 1837," RAGHN 1 (1936–7): 304–5.

competing leaders could not fully trust. Leaders thus set out to "educate" the public in the ways of the world, drawing their lessons from the Manichean dictates of the colonial regime.

The official paper – *Aurora de Nicaragua*, or *Nicaragua's Dawn* – made the public's "moral" education its mission.[52] Similarly, the antigovernment paper *Nicaragua's Sentry* (published by political exiles) and countless anonymous broadsides made it their twin objectives to "reveal" to the public the merits of the "truly virtuous" while "unmasking" the vile men who "manufactured" so much "defamation."[53] The result was not the intended one. In 1826, a Central American notable had ventured:

If no punishment is set for those who slander in newspapers, those who have been slandered retaliate in kind.... From one libel we go to another. Vengeance leads to the spilling of blood ... political societies succumb to chaos, death, and horror.[54]

By 1838 this dark vision had attained such concrete shape that liberals and conservatives came to share a profound fear of "anarchy." One liberal notable condemned "excess" as the culprit:

To enjoy a passion, it is necessary to deliver oneself entirely into its arms, without thought or care for the consequences. This is what happened to us with Independence.[55]

Key to the construction of this argument was the idea that "excess" was caused by "divergence," and that divergence, in turn, arose where there was a plurality of opinions.[56] Grave consequences flowed from this conflation of uniformity and order on one side, and excess and pluralism on the other. First, by the early 1840s, dissenters were ipso facto labeled "anarchists."[57] Second, the public's moral education would now have to include instruction on how to distinguish between trustworthy and dangerous aspirants to positions of command. The first step toward this end was to draw a sharp distinction between "benevolent tutelage" and verbal "sorcery." Eloquence, after all, could be used to mislead the "innocent," to persuade them to commit deplorable acts they could not even imagine on their own.[58] But eloquence could also be used to bolster benevolent tutelage by fostering "good faith" – the very "tissue that keeps society together." The second step, of course, was for benevolent

[52] *Aurora de Nicaragua*, no. 2 (León: Imprenta del Fondo de Instrucción Pública: 9 September 1837), in *Catálogo de la Exposición Treinta Años de Periodismo en Nicaragua, 1830–1860* (Managua: Instituto Centroamericano de Historia, Universidad Centroamericana, n.d.), n.p.

[53] "Contestaciones al Centinela de Nicaragua" (León), 6 May 1837, in ibid., n.p.

[54] José del Valle, "Discursos Pronunciados en el Congreso Federal de Centroamérica el Año de 1826," *ASGHG* 2, no. 2 (December 1925): 265.

[55] Miguel Larreynaga, Presidente de la Corte Suprema de Apelaciones, "Discurso, Aniversario de la Independencia, 15 de Septiembre de 1838," *ASGHG* 15, no. 2 (December 1938): 220.

[56] Ibid.: 220–30.

[57] See the official monthly *NRO* (published under that name) for September 1838.

[58] *El Ojo del Pueblo* (Granada: Imprenta de la Libertad: 18 November, 1843). See also J. Estanislao González, "Al Señor Público" (León: Imprenta de la Libertad, 24 December 1851).

tutors to "disabuse" the people, and to lead them out of the "labyrinth of gossip."[59]

Most crucially, disabusing the people entailed "unmasking" evil impostors.[60] Government officials at every level became targets of inflammatory denunciations, which in turn provoked personalistic refutations. Hence prefects frequently resorted to broadsides to "satisfy" their "honor,"[61] and their repeated depictions of their posts as "dangerous" and "sacrificial." Hence also the impression grow that in Nicaraguan society both "familial ties" and "bonds of friendship" had been broken.[62] And hence it was generally understood, as it was also prevalently in other Central American countries, that having "tasted excessive freedom" after independence, the people were now prone to "continuous revolutions."

The revolutionary proclivity of the people, in fact, came to be seen in Central America as the cause of a perverse pattern of oscillation: governments wavered between "despotism"and "dejection," while their "subjects" tended either toward "servility" or "anarchy."[63] Responding to this perception, one Nicaraguan administration after another began in the mid-1840s to explore conciliatory policies. More specifically, they formed mixed cabinets that integrated "liberals" and "conservatives" drawn from their respective bastion cities, León and Granada. But mixed or not, administrations also continued their efforts to eradicate "factions."[64] Moreover, governments' pleas for more balanced rhetorical strategies remained anchored in the traditional notion of the "naive" masses as thoroughly pliable and ready to be "dazed" into disorderly behavior by irresponsible pamphleteers.[65] Finally, between 1845 and 1851, these administrations governed under the shadow of a military strongman who exercised his political influence by deploying the tactics of Manichean normative scheming. For example, he surreptitiously mobilized his followers, then challenged the primacy of civilian authority in acts of "obedience" to the "sacred constitution" in order to avoid "interminable" civil wars."[66] Incumbents, for their part, repudiated popular demonstrations of dissatisfaction as the work of "intrigue mongers" who incited the "simple" people.[67]

By mid-nineteenth century, the parameters of normative scheming in Nicaragua were clearly drawn by a binary opposition between "order" and

---

59 Militón Meneces and Sompronio Fernández, "Diálogo no. 3," October 1843, *Revista Conservadora del Peusamiento centroamericano* (*RCPC*) 27, no. 134 (November 1971): 69–72.
60 "Alcance al *Boletín* no. 8" (León: Imprenta del Gobierno, 6 May 1842).
61 Juan Ruiz, "Al Público" (Rivas: Imprenta de la Libertad, 31 January 1844), *RCPC* 27, no. 134 (November 1971): 93–4.
62 José L. Sandoval, "Pueblos" (Granada: Imprenta de la Libertad, 6 October 1844).
63 Rafael Miranda, "Consejo Federal" (San Vicente), 28 December 1844, *RAGHN* 1 (1936–7): 398–400.
64 *Registro Oficial*, March 1845.
65 José León Sandoval, "Al Público" (Managua), 22 September 1846.
66 J. T. Muñoz, "Acta de Limay," 23 March 1846.
67 "Al Público" (Granada), 11 July 1848, *RAGHN* 9, no. 2 (August 1947): 14–18.

"anarchy." Aspirants to power and incumbents alike routinely operated in accordance with this Manichean system of valorization and stigmatization. Indeed, "dictatorship" was increasingly formulated as the alternative to the postcolonial "degeneration" that, reaching a nadir, plunged Central America in "the chaos of immorality and anarchy," or as one liberal put it, into a "democratic frenzy."[68]

Within this context, the generalized craving for "order"[69] bolstered the emerging conception of good government as a paternal enterprise.[70] Sophisticated discussions of disciplinarian government, in fact, now hinged on the key differentiation between "despots," who "usurped" authority and ruled according to "caprice," and strong leaders, who ruled by "reason" and provided their followers with "paternal protection." On this view, the means by which a ruler assumed power were of secondary importance, because regardless of how he got there, a ruler could turn out to be either a capricious despot or a reasonable *pater*.[71]

All of this meant that electoral procedure did not primarily determine the legitimacy of elected rulers, as in Costa Rica. But unlike Costa Ricans, Central Americans in general and Nicaraguans in particular had no dominant substantive vision of good government. To the extent that they shared a vision at all, it was the paternalistic analogy between national governance and the "natural family." Thus, one national *pater* might pursue anticlerical policies and another might take the side of the Church; one might be a unitarian activist while another was an ardent separatist. But in no case were there common criteria for the evaluation of performance. Consequently one man's wise *paterfamilias* was another's capricious despot.

Further, unlike Costa Rican elites, who extolled the moral fiber of their people, the other regional elites based their distinction between justifiable and unjustifiable disobedience on explicitly demeaning views of subaltern groups. The liberals of El Salvador, for example, argued that "order" and "liberty" were not inherently incompatible because "only savages rebel against a just authority." Thus, rebellion against their country's liberal government was not justifiable, but it was more than justifiable in Guatemala, where the government was in the hands of the "hungry tiger," Ratael Carrera, and his hordes of "rapacious Indians."[72] Similarly, in Nicaragua, the conservatives of Granada, after emerging victorious from a military confrontation with León, set out to reverse "the moral degradation of the masses" in preparation for the next

[68] "Estado de los Pueblos al Establecerse la República Democrática," *Registro Oficial*, 1847, *RAGHN* 11, no. 1 (April 1951): 67–77.
[69] "Prospecto,"*Correo del Istmo de Nicaragua*, no. 1 (León: Inprenta del Estado, 1 May 1849), 1.
[70] "El Presidente del Estado de Honduras a sus Conciudadanos" (Comayagua: Imprenta de José M. Sánchez, 2 March 1852).
[71] *Correo del Istmo*, no. 4 (León), 16 June 1849, in *Catálogo de la Exposición Treinta Años del Periodismo*, n.p.
[72] "Continúa la Revuelta (?) de los Partidos en Guatemala," *El Progreso*, no. 5 (San Salvador), 9 May 1850, 18.

elections.[73] The liberals of León, for their part, set out to prove that the Granada conservatives, being an "assembly of monsters," were able to exert influence over the simple-minded electorate through "sinister machinations" and "intrigues."[74]

Within the context of this emerging field of imaginable possibilities, the elections went Granada's way, to a member of that city's powerful Chamorro clan. In his inaugural speech (1853), Fruto Chamorro summarized his role in unmistakable terms:

I consider myself a *paterfamilias*, a loving and stern father who, willingly and as a matter of duty, seeks the welfare of his children, and only in case of necessity and with an oppressed heart, raises the whip to punish he who gives him motive.[75]

Liberal notables soon began to wage a campaign of broadsides and pamphlets against the executive.[76] The executive responded by applying the old dictum "better to prevent than to lament," and citing reasons of state, arrested notables suspected of conspiracy.[77] From prison, one liberal *caudillo* issued a pamphlet condemning the executive's broad claim on discretionary power as "tyrannical."[78] To blunt further attacks on his rule – attacks that he deemed symptomatic of a deeper, constitutional problem – Chamorro convened a constituent assembly to take a hard look at the Constitution of 1838. Ever since the collapse of the Central American union, the 1838 charter had been the object of controversy. For some, the charter was an invitation to anarchy because it excessively constrained the executive. For others, the charter was far from ideal but unavoidable, since it blocked the tyrannical tendencies of the executive.

Chamorro firmly endorsed the first camp, arguing that the 1838 Constitution left lawful rulers "exposed to the illegitimate attacks of the disgruntled."[79] The constituent assembly he convened would change all that. The new charter (1854) changed the title of the executive from "supreme director" to "president," and extended presidential terms from two to four years.[80] Moreover, once the constitutional reform went into effect, the assembly declared that Chamorro was to finish his two-year term and then, without holding elections, serve for another four years.

The liberals' outrage merely intensified Chamorro's obstinacy. The ensuing civil war lasted three years. For the conservatives, the moral integrity of society

---

[73] "Prospecto," *Nueva Gaceta* (Granada), 11 November 1851.
[74] Francisco Zapata, "Breve Compendio" (León: Imprenta de la Paz, 24 October 1852), 1–20.
[75] Rivas, *Nicaragua: Su Pasado*, 29–30.
[76] "El Señor Obispo Viteri Que no Debe Tomarse en Cuenta el Libelo de Jerez," (Santa Barbara), 6 July 1853, *RAGHN* 4, no. 2 (1942): 186–7.
[77] Rivas, *Nicaragua: Su pasado*, 33–8.
[78] Los Defensores de la Constitución y de las Leyes, "Al Público" (León: Imprenta de la Paz, 30 November 1853).
[79] Rivas, *Nicaragua: Su Pasado*, 36–40.
[80] See "Decreto; Circular a Todos los Gobiernos, Nombre de República en Lugar de Estado," *Gaceta Oficial*, no. 9, 11 March 1854, *RAGHN* 6, no. 1 (April 1944): 63–7.

was at stake.[81] The liberals, for their part, denounced the reigning national *pater* as a capricious ruler of insignificant stature,[82] and warned that "heaven" would "punish" the conservatives for the "black crimes" they committed to "satisfy their brutal passions and to please their monster."[83] Both camps idealized the "natural" Christian family as a model for the organization of society because it more than any other paradigm clearly indicated the virtues worth striving for, as well as the sins to avoid and the sinners to shunn. And both camps committed every imaginable atrocity.[84]

Attempts at a mediated peace, needless to say, came to naught,[85] even as the military stalemate "consumed both armies in stubbornness, anguish, and despair."[86] To break the stalemate, the Liberals decided to recruit an American agent, William Walker, who arrived in Nicaragua in 1855 at the head of a small army of fifty-eight men. The decision would prove disastrous for all Nicaraguans, the Liberal leadership included.

Conclusion

Through the colonial crisis of 1808–12 and after independence in 1821, Central American political rivals sought to arbitrate their claims to power by electoral means.[87] Indeed, absent the monarchy, the legitimacy of postcolonial rulers hinged, rhetorically if not juridically, on the oft-exalted will of the people. The elites' veneration of popular sovereignty, however, coexisted with a discourse profoundly denigrating of the existing demos. In fact, throughout most of Spanish America, elites believed that the "true people" would have to be "created" by patrician governments whose enlightened policies might gradually produce acceptable replacements for the "urban riffraff" and the "ignorant peasants."[88]

At first glance, Latin America's founding elites seem no different from their counterparts in the United States, who harbored a deeply ambivalent attitude toward the demos. (Nor were the Americans the first to exhibit this ambivalence. European ruling and intellectual elites also had shown a long-standing fear of "the mob," which was perceived as a specter rising in contradistinction to the people.[89])

[81] *El Defensor del Orden*, nos. 7–44 (Granada: Imprenta del Orden, 19 June 1854–January 1855).

[82] Francisco Castellón, "Al Público" (León: Imprenta de la Paz, 8 December 1853).

[83] "Parte Oficial" (León: Imprenta del Gobierno Provisorio, 24 November 1854).

[84] E. Bradford Burns, *Patriarch and Folk: The Emergence of Nicaragua, 1798–1858* (Cambridge, MA: Harvard University Press, 1991), 192.

[85] "Documentos Sobre Pláticas de Paz" (Granada: Imprenta del Orden, 1854).

[86] Arturo Cruz, Jr., "Overcoming Mistrust: The Quest for Order in Nicaragua's Conservative Republic, 1858–1893" (Ph.D. diss., Oxford University, Michaelmas, 1997), 58.

[87] For an illuminating discussion, see Antonio Annino, "Introducción," in *Historia de las Elecciones en Iberoamérica: Siglo XIX* (Buenos Aires: Fondo de Cultura Económica, 1995).

[88] Francois-Xavier Guerra, "Spanish-American Representation," *Journal of Latin American Studies* 26 (February 1994): 11.

[89] Peter Hayes, *The People and the Mob: The Ideology of Civil Conflict in Modern Europe* (Westport, CT: Praeger, 1992), xvi–xvii, 24–5.

But these similarities notwithstanding, a crucial difference remains: The North Americans of the late eighteenth century were truly divided on the issue of the demos and suffrage, with eloquent and forceful advocates on either side.[90] Further, the North Americans' debates over the question of inclusion into the democratic process continued to attract forceful voices both in defense and opposition to enlargement throughout the nineteenth century.[91]

The Spanish Americans, in contrast, copied the North Americans' institutional mechanism, but managed to neglect and postpone the issue of individual rights indefinitely.[92] Nor did comparable talents with symmetrical resources conduct a lively debate about inclusion. If anything, by the late 1830s one of Central America's most distinguished founding fathers expressed a growing consensus when he warned that disaster would follow if Central Americans "indulged" themselves with such "lavish" notions as citizens' "inalienable rights." Now the most highly prized goal was "order," which, as he proceeded to argue, could only be established on the basis of two key conditions: "forgetfulness of the past" and "brotherhood for the future."[93]

When neither materialized, public opinion began to accumulate in favor of concentrating power in the hands of a paternalistic central government capable of protecting the "moral" fiber of republican institutions.[94] The tragic flaw in this reasoning was, of course, the self-serving uses that practitioners made of it, unleashing in the process cycles of "unmasking," "purification," and, ultimately, violence.

In these isthmian cycles of self-destruction, the Nicaraguans perceived themselves as *the* protagonists, caught in a great struggle between the champions of justice and order on one side, and anarchy and despotism on the other. In contrast, Costa Rica's exceptionalist system of normative scheming allowed rival elites ample space to impose and depose rulers while subjecting them to the central injunction of national preservation and development. In addition, its emerging field of imaginable possibilities was bounded by a normative realism that held Costa Ricans to be an inherently peaceable and diligent people fated by geography to live and toil in a dangerous region. By the mid-nineteenth century, the two neighboring countries could not have been more distant in their aspirations, fears, and competencies. But neither country had seen the end of history.

---

[90] Alexander Keyssar, *The Right to Vote: The Contested History of Democracy in the United States* (New York: Basic Books, 2000), 15.

[91] Ibid., 26, 84–7, 136–44.

[92] Iván Jaksic and Marcelo Leiras, "Life without the King," working paper 255, Kellogg Institute, University of Notre Dame, May 1998.

[93] Miguel Larreynaga, Presidente de la Corte Suprema de Apelaciones, "Discurso, Aniversario de la Independencia, 15 de Septiembre de 1838," *ASGHG* 15, no. 2 (December 1938): 220–30.

[94] *Un Vicentino, Reflecciones Dedicadas a las Lejislaturas [sic] de los Estados de Centro-América* (San Vicente), 1 January 1853 (San Salvador: Imprenta de Liévano, 16 March 1853), 1–11.

5

Costa Rica

Possibility Mongers

> To articulate the past historically does not mean to recognize it "the way it really was." ... It means to seize hold of a memory as it flashes up at a moment of danger.[1]
>
> –Walter Benjamin

Costa Rica's political elites confronted two defining moments of danger after they emerged into the light of day from the turbulent postcolonial period. One came at mid-nineteenth century, the other in the middle of the twentieth. In both instances, the elites perceived the threat as distinctly foreign. In both instances, as Benjamin would have it, they turned to the task of articulating history by seizing on their memorable past. The broad outcome, at both points, was a restored system of Manichean normative scheming in which the foe was, in contradistinction to the Nicaraguan system, foreign to the nation. But if at both points in Costa Rica the most tangible result was a reformist state characterized by a developmental bent, it was only at the latter point that the electoral principle of political democracy was finally sacralized. This chapter argues that the rhetorical politics of the 1948 Revolution show that this was possible because the existing political culture engendered its own rupture. Specifically, a group of political actors, though insignificant in numbers, managed to craft a compelling reason for themselves and others to bring down the government. This compelling reason they crafted out of traditional identity-based fears and convictions on the one hand, and new threats emerging in a changing world on the other. Fascism and communism at home, they argued, threatened moderate and peaceful Costa Rica. It was threatened, moreover, because rulers had deviated from their duty to provide for the welfare of the "good people."

Their rhetorical approach, however, was also novel because it claimed for this group the "scientific" competence to "study" dispassionately and objectively

---

[1] Walter Benjamin, *Illuminations*, Hannah Arendt, ed. (New York: Harcourt Brace Jovanovich, 1968), 255.

the country's authentic identity, and to devise appropriate, domestic solutions to its problems. This approach constituted, in essence, a profound criticism, on substantive grounds, of the Liberal Republic. This critique, in the context of an electoral dispute, would usher in civil war and, ultimately, a social democracy pledged both to the substantive and electoral criteria.

First Moment: Elaborations and Early Ramifications

At mid-nineteenth century, Costa Rica's elites perceived the world outside their borders as more unhealthy and intrusive than ever. In 1855, the warring camps in Nicaragua reached a military stalemate that León's Democrats (later to be known as Liberals) sought to break by bringing in the American adventurer William Walker and his band of mercenaries. In a matter of months, Walker had taken over the country. From the Costa Ricans' perspective, Walker's ambitious exploitation of the Nicaraguan Civil War loomed on the horizon like a "lethal pandemic."

The epidemiological simile employed by the Costa Rican government in its official request to the French and English governments for assistance conformed to the traditional view of a pristine Costa Rica. But as the request for assistance made plain, the simile also reflected the old fear that the nation was keenly vulnerable to contagion. Costa Rica's exceptional civility, after all, entailed a lack of martial competence, which meant that at this moment of peril, intervention by a "civilized" power was of the essence.

In its diplomatic note (November 8, 1855), the Costa Rican government averred that a "single French or English warship" would help discourage foreign adventurers from exploiting Central America's perilous condition, which, if left unattended, would surely have calamitous consequences for European property owners in the area. The note also explained that Costa Rica was prepared to do its part – an effort that, in combination with the desired foreign warship, would safeguard the interests of the major parties involved. The argument of the Costa Rican government went as follows: France and England would retain free access to the country's "rich natural resources," and the country in turn would keep the "peaceful and industrious" customs that since independence from Spain had been preserved in a sea of regional turmoil by the "equanimity" of the Costa Rican people.[2]

In truth, of course, Costa Rican governments had relied not only on the people's equanimity but also on an official policy of deliberate insulation. But this policy rested on two assumptions, each quite telling. First, given the exceptionally civil character of the Costa Rican people, as well as the country's inferior military capabilities, intense socioeconomic development was the logical approach to national fortification. Second, given the bellicose nature of other Central Americans, particularly Nicaraguans, it was incumbent upon

[2] Francisco Montero Barrantes, *Elementos de Historia de Costa Rica*, vol. 2 (San José: Tipografía Nacional, 1892), 83.

Costa Rican governments to keep at arm's length from the rest of the region. Walker's presence on the isthmus, however, introduced the terrifying possibility that Costa Ricans might lose both their socioeconomic accomplishments and their insularity. Worse yet, Walker's potentially expansionist designs confronted Costa Rica's political elites with a grave dilemma: Absent the intervention of a major power, the risks associated with a belligerent response on the part of Costa Ricans seemed as high as the risks associated with passivity.

Controversy ensued around this dilemma. The executive argued that involvement in their neighbor's troubles was inevitable, since Walker planned to "enslave" the Costa Rican people. His opponents countered that waging war against Walker was an "insane adventure" that could only bring "prejudicial" consequences to the nation.[3] The executive prevailed. On March 1, 1856, President Juan Rafael Mora Porras declared war on the American. But while President Mora Porras personally led his troops in Nicaragua, the opposition at home attempted a coup. Although the attempt failed, in order to hasten home to reassert political control, the president was forced to appoint a military successor on the field.

In May of 1857, Walker surrendered. Costa Rica was not only victorious but ennobled. As in any other country under similar circumstances, this accomplishment strengthened the incumbent, at least enough to seek perpetuation in power. But President Mora Porras, having led his people into alien terrain, was now also more vulnerable to attacks by domestic rivals, who kept a close watch on his ability to balance his interests with those of other notables and the coffee economy. By 1859, that balancing was less than perfect.[4] The president was removed and executed.

The coup flexed the political muscle of the military corps that the National War against Walker had left in place. In fact, having brought to political prominence high-ranking officers who had distinguished themselves in battle, the coup signaled the emergence of a destabilizing pattern. Rival blocs of the coffee elite – theretofore constrained by the substantive logic of rule legitimation in general, and by the process of *transacción*, or bargaining, in particular – could now turn to the military to impose or depose presidents from this or that notable family (virtually all of them direct descendants of the conqueror Juan Vázquez de Coronado).[5]

The military's new political role, however, proved unsustainable. To begin with, while chief executives were still expected to fulfill a developmental mission

---

[3] Orlando Salazar Mora, *El Apogeo de la República Liberal en Costa Rica, 1870–1914* (San José: Editorial de la Universidad de Costa Rica, 1990), 23–4. See also Ricardo Fernández Guardia, *Cartilla Histórica de Costa Rica* (San José: Imprenta de Avelino Alsina, 1909).

[4] A powerful coffee processor and exporter, Mora had made plans to create a bank that would have benefited the coffee economy as a whole, but also threatened to break the dominance of other exporters over the coffee trade. From their perspective, the executive had lost his balance. See Jeffery Paige, *Coffee and Power: Revolution and the Rise of Democracy in Central America* (Cambridge, MA: Harvard University Press, 1997), 16–17.

[5] For a discussion of elite lineages, see ibid.

on behalf of the nation, the standards of performance were now enforced from the particularistic perspective of whichever elite family managed to make the most effective bid for the military's support. Thus competing elites continued to operate under old normative exigencies but lost the stabilizing sense of "fairness" once provided by the postcolonial system of exceptionalist normative scheming.[6] Under that system, as the previous chapter showed, power went to those who, by elite consensus, were perceived as capable of generating positive-sum outcomes, and, conversely, power was denied to those who proved either ineffectual or overly ambitious. Moreover, by delving deep into the fray, the military risked losing its incipient identity and sense of mission as defender of the nation's sovereignty. Thus by the late 1860s, all concerned were prepared to resurrect the Braulio Carrillo formula which, based on dictatorial conciliation of particularist and collective interests, called for a *primus inter pares* to lead the state's developmental efforts while safeguarding governmental impartiality.

Legitimate Arbitration: The Substantive Criterion

The most effective bid for the role of *primus inter pares* came from the National War hero, General Tomás Guardia (1870–82). Guardia bolstered his bid by exploiting the long-standing fear of external contamination. His rhetorical approach was best exemplified by his 1873 manifesto, in which he argued that Costa Rica had for many years "purchased" its internal "quiet and calm" at the "expense of its national honor and dignity." To substantiate this claim, Guardia pointed to Costa Rica's "history with the other Central American republics" and, more specifically, to Nicaraguans' frequent "violations" of Costa Rica's national territory.[7]

Clinging to this argument, Guardia swiftly reorganized and solidified the army, then severed officers' ties to the coffee notables and turned the institution into a personal buffer against domestic revolution. More importantly, Guardia reinstated Carrillo's approach to governance through a developmental agenda aimed simultaneously at strengthening the national economy and satisfying different elite sectors. Guardia built railways and ports for coffee exporters and commercial groups. He favored cattle ranchers by raising protectionist barriers. He protected liberal intellectuals and professionals and even actively fomented the formation of elite circles of political thinkers. He accommodated the Church by opening the country to various religious orders, most notably the Jesuits.[8] And he enlarged and elaborated the state apparatus. (The state's extractive capacity, for example, registered a dramatic expansion. Between 1870 and 1871

---

[6] President Mora's fate illustrates the contradiction.
[7] Tomás Guardia, "Manifiesto del Presidente Don Tomás Guardia, A sus Conciudadanos," 21 November 1873, in Carlos Meléndez Chaverri, ed., *Documentos Fundamentales del Siglo XIX* (San José: Editorial Costa Rica, 1978), 306–9.
[8] Salazar Mora, *El Apogeo.*

alone, revenues increased in nominal terms by 54 percent, and by 90 percent between 1871 and 1880[9].)

Under Guardia's leadership, national elites cooperated in the restoration of the system of exceptionalist normative scheming. Elite competition could once again proceed with its usual intensity, but within the frame of a shared view of legitimate arbitration. Structured in this way, Costa Rican politics appeared simultaneously generic and unique within the Central American context. Clannish vying for preeminence, for example, was nearly as common in Costa Rica as it was in Nicaragua. But Costa Rican elites, unlike their Nicaraguan counterparts, were able to sustain early on a remarkable continuity in state policy.[10]

The expanding scope of popular participation in developmental gains was also noteworthy. Increased state capacity made possible intense infrastructural work in support of the coffee economy. Previous state policies had structured this economy in a pyramidlike shape that both reflected the coffee elite's dominance and their close dependence on a broad base of small and medium-size producers. Moreover, increased state capacity improved the chances for educational reform – a long-standing elite preoccupation that, given its implications for the political enfranchisement of the majority, must be considered here in some detail.

Well into the twentieth century, as John Peeler has shown, Costa Rican regimes

... employed variants of the indirect election: presidents (and sometimes deputies) were elected by electoral colleges, which were in turn popularly elected. The right to vote was normally restricted by literacy and property requirements, and the right to hold public office was restricted by higher property requirements ... literacy requirements alone would have excluded 90 percent of the population in the mid-nineteenth century.[11]

And indeed, in 1864, only 11 percent of the population knew how to read and write, and 76 percent of children stood outside the education system.[12] But it is also true that by then, Costa Rican elites had shown on repeated occasions an earnest intent to expand the reach of the educational system. The Constitution of 1844 declared that education was Costa Ricans' "sacred right," guaranteed by the state. The Constitution of 1847, in turn, made it the state's "sacred duty" to build the necessary schools. And the Constitution of 1859 charged the legislative branch with the task of earmarking adequate funds for

9   José Luís Vega Carballo, *Orden y Progreso: La Formación del Estado Nacional en Costa Rica* (San José: Instituto Centroamericano de Administración Pública, 1981), 271–4.
10 Lowell Gudmundson, *Costa Rica before Coffee: Society and Economy on the Eve of the Export Boom* (Baton Rouge, LA: Lousiana State University Press, 1986), 4.
11 John Peeler, *Latin American Democracies: Colombia, Costa Rica, Venezuela* (Chapel Hill, NC: University of North Carolina Press, 1985), 61.
12 Olger Avila Bolaños, "La Población de Costa Rica en el Siglo XIX," in Carmen Lila Gómez et al., eds., *Las Instituciones Costarricenses del Siglo XIX* (San José: Editorial Costa Rica, 1985), 85–111.

the advancement of education, with special attention to be paid to primary schooling.

Against this background, Congress seriously considered in 1867 the Plan for Educational Reform, which proposed state-sponsored public education for the entire national territory. The reform was not passed into law partly because the municipalities and the Church fought for continued control of education, and partly because Congress itself feared the emergence of an excessively interventionist state. Nonetheless, the Constitution of 1869 partially adopted the reform, making primary education for all boys and girls compulsory. (Although funded by the state, the actual delivery of primary education was to remain under direct municipal control.) Economic and fiscal crisis – not lack of vision or intent – ultimately thwarted the state's educational mission. Temporarily strapped for resources, the state suspended educational subsidies to the municipalities in 1881, and by 1884, after a failed experiment in the privatization of primary and secondary education, the state was finally forced to close the schools.[13]

The goal of a literate Costa Rica, however, remained at once a realistic and normatively desirable proposition in the field of imaginable possibilities. This was so for two reasons. First, just like Guardia's predecessors had provided the rhetorical groundwork for the prioritization of public education, Guardia's successors in government inherited the formal state structures that enabled them systematically to extract, administer, and distribute public revenues in the quest for educational reform. Second, Guardia left behind a critical mass of liberal intellectuals who in turn supplied a plan for the systematic implementation of educational reform. By the 1880s, these two legacies of the Guardia regime enabled ruling elites to renew their efforts at educational reform with greater success. The *Ley Fundamental de Educación* (1885) and the *Ley General de Educación Común* (1886) launched an effective campaign that aimed both to increase the number of schools and to professionalize the educational system.[14]

Extended Ramifications: Multivocality and Electoral Competition

The timing of educational reform was significant. The year 1882 inaugurated the era known as the Liberal Republic, which was to last until the Revolution of 1948. During this sixty-six-year period, a small educated minority "competed and cooperated in the control of political power" while simultaneously pursuing reformist policies that intensified preexisting developmental tendencies.[15] And yet it was also during this period that pressures for the democratization of political participation began to emerge. Political elites themselves contributed to these pressures, both in deliberate and unintended ways. Across

[13] Astrid Fishel Volio, "La Educación en el Proceso de Formación y Consolidación del Estado Costarricense," in ibid., 129–52.
[14] ibid., 129–52
[15] Peeler, *Latin American Democracies*, 64.

the political spectrum, leaders championed educational reform because by creating a broader base of literate citizens, they hoped to produce mass electoral victories for themselves. Moreover, by the late 1880s, political elites began in earnest to seek the political allegiances of the "popular classes," most notably by building political-electoral machines designed to reach into the grassroots of the polity.[16]

Indeed, by the first decades of the twentieth century, political elites had rapidly accelerated their march toward mass electoral politics in a direct response to three mutually reinforcing factors. First, literacy rates had improved. In 1892, only 20 percent of the population knew how to read and write,[17] but by 1929, the literacy rate had increased to 73 percent. Second, the success of presidents between 1906 and 1913 in curtailing the use of military personnel to intimidate electors seemed to validate elites' expectation that electoral mobilization could gain enough momentum to preclude "official" use of the military for political purposes.[18] Third, as improved literacy rates made increasing the electorate feasible, prior developmentalist policies engendered a new range of vocal social actors whose identities and claims were perceived as legitimate by elites themselves, thus rendering mass electoral politics both appealing and urgent.[19]

The state-led distribution of land that had begun in the 1820s and gained momentum in the 1840s, for example, had created a class of agricultural small and medium-size holders who, dependent on large coffee producers for financing, clamored for relief when periodic economic crises closed off capital flows and left them unable to cultivate the land. Similarly, the state-sponsored construction of railways and ports in the late nineteenth century resulted in the first critical mass of workers.

These factors – from the national elites' bid for the creation and support of a mass electorate to the incontestable legitimacy of subaltern vocality – were part and parcel of the field of imaginable possibilities engendered by nearly a century of exceptionalist normative scheming. That is, the voices of farmers and workers were both normatively commanding and politically alluring because they deployed the *lingua franca* of the "Costa Rican people" – that amorphous yet numinous identity exalted by elites since the birth of the nation. Thus, when capital shortages and declines in coffee prices incited small and medium-size holders' dissatisfaction, it was impossible to deny that these were the same farmers who generations of rulers and patriarchs had celebrated as "peaceful" and "industrious." When increases in consumer prices and scarcity of goods similarly provoked discontent among artisans and small-industry workers, it was impossible to deny that these were same civic-minded artisans and workers

---

[16] Victoria Ramírez, *Jorge Volio y la Revolución Viviente* (San José: Ediciones Guayacán, 1989), 27.

[17] O. Avila Bolaños, "La Población de Costa Rica en el Siglo XIX," in Gómez et al., *Las Instituciones Costarricenses*, 85–111.

[18] Salazar Mora, *El Apogeo*, 56–9.

[19] Ibid.

whose moderate newspapers, mutualist societies, cooperatives, and political clubs gave new life to the exceptionalist themes that the elites themselves had extolled in forging the nation's identity.

In this context, the confrontational and coercive approach that state and socioeconomic elites could well imagine as suitable for dealing with "foreign" (migrant) workers in the country's peripheral zones[20] was not an appropriate response to the grievances of the "Costa Rican" small and medium-size coffee producers concentrated in the zone of the Central Valley. In fact, the political rhetoric and tactics of the small and medium-size holders themselves – groups whose emblematic characteristics were civility and reasonableness – endorsed the controlling notion that in politics, as in work, the Costa Rican people were truly exceptional. Even in the Central Valley's urban sectors, the enlarging state apparatus relied on a growing number of Costa Rican public employees and professionals who often joined artisans (and an incipient class of small-industry workers) in the creation of civic-minded newspapers, mutualist societies, co-operatives, and political clubs. Like the small and medium-size holders, these publications, societies, cooperatives, and clubs revealed labor's strong conviction that the state, far from being its enemy, was a potential ally in labor's struggle for better wages, improved working conditions, and a solution to unemployment.

The upshot of all this was that in the field of imaginable possibilities, the creation of electoral-political machines appeared to national elites as a logical, prudent, and perhaps even desirable step toward an even more effective arbitration regime. Further, by intensifying national elites' competition for popular support, party machines forced those same elites to reconsider the old rules of the electoral game. Here, two closely related flaws stood out. First, by emphasizing substantive legitimation, national elites had left the electoral process open to such fraudulent practices as vote buying and coercion of electors (with presidential incumbents often playing the lead corrupting role). The second flaw stemmed from the system of indirect elections. Specifically, because local electoral colleges were vulnerable to bribery and coercive pressures, national elites could not take their electors' loyalties for granted. In the intervening period when citizens cast their vote for electors and the time the electors cast their ballot for the different candidates, typically an extensive round of intrigue and bargaining ensued between electors and local party bosses vying for soft votes.[21]

---

[20] Typically Chinese and Jamaican in origin, these "foreign" workers agitated, unsuccessfully, for better wages and working conditions. Italian migrant workers proved more effective at extracting concessions from employers, both because they were more experienced in the art of protest and because they garnered significant solidaristic support from national workers. See Vladimir de la Cruz, "Características y rasgos históricos del movimiento sindical en Costa Rica," in Jorge Nowalski, ed., *El Sindicalismo Frente al Cambio: Entre la Pasividad y el Protagonismo* (San José: Editorial Departamento Ecuménico de Investigaciones, EDEI, 1997), 19.

[21] Iván Molina, "Fraude Electoral y Cultura Popular en Costa Rica (1902–1948)" (paper presented at the XX International Congress of the Latin American Studies Association, Guadalajara, Mexico, 17–19 April, 1997).

Already in the late nineteenth century, the Republican Party had been created as an institutional platform for the denunciation of "official" electoral fraud. But by the early decades of the twentieth century, the need for a structural solution was glaringly obvious. National elites, though hopeful that their political-electoral machines would prove effective at "firming up" the loyalties of their respective electors, were still left with the logistical and institutional burdens associated with the process of loyalty solidification amid heightened competition. National elites, moreover, discovered that the more effective their political-electoral machines proved at controlling local politics, the more they continued to depend on local bosses and "electors' circles" for the actual delivery of votes. For national elites, then, the next logical step seemed to be electoral reform.

Crafted under the leadership of President Ricardo Jiménez (of the Republican Party), the electoral law of 1913 did three things: It introduced the direct vote for congressional and presidential elections, stipulated the requirement of an absolute majority for presidential victories, and assigned Congress the task of selecting a winner when any one candidate failed to garner such a majority. The reform law appealed to national elites on several counts. First, by removing electors from the scene and relying exclusively on the popular vote, the reform presumably minimized the danger of dissidence among local electors. Second, because electors were few in number and so visible, they were also an easy target for official pressure; their removal was thus meant as a blow to presidential incumbents' capacity to "impose" their successors. Third, by making Congress the great arbiter of the political game, the reform further enabled partisan leaders to impose party discipline on local politicians. And fourth, by eliminating the middlemen (the electors), it cleared candidates' paths to the electoral market.[22]

Exceptionalist Realism: Substantive and Procedural Legitimation

The electoral market and politics more broadly were shaped in the early decades of the twentieth century by exceptionalist realism. The nineteenth century notion of a Costa Rican exceptional character continued to organize the system of normative scheming and its rhetorical culture, thus shaping the field of imaginable possibilities – that is, the range of options that appeared both feasible and proper to political actors. Even reformers who characterized Costa Rican "democracy" as an illusion also conceded the power that that illusion exercised over the national imagination. One prominent critic declared Costa Rican democracy a "myth," but in the same breath argued that a noble false consciousness deluded his "sincere and patriotic" countrymen into believing that they lived in "the best of all worlds." Hence our critic concluded that Costa Ricans had no choice but to make their democratic "myth" a "reality."[23]

---

[22] Ibid.
[23] This was Salomón Castro, whose critique appeared under the title "Democracia Integral" in *Magazín Costarricense*. See Juan Rafael Quesada, "Educación y Democracia en Costa Rica,"

So enthralling was this myth that even those who sought to dispel it revealed an implicit affection for its presumably false charms. Here is another prominent educator and reformer, writing in 1915:

We must put an end to the legend that we are an essentially cultivated people; that we live in the Switzerland of Central America; that this is the best of democracies; and that San José is Paris in miniature. We must strangle this fallacious legend – although I don't know if we will have strangled a swan or a serpent.[24]

Even this more ironic strain in the exceptionalist rhetorical culture, with its attendant understanding of "realism," reinforced the traditional system of exceptionalist normative scheming. But the system itself – having generated a field of imaginable possibilities open to the prospect of a more transparent political democracy – endogenously complicated political actors' conciliation of collective and self-seeking goals. Thus political leaders continued to view developmental success as the primary source of political legitimacy; incumbents and aspirants to power were judged on the basis of their substantive accomplishments and promises (for the nation in general and the coffee elite in particular). But the "judges" – the range of vocal actors – also increasingly valorized the vote as an essential, if not natural, attribute of the Liberal Republic.

The friction between these two legitimating logics was brought to the surface by the presidential election of 1914 and the economic depression triggered by World War I. (To gauge the impact of the war on the national economy, one only has to consider the fact that the English markets, now closing, by then absorbed 75 percent of coffee exports.) On the one hand, political elites pressed emphatically for electoral reform. President Jiménez, for one, engineered the Reform Law of 1913; and Congressman Alfredo González Flores argued for the approval of the direct vote on the grounds that "the citizens' right to elect those who will be in charge of administering their interests [was] the very basis of a republican regime."[25] On the other hand, these same elites, in an effort to control policy making in the face of crisis, flagrantly violated the Reform Law they themselves had sponsored. The outgoing President Jiménez "imposed" González Flores – not even a candidate in the race – as his successor.

The "imposition" outraged organized workers who, increasingly persuaded of the advantages of political representation in general and of sending representatives to Congress in particular, argued that González Flores' selection made a "sham" of the poll. Such a sham, of course, was neither a novelty nor a fundamental concern in traditional politics. Its implications, however, would be quite different this time around. President González Flores was now the system's principal developmental agent, and as such was bound to meet the socioeconomic crisis head on without damaging the nation's exceptional

---

in Jorge Mario Salazar, ed., *Democracia y Cultura Política en Costa Rica* (San José: Ministerio de Cultura, Universidad de Costa Rica, 1990), 67–8.

[24] Ibid., 67–8.

[25] Molina, "Fraude Electoral y Cultura Popular," 22.

character. The more traditional tenets of this exceptional character could be easily upheld. And in fact, Gonzalez Flores' 1914 address to Congress was a veritable list of traditional precommitments. Consider the following sample:

1. I would not be a good Costa Rican if I made even the slightest attempt to alter our traditional way of being, or our well-known habit of total non-interference in the affairs of other Central American countries.
2. The pragmatic Costa Rican character has established a relationship of reciprocal respect between church and state. [Under my administration] no conflict between the two shall disturb Costa Rica's peace.
3. I will not carry on my conscience the stigma of undermining freedom of the press, whose exercise is ingrained in our people.
4. The Military and the Police [have come to] play an honorable and important role in the administration of the Republic, and each day become increasingly attuned to this society's way of being: They are becoming the sentinels of the Constitution.[26]

But now the exceptional core of the Republic called for electoral legitimation as well. Lacking such legitimation yet pressed to craft a governmental response to the deepening economic crisis, González Flores made a bid at resolving the contradiction in his landmark speech of 1915. His rhetorical strategy was at once conventional and bold. On the one hand, he conceded that his countrymen's respect for the nation's "characteristic peace and order" provided evidence of their "ample capacity" to lead a "republican life." On the other, he pointed to the "naked truth" that the free and effective exercise of the "right to vote" was hardly the hallmark of Costa Rican political history. From there, the president went on to argue that the vote was of "relative value," since its weight varied according to each citizen's social and economic standing. Accordingly, the improvement of the citizenry's socioeconomic conditions was the state's first priority. The prioritization of progressive socioeconomic policies, however, had to be tied to the higher notion of domestic harmony. The president thus contended that if Costa Ricans were to avoid the internal strife they had always dreaded, then the state had no choice but to meet its obligation to uplift the "less fortunate." Only in this way could the state fulfill its principal task: to "avoid, at any cost, a war of all against all."[27]

Having restored the traditional fear of national disharmony and the logic of substantive legitimation to the center of political rhetoric (while bracketing electoral legitimation), the president went on to press for a significant expansion of the state's traditional domain of arbitration. This entailed direct state intervention in the economy. Faced with constricting state revenues, he proceeded to issue a series of highly controversial fiscal decrees. Decree 71 imposed a general direct tax on property. Decree 72 taxed all real estate properties, from buildings

---

[26] Biblioteca Patria, ed., *Alfredo González Flores: Su Pensamiento* (San José: Biblioteca Patria, Editorial Costa Rica, 1980), 20–3.
[27] Ibid. 60–1.

to farms, and targeted fallow lands in ways that forced proprietors either to work them or lease them for use. Finally, and most importantly, Decree 73 introduced a progressive income tax.[28]

From the executive's perspective, the decrees were part and parcel of the state's "realistic" attempt to protect both the "entire community" and its "weak members" from the explosive effects of economic depression and inequity. Thus, the decrees – not the ballot box – were the true source of presidential legitimacy at this particular juncture in the nation's history.[29] The decrees, however, were also the crux of the matter for the economic elites that had brought González Flores to power, although from a different vantage point. Accustomed to judging the "adequacy" of the executive's performance as developmental agent, economic elites now judged the decrees an intolerable intrusion by the state into their property and revenue domains.[30] For organized workers, in turn, the González Flores presidency represented an affront to procedurally based normative standards, even if those standards, as the offender himself had pointed out, had been routinely manipulated and eviscerated. Similarly, for rival political elites, the presidential selection of a noncandidate signaled the potential irrelevance of the electoral competitive processes in which they were increasingly invested. Finally, for the traditional Republican leadership in general and for Jiménez in particular, the new president's tendency to craft policy without securing the party's internal consensus exemplified a dangerous departure from the tradition of *transacción*.

The coup d'etat that removed the president was led by his close ally, General Federico Tinoco, and met with near-universal approval, particularly among economic elites and worker organizations. For economic elites, the coup reestablished the proper boundaries between the developmental state and the economy. For labor, the coup delivered a well-deserved punishment for transgressions against the electoral principle. Approval of the coup, however, did not translate into support of the dictatorship, not even among workers, despite the fact that Tinoco, like Carrillo and Guardia in the nineteenth century, relied on dictatorial conciliation by partially adopting the program of the government he had just deposed. In a move meant to reassure workers in the short term and to open up space for future policy convergence among political elites, the new Constitution of 1917, crafted under Tinoco's tutelage, abrogated González Flores' tax reform, but enshrined a series of social "guarantees," such as the principle of social security and the state's obligation to safeguard the welfare of the working classes.

[28] González Flores also created the Banco Internacional de Costa Rica in an effort to promote and diversify economic activity through public credit (available also to peasant farmers). Jorge Mario Salazar Mora, *Política y Reforma en Costa Rica, 1914–1958* (San José: Editorial Porvenir, 1982), 44–5.

[29] Molina, "Fraude Electoral y Cultura Popular," 22.

[30] Eugenio Rodríguez, "Nuestros Liberales y sus Retadores," in Gómez et al., *Las Instituciones Costarricenses*, 205–19.

These guarantees would eventually serve as a basis for even more important reform legislation in the 1940s,[31] but they could not alter labor's position in the short term. After contributing to the pressures accumulating in favor of electoral reform, the *Confederación General de Trabajadores* (CGT), the most important labor confederation at the time, joined with students and opposition forces to precipitate the fall of the Tinoco dictatorship in 1919. In fact, by the early 1920s, political elites were plainly caught between the urgent need to respond to popular grievances and the equally pressing need to contend effectively with rivals on the electoral plane. Unable to combine in practice the substantive and electoral logics, presidential and congressional elites alike wavered between pragmatic accommodation and principled reform.[32]

Accommodation, however, generated elite fear – even in Congress – that the citizenry would grow disillusioned with their leaders. "The people," cried out one deputy, "must believe in our sincerity; we must act decisively." The fear was not baseless. Three reasons stand out. First, while the economic crisis associated with World War I inhibited labor's organizational proliferation and growth, surviving key labor organizations such as CGT announced their "radicalization," namely, their profound discontent with dubious electoral practices and a capitalist system that was said to have "failed" because it was "unjust" to workers. Second, anarchic and socialist ideologies gained impetus among workers, and syndicates began to emerge as a viable alternative to the predominant mutualist model of labor organization.[33] Third, public esteem of political "icons" declined palpably amid an unresolved economic crisis in 1920 that culminated in a general strike against rising prices and consumer goods shortages.

Political elites adapted to growing societal dissatisfaction by taking the position that personalistic political parties must yield, sooner rather than later, to parties organized along "popular" lines. Thus, even as personalistic political parties proved effective at mobilizing popular sectors for the election of 1920, political elites moved toward a more "substantive" approach to party formation. In the 1923 elections, three parties took initial steps in this direction. The Partido Agrícola, controlled by dominant coffee producers and powerful finance groups, proclaimed as its goal an "open democracy" in which "the general interest" would override "personal agendas" and the party itself would draw strength from "ideas" rather than "personalistic" attachments. Key political figures within the party, the Tinoco faction included, went further, criticizing the party's platform failure to address the plight of workers and peasants. The Republican Party, for its part, emphasized public education and the need to restore the public's faith in Costa Rican democracy, and criticized the Partido Agrícola as a group of large landowners and bankers whose extreme profit seeking kept down small producers and peasants. Finally, the

---

[31] Salazar Mora, *Política y Reforma*, 46.
[32] This was evident, for example, in the role of Congress in the electoral game. See Molina, "Fraude electoral y cultura popular."
[33] Salazar Mora, *El Apogeo*, 19–30.

newly founded Reformist Party set out to remedy the "failures" of the liberal state, most notably the failure to respond to workers' claims. The preeminent Reformist figure, General Jorge Volio Jiménez, proposed tearing down the "bourgeois capitalist regime" while simultaneously insisting that neither the leadership of his party nor its rank-and-file – including its contingent of socialist workers – were "Bolsheviks." And indeed, at the center of the Reformists' philosophy stood the inviolable principle of private property, though complemented by an activist state capable of mediating conflicts between capital and labor and addressing the grievances of the "poor and the weak."[34]

All three parties displayed a significant capacity for mass mobilization – a capacity now complemented by the fact that the liberal education policies first implemented in the 1880s had finally produced "the first literate generation among the mass of Costa Ricans," and thus expanded the electorate as "more and more voters were able to fulfill the literacy requirements."[35]

But even as citizenship participation increased overall, the problem of local fraud continued to taint congressional elections. (Given the role of congress in presidential selection, fraud polluted presidential politics indirectly[36].) Congress, for its part, continued to rubber-stamp controversial electoral results.

In this context, the presidential imperative to forge elite-serving compromises while advancing the national interest continued to push incumbents toward reform during the second administration of the Republican Ricardo Jiménez (1924–8).[37] Not only did Jiménez compromise heavily with the Reformists, but he seized once more the leadership of the electoral reform agenda, making possible, among other things, the creation of a national electoral council and the introduction of the secret ballot. (Theretofore, voters publicly delivered their ballots to the head of the local electoral junta, who would then read the content of the ballot to the other members of the junta – a procedure that left peasant workers exposed to political pressure from the *patrón* and local party operatives.) More importantly still, during his third and final administration (1932–6), Jiménez managed at a time of crisis to infuse new life into the system of exceptionalist normative scheming, thus reinforcing the parameters of the traditional field of imaginable possibilities.

In this field, the coffee economy figured both as the *sine qua non* of developmental success and as tangible proof of the mutually beneficial relations between the dominant coffee elites and a wide sector of industrious small and medium-size producers. The coffee economy's virtuous equilibrium, in short, was emblematic of Costa Rica's exceptional identity. But this virtuous equilibrium, like the nation's identity, was no to be taken for granted. Mortal threats

---

[34] Ibid., 51–3, 91.
[35] Peeler, *Latin American Democracies*, 65–6.
[36] See, for example, the controversial congressional elections of 1923, in Molina, "Fraude electoral y cultura popular," 17
[37] Ibid., 17.

always lurked just outside the national borders. By the mid-1930s, these threats were making their way into the domestic arena. Communism, for one, had arrived on the scene in 1931, with the creation of the Bloque de Obreros y Campesinos (Bloc of Workers and Peasants). In addition, sharp declines in world coffee prices destabilized the normally sociable relations between the coffee elite and their small and medium-size suppliers. As world coffee prices declined, processor and exporters offset the attendant fall in profits by hiking the processing and export prices they charged producers, and by delaying payment for deliveries already made. Aggrieved producers turned to the state for fairness, and the state, under Jiménez' leadership, responded. As Deborah Yashar writes:

> The small and medium producers confronted what they considered unfair economic relations. When they appealed to the state, President Jiménez, in his third term (1932–36), created the Institute for the Defense of Coffee (INDECAFE) in order to regulate the relationship between smaller producers and processors of the crop.[38]

In its first three years of operations (1933–6), INDECAFE functioned not as a neutral arbiter of relations among producers and processors and exporters, but as the latter's instrument. And yet, after 1936, INDECAFE – established by law as a semi-autonomous body – underwent swift internal evolution as its own elite-dominated board pushed the Institute to meet its tasks. Thus the Institute began actually to regulate prices and to impose sanctions on exporters who went against regulation. The board's transformation is no puzzle. In a clear manifestation of exceptionalist realism at work, the board recognized that, given the special sociability of Costa Rica's rural conditions, effective arbitration through INDECAFE could achieve three goals simultaneously. It could satisfy the "reasonable" demands of small and medium-size producers (theretofore exalted by elites as peaceful and industrious), reequilibrate the coffee economy's previously harmonious socioeconomic relations, and preserve the coffee elites' overall dominance. And indeed, precisely because INDECAFE proved able to meet these three challenges simultaneously, it emerged as the first institutional emblem of conciliatory developmentalism and substantive arbitration. To this day, INDECAFE (renamed the Office of Coffee in 1948, and later still renamed the Institute of Coffee) remains under elite control; to this day, too, it continuously resolves class conflict between the small farmer and the processing elite; and to this day, producers, processors and exporters alike perceive the Institute as "the principal guarantor of Costa Rican tranquility."[39]

Normality, in fact, seemed to reassert itself on the entire political spectrum. Even the Communist Party (Bloque de Obreros y Campesinos) had by then abandoned its radical rhetoric and embraced peaceful reformism. Normality certainly returned to the process of presidential succession, a process whereby

---

[38] Deborah Yashar, *Demanding Democracy: Reform and Reaction in Costa Rica and Guatemala, 1870's–1950's* (Stanford, CA: Stanford University Press, 1997), 64.

[39] Paige, *Coffee and Power*, 236.

the presidential incumbent – typically a notable of the Republican Party – selected the party's nominee and, for all practical purposes, the next president of the Republic. Thus, just like at the end of his third and final term Jiménez had selected León Cortés for the Republican candidacy, now Cortés at the end of his term (1936–40) anointed the notable Rafael Angel Calderón as the candidate for the Republican Party. Backed by socioeconomic elites and with Republican Party machinery behind him, Calderón carried 84 percent of the vote.

Second Moment of Danger: Reconfiguring the Field of Imaginable Possibilities

It was in this context of restored normality that the Costa Rican polity began a seemingly paradoxical process of internal polarization that would culminate in the Civil War of 1948. Scholars have typically pointed to three interrelated factors to explain this paradox. The first is Calderón's antifascist stance and, by extension, his declaration of war on Germany – a problematic move since coffee exporters traded heavily with Germany and depended on German nationals for export financing.[40] (The government also seized all property held by coffee growers, processors, and exporters of German origin.) The government's German policy, to be sure, strained relations between the government and coffee elites, not only for obvious self-regarding reasons, but also because these elites equated the coffee economy – indeed, coffee itself – with the national welfare.[41] But the polarizing effect of the government's German policy was significantly tempered because the Calderón government understood the vital importance of coffee and thus implemented policies meant to benefit the coffee elites, promote coffee production, and keep coffee exports from declining during World War II. (Calderón, for example, lifted taxes on coffee exports, even if it meant aggravating the fiscal deficit.)

The second polarizing factor identified by scholars is Calderón's strategic response to the erosion of elite support and to increasing popular dissatisfaction amid economic crisis – namely, the formation in 1942 of a governing coalition with the Church and the Communist Party (Bloque de Obreros y Campesinos). Here the underlying argument is that socioeconomic elites were further alienated from Calderón by the communists' participation in his administration and by its comprehensive social security legislation, which required both capital and labor to make contributions to the social security fund. But in this instance, too, we must bear in mind that the legislation was opposed most strongly by elites not in the agricultural sector – a sacred area that Calderón never intended to transform – but in the "secondary" commercial and industrial sectors. Moreover, the social security law in itself did not inherently imperil the socioeconomic

---

[40] Samuel Stone, *La Dinastía de los Conquistadores: La Crisis del Poder en La Costa Rica Contemporánea* (San José: Educa, 1975) 127.

[41] Through the twentieth century, Costa Rican elites would remain almost exclusively dedicated to coffee, leaving industrial development to foreign capital. Paige, *Coffee and Power*, 231.

elites' dominance. After all, as Yashar points out, the law could have augmented the system's capacity for arbitration.[42]

The communists' role in government was far more problematic, although here again mitigating circumstances came into play. To begin with, the coalition was itself a microrepresentation of Costa Rican reformism. The Church leadership, for example, threw its weight behind labor's struggles in an effort to promote "class conciliation" and to block the ascendance of the communist labor movement, whose ideas about "class conflict" it deemed "alien" to the nation's character. The Communist Party, for its part, had credibly embraced reformism since the mid-1930s, and was now even prepared to change its name from Bloc of Workers and Peasants – with its connotation of class conflict – to the more neutral Vanguardia Popular. As for the communist labor movement, it continued like the rest of organized labor to press nonthreatening demands centered on increasing salaries and improving working conditions. And it continued to demonstrate a clear willingness to cooperate with capital.[43] In fact, socioeconomic elites themselves understood by 1943 that anticommunist sentiment reached deep into key popular sectors, most notably peasants, small and medium-size farmers, and state employees. And even the governing coalition itself recognized these sectors' aversion to communist unionization.[44]

Actors across the spectrum share in the presumption that communism in its unalloyed, alien form could never take hold in Costa Rica. Only three years before the Civil War, very influential members of the old Republican leadership still expressed their faith in the power of the Costa Rican character to resist and even reshape communism. As Ricardo Jiménez – the Republican standard bearer who had served three presidential terms between 1910 and 1936 – wrote in 1945:

Our people instinctively repudiate [the communists'] violent lexicon. In other environments this [lexicon] might be appropriate, but [in Costa Rica] it merely inspires fear and caution. . . . I am not afraid of communism because if its ideology is to reign in this country it will first have to make itself Costa Rican. All the ideologies that have resonated and endured in our country have [first undergone this transformation].[45]

The communists themselves had long ago come openly to share this view. Here is Manuel Mora, the leader of the Communist Party, addressing the rank-and-file:

Comrades, we [communists] are not the only honest [Costa Ricans]. We are not the only ones who wish our country well. There are many others who, while not in total agreement with our point of view, do share several of our fundamental aspirations.

[42] Yashar, *Demanding Democracy*, 111, 115, 118.
[43] A division of labor evolved between 1943 and 1945. The Catholic labor federation (CCTRN) concentrated its organizational efforts on sectors that had spurned communist organizers, while the communist federation targeted urban workers. Yashar, *Demanding Democracy*, 142.
[44] Ibid.
[45] Biblioteca Patria, ed., *Ricardo Jiménez: Su Pensamiento* (San José: Biblioteca Patria, Editorial Costa Rica), 411.

So we must not hesitate, when it is in the country's interest, in uniting our forces with theirs ... What, then, are our party's immediate goals? To organize and orient our people. To propel our economy toward a more advanced form of organization. And to do all this *realistically*, taking into account the level of education of our masses, their political and philosophical traditions. This is what it means to do revolution in Costa Rica. All the rest is low-grade utopianism. . . . *Costa Ricans need a Costa Rican brand of communism.* . . . [emphasis added].[46]

The third and final polarizing factor that often figures prominently in analyses of the Costa Rican Civil War is the tendency of political actors at that time to conflate disagreements over socioeconomic policy with procedural grievances. The opposition to the Calderón administration, for example, sought to undermine the president's legitimacy by leveling charges of electoral corruption, while the government countered that in truth the opposition was seeking to reverse its reform agenda. This conflation, of course, fomented mutual mistrust. But it did not diminish actors' allegiance to the Republic and its stated commitment to electoral politics. If anything, actors intensified their competitive bids for power by playing the electoral game to the hilt. Thus, opposition leaders scrambled to gain the allegiance of particular segments of the fragmented multiclass continuum that characterized the electorate. To this end, they created party vehicles for compelling political figures. Cortés organized the Partido Demócrata; Otilio Ulate founded the Unión Nacional; and when it became obvious that they would have to unite in order to defeat Teodoro Picado, the Republican candidate anointed by Calderón, the opposition rallied behind a single leader, Cortés.[47]

The opposition, moreover, waged a keenly competitive campaign. Opposition leaders branded the government as "communist" while appropriating themes associated with the exceptionalist system of normative scheming. Cortés proposed to rescue the best of the Liberal Republic by emphasizing such substantive aims as administrative efficiency and probity, and, of course, he also trumpeted his own past accomplishments as public administrator and his undisputed honesty. Simultaneously, the newspaper publisher Otilio Ulate stressed the notion – first developed in the nineteenth century – that Costa Rican history moved at a tempo all its own. If in the nineteenth century developmental impatience had branded "timid" administrations as ineffectual, now in the middle of the twentieth, Ulate inverted the argument. He admitted that while social reform was laudable, the pace at which reform measures were implemented ought to match the country's capabilities. Outstripping those capabilities – something that Ulate claimed the Calderón government had tried to do – was an "extravagance" unbefitting the moderate character of Costa Rican history.

---

[46] Cited in Arnoldo Mora Rodríguez, *Historia del Pensamiento Costarricense* (San José: Editorial Estatal a Distancia, 1992), 155–56.

[47] For the opposition, Cortés was the "natural" candidate: He was a great notable of the Republican Party, and possessed an impeccable reputation for probity and administrative efficiency. His claim to leadership was firmly rooted in the logic of substantive legitimation.

Thus, polarizing trends were clearly in evidence during the Calderón administration, but so too were tempering forces that pushed both government and opposition leaders toward a peaceful, electoral resolution. This pattern, in fact, continued even during the highly turbulent Picado administration. After losing the election to Picado, the opposition accused the new government of electoral fraud. These allegations notwithstanding, in 1946 Picado saw through tax legislation that raised the property tax for large landowners and introduced direct and progressive taxation. Echoing the argument of postcolonial elites, Picado asserted that the law was not meant to impoverish the rich nor to enrich the state, but rather to impart a measure of fairness on the distribution of the fiscal burden. The opposition, however, responded to the "communist" measure by closing commercial and banking establishments. After the opposition's defeat in the 1946 midterm elections, it set in motion the 1947 commercial strike known as the *huelga de brazos caídos*. The opposition claimed to be seeking broader electoral guarantees against fraud. The government perceived the strike as a counterreform move. Either way, polarization reached deep into the social bases. Workers from Rerum Novarum (CCTRN) supported the strike, whereas the communist CTRC supported the government. Street clashes took place between government and opposition sympathizers.[48]

But even at this critical point, President Picado continued to base his hopes for a peaceful outcome on the long-standing process of conciliation whereby leaders adjusted their self-interested calculations to Costa Rica's exceptional reality:

Because Costa Ricans are *by habit peaceful and rational*, they have been able to develop the country despite their scarce resources.... I have thus made it my task to advocate peacefulness. *The leaders of the opposition will have to follow suit. After all, disorder is not in their interest either*, since the Costa Rican people, by tradition, repudiate violence and prefer to follow the channels of legality [emphasis added].[49]

And indeed, the government and the opposition began intense negotiations that put an end to the strike in August 1947. The president agreed that Ulate, as the opposition's presidential candidate for the upcoming elections (February 1948), could determine the composition of the new Electoral Tribunal. Moreover, under pressure from the Tribunal, parties to the negotiations recognized the Tribunal's supervisory authority and final judgment in the upcoming elections. Partisan newspapers – from the pro-government *Tribuna* to Ulate's *Diario* – publicized the agreement, which in essence elevated the Electoral Tribunal to the position of ultimate arbiter, thus displacing the army's traditional de facto arbitration powers as well as the legal arbitration powers of Congress.

Despite this agreement, however, the electoral contest between the opposition (led by Ulate) and Calderón, now making a second run for the presidency,

---

[48] Yashar, *Demanding Democracy*, 117–18, 177–8.
[49] Guillermo Villegas Hoffmeister, *Testimonios del 48* (San José: Editorial Costa Rica, 1989), 41–2.

was marred by allegations and counterallegations of fraud. Worse yet, the electoral process caused a series of unfamiliar, frightening events: violent encounters between opposition and pro-government forces; the political assassination of an opposition journalist; and, in the words of Archbishop Victor Sanabria, the loss of "mutual trust" that had "traditionally governed relations among Costa Ricans."[50] It was in this explosive context that the ballots of the 1948 election were processed. The Electoral Tribunal declared Ulate the presidential winner, but announced that Calderón's coalition had won a majority in Congress. Mutual allegations of fraud ignited the Civil War.[51]

If we concentrate on the intense contestation over the electoral process itself, we might be tempted to conclude that a profound disagreement over the rules of the electoral game provoked the war. If we concentrate on the conflict over social security and tax legislation, then we might say that the war was about key groups' vital interests. If we focus instead on the opposition's fear of communism, then we could point to ideological suspicion as the war's main cause. Finally, if we were to weave all these strands together, we would have a story of cumulative factors. While all are plausible explanations, none can account for the historical fact that as early as 1942 the opposition leader José Figueres had begun making war plans. None, moreover, can account for the fact that for all practical purposes, the military remained uninvolved in the war, which was fought instead by Figueres' "liberation" army and the governing coalition's "shock troops" and supporters. In other words, none can account for the emergence of a political group – Figueres' camp – willing and ready to break with the Costa Rican tradition of civic electioneering. And finally, none can account for the curious fact that, once victorious, the Figueres camp not only resumed but accelerated preexisting reformist trends, both in the realm of socioeconomic policy and in the electoral game.

To understand both how this "exceptional" system imploded and how a more democratic variant was subsequently restored, we must understand the origins and development of the political forces that set it ablaze only to reestablish it on firmer ground. This requires that we turn our attention to the establishment in 1940 of a progressive think-tank known as the Center for the Study of National Problems. For this think-tank would seize two key issues – socioeconomic reform and electoral legitimacy – and effectively tie them to the deeply embedded notion of Costa Rica as a unique nation imperiled by alien vices. More specifically, it was the Center that would credibly argue that the flaws of the Liberal Republic rendered the nation vulnerable to communist and fascist "orthodoxies." And so it was the Center that gradually but insistently fostered a climate of moral alarm, ultimately introducing the possibility that salvaging the nation's venerable past might require a temporary but radical departure from civil politics.

---

[50] Ibid., 169.
[51] For the Tribunal's complex role, see James Dunkerley, *Power in the Isthmus: A Political History of Modern Central America* (New York: Verso, 1988), 129–30.

Explaining the Civil War: Emerging Internal Manicheanism

Shifts in rhetorical politics indicate that it was during the Calderón years that the entire range of political actors came close to blurring the boundary between the foreign and domestic realms in the system of normative scheming. The Manichean logic had been traditionally used exclusively to position Costa Rica as an exceptional place in a dangerous world – a haven for virtue perpetually endangered by the political evils emanating from its neighboring states. But now a different version began to gain currency: Foreign ideologies like fascism and communism might very well gain adherents among Costa Ricans. This was a momentous shift in the field of imaginable possibilities because it rendered the idea of confrontation between Costa Ricans "conceivable."

But how did Costa Ricans get to this dangerous point? From their different positions in the system of normative scheming, political rivals employed the traditional rhetorical strategy of pitting Costa Rica against outsiders, and from this competitive process a rhetorical innovator emerged who raised the stakes and altered the course of history. In other words, the system of normative scheming engendered its own crisis. This rhetorical innovator was the Center for the Study of National Problems, a small think-tank whose politically minded leaders managed, all at once, to applaud existing reforms, press for more comprehensive institutional and structural change, argue for the protection of Costa Rica's inherent moderation, *and* instigate a sense of deep moral crisis.

Indeed, between 1940 and 1945, the Center made a bid for a new exceptionalist realism based on a "scientific" understanding of the country's virtuous identity and its potential for a more "perfect" society. The Center's leading lights worked from the premise that Costa Rica did indeed possess a unique "collective soul." But they also claimed that the characteristics of this soul would have to be discerned through a cool investigation of the nation's history. On their view, much like an archaeological expedition might lead to the discovery of an ancient civilization's remains, a level-headed incursion into the nation's past could be expected to reveal its "real" institutional foundations. Absent a precise knowledge of these characteristics and foundations, they further argued, innovative continuity with Costa Rica's venerable tradition was impossible.

This claim to scientific competence clearly gave the Center's leaders a competitive edge over the traditional republican leadership, who made no such claim. But the Center also implicitly challenged the traditional leadership by arguing that continuity required a careful study of "basic democratic principles" – principles that the Center hoped to propagate in order to establish the cultural conditions necessary for the "perfecting" process inherent in democratic development. In fact, blending together knowledge of Costa Rican reality and the democratic credo, the Center proposed to transcend "electioneering" and to engage in "politics," with the latter defined as "collective action aimed at influencing others through the creation of sentiments, tendencies, and ideas."[52]

---

[52] See Carlos José Gutiérrez, *El Pensamiento Político Costarricense: La Social Democracia*, vol. 1 (San José: Libro Libre, 1986), 71–7.

Precise knowledge of domestic reality, however, was not enough. At the most practical level, the Center proposed to build a bridge between understanding and action. This bridge would be partly provided by the creation of a political party which, rooted in democratic principles, would uphold an ideology "rigorously adapted to the national reality." One of the central attributes of this reality was an innate repudiation of "extremism." And so, in an updated version of the traditional fear of external contamination, Article 4 of the Center's Code of Regulations barred from membership any person "affiliated with a group of extremist tendency."[53]

The bridge between understanding and action also required a developmental state that would acknowledge and remedy deplorable flaws in the nation's socioeconomic system. As the Center's leading thinker, Rodrigo Facio, wrote in *Surco*, the Center's journal:

It is astonishing that [extremist doctrines] have not yet conquered . . . the long-suffering people of Costa Rica, especially in the countryside, where for fifty sad years, people have been taught that democracy means starvation salaries . . . malnutrition . . . inadequate schools, ignorance, exploitation by the *patrón*, and every four years, empty speeches, vain promises, vote-buying. . . .

The Center laid out a plan to protect Costa Rica's "democratic institutions" from the opportunistic doctrines that might gain ground with the nation's "long-suffering people." The first and most obvious step was to instruct the people – "to raise consciousness" – on the dangerous "theories and practices" of "authoritarian and totalitarian systems." The second step was much more subtle, and required Costa Ricans "to transform – according to the democratic thesis – the institutions bequeathed to them by [their] elders." Here the challenge for the Center was twofold: a) Identify the systemic failures that called for democratic transformation; and b) articulate the vital connection between transformative action on the one hand, and the perpetuation of cherished legacies on the other. To these ends, Facio argued:

The fundamental error of liberalism lies in the belief that economic relations are natural and therefore inalterable. [This erroneous belief accounts for] the economy's untouchable status; and for the abdication of the state's responsibility to press for social reforms that would make the system of production perform in accordance with contemporary ethical demands for justice.[54]

This kind of argumentation enabled the Center to assume a stance at once critical and "dispassionate" in a polarized political spectrum. The Center, for example, supported the Labor Code promulgated by Calderón. As Carlos Monge, another Center luminary, explained to a radio audience:

The Center . . . supports measures that fortify the socioeconomic basis for democracy. . . . Costa Rica is not as socioeconomically backward as certain Latin

---

[53] Ibid., 71–7.
[54] Rodrigo Facio, "Autoridad y Libertad," *Surco* 1, no. 1 (15 September 1940), in ibid., vol. 1, 78–107.

American republics, and with some good fortune the results of social legislation will be much superior in our country.[55]

But pointing to the results of a recent national opinion poll, the Center also claimed that Costa Rica was descending into "political, economic, moral and social chaos." Here, the Center argued that Costa Ricans had gradually "abandoned" their "republican tradition," and that only through its recovery could they find national salvation. "We must evoke, within this tradition, the exemplary phase of progressive accomplishments collectively attained by the liberals of 1889."

Innovative continuity – "resuming tradition while seeking to remedy its flaws" – meant facing up to the fact that the liberals of 1889 had underestimated two basic facts of social life: a) "the economic foundation of freedom"; and b) the need to "structure the popular forces that give life to a democratic regime."[56] Innovative continuity, moreover, entailed the urgent, if not radical proposition that grappling with the political economy's structurally flawed "reality" called for "a critical revision of [Costa Rican] values" – a revision that might well usher in the "destruction of myths and the formation of a real national culture at the service of the real people."[57] In other words, the quest for the country's socioeconomic and institutional "reality" was also a quest for national authenticity.

Structural and normative exigencies were thus tied inextricably by an emerging new variant of exceptionalist realism. The Center, moreover, began to foment a climate of practical and moral urgency, especially after the "fraudulent" elections of 1944, in which Calderón's protegé, Picado, crushed Cortés, the opposition's candidate. Sharpening the dual themes of an imperiled national tradition and the attendant need for "democratic perfecting," the Center raised the stakes:

The socioeconomic problems that the nation has faced since the beginning of this century have grown more acute in recent years, to the point that *they now compromise. . . . . even the traditions of freedom, peace and security that once characterized little Costa Rica.*[58]

The Center thus redirected critical attention back to the unresolved contradiction that had first emerged with great force under the failed administration of González Flores. The next step for the numerically weak Center was to find an organized partner – a political machine – to propagate its alarming message. The Center accomplished this by merging with Acción Democrática, the wing of young intellectuals that emerged within the Partido Demócrata during the electoral struggle of 1943. The merger, in turn, resulted in the creation of the Partido Social Demócrata, whose purpose, as

---

[55] Carlos Monge, "Legislación Social en una Democracia" (1943), in ibid., 111–24.
[56] Centro para el Estudio de Problemas Nacionales, "Repuesta a Ideario Costarriscense" (1943), in ibid., vol. 1, 145–62.
[57] Centro para el Estudio de Problemas Nacionales, "Repuesta a Ideario Costarriscense" (1943), in ibid., 45–162.
[58] *Surco* 5, no. 52 (February 1945), in ibid., 237.

stated by Figueres, one of its most charismatic leaders, was to "found the second republic."

The "second republic" motif signaled the new party's commitment to innovative preservation of the "best" Costa Rican traditions, and it differentiated the party from politicians closely identified with the old Liberal Republic, who seemed incapable of grasping the "urgent" need for change now stressed by the Social Democrats. Thus, while as late as 1945, Cortés, Ulate, and Jorge Volio – together representing virtually the entire spectrum of conservative and reform liberalism – resorted to old-fashioned coalition building by forming the Movimiento de Compactación Nacional,[59] Figueres began openly exploring more radical alternatives at the Social Democratic Party's Constitutional Convention:

We prepare to fight for future conquests, while maintaining and perfecting the achievements of the past.... The first republic [has] died...if we are men of dignity, we shall return the blow dealt to the *patria* by irresponsible men.[60]

From Figueres' perspective, the challenge at hand was "to transform a peaceful people into potential warriors" – a challenge he found difficult but not unmanageable. As he would later admit, he began making war plans as early as 1942, emboldened by the conviction that, like him, the majority of the citizenry understood that "the era of public freedoms had come to an end in Costa Rica, and that their vindication would probably require the greatest sacrifice."[61] For the next six years, Figueres participated in the formal political game while simultaneously pursuing military readiness in the mountains. Rooted in the sense of crisis first developed by the Center and then fomented by the Social Democratic Party, this readiness provided opposition forces with a viable, even compelling alternative to negotiation and compromise in the face of the 1948 political impasse. In one early sign of the importance of a "justifiable" armed alternative to the conventional political game, the president of the three-man Electoral Tribunal left the bench and joined Figueres' National Liberation Army on the hills. This action led to the Tribunal's dissolution and to Congress's partisan decision to ratify the governing coalition's legislative victory while annulling the opposition's presidential victory. Soon, a wide range of citizens – from peasants to opposition militants – would follow suit. By March 11, 1948, the Social Democrats' slogan – "We shall found the second republic" – had become Figueres' call to arms,[62] and by the next day the war had

---

59 The alliance was a logical step given the loss of electoral support for the governing coalition. See Salazar Mora, *Política y Reforma*, 122.
60 José Figueres, "Discurso de Clausura de la Convención Constitutiva del Partido Social Demócrata: Fundaremos la Segunda República," in Gutiérrez, ed., *El Pensamiento Político*, vol. I, 211–12.
61 José Figueres, "Discurso de Apertura de la Asamblea Constituyente: La Orientación General de la Segunda República," 16 January 1949, in ibid., vol.I, 279–92.
62 "El Chuzo y el Raspa-dulce: Primera Proclama del Ejército Nacional," 23 March 1948, in ibid., vol. I, 275–6.

exploded. The Calderón camp accused Figueres of "betrayal" and labeled him a Nazi-Fascist.[63]

The Costa Rican army had little if any involvement in the war. By mid-April, the war was over. An interim president held office briefly, and then, in accordance with the Ulate–Figueres pact, Figueres presided over a revolutionary junta that governed for a year and a half, at the end of which Ulate assumed the presidency (1949–53).[64]

Upon assuming power on May 8, 1948, the junta declared the founding of the Second Republic. The junta governed for eighteen months without any formal restraints. The junta abrogated the Constitution of 1871 closed, Congress, suspended freedom of the press, and outlawed all parties espousing "antidemocratic ideologies," thus excluding the communists from the political arena. Followers of Calderón and Picado had thier property expropriated or were exiled or incarcerated, and several labor leaders suffered a similar fate.

The junta itself weathered financial crisis as well as political opposition from various quarters. Conservative groups from the old Republic, after having fought side by side with Figueres, now balked at the fiscal costs associated with a reformist, interventionist state. Monseñor Victor Sanabria, for his part, criticized the persecution of the opposition.

The incipient regime, however, was unwittingly fortified by the Calderón–Picado forces, which from exile in Nicaragua prepared an invasion of Costa Rica with the support of the Somoza regime. The invasion, launched on December 10, 1948, prompted the whole ideological spectrum to rally around the flag. Figueres' leadership was now assured.[65]

Rhetorical Settlement: Outward-Looking Manicheanism Restored

Figueres characterized the 1941–9 period as an "abnormality" in the country's history – a time when government violated "tradition," and a peaceful nation was forced to rebel against "the criminals" in power and the "communists' shock troops." At the end of this anomalous period, however, Figueres claimed to discern two "great historical truths." First, "Costa Ricans had exhausted all peaceful means available to them before resorting to armed force in defense of their rights." Second, although law-abiding and peaceful, Costa Ricans were no passive dupes: In successfully fighting for their rights, they had displayed the requisite courage and competence of democratic citizens. Now they could proceed to build the Second Republic.[66] Government in Costa Rica, Figueres promised, "would once again be one of the most respectful and respected on earth." Government, he further vowed, would be based on "technical administration," as

---

[63] *La Tribuna*, 13 March 1948. See Villegas Hoffmeister, *Testimonios del 48*, 184.
[64] Yashar, *Demanding Democracy*, 183.
[65] Salazar Mora, *Política y Reforma*, 154–5, 160.
[66] Figueres, "Discurso de Apertura . . . Orientación General," in Gutiérrez, ed., *El Pensamiento Político*, vol.1, 279–92.

opposed to *politiquería* (petty politics), and the nation would enjoy "social progress *without* communism."[67]

The junta nationalized the banking system and electricity production, promoted agricultural diversification and industrial development, established the foundations of a welfare state, and committed itself to electoral democracy.[68] These reforms altered power relations to such an extent that the junta's successor, the Ulate administration, had to leave the reforms virtually intact. Moreover, shifts in power relations were reinforced in 1951, when the founding of Figueres' Liberación Party drew vital support from several political groups, most notably, the Social Democratic Party, other opposition groups that had emerged during the Calderón-Picado decade, and combatants in Figueres' rebel army.

The party was founded to create an electoral machinery that could simultaneously propel to power an ideological movement and the most popular leader of the movement, namely Figueres himself. Through the 1950s, the party consolidated its identity as the "nation's savior," capable of integrating the traditional concept of political democracy with the "modern" exigencies implicit in a mass society demanding social welfare. In the 1953 elections, two major political camps emerged. The pro-reform Figueres camp, organized under the Liberación Nacional, and the anti-reform camp, organized into two major parties, the Partido Unión Nacional and the Partido Demócrata. These two were joined by the old and weakened Republican Party in order to take on Liberación.[69]

But the rhetorical strategy of "national salvation" enabled Figueres in 1953 to gain the electoral support of the following key sectors: small and medium-size farmers from major rural zones; the cantons of San José just outside the Central Valley; and the middle classes in the urban centers.[70] This winning rhetorical strategy was "preserved" in a series of public letters that Figueres wrote in 1955 to the Costa Rican citizenry. The letters also defined the essence – at that particular juncture – of social democratic exceptionalism, and at last pronounced the electoral principle equally important to the substantive criterion of legitimation.

The narrative underlying this new equality between the two principles went as follows. Nineteenth century Costa Ricans sought to preserve harmony and worked hard both because they were inherently peaceful and industrious and because, as rational beings, they understood that these were the habits that both strengthened the nation and secured their personal happiness and private

[67] Ibid.
[68] These measures solidified the dominance of agroexporters while simultaneously entrenching support for the junta among the urban and agrarian middle classes. Opposition arose among several members of the junta, including the minister of security, who threatened a coup d'etat unless the banking system's nationalization was reversed. But Figueres easily reasserted control over the military, removed the rebellious minister from the junta, and then pardoned the other officers involved. Salazar Mora, *Política y Reforma*, 152, 163.
[69] ibid., 186, 191.
[70] Wilburg Jiménez, *Análisis Electoral de una Democracia* (San José: Editorial Costa Rica, 1977).

property. After 1948, however, citizens finally acquired an explicit proprietary stake in the procedural aspects of power construction. Figueres even argued that electoral mechanisms had now been perfected to the point that if an opposition leader resorted to arms – much as he himself had done only seven years earlier – that leader would be "stealing" power from the citizens as plainly as he if he were to assault the citizens' "businesses and homes."[71]

This narrative, as a new rhetorical frame, synthesized the traditional understanding of national identity with an expanded view of rule legitimation. Costa Rica, said Figueres, was a country with an "established democratic tradition, generalized public education, and habits of work and peace" – all of them "possessions" that Costa Rica owed to "specific characteristics" of its people and to "the vision of the educators and statesmen of its past."[72] But the clamor for social reform now made developmental "planning" crucial.[73] Such planning was the primary challenge confronting would-be rulers[74] – a challenge rendered all the more delicate by the strictures of exceptionalist realism. For as Figueres claimed, the nation's socioeconomic development would have to be carried out without recourse to foreign "orthodoxies," namely fascism and communism, both of which were deemed "evil" and thus "alien" to the Costa Rican character.

The new brand of exceptionalist realism, in fact, dictated that a middle path between socialism and capitalism was inevitable, since Costa Rican "authenticity" by definition rejected extremes and firmly adhered to political democracy. Finding this unique path required "scientific" knowledge, for it was precisely the dispassionate "study" of indigenous problems that would both accurately diagnose the nation's ills and reveal the local capabilities – the local knowledge – best suited to remedy those ills. For Figueres, Liberación's singular contribution – its central claim to governmental competence – was its discovery of the vital link between the scientific study of the national reality and that reality's improvement.[75]

Exceptionalist realism based on a "scientific" reverence for national tradition was continuously developed by the Liberación leadership. In 1965, Liberación's candidate, Daniel Oduber, cast his party's rivals as nostalgically fixated on the glories of the nineteenth century yet unable to meet the exigencies of a changing world. In contrast, he argued, Liberación had managed to blend the most desirable aspects of foreign models with the loftiest Costa Rican virtues. His party was, all at once, social democratic in its socioeconomic policies (as in Western Europe), liberal in its politics (as in the United States), deeply respectful of the great Costa Rican leaders of the past (who, despite their undeniable

---

[71] José Figueres Ferrer, *Cartas a un Ciudadano* (San José: Editorial Universidad Estatal a Distancia, 1980), 3.
[72] ibid., 11.
[73] ibid., 11–12.
[74] ibid., 15.
[75] ibid., 16, 21, 23.

accomplishments, had failed to solve the problems of "modernity"), and technically capable of crafting "scientific" developmental "formulas."[76]

Exceptionalist Realism and Socioeconomic Development

The first National Developmental Plan (1965–8) was the emblematic representation of this scientific traditionalism, aiming simultaneously for import-substitution industrialization and increased agricultural diversification and production.[77] But exceptionalist realism, as articulated by Liberación, did more than shape the party's competitive rhetoric and its approach to national development. It forced its opponents into the same field of imaginable possibilities. By the time of the 1966 presidential race, the opposition's candidate, José Joaquín Trejos of Unificación Nacional, self-consciously avoided taking either a "leftist" or "rightist" stance, on the grounds that the people could only "comprehend" a "purely Costa Rican message." The content of this message was rooted both in the rhetorical legacies of the nineteenth century and in the more recent rhetorical contributions of Liberación. Development, claimed Trejos, could not be attained without peace or education, both of which were "characteristic traits" of the Costa Rican nation. Nor was development possible unless Costa Ricans solved their developmental problems by making "rational use" of the nation's available instruments and resources, most notably the advantages inherent in local knowledge and in its people's peculiar qualities.

Such "knowledge" and "qualities" flowed from an apparently seamless past that spanned the entirety of the country's known history. The country's natives, Trejos averred, had been "especially poor." Its first conquerors had been uniquely "noble in spirit." And its postcolonial leaders never failed "to combine ideology with constant concern for the weak and impoverished." It was this "natural" history that, according to Trejos, made Costa Ricans "duty-bound to seek social solidarity." But this same history, Trejos also argued, showed Costa Ricans' inclination toward "self-reliance," "self-motivation," "individual effort," and "personal responsibility." Government, he concluded, should promote this healthy inclination, among other things, by denationalizing the banking system.[78]

The glorification of popular wisdom, then, became a platform for Trejos' attack on one of the great symbols of the 1948 Revolution: the nationalized banking system. But glorification of popular opinion also led Trejos to take the logical step of conducting public opinion polls.[79] The polls indicated that the electorate

[76] Daniel Oduber, "De Dónde Venimos" (1965), in Gutiérrez, ed., *El Pensamiento Político*, vol. 2, 109–28.

[77] Wilburg Jiménez Castro, *Genesis del Gobierno de Costa Rica: 1821, 1981* (San José: Editorial Alma Mater, 1986), 32–3.

[78] José Joaquín Trejos Fernández, *Ocho Años en la Política Costarricense* (San José: Editorial Hombre y Sociedad, 1973), 38–47.

[79] José Manuel Salazar Navarrete, *Oduber: Elección Presidencial de 1974* (San José: EDARASA, 1978).

valued continuity with previous reform policies, including the nationalization of the banking system. Indeed, the polls vindicated the elites' traditional view of Costa Ricans, who came across as moderate citizens inclined to show respect for historical accomplishments and reluctant to approve radical departures from the tried and true. The Trejos campaign adjusted immediately. The candidate fell silent on the issue of denationalization[80] and accorded Liberación its rightful place in the nation's history, in much the same way as he credited more distant ancestors.[81]

After narrowly defeating Oduber in 1966, Trejos went further. Like the outgoing Liberación administration, his government crafted a National Developmental Plan for 1969–72. The plan was a departure from the previous one in that it emphasized the conventional principle of comparative advantage, which for Costa Rica entailed a concentrated return to the promotion of agricultural exports. But a plan there was. Moreover, the 1969–72 plan was sufficiently compatible with its predecessor to be integrated into the next plan (1972–8), which in essence became a hybrid of past blueprints, fomenting import substitution while exploiting full force the country's comparative advantage in agriculture. The next plan (1979–82) was merely an extension of this blend, premised as it was on the idea that the country was by "vocation" agrarian and that, if exploited "scientifically and rationally," agriculture could serve as a foundation for the development of "secondary" industrial activities.[82]

By bringing both Liberación and its opponents onto the same field of imaginable possibilities, the new exceptionalist realism engendered a convergence dynamic in political practices. If Trejos had imitated Liberación to good effect, now Liberación was prepared to learn from Trejos' experience with the constraining effect of the Costa Ricans' "moderation." As one Liberación intellectual and activist observed:

There are nations which display a rare but constant tendency to forge a common understanding of fundamental interests, and to elevate such interests above secondary differences. This seems to be the case in Costa Rica. In other societies, disagreement prevails. Such societies lack an accurate national diagnosis which, deeply rooted in their own history, might lead to politically viable solutions. And as with nations, so it is with political parties... parties that can supply an exact diagnosis of the national reality, and can articulate a transformative agenda that is both feasible and widely accepted, will gain strength and permanence.... *Liberación's relevance stems precisely from its ability... to generate solutions that [among competing programs] are the most congruent with the best of Costa Rican history and traditions* [emphasis added].[83]

---

[80] Trejos Fernández, *Ocho Años*, 20–9.

[81] Trejos, for example, argued that education represented the oldest and deepest longing of the nation because – like the exemplary conqueror Coronado – Costa Ricans wished to "persuade through reason" rather than "prevail by force of arms." Ibid.

[82] Jiménez Castro, *Génesis*, 32–3.

[83] Salazar Navarrete, *Oduber: Elección Presidencial*, 40–1.

In the late 1960s, this meant sharpening Liberación's competitive edge over its rivals. This edge, as the party's leaders knew well, consisted in their successful political use of "reflection" and "study." To this end, Liberación began to hold "ideological congresses" – brainstorming sessions aimed at refining and renovating the party's version of exceptionalist realism. By 1969, Liberación was able to respond to the social movements rocking the United States and Western Europe. Oduber, for one, reworked the old theme of autochthonous development. Making a distinction between "possible" and "impossible" revolutions, Oduber argued that only Costa Rica's "real" conditions could determine the "appropriateness" of innovative policies. And any assessment of those conditions now had to take the Revolution of 1948 as its point of reference.

As Oduber put it, the Revolution was neither chained to nineteenth century liberalism nor open to communism, and as a consequence was able to alter the parameters of political "realism." That is to say, the Revolution rendered alternative programs "unreal" and "unfeasible." The Revolution, after all, had preempted the left by establishing a welfarist-entrepreneurial state. The Revolution had also outstripped the right, because by introducing a "scientific" approach to governance, it had modernized political institutions while increasing individual security. To propose anything different – either from the left or the right – was to propose the "impossible," and proposing the impossible, in turn, was tantamount to "inhibiting" the continued progress of the "possible revolution."[84] From this chain of reasoning, Oduber went on to argue that if the people returned Liberación to power, the possible revolution was not only viable but enticing; in a mere twenty-five years, he promised, Liberación could deepen social change "without destroying private property."[85]

Liberación thus explicitly renovated for modern times the theme of possibility mongering that had laced the rhetoric of early postcolonial leaders. Indeed, in a show of self-confidence, Liberación followed the example set by Unificación in 1966, turning during the 1970 race to public opinion polls (which accurately predicted the victory of its candidate, Figueres). By the time of the 1973–4 campaign, Liberación was ready to launch an intense wave of surveys, querying citizens about fundamental preferences as follows:

Which of the following systems do you believe should be used to organize the country? 1. Socialism: a system in which private property and private enterprise do not exist. 2. Capitalism: a system in property and enterprise are in the hands of private individuals, and government concentrates on maintaining order. Or 3. A combination of these two systems, with some tasks assigned to the government and others to private enterprise.

Nine percent chose socialism, 13 percent capitalism, and an overwhleming 73 percent the hybrid. The remaining 5 percent abstained.[86]

---

[84] Daniel Oduber, "Apuntes para un Congreso Ideológico del Partido de Liberación Nacional," in Gutiérrez, ed., *El Pensamiento Político*, vol. 2, 207–33.

[85] Ibid., Vol. 2, 233–40.

[86] Salazar Navarrete, *Oduber: Elección Presidencial*, 42, 50.

Liberación interpreted these results as further evidence that Costa Rica's "national character" repudiated "ideological extremes." As one Liberación intellectual surmised, the "Costa Rican peculiar way of being" was so deeply embedded in "democratic sentiment" that democracy could be considered almost "second nature" to the nation.[87] In fact, elite confidence in the people's exceptional virtues reached a new peak, culminating in the 1975 constitutional amendment that granted leftist and radical political groups – such as Acción Socialista, Pueblo Unido, and Alianza Popular – the right to organize and to compete freely in the electoral process.[88]

Liberación also saw the survey results as resounding proof of its unerring and intimate understanding of the people. What Liberación could not discern, much less control, was the extent to which its rhetorical frame – its communicative link to the virtuous nation – was becoming the opposition's frame as well. And neither Liberación nor the opposition could fully grasp how this rhetorical convergence both narrowed the parties' substantive differences and intensified the political system's tendency to "alternate" power between them. By the mid-1970s, they were both not only multiclass parties, but their bases of support were virtually identical.[89]

By the mid-1970s, it was also clear that neither major party could aspire to political hegemony precisely because both parties operated within the same rhetorical frame and the same field of imaginable possibilities. Routinely reinforced by the rhetorical practices of competing politicians,[90] this field was formalized by professional historians. One modern student of Costa Rica's conquest proclaimed Coronado "the most humanitarian and least covetous of all the captains," while another prominent historian proudly pronounced him "founder of Costa Rica."[91] A "biography" of Costa Rica went on in 1981 to depict the conqueror as a "skillful politician" who was able to combine "compassion" with "firmness" and military tact with sheer force of arms. Mainstream Costa Rican historiography took the story a step further by depicting Costa Rica's early explorers as "conciliatory" and Nicaragua's conquerors as bent on obstructing the "peaceful" conquest of the Talamananca region in Costa Rica.[92] For his part, one of the country's foremost Marxist scholars interpreted the conciliatory preferences demonstrated at critical junctures by

---

[87] Ibid., 42, 50.

[88] Jorge Mario Salazar, "Partidos Políticos y Participación," in Salazar Mora, ed., *Democracia y Cultura Política en Costa Rica,* 129.

[89] Mario Sánchez Machado, *Las Bases Sociales del Voto en Costa Rica: 1974–1978* (San José: URUK Editores, 1985), 37–8.

[90] In the 1970s, for example, the opposition to Liberación administrations hammered home the point that increases in inflationary pressures, and the related discontent among the urban petit bourgeoisie, were due to Liberación's break with tradition. Ibid., 17–18.

[91] Eugenio Rodríguez Vega, *Biografía de Costa Rica* (San José: Editorial Costa Rica, 1981), 20.

[92] Jorge Lines, "Integración de la Provincia de Costa Rica bajo el Reinado de Carlos V," and Carlos Meléndez, "Los Poderes Conferidos al Alcalde Mayor Licenciado Juan de Cavallón," both in Academia Costarricense de la Historia, *IVCentenario de la Entrada de Cavallón a Costa Rica, 1561–1961* (San José: Inprenta Nacional, 1961), 21–31, 41.

the country's postcolonial leaders as early displays of an "eminently Costa Rican...attitude," a "characteristic of our people's idiosyncracy."[93]

As if directed by an invisible yet steady hand, Costa Rican historiography stylized the nation's history as a linear process in which, as the Academia de Geografía e Historia put it, the *patria* was "fashioned" as a "collective" product by the country's "elders." The historians gathered under the Academia's auspices suggested that the origins of this magnificent patrimony could be easily traced to the nation's first chief, Juan Mora Fernández 1824–33). Here was a man of "superior spirit" who, after peering into the distant future with his "penetrating gaze," was able to set the foundations for the nation's "happiness and ennoblement."

But remarkable as this "great patriot" might have been, in the end, he was no more than a quintessential expression of the Costa Rican character. For as Chief Mora himself had asserted at the nation's dawn, Costa Ricans were

...honest citizens and peaceable tillers, artisans and workers who, devoted to their private occupations, [were] able to subsist on their work alone while harboring no other interest than fulfilling their domestic duties and defending the state when called upon to do so by law.[94]

In recent years, tangible successes have rendered Costa Rica's claim to exceptionalism even more credible. In the 1920s, Costa Rica's gross domestic product (GDP)was the smallest in Central America, except for Nicaragua, whose GDP it barely exceeded. By 1991, Costa Rica's GDP was 20 percent larger than that of El Salvador, three times that of Nicaragua, double that of Honduras, and about 70 percent the size of Guatemala's (a remarkable figure when we consider Guatemala's population, which at 9.2 million trebles that of Costa Rica).[95]

Scholars have also noted that by 1980 the country's illiteracy rate had declined to 10 percent, and enrollment in higher education among the college age, population was higher than in the United Kingdom, Finland, Austria, and Switzerland. Between 1960 and 1980, infant mortality was reduced by 47 percent while life expectancy increased by twelve years. During those same two decades, social security coverage expanded from 25 percent of the population to 68 percent.[96] Finally, as Mitchell A. Seligson and Edward N. Muller observe:

Few other developing nations...have been able to achieve economic growth while at the same time reducing income inequality...the reduction in income inequality in Costa Rica [between 1961 and 1971] still left a distribution that was more highly skewed in

---

[93] Rodolfo Cerda Cruz, *Formación del Estado en Costa Rica* (San José: Editorial Universidad de Costa Rica, 1967), 96–9, 156–9.

[94] *Gobernantes de Costa Rica* (San José: Academia de Geografía e Historia de Costa Rica, 1978), 9, 13.

[95] Carlos Vargas Pagán, "La Evolución de la Pobreza en Costa Rica," in *Contribuciones* 47, no. 3 (July–September 1995): 95–6.

[96] See Mitchell A. Seligson and Edward N. Muller, "Democratic Stability and Economic Crisis," *International Studies Quarterly* 31, no. 3 (September 1987): 310.

favor of the rich than found among the industrialized nations, [but] the distribution no longer matched the typical pattern of extremely high inequality found in most developing nations.[97]

The country's political economy, of course, has not been free of problems. In the late 1970s, the Costa Rican model of state-led development reached stubborn limits. By the early 1980s, balance of payments disequilibria became more pronounced as the boom in world coffee prices came to an end and the global economy went into recession. The Rodrigo Carazo administration, moreover, eschewed structural adjustment while borrowing heavily in the international financial markets and expanding the monetary supply. The upshot was a severe crisis: a record-high inflation rate of 90 percent, 12 percent gross national product (GNP) contraction, an onerous external debt (4 billion U.S. dollars), a 10 percent unemployment rate, sharp reductions in real salaries, drastic reductions in public investment, and a steep decline in overall consumption levels.

Liberación returned to power in 1982 after holding an "ideological congress" whose purpose was to devise a dual strategy for tackling the economic crisis at home and the ascent of the Frente Sandinista de Liberación Nacional (FSLN) in neighboring Nicaragua. The Liberación program shows the basic elements of this strategy. First, just like the party's founding members had done in the 1940s, the party not only acknowledged but actually highlighted the "confusion, crisis, and disorder" emerging at the time. Second, echoing the promises made by its founding members in the 1940s, the party now pledged to engage in "scientific study" of the nation's problems and, on the basis of those findings, proceed to craft its solution.[98] Third, in a repeat performance of the pronouncements of the 1940s, party leaders made the point that their intent was not to "discard or abandon" the nation's political legacies, but rather to "rescue," "purify," and "perfect" them.[99]

Having framed the crisis in this way, the party pressed for a policy package that was at once traditional and novel. On the one hand, the party deviated from its traditional statism by pushing for administrative decentralization and increased flexibility. On the other hand, the party adhered closely to its hallmark pursuit of an "autonomous" and "Costa Rican" developmental approach that would be based less on "foreign" models and more on domestic "scientific, technological, and artistic research." The objectives of this "research" were declared as follows: The attainment of greater participation in social welfare by marginal groups, and the construction of a unification "method"

[97] Ibid., 310.

[98] Francisco J. Orlich, "Un Nuevo Objetivo Nacional, Más Democracia, Mayor Desarrollo Económico para una Sociedad de Bienestar General: Programa del Partido Liberación Nacional Aprobado por el Segundo Congreso Nacional" (San José: Secretaría de Planes y Programas del Partido Liberación Nacional, 1981), in Gutiérrez, ed., *El Pensamiento Político*, vol. 2, 305–6.

[99] Ibid., 306–7.

through the practice of cooperation and consensus building among divergent groups.[100]

The Liberación administration of Luis Alberto Monge (1982–6) came to power ready to broadcast an "emergency plan" designed to address a heavy fiscal deficit, a taxing external debt, a highly devalued currency, negative growth rates, and the dismal prospect of national "bankruptcy."[101] The new administration would also position Costa Rica firmly at the margin of isthmian conflicts:

[Central America] is at war, and Costa Rica's peace is at peril. . . . We Costa Ricans believe that war is the greatest irrationality and a political failure. . . . Costa Rica is not a major political player, nor can it be. *Costa Rica is not a military power, nor does it wish to be.* Costa Rica is a spiritual authority because its people adhere to their faith in the power of common sense and moral fortitude . . . [emphasis added].[102]

Conclusion

Costa Rica's democracy, by far the strongest in Latin America, is in essence a regime of arbitration whose legitimation is anchored in both substantive and electoral principles. But this double legitimation, which today renders the regime robust and supple, was not attained at a stroke. Rather, this double legitimation is entwined with an exceptionalist system of normative scheming whose construction and renovation could have failed at crucial points. Nor is this exceptionalist system without flaws. In the conclusion of this book, we will consider its limitations, particularly the constraints it places on organized labor. Its accomplishments, however, ought not be underestimated, especially when viewed in comparative perspective. The Nicaraguan alternative, to which we now turn, is both a lesson on the difficulties faced by national elites seeking peace and progress, and a cautionary tale of what happens to a people when they lose sight of their own potential to achieve these goals.

[100] Orlich, "Un Nuevo Objetivo Nacional," in ibid., vol. 2, 324–30.
[101] Luis Alberto Monge, "Los Cuatro Compromisos: Presentación del Plan Nacional de Emergencia" (San José), 30 April 1982, in ibid., 331–3.
[102] Luis Alberto Monge, "Proclama de Neutralidad," 17 November 1983," in ibid., 346–57.

6

Nicaragua

Hybrid Arbitration

Athenians: Since we are not allowed to speak to the people, lest forsooth, they should be deceived by seductive and unanswerable arguments, which they should hear set forth in a single uninterrupted oration . . . you who are sitting here may as well make assurance yet surer. Let us have no set speeches at all, but do you reply to each several statement of which you disapprove, and criticize it at once. Say first how you like this mode of proceeding.

Melians: The quiet interchange of explanations is a reasonable thing, and we do not object to that. But your warlike movements, which are present not only to our fears but to our eyes, seem to belie your words. We see that, although you may reason with us, you mean to be our judges; and that at the end of the discussion, if the justice of our cause prevail and we therefore refuse to yield, we may expect war; if we are convinced by you, slavery.

Athenians: Nay, but if you are only going to argue from fancies about the future, or if you meet us with any other purpose than that of facing your circumstances in the face and saving your city, we have done; but if this is your intention we will proceed.[1]

–Thucydides

The proceding passage hints not only at the dangers and the promises of communication, but also at the importance of who participates and how communication proceeds. The classic prisoners' dilemma arises because detained accomplices, isolated from one another, are unable to collude in the crafting of a mutually beneficial strategy.[2] In other words, the *sine qua non* of this non-cooperative game is the absence of communication between players. But in a Manichean system of normative scheming, it is the free flow of communication

---

[1] Thucydides, "The Sicilian Expedition," in W. H. Auden, ed., *The Portable Greek Reader* (New York: Penguin Books, 1977, 1982), 656–7.

[2] Roybin M. Dawes, *Rational Choice in an Uncertain World* (New York: Harcourt Brace Jovanovich, 1988).

that tends to foment mistrust and conflict even among players who might share strategic interests. As a result, Manichean communication blocks the construction of effective arbitration institutions, even though such institutions are meant to issue sustainable allocations of power resources to rival claimants.

Manichean communication has this deleterious effect because, to mix game-theoretic and Manichean parlance, actors share in the common knowledge that while they are rational *and* basically good, others are rational *and* basically nefarious. This means that, to the extent that rationality is consistently goal-oriented, actors specify the game in terms of an existential binary opposition. As a result, they come to see formal rules as objects of normative manipulation and evasion. Rules, to put it simply, become part of the repertoire of instruments at the disposal of normative schemers.[3]

So how does Manichean communication work? To begin with, Manichean communication is not reducible to the deliberately provocative pronouncements typically associated with divide-and-conquer tactics. Rather, Manichean communication is a specific but widely intelligible interplay between historical legacies and political agents. This dynamic unfolds as follows. Communication feeds off history because the articulated past renders credible, even intuitive, the claims that actors make in the present. But communication is also political because as these intuitive and credible present-tense articulations become subject to interpretative manipulation, they can open up the possibility for departures from entrenched visions and behavioral patterns. Finally, communication is widely intelligible because all the relevant actors share in the normative realism that is attached to their declarative identity – the prescriptions and proscriptions, as well as the sense of collective competence and notions of feasibility, that characterize their professed belief in who they are as a collective as well as their understanding of how the world works.

Implicit in this communicative dynamic, then, are the dangers associated with entrenched mistrust. But implicit too is the possibility for a constructive departure from fatalistic visions and destructive practices. The Spanish transition to democracy in the late 1970s, as we saw in the early chapters of this book, is a dramatic example of such a constructive departure. But this chapter argues that political-cultural transformation need not begin either with an onslaught against the corresponding field of imaginable possibilities, nor with a deep structural alteration of the *lingua franca* – the language that actors use when crafting their rhetorical strategies. Political-cultural transformation can begin modestly. It can begin with tinkering – the creation of something new through partial adaptations of the old. This chapter examines a particular type of tinkering, which I call *tailored communicative regulation*: the self-conscious

---

[3] For the standard assumptions of game theory, see Scott Gates and Brian D. Humes, *Games, Information, and Politics: Applying Game Theoretic Models to Political Science* (Ann Arbor, MI: University of Michigan Press, 1997), 8–10. For a succinct discussion of rationality, see James D. Morrow, *Game Theory for Political Scientists* (Princeton, NJ: Princeton University Press, 1994), 16–25.

act whereby key actors, rather than try to impose indiscriminate or purely self-serving censorship, take measure of their own destructive rhetorical practices and proceed to regulate speech selectively.

Tailored Communicative Regulation

Tailored communicative regulation is an identifiable learn-as-you-go process based on a blend of rhetorical prescriptions and proscriptions – regulatory techniques – that alter not only the play of persuasion strategies but also address actors' changing vulnerabilities and incentives. This latter reconfiguration, in turn, prompts – perhaps even forces – the construction of supportive institutions. In this case, such institutions consist of formal and informal rules that assuage the fears and constrain the ambitions that the new rhetorical regulations may incite or heighten.

Between 1857 and 1893, Nicaraguan elites devised and established regulation techniques and supportive institutions to create a growing sense of trust and cooperation between antagonistic camps, and to minimize the previously intractable forces of *caudillismo* and clannish and localist hostilities. In so doing, they showed that tailored communicative regulation can ultimately usher in major systemic changes. For if a synergy between rhetorical regulation and supportive institution building takes hold, then actors can safely begin to soften their rigid antagonistic positions and to reshape their seemingly obdurate identities. Thus, previously inconceivable strategic alliances may come to be generally regarded as both normatively justifiable and realistic.

Moreover, when embedded in this newly shared brand of normative realism, the enhanced elasticity of identity construction and alliance making can eventually generate a political momentum that shifts the boundaries of imaginable possibilities. The world appears at last transformable to actors, and this growing perception can begin to outweigh fatalistic views. Or to put it in political-historical terms, the extant system of normative scheming endogenously generates a critical juncture. In Nicaragua, this juncture resulted in a remarkable experiment known in the country's historiography interchangeably as the Thirty Years and the Conservative Republic. These three decades, in effect, witnessed the development and collapse of an effective arbitration regime based on an oligarchic arrangement comparable at the time to the democracies of Chile, Uruguay, and Costa Rica.

Under the Republic, political violence among elites diminished radically, their state-building competence grew rapidly, and the state's developmental capacity began to outpace even the most ambitious modernizing visions. Central to these advances was the solution of the "succession problem," which typically arose in postcolonial Latin America when incumbents sought either reelection or imposition of a favored successor. Almost invariably, these moves would trigger rebellion. Chile's oligarchic democracy, for example, suffered with this problem under the Conservatives, and was able to overcome it only in its Liberal phase.

The chief material benefit of Nicaragua's political stabilization under the Republic was the emergence of a dynamic coffee economy at a precarious point in its economic development, when European demand for Central American natural dyes was on the decline.[4] Just as importantly, the coffee economy provided the revenue base for further increases in state-building competence and, by extension, for further rounds of state-orchestrated development. This synergy theretofore had eluded Nicaraguans. For in the absence of encompassing arbitration, power positions were thoroughly unstable, and as a result economic policies were inchoate at best. The combination of rhetorical regulation and institutional adaptation changed all this by redefining identities, political roles, and lines of authority.

The initial regulatory experiments were more like improvisations based on experience and political learning. In the wake of the (successful) National War against Walker, for example, Nicaraguan elites faced the urgent task of breaking a new, postwar impasse. Given the high degree of militarized polarization, this task fell to the *caudillos* of the two contending camps. The two leaders turned to a simple regulatory technique: Close off the relevant areas of debate and decision-making to the vast majority of notables, and thus reduce the number of vocal claimants to authority and influence. In the context of postcolonial Latin America, this restrictive technique represented a sharp break with the royally sanctioned permissiveness of expression that had characterized encompassing arbitration under the ancien régime.

The institutional arrangement that the two *caudillos* established in support of restricted multivocality hinged on dictatorial rule by mutual consent. This arrangement, too, was a departure from postcolonial politics because it aimed to elevate one of two *caudillos* to the status of primary arbiter with the explicit cooperation of his rival, while at the same time it sought to insulate both *caudillos* from the clashing pressures of their respective followers and notable ranks. Although this initial experiment proved ephemeral, it taught actors important lessons about the opportunities and perils inherent in the processes studied in what today we call transitology, and thus created a set of legacies that helped make a subsequent, more lasting experiment possible.

This more durable experiment relied on a regulatory technique that shifted the burden of restrictions away from the notable ranks and onto a single but major actor, the president. This second technique was as seemingly straightforward as the first. Briefly stated, the president was subjected to a strict code of rhetorical conduct that prescribed presidential conciliatory statements and gestures while proscribing presidential participation in polarizing exchanges. Indeed, prior to assuming office, a president-elect was expected to make a public precommitment that tied the legitimate deployment of executive power to his own faithful fulfillment of the attitudinal and behavioral guidelines embodied in the presidential code of rhetorical conduct.

---

[4] John A. Booth, *The End and The Beginning: The Nicaraguan Revolution* (Boulder, CO: Westview Press, 1985), 20.

This technique – call it executive restraint – borrowed key features from the royal model of legitimate arbitration. It placed at the center of the rhetorical culture a single persona: Where once the king had stood as sovereign arbiter now stood the chief executive. Also like the royal model, it structured the president's public identity by specifying a set of constitutive virtues like benevolence and impartiality. Finally, in contradistinction to restricted multivocality, this technique closely regulated executive behavior, but allowed notables the full expression of their political opinions. This formula replicated to a significant degree the Crown's policy of expressive pluralism.

Regulation of presidential rhetoric, however, also represented a sharp break with colonial tradition. The executive was the exemplar, but unlike the royal sovereign, he was not above reproach. If anything, the executive was offered to fiery orators and pamphleteers as a fair target of direct criticism. Conversely, while the men around the "innocent monarch" had been generally perceived as "wicked" during the colonial period, now the notables around the president were seen as the voice of "public opinion" and by, extension, as rightful judges of presidential performance.

The result was the creation of a presidency that functioned as a relatively stable, neutral space around which robust and spontaneous multivocality could play itself out. But the reconfigured set of vocal roles and prerogatives also entailed new risks for all the major players, and thus called for a reconfiguration of the formal rules of the game as well. These rules would have to reassure exemplar and judges alike. The presidential incumbent needed to know that aspirants to the executive office would not misinterpret his self-moderation as a weakness to be exploited for self-seeking purposes. The ranking notables, for their part, needed to know that the incumbent's success as exemplar of moderation would not degenerate into a power base for a new variant of *caudillismo*.

A blend of institutional adaptations satisfied both. A constitutional ban on presidential reelection diminished the notables' fear of a superprestigious president entrenching himself as sole arbiter. The constitutionally mandated elimination of the vice-presidency, in turn, liberated the executive from the insecurities associated with the power bids of unruly vice-presidents.

The payoff was substantial. Justifiable power was both imaginable and possible. At the most obvious level, the seemingly insoluble problem of presidential succession was resolved: Five out of eight chiefs of state quietly and properly transferred the reins of power to their successor. One died of natural causes while in office. The two outliers, like bookends on an orderly shelf, came at the beginning and at the end of the Republic. Their ascent and decline, therefore, is entwined with the puzzle of regime creation and breakdown. But between these two points in time, the Republic's presidential center not only created a stable referent for the relatively free play of struggles, it also came to serve as a focal point for bipartisan power-sharing agreements and policy convergence.

This last accomplishment, though less obvious than the solution to the succession problem, was no small matter. Theretofore, bipartisan agreements had been a source of instability because rival leaders willing to share power and to reach policy compromises were perceived by their respective followers as engaging in "immoral" acts of "perfidy." Tailored communicative regulation based on presidential restraint cut through this Gordian knot: The more the executive demonstrated his willingness to receive criticism and to ignore personal attacks, the less his opponents could be accused of treason when they opted for bipartisan cooperation under the aegis of his administration. Opponents, in fact, not only could afford to get close to the president, they could actively seek proximity to him; they could even seek inclusion in his cabinet.

In effect, notables from various localities and clans were now able to legitimate their own role as judges of presidential performance and, in so doing, could partake in an increasingly equitable distribution of official sources of influence and prestige. Finally, as this process of inclusion gathered momentum, a mainstream of new ideas concerning political cooperation began to emerge – a mainstream whose most profound effect was to blur the distinction between Liberal and Conservative identities. Many of the leading lights of the Conservative camp began openly to describe themselves as "liberal" in spirit, something they did with the blessing of many of their Liberal counterparts.

On the Eve of the Republic: Internal versus External Manicheanism

Nicaragua's internal Manicheanism was patently evident in 1855. The Democrats (later to be called Liberals) of León and the Legitimists (later to be called Conservatives) were stubbornly locked in a debilitating military stalemate. Neither side, however, would relent. The Democrats, in fact, decided to try to break the stalemate by importing the American adventurer William Walker and his band of mercenaries to fight on their side. In optimistic anticipation, the Democrats conferred upon the American Nicaraguan citizenship as well as the rank of colonel in their army. They also authorized him to recruit more men, and gave him virtually unrestricted access to the territories under their control. The gambit seemed to pay off when Walker managed to seize Granada, the bastion of the Legitimist camp.[5]

The Democrats of León were not alone in their enthusiasm for Walker. The vanquished city of Granada received its conqueror with open arms, literally: Granada's military leader actually embraced Walker. Moreover, the city's most prominent priest – and one of the country's most influential political sermonizers – expressed the hope that the foreigner might act as "the tutelary Angel of Peace, and the North Star of the aspirations of an afflicted people."[6] The priest's hope hinged on the simple proposition that Walker was "an enlightened and talented man," and as such might just prove to be "the providential envoy

[5] Arturo Cruz, Jr., "Overcoming Mistrust: The Quest For Order in Nicaragua's Conservative Republic, 1858–1893" (PhD. diss., Oxford University, Michaelmas, 1997), 60.
[6] Francisco Vigil, *Manuscrítos Auténticos Compilados, Padre Vigil*, 119–122. Dating back to the middle of the nineteenth century, these documents were first published in Granada in 1930. They were privately reprinted in Managua in 1967.

who cures the wounds and reconciles the Nicaraguan family, which others have divided."[7]

The hope that Walker might play the role of temporary but effective arbiter to the country's intra-elite disputes proved ephemeral. The population's general exhaustion, to be sure, put considerable pressure on the belligerents to work out a truce through the foreigner.[8] But since the camps were at once mutually resentful and internally fragmented,[9] negotiations faded into double dealings, and double dealings backfired on elites.[10] Granada's military leader, the very same leader who had embraced Walker, soon found himself before the American's firing squad. León's commander watched the execution from a nearby balcony.

By July of 1856, Walker was ready to dispense with all Nicaraguan leaders, the Democrats included, and had himself elected president of the Republic. By August, Walker felt sufficiently confident to execute a Democratic leader. Although on the brink of utter chaos and mortally threatened by the foreigner, the Nicaraguan camps continued to fight each other. The camps' intransigence was such that it alarmed the other governments of Central America, which did their best to push the belligerents toward a peace agreement. But only as it became patently obvious to the leading belligerents that they stood to lose everything to their foreign arbiter, including life and property, did they finally forge a bipartisan alliance and join with other Central Americans to oust Walker.[11]

At this point it might seem reasonable to conclude that the severe shock of foreign conquest and the high cost of the subsequent war would be enough to alter the structure of incentives so that rational actors would overwhelmingly opt for a negotiated peace. A litany of factors certainly militated in favor of negotiations. To begin with, elite hubris by now had been tempered by the humiliation suffered at Walker's hands. Moreover, a general fear persisted that the American might return with a vengeance to the isthmus; the Nicaraguan economy was in shambles; the treasury was insolvent; and although partisan emotions still ran high, the pool of combatants had been decimated. Finally,

---

[7] "Sermón del Padre Vijil" (Granada), 14 October 1855. Quoted in Alejandro Reyes Huete, *Estampas de Nuestra Historia* (Granada: n.a., 1956), 51–5.

[8] Reyes Huetes, *Estampas*, 219–23, 230.

[9] Jerónimo Pérez, *Memoria para la Historia de la Revolución de Nicaragua en 1854*, 2nd ed. (Managua: Impreuta del Gobierno, 1883), 176–7.

[10] Rafael Carrera, "Guatemaltecos" (Guatemala), May 5, 1856; reprinted in *Gaceta del Salvador*, 15 May 1856. See also "Proclama del Presidente de la República de Nicaragua, a sus habitantes" (León), 3 June 1856 *Boletín Oficial*; "Otra del General William Walker" (León), 4 June 1856, *Boletín Oficial*, no. 9 (León), 5 June 1856.

[11] Democrats and Legitimists joined the armies of El Salvador, Guatemala, and Costa Rica, as well mercenaries hired for the campaign. Their combined efforts culminated in Walker's surrender on May 1, 1857. However, for the next three years, Central Americans lived in fear of Walker's return. For the ongoing political strife even in the face of Walker's power grab, see Esteban Escobar, *Biografía del General Don Pedro Joaquín Chamorro, 1818–1890* (Managua: Tipografía La Prensa, 1935), 8–9.

as if all this were not enough, Costa Rica seemed tempted to seize part of Nicaragua's territory.

But it is precisely at this point that it becomes most clear that incentives and rationality do not exist in a historical vacuum. Memories, too, shape the environment in which actors operate, exercising their power most directly, in this particular case, through the rhetoric of just retribution. The leading Democrats, for example, deeply resented the "fiery articles" written against them by their Legitimist counterparts. So did the Democrats' allies. General Gerardo Barrios of El Salvador, for one, was incensed by the Legitimists' pamphlets. "There were moments," he admitted to a Legitimist notable, "when I was on the verge of coming [from San Salvador] to Granada to break that printing press of yours that keeps the country divided." On the opposite side, predictably, the Legitimists resented the Democrats' own "hard-hitting publications." As one Legitimist pamphleteer explained to his counterpart in the Democratic camp: "I *had* to pay you back; remember: eye for eye, tooth for tooth."[12]

In a more didactic tone, the *Crónica de Costa Rica* cautioned its readers:

... if you wish to know the monstrous consequences of *giving free rein to everyone to say it all in a society without a solid constitution, education, or moral unity* ... then contemplate Nicaragua's catastrophes.... [In that country] save a few exceptions, *the press has been the rude word of anarchy, internal war, and the moral degradation of the people....*

Writers from one state [of Central America] to another have also spat on each other with ink ... thus weakening further a tenuous union.... Let us all preach: forgetfulness and forgiveness; unity and tolerance; faith and perseverance. *We are all in danger* [emphasis added].[13]

The *Crónica* traced back the chief cause of Nicaragua's ruin to the simultaneous presence of three factors: excessive freedom ("free rein"), extreme multivocality ("everyone"), and the lack of a regulatory collective structure ("solid constitution, or education, or moral unity"). However, the *Crónica* stopped short of an attack on liberty. What the *Crónica* did advocate explicitly at this new moment of "danger" was identity reform, recommending to all Central Americans the very deeds and qualities that, in the interpretation and construction of their own history, Costa Rican leaders had managed to claim as the emblematic traits of their national identity: forgiveness, unity, tolerance, and faith.

Implementing Regulatory Techniques and Supportive Institutions

The *Crónica*, of course, could offer no specific suggestion on how to attain this goal. But Nicaraguan political leaders obviously took note, and even reprinted

---

[12] Pedro Joaquín Chamorro, *Biografía del Licenciado Jerónimo Pérez* (Managua: Tipografía La Prensa, 1939), 14–21, 123.

[13] "La Prensa," published by the *Crónica de Costa Rica* and reprinted in Nicaragua's *Boletín Oficial*, no. 45 (León), 22 April 1857.

the essay for the edification of local readers. More importantly, they began a process of experimentation in speech regulation through selective restriction of multivocality. In essence, they established a mutually reinforcing relationship between rhetorical regulation and supportive institution building in four strategic steps. First, the two predominant *caudillos* drastically reduced the number of notables slated to participate in the peace negotiations. Indeed, each *caudillo* was accompanied by only one notable. This in itself was a remarkable move for a time and place dominated by *tertulias* – the political circles of notables that were common not only in Nicaraguan cities but also in Costa Rica and most of Latin America. Second, once insulated in this way, the two *caudillos* explicitly claimed to have the implicit "trust" of their respective camps; and having jointly staked this claim, they arrogated to themselves the authority to assume joint dictatorial powers of arbitration, without further consultation with their respective notable ranks.[14] Third, they left the military under the control of the Legitimist (Conservative) *caudillo*, and gave him the status of *primus inter pares* in the duopoly of power, making plain in the process that the Democrats (Liberals) bore responsibility for bringing Walker into the mix. Fourth and finally, unobserved by the top-ranking notables of his own camp, the Liberal *caudillo* was able to assume this responsibility by vowing never to become involved in "fratricidal wars" – a pledge that prompted the one attending Conservative notable to express the hope that the Liberal *caudillo* would indeed turn from "the spirit of evil" to the "spirit of good."[15]

The power-sharing agreement was formalized in the so-called Binary Government (1857). Its core idea, dictatorship by mutual consent between antagonists, was not implausible. By acting in concert and ruling with a strong hand, the duopoly's *primus* might just be able to impose order in his role of final arbiter; at the very least, he might help avoid the territorial partitions some notables were proposing. At the most specific level, consensual dictatorship implied that while one *caudillo* would rule, both *caudillos* would have the capacity to discipline the notable ranks while remaining free to solicit the advice of particular notables and to select their most trusted allies to serve in government positions. On both these counts, the arrangement hinged on the idea of future restrictions on multivocality – the very technique that had allowed for

---

[14] Claiming the "trust" of followers was not a peculiarity of the Nicaraguan historical moment. As John Dunn writes:

> 'Defenders of absolutism throughout the ages, from Bodin, Richelieu, and Louis XIV to Stalin and Mao Tse-tung, have sought to present their own putatively legitimate authority as founded in fact upon the profound and pervasive trust of its faithful and law-abiding subjects, contested only by the willfully and inexcusably contumacious.'

See John Dunn, "Trust and Political Agency," in Diego Gambetta, ed., *Trust: Making and Breaking Cooperative Relations* (Cambridge, UK: Basil Blackwell, 1988), 73–4.

[15] Chamorro, *Biografía del Licenciado Jerónimo Perez*, 21–3, 239–42. See also "Acta Patriótica" (San Salvador: Imprenta A. Liévano, 1857), *RAGHN* 9, no. 1 (April 1947): 23–6; *Boletín Oficial*, no. 48 (León), 17 May 1857.

the tentative transition to peace, as well as for the establishment of the Binary Government itself.

At the end of the day, however, neither *caudillo* was able to control his notable ranks. Quite the opposite. The prospect of future restrictions on multivocality generated vehement objections among Conservative (former Legitimists) and Liberals (former Democrats) alike. Moreover, the Conservatives managed to unify the notable ranks across partisan lines by marshaling the emotional power of historical memory. Their rhetorical strategy was simple yet creative for that time and place: Establish consensus around the idea of constitutional government by emphasizing the goals pursued by each camp during their postcolonial struggles – liberty for the Liberals, electoral order for the Conservatives. The strategy worked: The notables were able to combine forces to pressure the Binary Government into convening elections for a constitutional assembly and for president of the Republic.

The notables' calculus was self-serving as well. They called for an assembly because they themselves were the ones most likely to be elected deputies by their localities, which meant that they stood to gain control of the constitution-making and electoral processes. And indeed, once installed in the Constituent (November 1857), the notables seized the opportunity to dismantle the experiment in restricted multivocality and the attendant formal rules, namely the Binary Government.

The way in which the notables went about all this, and the replacement institutions they devised, point to a key aspect of political-cultural transformation: Even discarded experiments, by altering established notions of the possible, can provide actors both with a starting point for renewed experimentation and a chance to make credible normative claims.

To understand the mechanisms driving this process, consider first that the notables' "realism" impelled them to recognize the essential "facts" associated with significant changes in postwar conditions. The notables now recognized that the brief experiment in restricted multivocality and mutually agreed upon dictatorship, while undesirable in itself, had nonetheless proven instrumental in the transition from war to peace. Indeed, now that Nicaraguans had shown themselves capable of establishing a measure of tranquility, it was simply unacceptable, from a normative stance, not to build on that newly revealed competency. Second, the notables now understood that in order to present a viable alternative to the status quo, they needed to preserve the relative stability that the Binary Government had managed to provide. And last but not least, the notables themselves now saw the link between relative stability and rhetorical regulation.

The sequence of steps that the notables took in the direction of rhetorical regulation, in fact, sheds light on how a system of normative scheming can begin to change in virtually imperceptible yet crucial ways. The notables began by taking a hard look at General Tomás Martínez, the very same *caudillo* who had put together the Binary Government that they were so eager to dismantle. Three things were striking about the general. First, he was the country's only proven warrior, having amply demonstrated his military competence during the National War. This was a key factor, given that the unrepentant Walker remained a threat (until his execution three years later in Honduras). Second, and perhaps most importantly, all concerned parties knew of Martínez' willingness to assume a conciliatory stance. Third, this conciliatory inclination flowed from an old but still appealing sense of normative realism: To defend the nation from the Walker threat, Martínez reasoned, Nicaraguans would have to breathe new life into the ideal of the united national family and, by extension, resort to the traditional remedy of "forgetfulness."[16]

This normative realism resembled the Costa Rican prescription for a defensive posture vis-á-vis outsiders. But it also differed from it in two crucial ways. First, it relied on a familial formula for unity, as opposed to the Costa Rican emphasis on the exceptional character of "the people." Second, it stressed forgetting, as opposed to the Costa Ricans' emphasis on remembrance. This was Nicaragua, however, not Costa Rica, and Martínez was the ideal transitional figure for the notables, who used the Assembly to appoint him provisional president (1857–9).

In so doing, the notables not only divested the military *caudillo* of his dictatorial role, but also subjected him to a constitutional process that they aimed to control. The *caudillo*, for his part, explicitly acknowledged the power of the notables. In his inaugural speech of November 1857, he made two crucial rhetorical moves. First, he once again stressed reconciliation as an essential precondition for the nation's safety from foreign aggression.[17] Second, in the colonial tradition of the wise sovereign, he asked "all Nicaraguans" to "enlighten" him with "their counsel."[18] The signal was clear. The president was prepared to listen to the notables, Conservatives and Liberals alike.

This was a significant departure from previous presidential commitments to "listen," which had been typically extended as paternalistic, revocable concessions on the part of the executive (for contrast we need only recall Pedro Joaquín Chamorro's pronouncements prior to the National War). Moreover, this time the president's renunciation of arbitrary power was embedded in a constitutional process that was itself reassuring to the notables on two counts. First, by using the constitutional process to select a president already tied to his own conciliatory rhetoric, the notables minimized the risk of producing a destabilizing government. Second, the notables knew that they could retain the upper hand only if, through the constitutional process itself, they managed to establish cooperative links across partisan and localist boundaries.

[16] Gregorio Juarez and Rosalío Cortés, "Mensaje del Poder Ejecutivo Provisional de la República de Nicaragua en la Instalación de la Asamblea Constituyente en 1857" (Nicaragua: Imprenta del Gobierno, 8 November 1857).

[17] Excmo. Se. Jeneral (sic) Presidente Don Tomás Martínez, "Discurso, Acto de su Inaguración" (Managua: Imprenta del Gobierno, 15 November 1857).

[18] Ibid.

The Constituent Assembly began its work at the end of 1857 and finished in August of 1858. The Granada notables, in a striking and unprecedented show of deference to the localist sensibilities of their counterparts in León, supported the appointment of a high-ranking Leonese notable to the Assembly's presidency. Moreover, the new charter itself satisfied the antagonistic cities' longing for institutional prominence. The charter, for example, split the Supreme Court into two sections: one to be the domain of Granada, the other of León.[19] In fact, the notables' careful reach for geopolitical balance was palpable in the document they produced:

Each [territorial] department had the right to two senators, and two alternate senators. The deputies were apportioned according to the population; this resulted in two or three deputies per department, as well as two deputies assigned to the districts of Masaya and Managua.[20]

The notables also used the new constitution to level the playing field for notable clans and their various localities. As in Costa Rica, elections for president and deputies were held indirectly through an electoral college whose members were chosen at the canton level by a popular junta in which only citizens were allowed to participate. Senators were elected by a department junta of twelve electors chosen by their respective district colleges.[21]

As in the other oligarchic democracies of the nineteenth century, education and property requirements restricted the franchise. But at the same time, it is worth noting, that Nicaragua's electoral college steadily expanded from 570 members in 1858 to 940 members for the 1875–9 presidential term. This expansion was all the more significant since it stemmed partly from the creation of new districts within the camps' respective zones of influence, and as a result was geopolitically balanced.[22]

The Constitution's emphasis on geopolitical equilibrium reflected the notables' sense of realism. Experience had taught them never to underestimate the power of localist identities, or the destructive passions that perceived transgressions against such identities could unleash. But experience had also taught them about the potential benefits of political-institutional innovation. The very constitution-making process on which they had embarked provided them with immediate proof that in spite of their own past excesses, they were capable of constructive cooperation. This enhanced sense of competence, in fact, emboldened the notables to infuse the national electoral process with a significant measure of competitiveness.

To this end, the notables availed themselves of two devices. One was the requirement of no more than a simple majority of electors to elect a president. The

[19] Arturo Cruz, Jr., *Nicaragua's Conservative Republic, 1858–93* (New York: Palgrave/St. Antony's Oxford, 2002), 49.
[20] Ibid., 49.
[21] Ibid., 50.
[22] Ibid., 74.

other was a complex double-voting mechanism. This holdover from previous constitutions obliged electors

> ... to choose two candidates from the list, one of whom had to be a native of a district other than his own. It assumed that the first choice invariably would be the "favorite son". The elector's second vote, however, constitutionally required him to look beyond his immediate geographic constituency.... Further participation was encouraged by the device of having deputies and senators elected simultaneously with their own replacements, called *suplentes*, who would take the position in the event of incapacitation or removal from office of the primary holder. This in effect doubled the number of campaign slots.[23]

The notables well understood the long-term ramifications of the double vote. They were particularly aware of the fact that the double vote would stretch the geographical scope of the arbitration regime they were constructing. To be sure, even with the double-voting mechanism in place, the Conservatives of Granada and the Liberals of León would still be in an advantageous position to sway the votes of their respective satellite towns.[24] But the mechanism also introduced uncertainty into the fray, for if the candidates of one camp chose to exploit only their "natural" advantage by campaigning solely within the confines of their local clubs and native cities, they ran the risk that opposing candidates would choose to exploit the new rules and campaign on their rivals' turfs.

At a minimum, then, the stumping ground would be expanded. This expansion, in turn, would force competing candidates from the two rival power centers of Granada and León into closer contact not only with their old clienteles, but also with groups outside their traditional spheres of influence. In other words, candidates would have to transcend localist politics and contend with a more complex array of grievances and aspirations.

Partly in anticipation of the administrative challenges that lay ahead as a result of the more "national" character of the regime under construction, the Constitution provided for a system of department prefects. The objective here was twofold: Establish a web of communication between the administration and the multiple localities sprawled around it, and effectively deliver responses to the demands that the localities were now formally entitled to articulate. Appointed by the president,

> ... the prefect served as a liaison between the central authority and the local governments. *The prefects functioned as mini-presidents*: in each one of their departments they discharged a wide range of activities – such as finance, primary education, and policing – and were reminiscent of nothing so much as the old Bourbon intendants [emphasis added].[25]

---

[23] Ibid., 51.

[24] The Granada leaders were most influential in Rivas, Chontales, Masaya, Managua, and Matagalpa. The Liberals of León had the advantage with voters in Chinandega and Segovia.

[25] Cruz, *Nicaragua's Conservative Republic*, 51–2.

At every level, then, the Constitution crafted a framework for the vivacious play of multivocality and, more specifically, for the arbitration of the resultant competing claims to authority and resources. But the Constitution also created formal rules to address the new political vulnerabilities that resulted from the notables' ongoing experiment in tailored communicative regulation. Most strikingly, and as the notables could appreciate, the president was now exposed to new political dangers because power contenders might well mistake presidential tolerance for weakness. Conversely, if the president managed to play his conciliatory role to the hilt, he could well become the vital core of a super-prestigious presidency, thus exposing the notables themselves to the dangers of entrenched personalist rule.

To avoid either outcome, the notables embedded the rhetorical regulation of presidential conduct in a set of supportive institutions. In order to equilibrate power relations between the executive and the legislature, they gave the executive a longer (four-year) term, but they denied him the option of successive reelection. At the same time, to protect the president from illegitimate challenges, the notables followed the Constitution of 1838 in one key respect: They suppressed the office of the vice-presidency, which was widely regarded as an irresistible temptation for the second in command to let loose personal and disorderly ambitions.[26]

The notables' new charter went into effect on September 13, 1858, and the first presidential term under its aegis was slated for the period from March 1859 to March 1863. Martínez, at that moment the provisional incumbent, was elected president (1859–63). The new government immediately made an important inclusionary move: Though he was a Conservative with familial connections in Granada, Martínez appointed a Liberal from León to serve in his four-man cabinet as foreign minister. The Conservative government, moreover, concentrated vigorously on the promotion of coffee, cotton, and sugar exports – in retrospect, a striking initiative, since Latin American historiography has almost uniformly treated coffee as a "Liberal crop" and commercial expansion as a Liberal preoccupation.[27]

This developmental initiative worked as intended for coffee. Efforts at promoting cotton and sugar, in contrast, met at first with limited success given the acute shortage of labor. To tackle this problem, and in yet another move typically associated with Liberal regimes, the Conservative government issued laws designed to create a labor market. Agricultural judges, for example, were charged with the responsibility of "pursuing and capturing those who should fail to appear at work to which they had committed themselves, and punish[ing] them in accordance with this law, and [placing] them forthwith at the disposal of the *patrón*." The judges were also mandated to "prosecute as vagrants the

---

[26] See Cruz, Jr., *Nicaragua's Conservative Republic*, 49; Anselmo Rivas, *Nicaragua: Su Pasado, Ojeada Retrospectíva* (Managua: 1936), 186.

[27] A series of economic incentives were put into place by governmental decree, starting in 1858. See Cruz, Jr., *Nicaragua's Conservative Republic*, 52.

peons who are not inscribed in their respective districts, and those who on workdays should be wandering the streets, without visible occupation, unless they have matriculated with some *patrón*, who has granted them a license."[28]

In 1861, the Martínez administration proudly announced that "the program of peace and reconciliation" had yielded a degree of "confidence and harmony not seen since independence." And indeed, the land under cultivation expanded and coffee farms proliferated. Moreover, while the army in Costa Rica was reorganized and strengthened as a result of the National War against Walker, in Nicaragua the army shrank because the Conservative notables both wished to diminish the fiscal burden associated with a larger force and preferred a weak military. Put more directly, the Conservative notables did not hesitate to erode the coercive resources of their *own* General Martínez, now the president of the Republic.[29]

This move was both rational and normatively justifiable. The Costa Ricans, for example, might perceive harmony and a shared developmental agenda as part and parcel of their "natural" inclinations. But the Nicaraguans regarded them as fragile novelties to be politically fortified. From the perspective of the Conservative notables, this implied the purposeful debilitation of the military corps. Two reasons stand out. First, the Conservative notables had to protect themselves from a reversal to militarism, even if such a reversal were to be caused by one of their own. Second, and equally importantly, the Granada Conservatives understood that to build a developmental state, they needed to establish a relationship of sustained cooperation with the Liberals of León. They could hope to establish this relationship only if they first reassured the Liberals that the Conservative government had no intention of building up the military for self-seeking purposes.

Having provided the necessary reassurances, the Granada Conservatives took two crucial steps. First, they saw to it that the Conservative government handed over to the Liberals of León one of the most sensitive tasks of state building: the creation of civil, criminal, and procedural regulations.[30] Second, they began to minimize the tradition of anonymous broadsides, vitriolic pamphlets, and sweeping generalizations. Diverging from a rhetorical tradition previously closed to nuances of any sort, the notables began critically to assess their own camps' internal conduct and to eschew gross generalizations.[31] Indeed, they now claimed a "moderate identity" for themselves both in domestic and isthmian politics – the very identity previously monopolized by their Costa Rican counterparts.[32]

Their claim was credible. By 1862 Nicaragua had enjoyed five years of peace and progress. The elimination of the vice-presidency helped guarantee

---

[28] *Semanario La Unión de Nicaragua*, nos. 1, 2, 6 (Managua), January 5 and 12, and 9 February 1861.

[29] Ibid., no. 4 (Managua), 26 January 1861.

[30] Ibid., nos. 1, 2, 6 (Managua), January 5 and 12, and 9 February 1861.

[31] Ibid., no. 4 (Managua), 26 January 1861.

[32] Chamorro, *Biografía del Licenciado Jerónimo Perez*.

presidential preeminence, while the country's rapidly improving socioeconomic outlook lifted the fortunes of farmers, merchants, and the overlapping group of merchant farmers.[33]

Trust: Individuals or Institutions?

Nicaragua, it seemed, had emerged at last from the dark. As in Costa Rica, top-ranking Nicaraguan Conservatives now touted moderation and competence as essential attributes of the good president. Their Liberal counterparts agreed wholeheartedly. In fact, Liberals now proposed the reelection of the Conservative incumbent because, having demonstrated a "conciliatory character," he was ideally suited to serve as "pacific conciliator."[34]

The Liberal notables, in other words, clung to Martínez because he was the person who had actually delivered on the promise of bipartisan conciliation. Central to this notables' reason for depositing their trust in a Martínez was the fact that he had an established record that they could promote. The Conservative notables, for their part, repudiated his reelection precisely because he was no more than a personal embodiment of the practices they hoped to depersonalize, or, to use our contemporary parlance, the practices they hoped to institutionalize. Hence the strange paradox: While Conservative pamphleteers in Granada opposed the reelection of one of their own as unconstitutional,[35] Liberal pamphleteers in the city of León urged the citizens to accept his reelection for the sake of peace, and "to turn deaf" when others "speak to us of revolution."[36]

The clash between personalism and institutionalization shaped the behavior of the incumbent himself. At first reluctant to seek reelection, Martínez came to see it as a personal affront that his "own party" would object to his reelection.[37] The ensuing battle between personalism and institutionalization unleashed a round of Manichean struggles by entwining, once again, domestic and isthmian politics.[38] Here is how the Liberal leader of El Salvador, General Barrios, assessed the negative impact of Martínez' reelection on his project for Central American unification:

Passions and ignorance block the path that might lead [Central Americans] to form a single family. . . . So let them be happy with their impotent sovereignties, their ridiculous nations, and their localist interests . . . leave them submerged in misery . . . presenting to the world a parody of governments utterly without resources, incapable of affording

[33] Escobar, *Biografía del General Don Pedro Joaquín Chamorro*, 10.
[34] Ibid., 269–71.
[35] Ibid., 225, 257.
[36] Unos Amigos de la Paz, "Al Público" (León: Inprenta de Minerva, 24 August 1862).
[37] See Anselmo H. Rivas, *Los Partidos en Nicaragua* (Managua: La Prensa, 1936), 135, 138–9. First published in *El Centro-Americano*, 3 December 1881 to 14 January 1882.
[38] Pedro J. Cuadra Ch., *La Nacionalidad Centroamericana y la Guerra del 63* (Managua: La Prensa, 1952), 19–29. See also "Cartas Históricas del Presidente del Salvador Capitán General Gerardo Barrios" (San Salvador), 18 August 1862, and (La Libertad), 22 August 1862, both in *RAGHN* 11, no. 1 (April 1951): 26–30.

the paper and ink they use [on broadsides and pamphlets]; let them take pride in their comical smallness, and may they be damned by all generations to come [emphasis added].[39]

The idea that Central America could defend itself from foreign aggression through isthmian unity was an old one. Old, too, was the unification project – a project which had been historically undermined by national elites' obsession with the rank and prerogatives of their respective capital cities. It was no different this time. Isthmian unity remained at best a challenge, at worst a chimera.[40] Nicaragua's internal battles, in contrast, were now crucially different in the sense that the issues at stake now included, very explicitly, the debate of how best to foment trust. The Liberals, inclined to rely on the tried and true, argued for Martínez' reelection. The Conservatives, eager to solve once and for all the succession problem, firmly opposed it.

Martínez was reelected (1863–7), and personalized trust seemed to win the day.[41] The reelection, however, also set the stage for renewed violence. The leader of El Salvador issued this warning:

[Martínez'] triumph shall be ephemeral because it establishes *immorality* and produces general discontent.... If [the president] continues in power, anarchy is almost sure to follow....I still have three years to serve, and during these years *I will never trust in a weak and incompetent Chief who has an instinct for treason and is naturally hypocritical* . . . [emphasis added].[42]

The warning turned out to be an accurate prophecy.[43] Nicaraguan camps splintered and returned to Manichean rhetoric.[44] This rhetoric, in turn, deepened suspicions.[45] Suspicions led to preparations for war, and predictably, antagonists played into the hands of rivaling outsiders. One camp began to receive military support from El Salvador, the other from Guatemala. Finally, a rebellion exploded in 1863. All this ended with Martinez' victory on the battlefield.[46]

---

[39] "Cartas Históricas" (San Salvador), 10 September 1862, ibid.: 33–5.
[40] Chamorro, *Biografía del Licenciado Jerónimo Perez*, 280–97. For the impediments to the unification process, see Escobar, *Biografía del General Don Pedro Joaquín Chamorro*, 10.
[41] Anselmo H. Rivas, *La Elección del General Martínez* (Managua: La Prensa, 1936), 11, 273–6.
[42] "Cartas Históricas" (San Salvador), 25 November 1862, *RAGHN* 11, no. 1 (April 1951): 37–8.
[43] Barrios sided with the Nicaraguan Liberal *caudillo*. See Chamorro, *Biografía del Licenciado Jerónimo Perez*, 320.
[44] For resentment of betrayal, see Reyes Huete, *Estampas*, 75. For balance-of-power calculations, see Cuadra Ch., *La Nacionalidad*, 50, 65–6. See also "El Presidente de El Salvador, General Gerardo Barrios previene, bajo amenazas, al Gral. José María Medina" (San Salvador), 30 January 1862, *RAGHN* 11, no. 1 (April 1951): 194–5. For the aggravating role of "publications," see Pedro Joaquín Chamorro, *Máximo Jerez y sus Contemporáneos* (Managua: Editorial La Prensa, 1937), 253–4.
[45] See Cuadra Ch., *La Nacionalidad*, 18. See also *El Telegráfo del Pueblo*, 25 April 1863.
[46] See "Carta del General Tomás Martínez, Presidente de Nicaragua al General Rafael Carrera, Presidente de Guatemala" (Managua), 17 January 1864, *RAGHN* 3, no. 2 (December 1939): 160–1.

And yct, the notables' worst fear – reversal – did not materialize. Although victorious, Martínez from then on would waver in the face of a new dilemma in Nicaraguan politics. On the one hand, the presidency was constitutionally fortified, and thus the president himself felt strong enough to impose press censorship by decree. On the other hand, the president was also mindful of the fact that a new ideal of presidential conduct had begun to emerge, and that the virtue of moderation was at the core of this ideal.

The notables, too, were torn by divergent forces. One was the old fear of "demagoguery" and the damage it could inflict on vulnerable actors. The other was the emerging belief that, as five years of peace and prosperity had recently proved, Nicaraguans were capable of restraint.[47] Indeed, the twin goals of peace and prosperity had been established as realistic and feasible. These conflicting pressures made their way to the rhetorical arena itself. On one side stood those who argued that "demagoguery" was

...giving impetus to anarchy, exercising everywhere its *diabolical* influence.... possessed of the kind of guile and humility shown by a serpent that lowers its head the better to aim its *venom*...and which can be found in all the political circles of all the classes [emphasis added].[48]

On the other side stood those who argued that voices of moderation could indeed counterbalance fiery rhetoric. Newspapers, in fact, were created for the express purpose of placating, through "the sublime ministry" of the press, the "passions" of the moment.[49] This contingent deployed the recent memory of peace and prosperity to establish a link between enlightenment and dispassion, and to argue that both were possible in Nicaragua.

The argument not only resonated and prevailed, it also heightened the perception of the press as a potential source of enlightenment.[50] The president himself was forced to reconnect with the theme of moderation and conciliation.[51] And the emerging tendency among Conservative notables to define themselves as "liberal" in sentiment regained impetus.[52]

The presidential theme of moderation was not easy to sustain for Martínez, but sustain it he did. In fact, the climate of opinion made it necessary that he

...exhaust all political resources and apply all [his] faculties and those of the men in [his] government just to avoid [sending people] to prison and resorting to terrible, exemplary punishment....[53]

---

[47] The administration restricted freedom of the press through a decree that came to be known as the "Law of the Muzzle," a move that "scandalized" many Conservatives. Rivas, *Los Partidos en Nicaragua*, 148.

[48] *El Eco Meridional*, no. 4 (Rivas), 29 September 1864.

[49] *El Republicano*, no. 1 (Granada), 15 September 1866.

[50] *El Oriental*, no. 1 (Granada), 1 October 1866.

[51] Tomás Martínez, "Mensaje del Presidente de la República a la Legislatura Ordinaria de 1865" (Managua: Imprenta del Gobierno, 1865).

[52] *Amigo del Pueblo*, no. 1 (Granada), 21 June 1866.

[53] Señor Capitán General Presidente don Tomás Martínez, "Mensaje a la Legislatura de 1867" (Managua: Imprenta del Gobierno, 1867).

Innovative Silence

In 1867, Fernando Guzmán, a Granada notable, was elected to succeed Martínez. It became apparent at once that the Guzmán administration would continue the theme of conciliatory moderation that had consumed the last energies of its predecessor. In his inaugural manifesto to the citizenry, the president-elect emphasized the executive's role as a moderating influence:

I wish to extirpate, by means of a conciliatory policy if possible, the principal cause of our misfortune: the *dark political intolerance* that poisons the *patria*'s air by *pronouncing the dissident brother an irreconcilable foe....* As a private man, I can have my sympathies for any political camp, *but as a public man I recognize no political colors....*

This hybrid of colonial tradition and republican ideas in essence precommitted the incoming president to rules of rhetorical conduct now spelled out by the president himself:

...for the next four years I shall be the target of harsh criticism. But rather than fear criticism, I wish to listen constantly to the *frank, authoritative voice of the supreme judge of this era, the sovereign tribunal of civilization* [public opinion]. Opinion has its voice, and that voice is the press, a voice which I love and revere.... *[Even] calumny will find me indifferent; I shall despise it, but I will never persecute it* [emphasis added].[54]

This was also, in stylized form, a new hybrid model of arbitration. The rendition of the executive as a "fraternal" figure capable of tolerating "dissidence" amounted to a dual valorization of horizontal unity and pluralism. Moreover, this dual valorization was part and parcel of a modernizing vision. For it was precisely in the modern – the civilized – nations of the world that the notables gave "public opinion" pride of place.

The press, then, was explicitly recognized as the voice of the new sovereign judge. But how to recognize the press? The notables were the press. They were the men who founded, managed, and edited the influential journals and newspapers. Most of the time, they were also the pamphleteers who issued the anonymous letters and broadsides that inundated the public sphere. And invariably they were the respected orators who commanded the attention of the prestigious political clubs that dominated the various cities and towns.

So it was the notables who would play the role of sovereign judge and as such hold the power to reprimand and even attack the highest official in the land. It was the notables – Liberals and Conservatives alike – to whom the president offered himself as a permissible rhetorical target. And it was to the notables, whose freedom of expression previous governments had tried to constrain, that the president made two key points. First, governments, being fallible, are legitimate objects of criticism. Second, the motivations of opposition leaders

[54] S. E. el President D. Fernando Guzmán, "Manifiesto" (Managua: Imprenta del Gobierno, 1867).

can be valid, even laudable. Importantly, he buttressed these points with an explicit presidential promise to the notables:

Do not fear, there will never be a government agent who, armed with some wicked law, persecutes those who have the energy and patriotism to censure the abuse of power.[55]

The synergetic effects of presidential self-restraint turned out to be profound, even startling. To begin with, the government was able to move toward policy convergence. Most significantly, the new Conservative administration entered into an agreement with the Liberal camp whereby both sides committed to a "liberal" developmental agenda in the areas of education, transportation, and industry.[56]

Policy convergence was quickly complemented by a series of conciliatory moves, including an amnesty that brought the Liberal *caudillo* back from exile and bestowed upon him the status of cabinet minister without portfolio.[57] The dominant wing of the Liberal Party now argued for a "fusion" with the Conservatives, on the grounds that partisan divisions were no longer justifiable. As the Liberal leadership noted, Nicaraguans everywhere now liked to call themselves "liberals," and the partisan and localist boundaries that kept them apart had become "obsolete" and "petty."[58] For the Liberals, in fact, presidential resistance to the "merger" was tantamount to "rejection." This is how they put it:

The need to *fuse* the two parties was proved to [the president]. And let us not deny it, it was a beautiful hope. However, [the president] and his secretaries used this idea to practice their treacherous policy . . . [he] forged instruments of vengeance [and] became the separatist of the Nicaraguan family, provoking the present struggle . . . every initiative we made was maliciously misinterpreted, and gave rise to suspicion. *Every Nicaraguan who wanted to be close to him, he rejected* [emphasis added].[59]

The Liberals had reason to be confused. Wherever one turned, things seemed out of kilter. The Conservative administration openly declared its "liberal spirit." And the hierarchy of the Catholic Church, which in Central America had often

---

55 Reyes Huetes, *Estampas*, 98–9.
56 The administration also joined in a pacifist agreement sponsored by the Nicaraguan Liberal *caudillo* and several Costa Rican notables (1868). The agreement stipulated that the parties to the agreement would peacefully seek the "natural" union of Central America, a Liberal goal.
57 The president also pardoned the Conservative notables jailed by his mentor and predecessor. See Chamorro, *Máximo Jerez y sus Contemporáneos*, 338–9. The president's predecessor and mentor perceived this conciliatory gesture as personal betrayal. The former president was soon alienated from his successor and, in alliance with the Liberals, launched a revolution against the new president. See Tomás Martínez, "El General Martínez a sus compañeros," *RAGHN* 8, no. 1 (April 1946): 86–9.
58 "Carta de Jerez al Presidente Guzmán" (León), June 26, 1869; "Decreto de Instalación del Gobierno Provisional"; "Manifiesto de Jerez a los Nicaraguenses," *RAGHN* 8, no. 1 (April 1946): 69–72.
59 "La Revolución Actual I (sic) su Objeto," ibid.: 86–9.

been at odds with Liberals and labeled them "enemies" of religion, now leveled this very charge at the Conservative president.[60]

In this rapidly changing environment, the administration relied on the most influential Conservative notables for guidance. The solution they provided was simple but sagacious: The president, they specified, ought to consider as "foes" only those disgruntled Liberals who had actually taken up arms; everyone else, including nonbelligerent Liberals, ought to be treated as "friends."[61] In keeping with this more flexible distinction between friend and foe, the president proceeded to put down the rebellion, then used his victory as a platform to issue an unconditional amnesty for all involved.[62]

The amnesty decree explicitly stated the president's wish to show his "benevolence" to the rebels, whom he said had been either forced or misled into rebellion. Moreover, the decree was significant because it openly declared the president's hope of avoiding

...ruin and misfortune for the beautiful city of León and its prosperous department, whose fate is a matter of great and well-deserved concern to the Government.[63]

Coming from a Granada Conservative, the remark about León was momentous. Less obvious but even more important was the beginning of something new at that point: For the first time in the country's history, a government actually set out to create a conciliatory historiography. In the official account of the failed rebellion, the identity of the executive was inextricably tied – as the royal sovereign's once had been – to the virtues of benevolence and patience. The rebels' "subterfuge," to be sure, had compelled the president to launch a military offensive. But once victorious, he had recognized the fact that the vanquished were "brothers," and ought to be treated as such.[64]

Expanded Possibilities

The idea of presidential moderation as a core principle of government seized the imagination of the notable class. For it was this idea that would enable the notables as normative schemers, when faced with the difficult task of candidate selection, to craft a compelling reason that would simultaneously allow them to

---

[60] "Al Vicario General" (León), 4 November 1869, *RAGHN* 9, no. 3 (1947): 84–5. See also "Para Conocimiento del Público se dan a Luz" (León), 1869, *RAGHN* 9, no. 1 (April 1947): 94–5.

[61] Letter of 18 July 1869. Cited in Anselmo H. Rivas, *La Situación en 1869* (Managua: La Prensa, 1936).

[62] The revolution, it is worth pointing out, took no account of the Central American balance of power, which at that moment precluded assistance to the Nicaraguan rebels from any of the neighboring governments. See Enrique Guzmán, "Retrato a Pluma de Máximo Jerez," *Revista Conservadora* 2, no. 8 (March/April/May 1961): 118.

[63] "Decreto Concediendo a los Rebeldes Amnistía General," 24 October 1869, *RAGHN* 8, no. 1 (April 1946): 42–4; Rivas, *Nicaragua: Su Pasado, Ojeada Retrospectiva*, 60.

[64] See Anselmo H. Rivas, *Reseña de la Revolución de 1869* (Managua: La Prensa, 1936), 207–16. First published as *Exposición del Informe del Ministro de la Gobernación y Guerra* (Managua: n.a., 1870).

champion different candidates *and* improve their collective chances of getting the winner "right." From then on, only notables endowed with the appropriate "temperament" would be considered viable contenders. Indeed, the Conservatives chose their next candidate on the basis of his unassuming character. The candidate, however, refused the nomination, and even wrote electors around the country, warning them that he was unqualified to hold the office of the presidency.

The candidate's reticence served only to reassure the electors, who not only disregarded his warning but gave him an overwhelming victory. The candidate, for his part, tried one more time to avoid his fate by declaring himself "unfamiliar with the science of government."[65]

Claiming lack of competence was an ingenious tactic, since competence was now regarded as an essential trait of a good president. The tactic, however, proved ineffective: Congress refused to release the president-elect from his duty. As the congressional resolution stated, his refusal to take office might lead Nicaraguans to "a new partisan fight which, by reviving passions, might usher into anarchy.... If the sacrifice demanded of [the president-elect] is great, so is his celebrated patriotism and his love for the preservation of public order."[66]

The reticent president performed very well. He managed to keep Nicaragua out of isthmian entanglements. More importantly, he maintained harmony between the branches of government, actually begging Congress *not* to delegate to the executive the task of drafting the necessary legislature, as Congress was planning to do. Thus, in a strange reversal of historical patterns, the executive and the legislature struggled not for the prerogative to legislate, but for the opportunity to delegate legislative authority. Indeed, the executive went so far as to request that Congress both assume and execute that authority. In short, he asked Congress to govern.[67]

The more harmonious the relations between the two branches of government, the less incentive the political parties had to seek external alliances. The frequent isthmian entanglements of the past began to yield ground to a controlled isthmian policy based on flexible neutrality. As rulers in neighboring countries fell and rose, Nicaragua quickly turned its back on the deposed, and just as swiftly recognized those ascending to the office. This capacity to respond to external turmoil without embroilment contributed to the growing sense that while previously one could speak only of Nicaraguan governments, now a Nicaraguan *regime* was emerging – one whose presidents called themselves

---

[65] Vicente Quadra, the president-elect, went so far as to plead with Congress: "You must take into account my frail constitution. As you will see from the attached documents, I suffer from illnesses which prevent me periodically from engaging in active exercise and more especially in mental work." See "Renuncias a la Presidencia de 3 Personajes de Nicaragua, La Renuncia de don Vicente Quadra," *RCPC* 26, no. 127 (April 1971): 26–9.

[66] Ibid., 26–9.

[67] Vicente Quadra, "Mensaje Dirijido [sic] al Soberano Congreso por el Señor Presidente de la República [Vicente Quadra] en Marzo de 1871" (Managua: Imprenta del Gobierno, March 1871).

Conservative but could also be perceived as Liberals. Granada itself had become the bastion of a hybrid Conservatism.[68]

The growing perception of an emerging regime and a dawning "liberal era" was also reinforced by the increasingly common occurrence of peaceful power transfers from one elected president to the next. The longer the electoral mechanism proved effective, the more progressive and civilized the notables felt. The mechanism, however, did not work in a vacuum. The electoral victor invariably enjoyed the endorsement of the incumbent, whose prestige, in turn, depended heavily on his public conduct while in office. And his conduct, as in Costa Rica, was deemed appropriate so long as he displayed the defining virtues of a good president. In Nicaragua, these virtues were moderation and competence.[69] Similarly, the outgoing incumbent looked for those same qualities in the candidate he chose to support.

The self-identification of Conservative administrations with "liberalism" was accompanied by an ever firmer policy of freedom of the press.[70] This policy increased the vibrancy of political opinions and enhanced the geographic scope of multivocality. Most likely to keep these two powerful trends under control, the notables began to identify "seriousness, calm, and repose" in the public realm with "civilization."[71]

This identification became particularly salient with regard to the lesser municipalities, which often turned into a stage for violent, albeit contained, conflict during congressional elections.[72] Also noticeable was the declining use of familial metaphors by leading elites and their more frequent use by minor elites. Specifically, as the notables of the leading cities converged into a mainstream, they began to forge a new, more flexible construct; however, the elites of the lesser localities, now demanding "equality" and "justice" from the regime, found the rhetoric of the familial model quite useful for expressing their grievances.

This was especially the case with the subaltern municipalities as they set out to convey exactly what they meant by equality and justice. The Conservative town of Masaya, for example, merely wanted one of its "sons" to be elected deputy. Other localities shared the sentiment. One newspaper declared that

...the departments...take it as an affront and an injustice that they are obligated to elect the sons of mothers [cities] other than their own.[73]

---

[68] In a letter of 4 October 1871, Guatemalan Liberals even reached out to one of Granada's notables as if he were a fellow partisan. See *RAGHN*, 9, no. 3 (1947): 24.

[69] The Liberal historian José Dolores Gámez actually saw the transfer of power as a process of inheritance, whereby the incumbent invariably "left" the presidency to a trusted associate. See Gámez, "Promesa Cumplida," 10 February 1899, reprinted in *RAGHN* 16–17, nos. 1–4 (1957–8): 20–30.

[70] This often meant that "conciliators" were exposed to the dangers of "demagoguery" – dangers they sought to preempt through additional demonstrations of tolerance and conciliatory gestures. See Unos Ciudadanos, "Nuestra Opinion" (León: Imprenta del Istmo, 22 June 1872).

[71] *Los Anales*, no. 3 (Masaya: Imprenta del Orden, 1 August 1872).

[72] For illustration, see *Los Anales*, no. 9 (Masaya: Imprenta del Orden, 1 November 1872).

[73] *Los Anales*, no. 10 (Masaya: Imprenta del Orden, 15 November 1872).

The familial model also served the lesser notables particularly well because it enabled them to appeal for justice and equality in terms compatible with the clan-based structure of influence and distinction. They could, in short, equate justice and equality with "acceptance" into the national apex of prestige. As the notables of Masaya now stated, "We want [for deputies] men from the circle that prevails here *and* who are also members of the [Conservative] circle that prevails in the Republic."[74]

This meant, simply, that their local elites wished to be recognized as deserving of inclusion in the deliberations of the most distinguished citizens – that is, the national elites. But this aspiration, they claimed, had been denied to them when the winner in their congressional elections – a Granada notable – had been "elected" by a few against the will of an intimidated majority. So what did it matter, they concluded, if the official gazette published the government's guarantee of free election?[75]

Beyond the locals' wish "to figure on the national stage" – to belong to the president's circle – something else can be gleaned from the editors' complaint: their trust in the president himself.

The more honest the president is, and the more he wishes to grant constitutional guarantees, the less he is obeyed by some of his subordinates and circles of support . . . [76]

In this, too, the president was now perceived in the manner of a king: as wise and benevolent but surrounded by unworthy advisers. These advisers did treat localities differently. For example, in 1872 a conspiracy against the government was prepared in León. But this time, the government named one of the key conspirators as the city's chief of arms. It even allowed him to organize the local officialdom and troops. The former conspirator now controlled León, but he was also *part* of the national government.[77]

The ruling notables, in other words, dealt with localist complaints on a case-by-case basis. This approach, however, was less useful when dealing with the powerful intraparty reactions caused by the blurring of partisan identities. Specifically, the more the Liberal and Conservative camps developed a shared view of just governance, the more they provoked the emergence of "authentic" factions within their own ranks. Elections typically activated these emerging factions.

On the side of the Conservatives, the Authentics sought to isolate the "Liberals" in their midst, accusing them of "blasphemy" and "alerting" all

---

74 Ibid.
75 Ibid.
76 Ibid.
77 The power-sharing arrangement worked as planned. Reyes Huete, *Estampas*, 101–3. Against a background of domestic stability, Nicaragua entered into treaties of friendship with Guatemala, El Salvador, and Honduras, and on the basis of these treaties was able to maintain a neutral stance when in 1875 those three countries became embroiled once again in war. See "El Ministro de Relaciones de Nicaragua, Don A. H. Rivas, Explica la Conducta Leal y Pacífica de su País," 5 September 1876 (Managua: La Prensa, 1936), 217–32.

"Catholics" to repudiate the "detestable candidacy" of the suspect faction.[78] The True Liberals, for their part, warned their camp that election of a Conservative president would mean a return to "monstrosity."[79] In addition to partisan themes, the True Liberals deployed localist rhetoric. The *patria*, they argued, was in the hands of "four wicked men from Granada."[80] And, of course, they mixed localist and partisan appeals. Their own Liberal city of León, they claimed, had been "infested" by Conservatives after "being fed the poisoned bread of the Granadans." Most telling of all, the True Liberals implored their brethren to resist the tendency towards a de facto merger with "the other":

Be LIBERALS with honor and patriotism. Do not be Conservatives. Realize that their infernal farce only brings ruin to the country. . . .[81]

The True Liberals of lesser localities were similarly alarmed by their local populations' growing acceptance of Conservative candidates. Once again, the appeal to localist loyalty was salient:

Apart from a few honorable exceptions, [Nicaragua] has always been led by men lacking conscience, sense of abnegation, and patriotism. *Today the light of civilization finally shines on our horizon, and the progress of other pueblos stimulates us to follow their example.* So it is necessary that we emerge from the sepulchral stillness in which we are kept by the exclusionary and retrograde circle of Granada [emphasis added].[82]

The argument here seems to reveal a contradiction of sorts. On the one hand, the Conservative Republic had created the conditions that rendered civilization an attainable goal. On the other hand, the regime also generated the impression that a ruling circle was forming in the country. Dig a little deeper, though, and the roots of localist and partisan reaction become visible. The ruling circle was in fact made up of political hybrids whose emerging identity hinged on a declared commitment to conciliatory rhetoric and administrative competence. Delivering on this commitment, in fact, enabled the regime to attract new supporters across localist and partisan lines, and broadened the legitimacy of "judgments" handed down by the circle of hybrids. But the regime's success also threatened old political identities and attendant notions of fairness.

Rewards were no longer to be allocated on the basis of blind loyalty to *caudillo*, camp, and locality. Instead, the distribution of authority, prestige, and material resources now depended on the claimants' contributions to a political-developmental program that proceeded according to its own logic and required far more time than had the swift delivery of rewards from patron to client.

---

[78] Unos Católicos, "Una Advertencia" (Diriá: Imprenta del Orden, 19 July 1874).
[79] Los Amigos del Pueblo, "La Libertad en Lucha con la Intriga" (León: Imprenta de J. Hernández, 8 September 1874).
[80] Los Liberales, "Voto del Partido Liberal" (León: Imprenta de Minerva, 22 September 1874).
[81] Unos Patriotas Liberales, "Leoneses!" (León: Imprenta de J. Hernández, 3 October 1874).
[82] Los Verdaderos Labradores de Chichigalpa, "A los Libres Ciudadanos de Chichigalpa" (León: Imprenta de J. Hernández, 30 September 1874).

This shift in the meaning and delivery of justice created pockets of severe discontent and prompted renewed claims to authenticity:

We have recently seen an insignificant little paper which under the signature "Some Laborers of Chichigalpa" tried to deceive the naive making them believe that the [Conservative] candidacy is a symbol of peace. . . .

[They] appropriate our name in order to profane our high destiny. . . . For us the symbol of peace can never be a Conservative from [Granada and the Eastern Departments]. We the honest . . . have nothing to fear. . . . Our hopes and progress are deposited in [León and the Western Departments]. Signed: The True Laborers of Chichigalpa.[83]

This resistance notwithstanding, the drive toward integration of high-ranking Liberals into every new Conservative administration continued apace. Indeed, the pressure for conciliatory politics and policy convergence was unrelenting at the elite level. The mechanics of the momentum were reminiscent of the Costa Rican case. Each president actively sought intercamp agreement and policy convergence.[84] But the more a president succeeded in these tasks, the greater the pressure on his successor to build on these prior achievements, perhaps even transcend them.[85]

The Chamorro administration that came to power in 1875 illustrates the point. Its predecessors, individually and collectively, had made visible strides both on the political and economic fronts, strides that in turn raised expectations for succeeding administrations to deliver broader-based progress. Chamorro's notables responded to the pressure: In cooperation with prominent Liberals, they intensified the promotion of coffee through a series of economic reforms. Indian communal lands, or *ejidos*, were privatized – in the name of civilizational progress – to make room for the expanding coffee sector. Even the church's land was diminished.[86] In addition, as the Costa Ricans had done decades earlier, the state awarded prizes to efficient coffee producers, and it provided subsidies, technical information, and land grants in an all-out effort to stimulate the production of the bean. Finally, the state plowed ahead with its infrastructural development agenda, emphasizing the extension of telegraph nets and railways, and encouraging the construction of a credit system to finance coffee (mainly through British banks). By 1890, the reforms had yielded impressive results: Coffee was now the country's principal export.[87]

---

[83] Ibid.
[84] Reyes Huete, *Estampas*, 105.
[85] By publicly espousing this Liberal cause of Central American unity, and by actively pursuing the project diplomatically with other countries, President Chamorro made further inroads into the Liberal camp. See "Cartas Sobre Unión Centroamericana Cruzadas entre el General Máximo Jerez y el Presidente de Nicaragua don Pedro Joaquín Chamorro" (Tegucigalpa), 12 November 1875; (Managua), 9 December 1875, *RAGHN* 3, no. 1 (January 1939): 77–81.
[86] Dora María Tellez, *Muera la Gobierna: Colonización en Matagalpa y Jinotega (1820–1890)* (Managua: Universidad de las Regiones Autonomas de la Costa Caribe Nicaraguense [URACCAN], 1999), 15–18, 32–4.
[87] Booth, *The End and The Beginning, The Nicaraguan Revolution*, 20–1.

The upshot of all this was a gathering momentum that carried the regime to new heights of accomplishment. As at previous inflection points, the presidency became once again an intimidating prospect for potential candidates, especially now that they were selected on the basis of their unassuming character. In 1878, the Conservatives' nominee – favored even by the most outspoken Authentics – rejected the nomination.[88] He was, in fact, so determined to escape his fate that he publicly reminded the notables of his friendship and business ties to the sitting president, implying not so subtly that it would sully both the good name of the incumbent and his own if he were to accept the offer.[89]

The Conservatives began to look for a replacement, then thought the better of it and returned to the charge. This is the argument that one of their most influential notables made:

I am a friend of the nominee, but if I were a member of Congress and had to vote on this matter of the election, I would level against him the necessary fines to take away his fortune cent by cent. I certainly would not allow his will to prevail over that of the nation. This would be a scandal and a lethal precedent.... What man of honor would [in the future] accept the position that [the candidate] has renounced for no good reason?

The credible threat of financial punishment enabled the notables to extract compliance from their candidate. This method of coercion, interestingly enough, was proposed by the notable who in the next election would renounce the presidential nomination himself. "I lack the necessary capital," he would contend, referring to the expenses associated with the office. "I cannot be asked to drown out my conscience, and to expose my honor."[90]

Like his predecessor, he too was forced to serve. In his 1879 inaugural address, this new reluctant president, Joaquín Zavala, lamented journalistic excesses, but in the same breath extolled the "precious" value of freedom of the press, and guaranteed its exercise.[91] And like his predecessor, he fulfilled his commitment. The press freely engaged in lively, often acrimonious debates on a wide range of topics, from ideology and policy to the political virtues and vices of various notables.[92] Moreover, because the president stood in silence when publicly attacked, Conservatives and Liberals were able to continue their cooperation in government, and despite the intensity of public exchanges, their "views" continued to converge.[93]

---

[88] Rivas, *Los Partidos en Nicaragua.*

[89] "La Renuncia de don Joaquín Zavala" (El Pital), 1 May 1878. Reprinted in *RCPC* 26, no. 127 (April 1971): 29–30.

[90] Ibid., 29–30.

[91] Reyes Huete, *Estampas*, 109.

[92] Carlos Selva, *Un Poco de Historia* (Guatemala: Ediciones del Gobierno de Guatemala, Colección Los Clásicos del Istmo, 1948), xxii–xxiii, xxvi–xxvii.

[93] The new president, however, restricted the freedom of the Church to criticize the government in one particular way: No priest or cleric would have the right to characterize any government decree as inimical to religion. See "El Artículo 283," *Revista Conservadora*, 2, no. 9 (June 1961): 131.

Historiography at Stake

By the early 1880s, the Conservative Party, now entwined in a cooperative relation with its Liberal counterpart, had begun to write an official history of the regime. The narrative is revealing. To begin with, it was organized around the fall-from-grace theme, and went as follows: In the post-independence period, liberalism emerged as "the most compelling ideology" for "all enlightened men of good will." Such men were drawn to liberalism because they wished "to transform the old Spanish colonies" by guaranteeing "citizens' rights" and supporting their "legitimate aspirations." Unfortunately, these "Apostles of Liberalism" failed to deliver on their promises, and thus squandered the "prestige" that they had attained with their "seductive propaganda." Worse yet:

... filled with pride, they soon showed their disorderly appetites, and discarded their patriotism and love of the people, which as it turned out, had been nothing but a mask. At that point, all the sane elements of society that had supported them went their separate way; they left to establish the Conservative Party, which grew daily as more honest people became disillusioned. This is how the Conservative Party was formed by men of diverse ideas who nonetheless were linked by a shared love of order, which is the indispensable fountain of liberty and progress.

From the perspective of mainstream Conservatives, the theme was quite serviceable. On the one hand, it allowed them to keep their liberal ideas, which the narrative identified with enlightened men of goodwill. On the other hand, it allowed them to impugn the early advocates of those same ideas – the "Apostles of Liberalism."

The diversity of ideas that reigned among Conservatives, the narrative also explained, had a blurring effect on partisan lines. Political parties remained undefined in the near term, even as they sought in vain to carve out distinct identities.[94] And for as long as "true" political parties remained undefined, our historian concluded, the differences in the composition of the two camps would be a numerical one:

In both parties the same men, passions, weaknesses, and ambitions come into play. The difference has always consisted in the fact that the party which today calls itself Conservative invariably gathers a *greater number* of patriots who safeguard the interests of the majority while in the other camp these patriotic elements are the exception. . . . [95]

And yet the narrative also revealed a sense of optimism about the country's capacity for peaceful coexistence – an optimism that was far from groundless given the country's experience with orderly succession under the Republic:

On several peaceful occasions, during which order has seemed consolidated, there emerged the outline of the two political parties. Eventually, these two parties shall govern the country alternatively, and jointly bring it prosperity and greatness.[96]

[94] Rivas, *Los Partidos en Nicaragua*.
[95] Ibid., 135–6.
[96] Rivas, *Los Partidos en Nicaragua*, 140–4.

Intended as a historiographic foundation for the regime, the narrative aimed all at once to glorify the mainstream Conservatives, diminish the recalcitrant forces within both parties, bolster the bipartisan consensus at the core of the Republic, and render plausible a future based on partisan yet civil competition. But neither the account itself nor the normative judgments it made about would ever attain anything like hegemonic status.

At the most immediate level, this was so because the parties' internal fragmentation along authenticity cleavages triggered competing historiographic projects. To be sure, even the most recalcitrant Authentics acknowledged that the country now enjoyed previously unimaginable welfare. But they also held passionate and divergent opinions about the path that had ushered in this happy state of affairs. Indeed, each disappointment and failure in the country's political history was, once again, an object of contention. "True" partisans set out to assign blame for the post-independence wars, the breakup of the Central American Federal Republic, the recurrent political assassinations, the leaders' unholy alliances, and the disloyal maneuvers associated with their turbulent past.[97]

At a more subtle level, however, the regime's attempt to establish a historiographic foundation was trumped by its own contradictions. This was not obvious at first. If anything, even as True Liberals and Conservative Authentics castigated one another for their "filthy broadsides,"[98] mainstream leaders continued to share in a growing sense of national "regeneration." The newspaper of the intellectual society, *El Ateneo*, for example, asserted that even the most pessimistic now harbored hope. *El Ateneo* itself had been founded to promote the sciences and literature, precisely because its founders could at last envision a future in which knowledge, not brawn, would garner individuals public recognition.[99] *El Ateneo* even declared that

...the world marches inexorably towards religious, scientific and political unity. Progress means nothing if not the synthesis of all material and spiritual powers into the common expression of universal law.[100]

But significantly, the society of *El Ateneo* "absolutely" forbade all political discussions in its meetings and in its newspaper's articles. Exempted from this prohibition, of course, were all discussions "on the various forms of government, public law, or the ways that might help lead Central America toward national reconstruction."[101] The Athenian society's self-censure left ample space for theoretical investigations into the nature of government and its relation to the future of Central American institutions.[102]

---

[97] "*El Centro Americano* versus *El Termómetro*," no. 20, 12 May 1880, *RAGHN* 3, no. 1 (January 1939): 83–95.
[98] For a vivid example, see *El Termómetro*, no. 8 (Rivas), 18 June 1882.
[99] *El Ateneo*, no. 1 (León), 1 September 1881, *RCPC* 26, no. 129 (June 1971).
[100] *El Ateneo*, no. 3 (León), 1 November 1881, Ibid.
[101] *El Ateneo*, no. 4 (León), 1 December 1881, Ibid.
[102] These theoretical debates typically ignored the realities of the times, such as the complex connections between the 1881 Indian rebellion in Matagalpa and the conflict between the

These theoretical investigations came at a time when the regime seemed to reach its zenith. In 1882, the True Liberals warmly endorsed the Conservative candidate, Adán Cárdenas, broadly perceived as a Liberal at heart. Not too long before, this faction of the Liberal Party had denounced the historical duplicity of the Conservatives. But now they declared that the Conservative Party had

... finally opened their eyes to the light. At last convinced of their impotence to oppose the torrent of our progress, they now begin to capitulate by accepting Adán Cárdenas as future president, a capitulation which bestows honor upon them.[103]

The problem was, of course, that the Conservative candidate was such a Liberal that he even favored the Jesuits' expulsion from the country, and as a result was repudiated by the Conservative Authentics. To complicate matters further, because the regime had delivered "justice" to the various political forces partly through a policy of geopolitical balance, Authentic Conservatives, once concentrated in Granada, were now a visible force in the Liberal bastion of León. And in fact, the Conservative Society of León protested the Cárdenas candidacy, on the grounds that although the candidate was a nominal Conservative, in truth he was a Liberal "deserving of a place [in a gallery] of radicals."

Cárdenas' electoral victory deepened the Conservatives' internal cleavage to the point that the True Liberals of León felt sufficiently confident to predict the "death" of the Conservative Party.[104] Moreover, as it became clear that the Conservative Party's majority was now liberal minded, mainstream Liberals began advocating a formal merger between the two parties:

All of us who profess liberal principles, regardless of our label [Conservative or Liberal]...let us form a single party, and adopt a unifying program....Let the [Conservative factions] of laggardly ideas go their way; let them form the nucleus of the true conservative party.[105]

Ultimately, the election of the Conservative Cárdenas filled Liberals with a sense of triumph. History, it seemed, was finally on their side:

... the past has crumbled ... and the sons of darkness – pallid and anguished – flee while covering their ears, trying to drown out their conscience, which shouts indignantly, Cain! What have you done with your brother's blood?![106]

Reversal

In 1884, a notable born to Nicaraguan parents in Costa Rica founded the *Diario de Nicaragua*, the country's first daily. His reasons are quite telling. Nicaragua,

---

regime and the Jesuits. See, for example, Enrique Miranda, "La Guerra Olvidada," *RCPC* 29, no. 144 (September 1972): 75–82.

[103] *El Termómetro*, no. 11 (Rivas), 16 July 1882.
[104] *El Termómetro*, nos. 18, 20, 3 and 17 September, 1882.
[105] *El Termómetro*, no. 20 (Rivas), 17 September 1882.
[106] *El Termómetro*, no. 23 (Rivas), 8 October 1882.

he said, had come to "enjoy unlimited freedom of the press." But the press, he added, had turned into an outlet for political "passions" in a country now split between the official press and the press of the opposition, both of which were perceived as "partial" in intent and "combatants" in practice. A daily, he believed, could provide a middle ground between antagonists; serve as a beacon of "science, patriotism and rectitude"; represent "rational interests;" and by dealing on a daily basis with a wide range of issues and reforms, function as a kind of "perennial plebiscite."[107]

The daily's experiment in impartiality was a clarion call for notables to deal explicitly with the problems engendered by the regime's paradoxical success. The Republic's incipient official historiography, with its accusatory thrust aimed directly at the first "apostles of Liberalism," was obviously not the answer. On the contrary, it accentuated the emerging conflict. The Authentic Conservatives and the True Liberals believed their parties to be in imminent danger of succumbing to the enemy within. And the mainstream – the enemy within – sharing the *lingua franca* of the extremes, had no alternative cognitive framework to combat the notion that further convergence was in fact one more step toward existential catastrophe.

Two examples illustrate the point. One is the president himself. A nominal Conservative generally perceived to be a Liberal at heart, he both carried on with the regime's tradition of executive self-restraint *and* took the regime's increasingly Liberal agenda to a new level by challenging the power of the Jesuits. This daring move pleased the True Liberals, offended the Conservative Authentics, and alarmed everyone in between. Such a variety of reactions was not inherently perilous. Rather, the threat to the regime lay in the shifting boundaries of the permissible that resulted from actors' changing vulnerabilities as they came up against the limits of the new "reality." The Conservative president, by taking a new, more radical step in the direction of Liberalism, lost the active support of mainstream Conservatives, who envisioned the future of government as an exercise in partisan alternation but nevertheless identified the founding Liberals as the guilty party in the country's disastrous history. The Authentics, for their part, became vulnerable to their new president, who now was determined to defend his progressive credentials. The result was that all the principals, including the president, vowed to respect the regime's rhetorical norms, but only so long as this respect made realistic sense from their particularist perspectives:

As a slave to duty, I have restrained all spontaneous impulse to repress the unjust and malicious attacks leveled against my dignity as president. . . . by the enemies of order. . . . I showed boundless tolerance for their abuses, and met their libels with contempt. *Still, they interpreted my moderation as weakness* . . . engaging in one conspiracy after another, they went so far as to attempt to seize the military garrison of Granada. My tolerance reached its limits . . . [emphasis added].

[107] Rigoberto Cabezas, "Fundación de un Diario, 1884," *RAGHN* 8, no. 1 (April 1946): 76–87.

The government "discovered" subversive plans, frustrated them, and sent the accomplices in this "criminal project" to trial. But "incendiary" publications against the government continued, and some "enemies of order" even went outside the country to look for allies.[108]

The second example that illustrates the dangers associated with identity transformation in a context of fundamental Manicheanism is the founder of the daily *El Diario de Nicaragua*. Taking to heart the regime's dictum that the press was "the sovereign judge" of governmental behavior, the daily's founder dared criticize the president. Theretofore, such criticism had not only been allowed but expected. However, unlike his predecessors, this president felt unprotected by the formal rules of the game. After all, what good were these rules if his opponents were willing and ready to break them? The president, once a symbol of self-restraint, was now compelled to participate directly in the clash of politics. He sent the daily's founder into exile.

The official gazette justified the president's harsh measure as "constitutional" on two counts: Since the journalist had been born in Costa Rica, he was a "foreigner"; in addition, the government "suspected" him of illicit intent. In his address to Congress in 1885, the president himself alluded to the incident when he spoke vaguely of individuals who "had scandalized the country by promoting disturbance and commotion through calumny and slander."

The letter that the exiled editor wrote the president from abroad captures the Republic's progress and its limits. The journalist reminded the president that "honorable men do not fear the press," and singled out his administration as unworthy of its predecessors because rather than gather around the presidential seat "ethical and wise advisors," the president had formed a "black circle" of "inept yes-men" who had allowed him to "violate" the most "precious" of Nicaraguan freedoms: freedom of the press.[109]

Controlled turmoil now became the hallmark of partisan politics as political leaders and followers alike wavered between established norms and new fears. Institutions were heralded as victorious over *caudillismo*, yet the True Liberals and Authentic Conservatives perceived themselves as engaged in combat with "the enemy within."[110] For the Authentics, the "progressive" elements of the Conservative Party were dangerous "impostors" unworthy of the Conservative identity.[111] The Liberal Party was similarly torn.[112] And like the Conservatives, the Liberals were also increasingly bitter in their attacks across party

---

[108] Dr. D. Adán Cárdenas, "Mensaje Dirigido por el Señor Presidente de la República al Soberano Congreso en su XIV Período Constitucional y Contestación del Señor Presidente del Congreso," 15 January 1885 (Managua: Tipografía Nacional, 1885).

[109] Letter to President Adán Cárdenas from Rigoberto Cabezas (Guatemala), 14 December 1884. Reprinted in *RAGHN* 8, no.1 (1946): 90–8.

[110] *El Mercado*, no. 491, Managua, 19 January 1886; no. 504, February 4, 1886.

[111] Ibid.

[112] Federico Navarro, "Segunda Carta Abierta a D. Vicente Navas" (León: Imprenta del Istmo, 1886).

lines, reverting to postcolonial dichotomies, such as order versus anarchy and progress versus reaction.[113]

Against this ominous background, a "progressive" Conservative, Evaristo Carazo, won the election of 1887. By then, the gulf between the "authentic" and the "progressive" factions of the Conservative Party was such that when the latter's candidate won, the former felt they had been "defeated" by a foe.[114] Conversely, supporters among Conservatives and Liberals touted both the outgoing and incoming presidents as "trustworthy" men, and took pride in the peaceful transfer of power from the one to the other.[115]

In his inaugural address, the president-elect stressed a lesson from the past. "Liberties," he asserted, "are meaningless amidst disorder." Though a "progressive" Conservative with many Liberal sympathizers, the president now returned to a theme that had lost prominence under his predecessors: the executive's role of disciplinarian and guardian of order.[116] The combination of progressive ideas and a paternalistic approach garnered the president few allies. In fact, when two years later he died in office, the president had few mourners. The Conservative Authentics even celebrated his demise with open displays of jubilation, and looked forward to the commencement of the succession process.

In the absence of a vice-president (recall that the office had been deliberately eliminated to protect the presidential incumbent from vice-presidential jealousies and transgressions), the new president was chosen through a *sui generis* but constitutionally mandated procedure. Like a lottery, this procedure hinged on the blind selection of a successor from among a pool of five senators. One Conservative notable of the period observed that while this procedure might seem like an "absurd extravagance" to an outsider, in Nicaragua it had "closed the door to civil war."[117]

The procedure did indeed work in 1889, infusing Conservatives and Liberals alike with a renewed sense of optimism. The editors of the Conservative newspaper *El Diario Nicaraguense* explained that because the new president, Roberto Sacasa, had been selected through this semirandom process, his administration was of "noble origin," that is, "not beholden to any political personage, locality, circle, or party." The editors also gave the new president good marks for his choice of close advisers; more significantly, the editors reasserted their own authoritative voice:

El Diario Nicaraguense shall continue to ... *censure* and *applaud* the government as it sees fit ... [emphasis added].[118]

[113] Idem. "Quincenal Leonés, Dedicado a Servir los Intereses del Partido Liberal" (León: Tipografía de J. Hernández, 1 January 1887).

[114] Selva, *Un Poco de Historia,* xlii.

[115] *El Imparcial,* no. 56 (Managua), 4 March 1887.

[116] Crnel. D. Evaristo Carazo, "Discurso Inagural del Señor Presidente de la República, 10. de Marzo de 1887" (Managua: Tipografía Nacional, 1887).

[117] Anselmo H. Rivas, *La Candidatura de Zacate* (Managua: La Prensa, 1936), 186. Originally published in *El Centro Americano,* 22 July 1882.

[118] *El Diario Nicaraguense* (Granada), 23 August 1889.

The stress placed by *El Diario* on the selection's randomness suggested that *fortuna* had given the regime the gift that all Central Americans had wished for so long: a new beginning. *Fortuna*, it seemed, was even generous enough to ensure that the new president should be not only a notable who hailed from León but was also renowned for his pleasant nature and rectitude. This felicitous combination, in fact, earned the new administration the label of "Providential Government," and garnered it the explicit and enthusiastic support of "various political circles, as well as the municipal corporations, the clergy, the merchants, the farmers, the colleges, the schools, the entire nation."[119]

Anchoring their hopes on Sacasa's sterling reputation – the key factor in the crafting of compelling reasons for leadership selection under the Republic – the notables turned a blind eye when the president-elect first arrived in the capital city surrounded by a Leonese entourage shouting the localist slogan "Long Live León!"[120] The notables even ignored Sacasa's reliance on the Liberal intellectual José Dolores Gámez, whose view of history "as an avenging torch against the wicked" would help shape both Nicaraguan historiography and politics.[121] Indeed, *El Diario* gave the new administration the benefit of the doubt, and only mildly criticized its delay in making appointments to secondary positions in the cabinet because such a delay – fifteen days – generated "uncertainty, political intrigue, absurd claims, and attempts to revive the fatal spirit of localism." *El Diario*, in fact, defended the administration from the increasingly frequent charge of "localism."[122]

But as Sacasa began to select his government functionaries mostly from León, he gave the impression of breaking what was by now a defining feature of the arbitration regime: the appointment to the cabinet of notables from various localities. The new president also affirmed his identity as a son of the city of León; disarmed Granada; and proceeded to form small loyalist circles in the major cities, thus reducing the executive's dependence on the parties and their leading notables. Finally, although he integrated Liberals into his government, he kept them at a distance, as distrustful of them as he was of his own Conservative Party. For this reason, he received no credit from the Liberals, but still provoked localist anxieties among fellow Conservatives in Granada, who watched nervously as he gave increasing prominence to Leonese government officials and increased León's military preponderance.[123]

The more the new administration distributed employment and business opportunities among those who offered their loyalty, and as the two parties grew mutually suspicious, Manichean identity formation and historiographical battles gained renewed intensity.[124] Words like "virulence" and "calumny" were

---

[119] Selva, *Un Poco de Historia*, 5.

[120] Ibid., 6.

[121] Quoted in Chamorro, *Máximo Jerez y sus Contemporáneos*, 7.

[122] *El Diario Nicaraguense*, no. 1526 (Granada), 23 August 1889.

[123] Selva, *Un Poco de Historia.*, 7–10.

[124] This dispute had partial origins in previous debates about the 1824 war and in the guilt of various rival clans and localities. See Juan Bautista Sacasa's defense of his father's posthumous

again commonplace. So were categorical oppositions. The Liberals claimed that the Conservative *El Diario* characterized the typical Liberal as "an assassin, as well as a thief, an alarmist, and a blasphemous scoundrel," while the typical Conservative was depicted as "honest, decent, immaculate, virile, and dignified." Naturally, the Liberals found this distinction "laughable," and went on to demonstrate that Nicaraguan history since independence had been tainted not by Liberals, as *El Diario* claimed, but by the Conservatives. Every assassination, every civil war, every invasion, and every period of anarchy was attributed to the Conservatives before concluding, "We repeat, the history [of the Conservatives] is full of perfidy and treachery, thievery, fire, torture, tears and blood."[125]

The Liberals, too, ultimately abandoned Sacasa.[126] The precariousness of his position notwithstanding, Sacasa chose to seek the presidency in the next elections. Supported by Leonese localists, state employees, and the police, he won the vote in elections marred by violence at the polls and by the opposition's abstention. Congress, however, still had to ratify the procedure and declare a victor. At that point, León was armed, and Sacasa's followers, through a series of deals and corrupt maneuvers, managed to gain control of various congressional committees. Only one problem remained: The opposition controlled the Senate, and had enough members in the House to render the outcome unpredictable. Faced with this last uncertainty, Sacasa opted to bring to Managua a Leonese mob, which invaded the Congress and, as the procedures were under way, "spontaneously" demanded the election of Sacasa – a combined replay of the colonial and postcolonial practices of dramaturgical obedience and inexorable collective ire. Soon thereafter came the suppression of the press and the expulsion of opponents accused of conspiracy.[127]

In 1891, President Sacasa justified his "deeds" by claiming that they had been shaped by the belief that "our calamitous political divisions ought to be relegated to oblivion." Referring to the expulsion decree, he added:

I was able to issue this grave and transcendental order only after doing violence to the sentiments in my heart, which is always inclined toward benevolence. And I had to go against the tendency of my tolerant and self-abnegating character.[128]

By 1892, the president had made numerous enemies in both parties. The Liberals felt insulted by the president's restrictive policies.[129] The Conservatives saw

---

reputation (León), 28 December 1874, in Tomás Ayón, *Apuntes Sobre Algunos de los Aconte cimientos Políticos de Nicaragua: De Los Años De 1811 A 1824* (León: Imprenta del Istmo, 1875, 1–7, and Ayón's letter to Sacasa (León), 26 December 1874, in his *Apuntes*, 9.

[125] "Defensa del Manifiesto de los Liberales de Chinandega contra Ataques de El Diario Nicaraguense que Dirije don Anselmo H. Rivas" (León: Tipografía de J. Hernández, 1889).

[126] Selva, *Un Poco de Historia*, 11–14, 24.

[127] Ibid., 14–19, 24–5.

[128] Señor Presidente Dr. D. Roberto Sacasa, "Manifiesto" (Managua: Tipografía Nacional, 1891).

[129] See Pedro Ortiz, "Ultrajes Reales y Delitos Imaginarios" (Nicaragua: Tipografía el Centro-Americano, August, 1891), *RAGHN* 8, no. 1 (1946): 71–80.

in the president a mortal foe of the Republic, which they claimed had brought such prestige to Nicaraguan politics that the country had come to be regarded as "the Switzerland of Central America."[130]

And yet, as late as January 1893, President Sacasa trivialized the creeping instability as "little summer clouds," and continued to justify his restriction of freedom of the press:

We must confess that [in Nicaragua] not the best use has been made of this freedom. Its passionate and hurtful language has been frequently aimed at the government.... I have willingly tolerated it, as I consider it one of our most valuable guarantees. It was only when it brazenly proclaimed rebellion and advocated the use of crime to obliterate authority that the police, in the name of public security, intervened temporarily.[131]

His opponents saw something else: a villain unmasked by his own intractable vices:

In a short time, he who had seemed humble became arrogant. Once having appeared upright, he now revealed himself to be perverse...frantic with ambition.... *Seduced by the Devil*, he has gone down that tortuous path which leads to the ruin of nations... and earns the hatred of the living generations, the execration of those yet to come, and history's eternal damnation [emphasis added].[132]

By April of 1893, Conservatives (mostly notables from Granada) and the Managua Liberals, led by a powerful coffee grower, General José Santos Zelaya, were allied and in armed rebellion against President Sacasa. An insignificant locality by all accounts, Managua had been designated capital city in the middle of the nineteenth century, in an effort to minimize the localist disputes between Granada and León over the seat of the national government. With the Conservatives' successful promotion of the coffee economy, the Republic transformed Managua and its surrounding sierras into a potent engine for the production of coffee. The pueblos of the sierras, for so long the satellites of Granada, began by century's end to gravitate politically toward Managua.[133]

The Conservative rebels, who in league with the Liberal Zelaya finally dealt the Republic its death blow, initially believed that the rebellion would usher in its restoration. As the Conservative notable who had once lauded President Sacasa in *El Diario* now put it:

[This revolution] is not the consequence of a shadowy conspiracy...*this [is] not a violent revolution but an insurrection, the psychological pinnacle of a peaceful evolution that has been in effect for the last three years*...[emphasis added].[134]

---

[130] "Lo que Va de Ayer a Hoy: o El Pasado y el Presente de la República" (Managua: Tipografía de Dionisio Estrada, 1892).

[131] S. E. Sr. General Presidente Doctor Don Roberto Sacasa "Mensaje al Congreso de la República, Inauguración XVIII Período Constitucional" (Managua: Tipografía Nacional, 1893).

[132] Selva, *Un Poco de Historia*, 9.

[133] Cruz, Jr., *Nicaragua's Conservative Republic*, 19.

[134] Anselmo H. Rivas, *El 28 de Abril* (Managua: La Prensa, 1936), 251–5. First published in *El Diario Nicaraguense*, 2 July 1893.

The bipartisan revolution against Sacasa triumphed to the extent that the offending incumbent was removed. But the hopes that the leading Conservative elders harbored for bipartisan regime construction were soon dashed. The young Conservatives who participated in the fighting now enthusiastically embraced the ideals associated with military prowess, while the Liberal leadership quickly turned against their Conservative allies. Liberals and Conservatives once again plunged the country into civil war.[135] Worse yet, thirty years of institutional learning were about to be obscured by the unrestrained return of Manichean historiography.

Conclusion

The links that connect normative scheming, political vocality, and regimes of arbitration are complex but not impossible to trace. The Nicaraguan experience is a case in point. Arbitration models based on familial logics of justice and cohesion not only prescribed uniformity of opinion but also stunted individuals' "meaningful participation" through civic "speech" and "acts of decision."[136] Indeed, the imperatives of compliance and fealty led "communicatively competent individuals" to form camps incapable of external dialogue. Worse yet, camps proved vulnerable to internal discord precisely because elites diminished their own communicative competence by strictly adhering to familial visions and articulations of good government. Elites thus simply could not get past their understanding of civil wars as "fratricidal" clashes – "abominations" for which no camp was willing to take any measure of responsibility.[137]

By mid-nineteenth century, no arbitration institution or individual arbiter could attain broad legitimacy. Locked in yet another mutually debilitating war, the Nicaraguans turned to a foreign soldier of adventure with grand political ambitions of his own. Next door, the Costa Ricans were aghast. As one of their diplomats put it:

The light and indolent Nicaraguans, driven by rancorous sentiments, will more readily join with the enemy of their own kind than with each other. Presumptuous, envious, and clinging to their backward habits and vicious customs, they will be deaf to all counsel; perhaps they will breathe war, and offer themselves as the instrument that spreads conflict to their neighboring republics.[138]

---

[135] For the convoluted alliances and counteralliances between Liberals and Conservatives that brought down the Republic, see José Madriz, "Por Nicaragua" (San José), 1904–5, *RAGHN* 28–9, nos. 1–4 (January–December 1964): 41–52.

[136] J. G. A. Pocock, "The Ideal of Citizenship since Classical Times," in Gerson Shafir, ed., *The Citizenship Debates* (Minneapolis, MN: University of Minnesota Press, 1998), 32.

[137] See the official monthly *NRO*, September 1838, see also "Discurso del Presidente del Congreso Federal Diputado J. B. Basilio Porras, 20 de Julio de 1838, y Otros Documents," *AGHG* 13, no. 3 (March 1937): 317–30.

[138] Comisión de Investigación Histórica de la Campaña de 1856–5, *Documentos Relativos a la Guerra contra los Filibusteros* (San José, 1856), Document No. 215.

War they breathed. It took a Central American effort to oust the foreigner, and even after all the suffering and devastation, the Nicaraguans could not negotiate a peace agreement. Yet it was this postwar negotiation stalemate that prompted the first political-cultural improvisations, so tentative and fragile that only in retrospect can they be identified as the beginnings of the Republic.

More deliberate and dramatic were the subsequent attempts by the Republic's notable class to regulate Manichean communication and to build the companion institutions to communicative regulation. The results were dramatic as well. By mitigating both the realistic calculations and the normative injunctions that had blocked bipartisan dialogue and cooperation, the Republic's political-cultural and institutional adaptations expanded the horizon of legitimate political alternatives. Most strikingly, an effective regime of encompassing arbitration began to emerge. Clannish, partisan, and localist grievances were increasingly addressed in simultaneous and comprehensive fashion. Moreover, the state addressed those grievances through oligarchic balancing rather than *caudillo*-led violence. This meant, among other things, that the resultant distribution of vocal influence and material resources among notables and localities, now much more stable and equitable, forged a combination of interests, ideas, and loyalties that in turn allowed for sustainable policy making. The state's developmental capacity surpassed all expectations, as the nation, left prostrate by successive wars, began to construct and expand a robust coffee economy.

Yet even the most successful experiments in political-cultural and institutional innovation must ultimately reveal their own flaws. How those flaws are addressed becomes both the measure and the defining challenge of the regime that sponsors them. The Republic was no exception. By concentrating on the regulation of Manichean practices without eradicating or at least reshaping its *lingua franca*, the notables left the regime open to the destructive uses the *lingua franca* of Manicheanism. And these uses did become a pressing problem precisely because the regime's successes had a powerful transformative impact on every aspect of political, social, and economic life. The emergence of a bipartisan mainstream of ideas, opinions, and practices, for example, generated cleavages within both political parties along identity lines, with "authentic" factions rising to castigate and expel the enemy within.

This dynamic was compounded by the consequences of yet another success. Specifically, by effectively promoting socioeconomic progress, the notables triggered the dramatic rise of new economic power centers; yet by politically integrating these centers at a pace too slow to keep up with the centers' growing fortunes, the regime engendered "outsiders" willing to exploit the parties' internal contradictions. These economically powerful political outsiders, in fact, would in short order connect with the regime's incipient historiography and its residual Manicheanism to reorganize identity construction in particular and politics more generally. As we are about to see, the regimes that succeeded the Republic borrowed little else from its decades-long experience. Determined to establish their own understandings of justice and fairness, and operating within the contours of what they deemed realistic, these new regimes cast aside the Republic's delicate equilibrations. Ultimately, they too would find themselves in the hands of yet another foreign arbiter, this one vastly superior in strength and prestige. The twentieth century was just around the corner.

7

Tropical Histories

Paradise and Hell on Earth

> A history is absorbed by its effects. At the same time... these effects change themselves without the past history ceasing to assist in [their] promotion. Each retrospective interpretation feeds off the pastness of an occurrence and seeks to articulate it anew in the present.[1]
>
> –Reinhart Koselleck

The complex dynamic outlined above by Koselleck is actually observable in part because political leaders make rhetorical use of "authorizing figures" – the icons of their nation's history – to bolster their own stature and plans of action. Think of American leaders' frequent invocation of great predecessors such as Thomas Jefferson and Abraham Lincoln.[2] In Nicaragua, however, the notables who built the Regime of the Thirty Years, worthy as they might have been of enduring recognition, were never to become national authorizing figures. By way of contrast, the nineteenth century notables who built the Costa Rican polity are to this day publicly revered by new generations, both at the elite and popular levels. This reverence is especially evident at moments of perceived or real danger. In 1983, for example, as civil wars raged in Guatemala, El Salvador, and Nicaragua, the government of Costa Rica linked its proclamation of "perpetual neutrality" to the country's exceptionalist history.[3] More significantly still, the country's president framed the proclamation as a direct extension of a policy established by the nation's founders – authorizing figures who from the distant past could still speak

---

[1] Reinhart Koselleck, *Futures Past: On the Semantics of Historical Time* (Cambridge, MA: MIT Press, 1985), 216.

[2] See Donald Rice, *The Rhetorical Uses of the Authorizing Figure: Fidel Castro and José Martí* (New York: Praeger, 1992), xi.

[3] The proclamation was the result of pressure applied on the government by a large segment of the political class. One of their chief concerns was the presence of anti-Sandinista leaders and rebels in Costa Rica.

persuasively to those living in the present. Consider a key passage from the declaration:

> ... our first chief of state was a countryside teacher ... who told Congress in 1829 that Costa Rica was simple and small, but that its government ... rooted in the virtues, morality, and good judgment of its people, was able to keep the peace. ... Three decades later, another teacher was elected president of the Republic ... and he informed Congress that Costa Rica had tried to no avail to stop violent conflict in Central America. ... Later, a young lawyer ... became president. He said then: our government, respectful of the law, will not interfere in the affairs of others, save to ... mediate and restore harmony. This policy [he believed] "flow[ed] from the Costa Rican people's character, which is an enemy of complications and not at all fond of adventures."[4]

The portrait, though naive in form, conveyed a powerful tripartite message. First, Costa Rica's statesmen were not generals or *caudillos*; they were educators and men of law. Second, they had preserved domestic peace by avoiding isthmian entanglements, and ventured beyond the nation's limits only to proffer their good offices. Third and finally, these leaders derived their sense of confidence from their conviction that their policy of neutrality stemmed from the defining virtues of the Costa Rican people.

Now consider a passage from a historical essay by one of Nicaragua's foremost Sandinista intellectuals and political leaders. The essay, it is worth noting, was written in 1975, scarcely three years before the Sandinista Revolution rocked Central America and ultimately led the Costa Ricans to reinforce their traditional neutrality.

> From its beginning, the history of Nicaragua has been nocturnal; a closed night in whose confines the humble can only whimper; a night of tyranny, dispossession, and inquisitorial intolerance; a night of centuries-long dominion by an obscurantist church and by *señores* who, with hanging noose and knife in hand, are the owners of human lives and farming estates.[5]

In its own dismal way, this depiction, too, is naive. It provides only inhumanity, oppression, and misery. And in its own way, it too conveys a powerful image: hell on earth. But a ray of light is implied. If someone were to crack open that "closed night," then the "humble" might be rescued from the anonymous yet despotic figures who rule in the dark and impose their rapacious injustice on the weak.

On this reading of Nicaraguan history, the man who would dare to take on this daunting task was Augusto César Sandino, later to become the authorizing figure of the Frente Sandinista de Liberación Nacional (FSLN). But so daunting was this task and so despondent the retrospective that Sandino's "appearance"

---

4 Luis Alberto Monge, "Proclama de Neutralidad," 17 November 1983, in Carlos José Gutiérrez, ed., *El Pensamiento Político Costarricense: La Social Democracia*, vol. 2 (San José: Libro Libre, 1986), 346–57.
5 Sergio Ramírez, "El Alba de los Desterrados," written in Berlin, 1975, and published in Ramirez' *El Alba de Oro: La Historia Viva de Nicaragua* (Mexico: Siglo Veintiuno Editores, 1983), 55.

on the scene was literally a "phenomenon" that required explanation. In 1980, the FSLN intellectual who had crafted this historical narrative of hell on earth, Sergio Ramírez, set out to do just that in a lecture to the Escuela de Cuadros (Academy) of the newly victorious FSLN. The first step in Ramírez' disquisition was to establish the historical-political context in which the redeemer first appeared:

By 1910, what we [had] in Nicaragua [was] an oligarchic faction, reduced to the role of bureaucratic intermediary. This faction [was] not even part of an alliance with the United States' financial axis of power, which by then had nailed its claws into Nicaragua. In docile submission, this [oligarchic] faction simply allowed the country to be dispossessed of its economic means.[6]

At this point in Ramírez' historical account, the Manichean view of politics seems on the verge of turning outward, in the direction of the north. But then, almost in the same breath, Ramírez also acknowledges that at that historical moment, Nicaragua's elite factions were embroiled in their own cutthroat conflicts. In fact, the Conservative *caudillo* Emiliano Chamorro – derided by Ramírez as one of the United States' "most beloved proteges" and one of "the favorite godchildren of imperialism" – showed no compunction about rebelling against a government that had come to power as a result of a U.S.-sponsored election.[7]

In this narrative, then, Nicaraguan elites' docile submission to foreign interests is momentarily trumped by those same elites' internecine hostilities. And it is here that the account, almost imperceptibly, turns complex enough to make space for Sandino:

Amidst factional wars, Sandino introduces for the first time the popular variable; but also at this moment, Nicaragua is about to enter the constitutionalist war of 1926 [over the issue of presidential succession].[8]

The last sentence alludes to the inescapable historical fact that Nicaraguan political leaders were once again about to wage war in to settle competing claims to the highest position of authority in the land. In other words, the polity was in the midst of yet another succession crisis. The issue at stake was the most basic: Who is to be the great arbiter? But this issue implicated other key points, such as the meaning of justifiable power, the assignation of rights to vocality, and the establishment of just claims to material rewards and status.

As in Costa Rica, moreover, two different types of regime legitimation were also at stake: One was based on the substantive criterion, the other on the electoral principle. The Costa Ricans, as we saw, managed to conciliate the two only after the Revolution of 1948. The Nicaraguans, in contrast, continued to struggle violently over the proper balance between the two. Their Manichean

---

[6] Ramírez, "Sandino: Clase e Ideología; Entorno Social de la Lucha Sandinista," in Ramírez, *El Alba de Oro*, 119.

[7] Ibid., 123–6.

[8] Ibid., 126.

system of normative scheming, in the end, precluded a sustainable balance; indeed, this system gave rise both to performance-based regimes and to the opposition groups that brought them down.

Dictatorial Arbitration and the Substantive Criterion

The Liberal regime of General José Santos Zelaya began to take shape in a very exclusive meeting in 1893. Those in attendance included two of the most important political figures of the city of León: General Anastasio Ortiz and the notable Francisco Baca. Now that the Regime of Thirty Years was nearly in ruins, General Zelaya, the powerful coffee grower from Managua we met in the previous chapter, had joined the Leonese to form the revolutionary junta that was to impose Liberal dominance over the nation. A rapporteur was present as well. After the principals – Ortiz, Baca, and Zelaya – worked out the details, the agreement was committed to paper. The deciding moment then came when the rapporteur intoned a question: "This *junta* shall be presided by . . . ?"

The scribe lifted his pen and waited for an answer – for someone to utter the name of the man who was to lead the Liberal revolution. General Ortiz and the notable Baca, long-standing rivals, glanced at each other suspiciously. As a heavy, awkward silence fell over the room, General Zelaya rose to his feet with great aplomb and, as if history had whispered the answer into his ear, he dictated to the scribe: "This *Junta* shall be presided by General José Santos Zelaya." A new exchange of glances and awkward silence followed. Zelaya, however, remained standing. When the scribe finally wrote in Zelaya's name, the general "showed much satisfaction."[9] The meeting was over, and the revolution was on.

The Republic's successful developmental policies had turned Zelaya's regional department, Managua, into a new center of economic power, brimming with the restless ambitions of its coffee magnates.[10] But while the Republic had made them prosperous, it had been slow to accord them oligarchic vocality. Zelaya was among these voiceless magnates. Although he had married into a prominent Granada family, he hailed from a locality not yet fully integrated into the geopolitical balancing act of the Republic, and so he was, for all practical purposes, from another world. Also left out were the magnates' second-rank allies: more modest coffee growers from Managua's surrounding regions.[11]

The Republic's regime of arbitration had given these actors material puissance but not the kind of political voice enjoyed by the notables of Granada, León, and their old provincial allies. This disjuncture helps explains why the

---

[9] Events of the meeting related by the scribe to Carlos Cuadra Pasos. See the latter's *Obras II* (Managua: Colección Cultural, Banco de América, 1977), 218–19.

[10] Humberto Belli, "Un Ensayo de Interpretación Sobre las Luchas Políticas Nicaraguenses," RCPC 32, no. 157 (October–December 1977): 53–4.

[11] For the sources of Zelaya's preeminence among Managua Liberals and the "coffee aristocracy," see José Madriz, "Por Nicaragua" (San José: Imprenta de Avelino Alsina, 1904–5). Reprinted in *RAGHN* 28–9, nos. 1–4 (January–December 1964): 43–4, 47–9.

Managuans who participated in the bipartisan rebellion against the Republic's last president, and subsequently fought their own war (ushering in Zelaya's reign), showed little familiarity with and even less respect for the Republic's rhetorical practices and companion institutions. Indeed, the Manichean persuasion strategies that the Republic had regulated once again stirred the emotions that animated the revolutionary war and motivated the soldiers who waged it. From the perspective of Zelaya and his closest allies, the end of the Republic signaled the end of thirty years during which Liberals, "noble" and "progressive," had suffered "persecution" at the hand of the "perfidious" Conservatives.[12]

This persecution, in truth, had really been more like political indifference, or exclusion at worst. And even this did not apply to the old ranking Liberals. It was the ascending Liberals from the new localities whom the Republic failed to include with sufficient speed. But the Republic's account of its own history, and its view of the two political parties' development, did persecute the Liberals, if only in figurative terms. Recall that in this account, the country's first Liberals figured as impostors, while their Conservative counterparts figured as the worthy carriers of Liberal ideas.

Zelaya and his circle connected passionately with this partisan rendition of history, and set out to replace it with their own, but they threw into oblivion the Republic's other legacies. Most notably, once in power, Zelaya dispensed with the practice of presidential abstention from rhetorical politics. If anything, as his own regime of arbitration lost legitimacy, he staked an increasingly strong claim to univocality. The justification for this dangerous move was present from the start, precisely because Zelaya brought with him the resonant themes that had prevailed in the public sphere prior to the Republic. One familiar theme from the postcolonial period was reconciliation based on deliberate forgetting of the past. The second theme was the justifiable use of power against disorderly elements.[13]

After being elected president by the Constituent Assembly of 1893, Zelaya also gave prominence to less profound but equally recognizable preoccupations dating back to the postcolonial period. These ranged from the lofty, such as the project of Central American unification, to the remedial, such as curing the moral "vices" that accounted for the country's degeneration. These preoccupations were already prominent in Zelaya's inaugural address.[14]

Viewed retrospectively, Zelaya seems caught in a time warp, oblivious to the strides the Republic had made prior to its turbulent final years, and unaware of the benefits the country had reaped from avoiding isthmian entanglements. But if we put ourselves in his place, it is possible to appreciate how his status as a

---

[12] Adolfo Altamirano, "Por Nicaragua, por el Partido Liberal por el General Zelaya" (Managua: Tipografía Nacional, 11 July 1904), *RAGHN* 28–9, nos. 1–4 (December 1964): 78–9.

[13] José Santos Zelaya, Anastasio Ortiz, and Pedro Balladares, "Mensaje Dirigido por la Junta de Gobierno a la Asamblea Nacional Constituyente, y Contestación del Presidente de Esta Ultima" (Managua: Tipografía Nacional, 1893).

[14] Gral. D. J. Santos Zelaya, "Manifiesto Inaugural del Presidente de la República de Nicaragua" (Managua: Tipografía Nacional, 1893).

political outsider to the Republic shaped his understanding of Nicaraguan reality. From his vantage point, the fact that the Republic had for over thirty years
managed to tame the country's postcolonial nightmare was nowhere near as
prominent as the fact that this nightmare had been tamed in part by suppressing
postcolonial dreams. These dreams still held sway over Zelaya. As many before
him had hoped, he believed that a Central American union would bestow dignity and stature upon its member states, as well as protect them from external
threats. A highly visible and muscular bureaucratic apparatus, he was also convinced, would endow the state with the power to evoke pride and awe in the
citizenry. Under his rule, Zelaya hoped, the country would attain such rapid
progress that peace and liberty would at last appear as one on the national
stage.

The Republic had come close to reconciling those two seemingly alien goals
by imposing oligarchic arbitration over *caudillismo*. But the imposition of this
regime had required more profound innovations. Recall the patient construction of cooperative links between Conservative Granada and Liberal León,
and the careful calibration of power relations between the branches of government. Recall further the fine balancing act between the notable ranks and the
president. And above all, recall the self-conscious regulation of political argumentation that made possible these formal and informal institutional redesigns.

Under Zelaya, all these advances were discarded. Even the Republic's measured view of progress was now challenged:

> The Liberals likened progress to a "violent and explosive volcano," while the
> Conservatives . . . saw progress as "slow development . . . a transformation which is first
> verified through ideas, subsequently through customs, and only then, through laws."[15]

For Zelaya, the logical starting point was the establishment of a formal, legal
structure meant to reshape existing customs. The Constituent Assembly, which
elected Zelaya president, produced a charter that enshrined every strand of
postcolonial Liberal idealism, and like the earliest post-colonial programs of
both Conservatives and Liberals, it guaranteed unrestricted freedom of expression.[16] These legal changes, though old in inspiration, would require a change of
established practices. The Republic's customary avoidance of Central American
politics, for example, would have to be replaced by an activist policy, and the
president would have license to speak without restraint.

The notion of reshaping customs by legal fiat alarmed the more experienced
members of Zelaya's cabinet. José Madriz, for one, even tried to moderate the
Constituent Assembly's hand, warning that

> . . . in no way can one break fully with the past without courting the danger of a violent
> reaction. . . . It is possible for thoughts to soar too high in the realm of theory.[17]

[15] Arturo J. Cruz, Jr., *Nicaragua's Conservative Republic, 1858–93* (New York: Palgrave/Saint
    Antony's Oxford, 2002), 134–5.
[16] Ibid., 134.
[17] Ibid., 133.

Madriz based his argument on a "realistic" assessment of the overly ambitious nature of the charter. But he also worried about the Assembly's disregard for the formal and informal institutions that the Republic's notables had tailor-made for the Nicaraguan "reality."[18] From this perspective, moreover, the Republic's controlling norm, moderation, was also at peril. The Assembly, for example, put an end to the custom of splitting the Supreme Court into two chambers: one for Granada and the other for León. The new unified court was to be located solely in León. This decision – itself an act of arbitration – was meant to satisfy the localist pride of Zelaya's Leonese allies. But the decision also managed to aggrieve both the Conservative bastion of Granada and the up-and-coming capital city, Managua, which was the focal point for the new and powerful Liberal coffee growers like Zelaya himself. In addition, the Assembly introduced the office of the vice-presidency, which went to a Leonese notable, General Ortiz. This too was meant as a recognition of León's importance. But on the flip side, the decision placed two military *caudillos* – Zelaya and Ortiz – in close proximity to each other and, to boot, at the very apex of power.

Soon, Madriz's concerns, grounded in the residual normative realism of the Republic, began to look like an accurate prophecy. The interim Law of Public Order, although drafted by progressive Liberal intellectuals, violated the spirit of the Liberal constitution waiting in the wings. The Law, for example, gave the president the discretionary power to judge whether "false news of subversion" was being propagated, to determine guilt, to identify the guilty, and to mete out punishment, which could consist of prison sentences and/or steep fines.

Other departures became evident once the new constitution went into effect. Here it is important to note that Zelaya relied heavily on two Liberal notables for ministerial advice. One was an ardent advocate of Manicheanism; the other sought moderation of the type he had observed among the Republic's notables.[19] The former prevailed, in part because he was the more persuasive of the two. But he also prevailed because by arguing that the progressive faction of Nicaraguan Conservatives was in league with the Conservative president of Honduras, he gave Zelaya a compelling reason to invade the neighboring country. This was key. Zelaya's ascent, after all, was bolstered by his promise of national greatness. By invading Honduras, he could begin to pursue his ultimate ambition: to establish a chain of Liberal governments across Central America – with Nicaragua and himself as the strongest links in that chain.[20]

In 1894, Zelaya invaded Honduras. His vice-president, General Ortiz, was the commander of the Nicaraguan troops. They seized the Honduran capital, expelled the Honduran president from the country, and installed a Liberal in his stead.[21] Not surprisingly, when General Ortiz returned home to his native city

---

[18] Madriz, "Por Nicaragua," 38–9.
[19] Cruz, Jr., *Nicaragua's Conservative Republic*, 135.
[20] Ibid., 136.
[21] Cipriano Orúe, *Presidentes de Nicaragua: Investigación Histórica, Biografías y Retratos al Óleo* (Miami, FL: NicArts Productions, and Managua: Multi Impresos Nicaraguenses, n.d.), 66.

of León, he was received as a military hero amid great pomp. From Zelaya's perspective, his own vice-president was now a political threat. Zelaya immediately left Managua to join Ortiz in León, a hasty move that triggered speculation about possible jealousies between the two Liberal *caudillos*.

This dangerous notion had to be dispelled at once, for history repeatedly had shown that the time line between rumor and fact was lethally short. A spat between two generals who also happened to be president and vice-president was bad enough. A spat between two leaders from different localities made it even worse. To avoid implosion, the Liberal Party's image makers were pressed into action. In their skillful hands, the encounter between Zelaya and Ortiz in León became not a meeting of two rivals, but quite the contrary – it became a magnificent exchange in which one conferred honor and the other submission:

Nicaragua [has] never witnessed such a solemn and majestic spectacle. Indeed, a century may have to pass before the nation sees anything like it again. This was the apotheosis of Zelaya and Ortiz. Noble and magnanimous, [Zelaya] raised the pedestal of glory with his own hands for [Ortiz], whom viciousness, envy and petty passions have tried in vain to portray as a rival, when in fact [Zelaya and Ortiz] are the best of friends. [Ortiz,] humble and modest, readily offered the [military] victory to his chief, publicly declaring: the glory is all yours, Señor Presidente Zelaya; I have merely fulfilled your mandate to the best of my abilities.[22]

From then on, Zelaya would press ahead feverishly with his developmental agenda, marking every accomplishment with celebratory displays at the center of which he stood alone – the single force behind the country's forward march. Many students of this period have attributed Zelaya's penchant for self-centered pageantry as an indication of limitless vainglory. But this view, while containing an element of truth, ignores the imperative of legitimation facing the *caudillo*. After all, here was a ruler who having sponsored a constitution that mandated the establishment of an arbitration regime based on electoral legitimacy now increasingly justified his power on substantive grounds. One crucial promise in this regard was the promotion of order and peace. Another was the promise to make the nation modern, wealthy, and mighty, if only on a regional scale. Highlighting his role in fulfilling these promises was a logical extension of the substantive legitimation on which he had come to rely.[23]

But the substantive criterion, which for decades had sufficed to make the Costa Rican regime of arbitration work, was much more problematic in Nicaragua. From the very start, unlike their Costa Rican counterparts, Nicaraguans had valorized the principle of election to the point of going to war over the perceived corruption of electoral processes by "evil" foes. Zelaya's own Liberal intellectuals had produced a charter that expressed, in the strongest

[22] *El Gobierno Liberal de Nicaragua: Documentos, 1893–1908* (Managua: Tipografía Nacional, 1909), 109.

[23] The military victory in Honduras, for example, gained Zelaya much prestige among Latin American liberals, a prestige that translated into admiration among liberals at home. See Orúe, *Presidentes de Nicaragua*, 66.

possible terms, the primacy of the voters' voice. The more Zelaya deviated in practice from this ideal, the more he eroded the foundational legitimacy of his regime. And the more he subverted his initial claim to justifiable power, the more he was forced to embed his rule in Manichean arbitration when settling disputes among competing localities and ambitious notables.

As grand arbiter, Zelaya distributed rewards and punishment according to an unmistakable Manichean logic – the only logic that others could understand without much effort. At the level of exemplary symbolism, Zelaya's regime began early on to mount displays of disciplinary retribution, such as the public caning of selected Conservative notables.[24] At the level of large-scale state action, the regime aimed its extractive capacity at those considered to be disloyal elements. To finance the war with Honduras, for example, Zelaya levied taxes and extracted forced loans from various cities. The most onerous loans, which verged on extortion, were heaped upon Granada, simply because the city was the bastion of the Conservatives. Zelaya's close adviser, the polarizing José Dolores Gámez, and his vice-president, General Ortiz, even proposed that the amounts of the loans be calibrated so as to "destroy the enemy." Liberal León, in contrast, put up with the least onerous loans, simply because it was a city of "friends."

That these punitive policies were also potentially divisive was not lost on Zelaya. After targeting Granada, Zelaya availed himself of informal but dense notable networks to spread the notion among that city's leaders that his government's harsh measures did not reflect any animosity on his part; rather, Zelaya let it be known, the measures were the result of localist pressures that the Leonese had brought to bear on him.[25]

This was a self-serving scheme, but it was not devoid of normative content. Like most Managua Liberals, Zelaya saw Granada's Conservatives as constantly promoting "fratricidal conflict."[26] So why not let them think that the Leonese were behind their misfortune? The ploy worked; it fed the Granadans' resentment of León. But ironically, as we will see, it made no difference to León when its elites and their followers became unhappy with the regime's allocation of offices, authority, and status.

Indeed, the growing dissatisfaction of important political groups only made it more pressing for Zelaya to accomplish his goals quickly, which helps explains why he began to finance his military expenditures and public works by running heavy government deficits. The Liberal notable, Luciano Gómez, the same notable who had tried to forge a bipartisan alliance with the Conservative progressives only to be thwarted by the combative Gámez, was "astonished" by the government's disregard for the state's "enormous monthly deficit."[27]

---

[24] Emiliano Chamorro, "General Emiliano Chamorro," *Revista Conservadora* 1, no. 1 (August 1960): 9.

[25] Madriz, "Por Nicaragua," 52.

[26] Altamirano, "Por Nicaragua, por el Partido Liberal, por el General Zelaya," 76–89.

[27] Cited in Cruz, Jr., *Nicaragua's Conservative Republic*, 139.

The notable's astonishment, although understandable, missed the fundamental point that Zelaya was driven by the need to justify in some tangible way his hold on power – by the need to produce impressive results. Thus, like the Conservatives before him, Zelaya put a premium on the coffee economy, which under his rule continued to thrive. And like the Conservatives, he prioritized the expansion of the railway. But for Zelaya in particular and the Liberals in general, the railway had even more acute significance, since it was nothing less than the very emblem of modernity. By 1895, Zelaya was embarked on the extension of the existing rail lines and branches. Unfortunately for Zelaya, the Conservative Republic had been able to develop the infrastructure impressively, leaving a visible legacy that made his own developmental task an exigent one.

The Republic had introduced both the telegraph and the railway in 1876 and 1877, respectively.[28] In 1882, the first locomotive arrived in the Liberal city of León. Work on the railway continued apace until 1887, when the presidential incumbent died in office, an unpredictable event that ultimately led to the debacle of the Republic in 1893.[29] Still, when all was said and done, the Republic had managed to lay down 150 kilometers of rail in the eight-year period between 1878 and 1886. The Republic's public works agenda, moreover, was fulfilled within the bounds of strict fiscal discipline. Zelaya, in contrast, was able to lay down 131.2 kilometers during the whole seventeen years of his reign,[30] precisely because fiscal imbalances, in great part due to the expenses associated with a standing army, simply rendered the construction of various projected rail lines unfeasible.[31]

Worse yet, while Zelaya made sure to inaugurate every new rail branch with great pomp, all the pageantry in the world could not suppress the resurgence of localist resentments. The Liberal clubs of León began to feel slighted by Managua's ascent, a resentment that in turn created a rift with Managua's Liberals. The Leonese Liberals, moreover, insisted on greater participation in government, and demanded that at the end of his term, Zelaya should consult with them on the anointment of the next Liberal candidate. These were demands to which Zelaya could not accede, since they implied, among other things, that the next candidate might not be Zelaya.

Zelaya's unwillingness to consider even the possibility of a more open nomination process was part and parcel of a larger argument that he had begun to articulate more fully by 1895. An "honest dictatorship," he posited, was

---

[28] For a view into some of the more controversial aspects of the Republic's infrastructural works, such as the use of Indian laborers, see Dora María Tellez, *Muera La Gobierna: Colonización en Matagalpa y Jinotega (1820–1890)* (Managua: Universidad de la Regiones Autónomas de la Costa Caribe Nicaraguense, [URACCAN], 1999), especially 221–46.

[29] Comisión de Liquidación del Ferrocarril de Nicaragua, *El Ferrocarril de Nicaragua: Historia y Liquidación* (Managua: Impresiones y Troqueles, 1997), 10–11, 17–18.

[30] Ibid., 19.

[31] Enrique Belli Cortés, *50 Años de Vida Republicana: 1859–1909* (Colombia: Impreandes Presencia, S.A., 1998), 347.

the most suitable form of government for the country. Dictatorship, he posited further, would bring order and peace. Finally, he posited, the 1893 Constitution was not "practical," by which he meant that the charter imposed restraints on the defenders of Liberalism, who were now called upon to do battle against its foes. In short, the very same Constitution that Zelaya had championed, and which had defined his initial claim to power, had become a liability on the political battlefield.[32]

This was nothing less than the outline of a dictatorial logic. And as had been the case in the postcolonial period, this outline represented – or at a minimum, suggested – the outline of an even greater vision in which the very definition of the possible and the desirable was at stake. Partly for this reason, as in the postcolonial case, Zelaya's argument met with bitter resistance from notables who understood its full implications. Indeed, the Leonese now possessed the compelling reason they had lacked to engage in destabilizing normative scheming. Prior to the open articulation of the dictatorial argument, their political ambitions and localist pride were just that: ambitions and pride. Now, they were in possession of a normative grievance that, in combination with their particularist interests, led them to choose defiance over loyalty, or even neutrality. General Ortiz, the Leonese Liberals' most prominent aspirant to the presidency – and Zelaya's own vice-president – prepared to mount a rebellion against the chief to whom presumably he had offered submission in exchange for glory.

By 1896, then, the traditional problems of *caudillismo*, localist claims, and the personalist ambitions of the vice-president – all the problems of encompassing arbitration that the Republic had painstakingly addressed – had come together to threaten Zelaya's hold on power. In brief, the regime was increasingly incapable of accumulating and exercising justifiable power. Even allies felt betrayed by allies, and a rebellion was afoot. The rebels justified their insubordination by accusing Zelaya of violating the Constitution of 1893. Underneath this accusation lay a thick web of suspicions at the center of which was a shared conviction among rivals that the "others" had been lying all along and that they were not really "friends" but "impostors... beyond redemption."[33]

As the mutual recriminations flew back and forth, Zelaya and his circle insisted that the rebellion was patently "unjust." Their reasoning is telling. Not only had they treated León kindly as far as the forced loans were concerned, but

... virtually all of the [cabinet] ministers were Leonese, as were the bulk of the military commanders, and the political bosses of the Republic; practically the entire judiciary was Leonese. And as if this were not enough, the majority in the legislature were from [Leon].[34]

---

[32] Madriz, "Por Nicaragua," 52–4.

[33] For the original exchange of accusations between these former Liberal allies, see the pamphlets and annexes assembled in *La Vindicación de Chico Baca: Vindicación Que No Vindica* (Managua: Nicaragua, 1896).

[34] Altamirano, "Por Nicaragua, por el Partido Liberal, por el General Zelaya," 82.

From a normative perspective, Zelaya not only harbored grievances of his own, but was also moved to fits of outrage, which the official paper *El Heraldo de la Guerra* conveyed to the public. One issue stated plainly:

León deserves extermination.... One can get a serpent to slither away by startling it. A monster, however, must be quartered; it must be burnt; and its ashes must be buried, for they might retain a residue of venom.[35]

Yet another issue of *El Heraldo* proposed that Nicaraguans unite

...to suffocate the demagogic spirit that has wreaked such havoc...and to render impotent the damnable and incurable localism of the Leonese; to render it impotent so it cannot block, as it has so often done before, the feeble stream of our moral and material progress.[36]

To back up this judgment, Zelaya raised an army of loyalists. He even persuaded Granada, now bent on taking revenge on León, to supply soldiers for the cause. (Honduras' Liberals also sent a contingent). At the end of the day, Zelaya prevailed. He then paid back his Granada allies by sending key notables into exile, and imposing new onerous loans on their city. Of course, this time, León was also severely punished. The relatively light loans that Zelaya had extracted from that city were now raised to a burdensome level.

Zelaya's next step was to call for a new Constitutional Assembly whose task would be to reform the existing charter *"as per* the president's instructions." The instructions were straightforward: to enhance considerably the authority that the state wielded over citizens; to nullify the provisions for direct, regular elections; and to lift the ban on reelection. The Assembly also named Zelaya president for the period 1898–1902. Finally, in 1905, another constitutional decree allowed the president unlimited succession.[37] The irony of it all was glaring: Zelaya's 1893 Constitution called for universal suffrage, yet in the one presidential election ever held under his rule, he won overwhelmingly because he ran unopposed.

Elections became purely a matter of form. Zelaya's true imperative was fast-paced economic development and, relatedly, the solidification of a new base of supporters who could believe in the justice of his power. To this end, he had turned from the start to intellectuals such as the historian Gámez and to the coffee growers, whose expanding fortunes had turned Managua and its vicinities into the country's new power center. With time, he also made these groups the beneficiaries of the enlarging state and of the monopolies he handed out to his loyal followers.[38]

The pattern that had been clear from the start was reinforced. Loyalty was a virtue to be rewarded; the disloyal were to be severely punished. This applied

---

[35] Madriz, "Por Nicaragua," 56.

[36] Ibid., 56.

[37] Cruz, Jr., *The Conservative Republic*, 143.

[38] Ramón Ignacio Matus, "Revoluciones contra Zelaya, 1893–1899," *Revista Conservadora* 3–4, nos. 19–21 (April/May/June 1962): 1–45.

to isthmian politics as well. In 1898, Zelaya offered his Costa Rican friend Ricardo Jiménez military assistance to overthrow President Rafael Iglesias, the object of Zelaya's keen dislike. In his polite reply to the Nicaraguan leader, the Costa Rican Jiménez made two points. First, he would have to decline the offer because no position of power was worth the shedding of blood. Second, if one weighed the benefits and costs of the offer, it became obvious that it would be less prejudicial to put up with the Iglesias administration than to unleash civil war, the source "of so many evils."[39]

But that was Costa Rica. In Nicaragua, things were done differently. In 1903, Zelaya executed the disloyal military officers who had orchestrated a failed revolt in Managua the previous year, and lavished the latest German equipment on his loyal standing army. The state's fiscal deterioration, predictably, continued apace throughout all this distribution of prizes and punishments. At one point, things got so bad that many schools – whose creation had been a source of pride for Zelaya – had to be closed across the country.

If Zelaya's failure to outdo the Conservative Republic amounted to a middling performance in terms of the substantive criterion, the state's fiscal crisis and its ramifications amounted to a dismal showing. At this point, two escape routes, each with its own risks, remained available to him. One was to revert expeditiously to the electoral criterion, and thus risk a humiliating defeat at the polls. The other was to reallocate favors to the Leonese elites, and to do so with enough generosity to placate them. The risk here was the possibility of being reduced to a *primus*, perhaps even *secundus inter pares*. Zelaya took neither route. To be sure, he spoke of forgiving the rebellious notables and popular groups of León, whom he also flattered by publicly calling their city the "cradle of Liberalism." But he kept them carefully controlled as he pressed ahead with one last attempt to justify his power on a substantive basis. More than ever, he was driven to perform modernist miracles, and so he set out to fulfill the most daring dream of nineteenth century Nicaraguans: to make the nation wealthy by exploiting its geographical advantage.

Like others before him, Zelaya was determined that a great foreign power should build an interoceanic canal through Nicaragua. To this end, he carefully nourished a "friendship" with President Theodore Roosevelt. By October 1903, however, it was becoming painfully clear that the United States was leaning in favor of a Panama route. By 1904, the Americans had settled on Panama, and now wanted from Zelaya guaranteed use of strategic Nicaraguan waterways for the military defense of the canal. Zelaya refused. He also persisted in his effort to establish Nicaragua as the dominant force in Central America.[40]

Zelaya's most articulate defenders set out to persuade Central Americans that Zelaya's most effective critics were not to be believed. If anything, Zelaya was a fair ruler whose actions were fully "justifiable." From his defenders'

---

[39] Cuadra Pasos, *Obras II*, 217–18.
[40] Belli Cortés, *50 Años de Vida Republicana*, 335–9.

perspective, what opponents saw as the violation of the 1893 Constitution was in fact a necessity imposed on the ruler by the "anarchy" of 1896. Here the logic was, once again, that the 1893 charter was too liberal given the Conservatives' determination to promote "disaster in order to seize power and destroy all Liberals." Under such circumstances, so went the argument, "laws ought not be obstacles to the attainment of higher ends."[41]

This argument subordinated the law to the incumbent arbiter, a move that in turn enhanced his decision-making prerogatives. The immediate result of this was that by 1907 Zelaya was again at war, this time with the Honduran and Salvadoran armies. As before, he prevailed. Nicaragua's public finances, however, were ruined. Moreover, Zelaya had made even more enemies at home. And as always, plenty of political exiles were scattered across Central America plotting against him. Rumors of a rebellion brewing at home intensified in 1908. A more damaging rumor also spread: Zelaya was peddling his canal project to the Japanese, the Germans, and the English – an affront to American exclusionary expansionism in the hemisphere. Against this backdrop, Zelaya backed an invasion of El Salvador by a group of mercenaries and Salvadorean political exiles bent on toppling that country's government. The invasion, launched in 1909, failed miserably.[42]

The Taft administration, by now convinced that Zelaya's isthmian ambitions posed a danger to U.S. interests in the region, prepared to destabilize his government. To accomplish this, the American government aided and abetted the forces up in arms against Zelaya. These forces represented the traditional mix of rebels: dissidents from the party in power, in this case Liberals; members of the opposing party, in this case Conservatives; and, of course, the indispensable military men and disenchanted civilians.[43]

The coup de grace against Zelaya was finally delivered when Secretary of State Philander Knox openly declared the United States' support for the ongoing rebellion against the ruler. Compelled to resign, President Zelaya

... sailed into exile in December 1909, on a Mexican warship provided by Porfirio Díaz. (Díaz had taken the precaution of clearing this generous gesture with the Taft White House beforehand.)[44]

A Fickle Arbiter: The Americans and the Nicaraguans

President Zelaya's departure left a vacuum in the Nicaraguan polity, a polity in which no one possessed either the necessary brute force or stature to arbitrate among conflicting claims to political and economic resources. To be sure, the

[41] Altamirano, "Por Nicaragua, por el Partido Liberal, por el General Zelaya," 110–11.
[42] Belli Cortés, *50 Años de Vida Republicana*, 388.
[43] For a brief description of the array of forces, see Knut Walter, "El Somocismo: del protectorado a la revolución," in Margarita Vannini, ed., *Encuentros con la Historia* (Managua: Instituto de Historia de Nicaragua y Centro de Estudios Mexicanos y Centroamericanos, 1995), 331.
[44] Cruz, Jr., *The Conservative Republic*, 149.

two *caudillos* who had rebelled against Zelaya – the Liberal Juan Estrada and the Conservative Emiliano Chamorro – assumed "power." But they enjoyed scant popular support. All they really had at their disposal was a bankrupt treasury. Worse yet, faced with this miserable state of affairs, the Taft administration effectively placed Nicaragua in receivership. The objective was to make the country, come what may, honor its debts to American and other foreign creditors. The result was that the new Nicaraguan government exercised only very limited control over the national economy.[45]

All this happened in 1910, the year that Sergio Ramírez takes as a starting point for his explanation of the "phenomenon" of Sandino's "appearance." That year was indeed an interesting one. To begin with, the Conservatives installed Adolfo Díaz in power through an election which, as Robert Kagan puts it, "the Liberals had no chance of winning and in which they did not participate." Two years later, the Liberals revolted "under the leadership of a dissident Conservative general." As Kagan further notes, their slogan was, "Down with Yankee imperialists."[46]

The revolt prompted the Taft administration to dispatch a contingent of marines, who stayed to "protect" a government that was patently incapable of withstanding the intractable domestic forces at play.[47] Also in 1912, Secretary of State Knox paid a goodwill visit to Nicaragua. On the occasion, the Conservative president, Díaz, delivered a welcoming speech in which he gave the defunct Conservative Republic no more than a passing nod before proceeding to depict a nation defeated by its own internal conflicts:

My . . . country . . . has been a republic for almost a hundred years without having known republican methods in all that time, except at brief intervals. *Our political struggles have unfortunately not been a luminous contest of ideas and principles; they have been a struggle between despotism, on the one hand, and, on the other, the ill-directed efforts of the people in search of happiness never attained* – a duel, a horrible duel, which has at length left the republic, if not dead, at least almost utterly exhausted [emphasis added].

Díaz' understanding of the past captured the paradox of Nicaragua's collective identity. This identity bound Nicaraguans together by locking them in an antagonistic logic, which in turn reinforced the narrative of collective (in)competence, and embedded them in an impoverished field of imaginable possibilities. As Díaz explained to Knox:

. . . *we are weak* and we need your strong help for the regeneration of our debilitated land. The hand which your government generously and fraternally extends us I accept without reserve or fear, for I know it belongs to a people which has made a religion of

[45] For a succinct treatment of Taft's Dollar Diplomacy and its effects on the Nicaraguan political economy, see Robert Kagan, *A Twilight Struggle: American Power and Nicaragua, 1977–1990* (New York: Free Press, 1996), 4–5.

[46] Ibid., 6.

[47] Walter, "El Somocismo: del protectorado a la revolución," 331.

liberty and, educated in and for freedom, loves its independence above everything and respects the independence of others... [emphasis added].[48]

American arbitration, however, was unreliable. By 1925, the United States was in an isolationist mood, and eager to leave Nicaragua. Kagan writes of one State Department official who recalled, "If we could bring about the election in 1924 of a government which had real popular support, we could extricate ourselves from a situation which was increasingly embarrassing."[49] On this score, the United States succeeded, at least in the immediate term. The election, partially supervised by the marines, produced a sweeping victory for the Liberal-Conservative coalition mounted against the incumbent, the Conservative *caudillo* Emiliano Chamorro. Once this had been accomplished, the State Department arranged for the marines' prompt departure.

The new bipartisan government, which perceived its mission as a last-ditch effort at national reconciliation, tried in vain to impress upon the Americans the need for protection from Chamorro's army. Like everyone else familiar with the polity's internal points of contention, the government knew that Chamorro was outraged by the two parties' collaboration, which he deemed inappropriate.[50] Chamorro's self-interest, of course, also played a role: He was jealous of the close ties between certain Liberal notables, on the one hand, and the president and vice-president, on the other.[51] Chamorro, it was clear to anyone who cared to notice, would seize the first opportunity to right these perceived wrongs. And indeed, two weeks after the marines left in August 1925, Chamorro's army staged a coup and seized power.

Kagan nicely summarizes subsequent events: "Chamorro purged his opponents from the Congress, drove the newly-elected Liberal Vice-President Juan Sacasa into exile, and had himself named president."[52] Chamorro also exiled the newly elected Conservative president, Carlos Solórzano. But it was Vice-President Sacasa who defiantly returned to Nicaragua and declared himself the constitutional president of the Republic.

Chamorro, described earlier by Ramírez as a favorite godchild of imperialism, had spoiled his godfather's plan. In 1926, the Coolidge administration forced Chamorro to resign. At the same time, knowing that an unhappy Chamorro would resort to violence and thus force the return of the marines, the administration would not recognize Sacasa.[53] Looking for a third alternative,

---

[48] "Speech of His Excellency Don Adolfo Díaz, President of Nicaragua, Welcoming Mr. Knox" (Managua), 6 March 1912, in Robert H. Holden and Eric Zolov, eds., *Latin America and the United States: A Documentary History* (New York: Oxford University Press, 2000), 105–6.

[49] Kagan, *A Twilight Struggle*, 7.

[50] For the *caudillo's* formative experiences, see Chamorro, "General Emiliano Chamorro."

[51] A Liberal notable from Jinotepe, Segundo Albino Román, was arguably the most influential. Román's opinions carried so much weight with the Conservative President Carlos Solórzano and the Liberal Vice-President Juan Sacasa that many considered him the true power behind the throne.

[52] Kagan, *A Twilight Struggle*, 7.

[53] Ibid., 8.

the Coolidge administration settled on the Conservative Adolfo Díaz, who, as we just saw, had already served as president under the American protectorate. But the Liberals, like Chamorro before them, did not fit into the stereotypical assignation of mere "lackeys" of imperialist power. They not only refused to recognize Díaz as president, they also launched the so-called Constitutionalist War under the leadership of General José María Moncada.

The Constitutionalist War brought the Liberal Sandino into the picture, along with other lesser Liberal generals, including one Anastasio Somoza García.[54] So what was the claim propelling this war in which General Sandino and General Somoza García fought on the same side? What was the compelling reason that led them to abandon the safety of the sidelines for the perils of active involvement? A familiar combination of normative grievances and selfish ambitions. First, as the name of the war suggests, a constitutional principle was at stake. For if one adhered to the full logic of constitutionally mandated elections and binding results, then the legitimate heir to the deposed president was *not* the Conservative Díaz, whom the Americans had recognized. Rather, the legitimate heir was the deposed vice-president, the Liberal Juan Sacasa, who was back on national soil. This was the principle that the Liberal Constitutionalist Army sought to vindicate. Second, there was a keen sense of partisan injustice. Both Somoza García and Sandino found it offensive that a Conservative had usurped Sacasa's position of authority, to which he had been legitimately elevated through elections they knew to be fair precisely because the marines had played the role of supervisor. This is why the purpose of the war was to restore Sacasa to power immediately. Finally, there was the matter of self-interest. Unlike Sacasa, who had been born into a distinguished Leonese family and was a high-ranking notable of the Liberal Party, both Sandino and Somoza García were "new men" – individuals of some means who hailed from Managua's relatively obscure satellite towns. If an unconstitutional injustice of such magnitude could be inflicted on a Liberal notable such as Sacasa, then new men such as Sandino and Somoza García could nurse no realistic hope for a brighter future. (Like Zelaya before him, Somoza García married into a notable family, but as with Zelaya, the marriage could get him only so far. This limitation applied even though the young woman Somoza García had wed happened to be the niece of President Sacasa.)

The Liberal warriors wrapped all these normative concerns and self-seeking considerations into a clear Manichean formulation. Sandino's storied assertion said it best: They were fighting to debunk Díaz, who was held in "contempt by every good Nicaraguan."

---

[54] Somoza García had converted to Liberalism. He was the son of a relatively successful Conservative coffee grower from San Marcos, one of Managua's surrounding towns. This second-rank town was in close proximity to an even less distinguished pueblo, Niquinohomo, from which Sandino hailed. Born out of wedlock, Sandino nevertheless had been recognized by his father, who, like Somoza García's father, was a coffee grower, but on a more modest scale. General Moncada, the chief of the Constitutionalist Army, came from Masatepe, another town from this same area of coffee producers.

As the war raged, the Coolidge administration eschewed intervention. Finally, in 1927, with the Nicaraguan government on the verge of breakdown, the administration gave in. Coolidge dispatched Secretary of State Henry Stimson to "clean up the mess."[55] To this end, Stimson held talks with another "new man," General Moncada, the commander of the Constitutionalist Army. The American and the Nicaraguan agreed on the following terms: The Liberals would put down their weapons, and in exchange the United States would supervise the elections of 1928.

The agreement, as Kagan points out, portended well for Moncada because, as most Nicaraguans knew, U.S.-supervised elections were likely to be transparent, which meant that the Liberals were almost sure to win, and that Moncada, as the Liberals' preeminent leader, was bound to be elected president. All the Liberal generals, save one, agreed to the terms. The one dissenting general was Sandino. The reasons, again, are complex. He feared that the agreement would backfire on the Liberals and that the 1928 election would produce yet another Conservative government. He also held a personal grudge against Moncada, who on more than one occasion had denied his requests for weapons and rebuffed his offer to serve in the Constitutionalist Army with the rank of general. Finally, and relatedly, Sandino's preferred scenario was one in which Nicaragua would be ruled directly by an American "military governor" until the 1928 election, which he thought should be held under the marines' supervision.[56]

Sandino's proposal reflected the growing conviction among Nicaraguan leaders that, since they could not trust one another, they needed a powerful, hands-on external arbiter. This trend was so pronounced by the mid-1920s that a radical Nicaraguan intellectual and poet lamented that no one knew what Nicaragua actually was, only what it was not. The poet even complained that Nicaraguans – "government and people alike" – had abandoned themselves to "sloth" while they waited for "a redemption that [could] only come from within to arrive from outside."[57]

Manicheanism Unleashed

The poet was only partly right. Nicaraguan leaders saw themselves also as agents capable of manipulating their external arbiter, either through ingratiation or political dexterity. Sandino failed at both. The Americans left Díaz in power until the election, which, supervised by American military officials, produced a high turnout of voters who gave the presidency to the Liberal Moncada. Unwilling to submit to Moncada's authority, Sandino's army

---

[55] Ibid., 9.
[56] Ibid., 10–11, 13, 15.
[57] This "radical" was the brilliant and influential Salomón de la Selva. Cited in Volker Wundrich, "El Nacionalismo y el Espiritualismo de Augusto C. Sandino en su Tiempo," in Vannini, ed., *Encuentros con la Historia*, 289–90.

continued to wage a skillful guerrilla war – now evading, then engaging the marines. But Sandino's troops reserved their most bitter wrath for Nicaraguan "traitors." The execution techniques they employed are instructive. With a sharp machete, the executioner would slice off the top of "the traitor's" skull. This was known as the "gourd cut." Another technique was the "vest cut," which removed the head and arms. Finally, there was the "bloomers cut," which did away with the legs. Sandino thought the cruelty justifiable. "Liberty is not conquered with flowers," he stated. "For this reason, we must resort to the cuts of vest, gourd, and bloomers."[58]

This justification was buttressed by Sandino's Manichean view of Nicaraguan reality, which he repeatedly articulated in his correspondence with various Latin American presidents and notables. Here is one example:

I saw that the Liberal and Conservative leaders were *one* ball of cowards, villains, and traitors, incapable of leading a courageous and patriotic people. We have turned away from those leaders, and we . . . workers and peasants have improvised our own chiefs. Even in these days of such brilliant and exemplary lights, these failed politicians, [like] dogs and cats trapped in a sack . . . struggle to attain the presidency based on foreign supervision. . . . [59]

The days of such brilliant and exemplary lights was a reference to the nationalist and populist sentiment sweeping Latin America, where Sandino's exploits against the marines were by now widely admired. More telling, however, was the reference to the courageous and patriotic people fighting under him. It had been a long time since a Nicaraguan leader had used such positive terms to describe his humble followers. But Sandino also inserted this courageous and patriotic people into a familiar world of dark and light, with Sandino and his people on one side, and all other Nicaraguan leaders, without nuance or distinction, on the other.

This Manicheanism resonated with his troops, most of whom were faithful practitioners of the principle of just war as they understood it. Propelled by a syncretistic formulation of indigenous conceptions of the "foe" and Catholic articles of faith, "just war" was a terrifying endeavor, especially for those who waged it. This is why Sandinista and non-Sandinista combatants alike routinely elevated pleas to the Virgin Mary and all the saints for personal protection on the battlefield. One Sandinista corpse, for example, was found with a copy of the "Just Judge's Prayer," an ancient Spanish plea recited in the New World since the days of conquest. By now, it was more of an incantation than a prayer:

As I feel my enemies' vengeful wrath approaching, I repeat thrice: They may have eyes, may they not see me; they may have hands, may they not touch me; they may have mouths, may they not address me; they may have feet, may they not overtake me. I see them; I talk to them; I drink their blood and slice their hearts.[60]

---

[58] Kagan, *A Twilight Struggle*, 15.
[59] Cited in Ramírez, "Sandino: Clase e Ideología," 133–4.
[60] Wundrich, "El Nacionalismo y el Espiritualismo de Augusto C. Sandino," 297.

The butchery that accompanied the incantation, as we saw previously, was reminiscent of the postcolonial wars. So too was Sandino's political self-portrait. Just as postcolonial political rhetors distinguished their meritorious deeds from the wrongdoings of their "wicked" rivals, Sandino described himself as a man of "sincere character" looking for a way to resist "the advance of hypocrisy"; a man with "high ideals of honor and patriotism"; a man whose "arduous labor" had earned his "campaigns" much "luster."[61] And like the *caudillos* who preceded him, Sandino was forced by the very logic of his rhetorical construct to explain the source of his atypical virtuousness. For this, he turned to the spiritualism he had discovered during the years he had lived in Mexico. In a letter to one of his key lieutenants, he wrote:

You and our other brothers must remember that *I am merely an instrument of Divine Justice seeking redemption for our people* [emphasis added].[62]

Unlike Costa Rican leaders, who justified their policies by associating them with the exceptional virtues of the earthly Costa Rican people, Sandino looked to the heavens for the source of his exceptional character. Such invocations of a higher power were traditional among *caudillos*.[63] But this is not to say that Sandino was incapable of innovation in the face of changed conditions. In confronting his Nicaraguan rivals against the backdrop of an American occupation, for example, he produced a rhetorical adaptation of internal Manicheanism whereby "the other" was vilified as worse than a traitor – as a sort of political masochist eagerly seeking "the caress of the foreign whip."[64]

Sandinista leaders who were to come on the scene long after Sandino's death would seize upon the despicable image of "the other" that this innovative rhetorical turn evoked. But ironically for Sandino, at that moment, his rhetorical turn was about to lose its practical trope. With each passing day, Washington grew more anxious to extricate itself from Nicaraguan affairs. In fact, the marines stayed only long enough to supervise the 1932 election, from which the Liberal Sacasa emerged victorious. This newly elected government, too, asked the United States for continued support, again to no avail. The Hoover administration withdrew the marines, leaving in their stead the newly created Guardia Nacional (National Guard).

With the marines gone, it became clear that the same old set of Nicaragua Liberal actors were the main contenders for authority. General Moncada, hoping to continue to exercise influence behind the scenes, had his subaltern ally, General Somoza García, named chief of the National Guard.[65] President Sacasa, still fearful of Sandino's powerful army, sought conciliation with the rebel leader. Sandino, now dispossessed of his foreign foe, agreed to a meeting. They reached

---

[61] Ibid., 291, 296.

[62] Ibid., 298–9.

[63] The postcolonial *caudillo* and powerful orator Cleto Ordoñez, for example, actively fomented the popular illusion that he possessed magical faculties.

[64] On Sandino and his guerrilla army, see Neill Macaulay, *The Sandino Affair* (Chicago: Quadrangle, 1967); Gregorio Selser, *El Pequeño Ejército Loco* (Havana: Imprenta Nacional, 1960).

[65] Prior to Somoza García, an American officer was the Guardia's commander.

the following settlement. For one year, Sandino would retain a small army to be supported with public funds. The rest of his soldiers – almost two thousand – were to turn in their weapons and disband. The agreement also granted Sandino control over a small part of the national territory, so he could establish an agricultural cooperative for his men.[66] At the meeting's conclusion, Sandino embraced Sacasa and Somoza García, who was also present.

Just as Sandino had repudiated the peace agreement of 1927, now some of Sandino's lieutenants repudiated his settlement with Sacasa and Somoza García. But while Moncada had allowed the dissenting Sandino to go off into the mountains, Sandino ordered the execution of his own dissenters. Their prompt elimination ensured that the set of relevant actors would remain unchanged for the moment. There were, however, two new elements. One was the National Guard. Presumably the state's instrument of coercion, the Guard was also a collection of middle-class officers and peasant soldiers who depended on Somoza García's capacity to extract resources from the government. The more he succeeded in providing the *guardias* with everything from their basic necessities and weapons to the opportunity to climb up the hierarchy, the more they found him to be a fair and effective judge of their *situación*. The other new element had to do with Sandino. Simply put, his army had turned in only a small fraction of their weapons; as result, his military capability remained virtually intact, all the more threatening to his rivals because it was *vox populi*.

As these two new realities became obvious to all in 1933, Washington grew ever more removed and disinterested in Nicaraguan affairs. President Sacasa and his officials saw clearly their rivals' presidential ambitions. Sacasa was suspicious of Somoza García, his niece's husband. Somoza García, after all, had garnered the loyalty of the *guardias*. Sacasa was also fearful of Sandino, who had garnered the loyalty of Sacasa's followers. Sacasa even had to contend with two other impatient presidential aspirants. These two men also happened to be Sandino's most detested foes: the Liberal Moncada (of the Constitutionalist War) and the Conservative Chamorro (who had staged the coup that in turn provoked the Constitutionalist War). In hopes of making political hay, these two *caudillos* set out to destabilize the president by throwing their support behind Somoza García.

This configuration was, at best, unstable. Sandino, whose army continued to engage in skirmishes with the National Guard even after the peace agreement, responded by declaring the Guard unconstitutional. This was a smart move because it enabled Sandino to argue that the Guard was operating outside the law and against the government.[67] The declaration enraged the Guard's officers. As Kagan puts it, "The Guard wanted to be let loose to destroy Sandino."[68]

---

[66] Knut Walter, *The Regime of Anastasio Somoza: 1936–1956* (Chapel Hill, NC: University of North Carolina, 1993), 31.

[67] Sergio Ramírez, ed., *El Pensamiento Vivo de Sandino* (Managua: Nueva Nicaragua, 1981), 304–5.

[68] Kagan, *A Twilight Struggle*, 21.

But President Sacasa stood in the way. Sandino's argument – that the National Guard habitually refused to follow presidential orders precisely because it was an illegal entity – resonated with Sacasa.[69] The president, moreover, was trying to cope with the blunt fact that he was now caught between two organized armed camps staking conflicting claims, each momentous for the future of the country and his own. On one side, the Guard staked claim to monopolistic control over the country's coercive power. On the other side, Sandino's army, already in control of a piece of the national territory, effectively blocked the Guard's claim to monopoly and, by its very existence if not its stance, established a de facto duopoly. Indeed, by declaring the Guard unconstitutional, Sandino had established a justifiable cause for his own army's war against the Guard. Sacasa tried simultaneously to arbitrate between the two leaders and to play them off against each other, giving both of them state resources for their respective armies.[70]

Against this background, various political leaders deployed their powers of persuasion to argue that the nation's peace and the welfare of the people required the removal of certain obstacles. The first obstacle to be identified was Sandino.[71] Soon thereafter, in February 1934, the National Guard murdered Sandino in cold blood. The murder did remove an obstacle – an obstacle to Somoza García's quest for the country's highest position of authority. This turn of events made President Sacasa and his allies all the more vulnerable and, by extension, all the more insistent on U.S. intervention against Somoza García.[72]

The Americans were unmoved. Once again, various political leaders claimed to speak on behalf of the nation's peace and the welfare of the people, this time urging the president to reach an "understanding" with the National Guard.[73] But Sacasa would not acquiesce. Instead, he and his cabinet asked Washington at least to make a public statement that might deter Somoza García in his attempt to depose the government. Washington granted not even a gesture. The die was cast. After brief battles between the forces of President Sacasa and the National Guard, Somoza García seized power. By 1936, the general was in de facto control of the country's *situación*. Preparing a guaranteed victory in the upcoming election was the new task at hand.

Dynastic Arbitration

Somoza García's 1936 electoral campaign was from the start closely entwined with the construction of a new regime of arbitration. The first step was the

---

[69] Ramírez, ed., *El Pensamiento Vivo de Sandino*, 304–5.

[70] Walter, *The Regime of Anastasio Somoza*, 33.

[71] Sofonías Salvatierra, *Sandino, O la Tragedia de un Pueblo* (Madrid: Talleres Tipográficos Europa, 1934), 269–71.

[72] Although General Somoza García was married to President Sacasa's niece, the president understood that the familial connection was not a constraint on the general.

[73] Reported by Sofonías Salvatierra, mutual friend and ally of Sacasa and Sandino, in Salvatierra's *Sandino*, 269–71.

clear articulation of a presumably collective goal. Using historical shorthand, Somoza García labeled this goal *democracia ordenada*, or orderly democracy. In this endeavor, he enjoyed the support of a new generation of Liberals who had risen to the top of the party's hierarchy after the coup against President Sacasa threw the party's traditional elites into disarray. These new party leaders obviously owed Somoza García their recent prominence. They also endorsed his interpretation and construction of *democracia ordenada*. Their endorsement, in fact, was carefully crafted. First, to bolster their rightful claim to the Liberal identity, they embraced Zelaya as their authorizing figure. Second, they specified Somoza García's role within the Liberal *democracia ordenada*. To this end, they articulated a vision of a capitalist system in which a regnant arbiter would harmonize the interests of different *groups* into an organic whole. The identity of the arbiter, although implicit, was well understood by everyone.

These different groups in need of harmonization from above ranged from landowners to workers and peasants. Harmonization required constant arbitration of various claims to political vocality, public resources, and legal settlements of conflicts between the pertinent groups. In this balancing act, all authority flowed from above. Consider the case of labor. Already in 1935, Somoza García had dealt with the more progressive activists in the Nicaraguan Workers' Party (Partido Trabajador Nicaraguense, henceforth PTN), whom he stigmatized as "communists" before quarantining them on the remote Atlantic Coast. In 1936, however, he courted the PTN by acting as friendly arbiter in an urban workers' strike. The moment the PTN showed any degree of autonomy, the arbiter reverted to repressive measures. From then on, any urban labor organization that acknowledged the arbiter's unquestionable wisdom received the regime's legal protection and material support.[74]

Somoza García also sponsored a modern and robust Labor Code that, together with the actual dispensation of official protection and resources, recognized workers' presence in the public sphere and granted them subaltern vocality. But Somoza García's most skillful arbitration move was the creation of a new union federation to be closely associated with the Liberal Party. This move enabled him to render judgments pertaining to specific labor demands while simultaneously separating organized workers from "the elite opposition, who divided the world into pro- and anti-Somoza forces."[75]

Somoza García divided the world in a similar fashion. The "aristocracy" and the "past" stood on one side, with nothing but turmoil and injustice to show for themselves. Casting himself in the role of "redeemer," he stood on the other side, hand in hand with the "future," which held in store many bright promises. These promises, as he plainly stated, were intended "for the motherland" and

---

[74] Walter, *The Regime of Anastasio Somoza*, 56–7.
[75] Lisa Haugaard, "In and Out of Power: Dilemmas for Grassroots Organizing in Nicaragua," *Socialism and Democracy* 7, no. 3 (Fall 1991): 160.

for his "friends."[76] To rural laborers, for example, he offered land distribution. He also granted an audience to the banana growers, who resented the low prices paid for their product by the North American banana company. Moreover, for the specific purpose of getting out the vote on election day, he developed "special" ties with partisan activists, who in turn worked the patron-client networks crisscrossing the Liberal agrarian zones. Finally, to ensure impressive rallies in the days leading up to the election, he ordered his campaign workers to distribute food, hard liquor, and tobacco among the peasantry.[77]

Despite this all-out effort, voters abstained in record numbers. One reason was the Conservative Party's decision to protest the election by withdrawing from the contest. (Instead, the Conservatives turned again to the United States, asking one last time for intervention against Somoza García. Again, the United States left them to their own devices.) Another important factor behind the large percentage of non-votes was the influence of dissident Liberals. Yet another cause was the effectiveness of patron-client networks, which, in the major strongholds of traditional Liberalism and Conservatism, pressed the voters to stay away from the polls.[78]

Somoza García received 80 percent of the votes cast. Most of the remaining votes went to the Partido Conservador Nacionalista (Nationalist Conservative Party). A splinter of the traditional Conservative Party, the Nationalist Conservatives relied for their campaign expenses on public funds made available by Somoza García. They also fully expected to lose. But their composition and their motives were complex, and can be properly understood only in the political-cultural context that caused multiple splintering and factions both within the Liberal and Conservative parties during the first two decades of the regime. The traditional Conservative Party, for example, offered no real hope of ascent for middle-level activists, who now realized that supporting Somoza García was the only "realistic" path to participation in the "government of the future." But more profound forces were at work.

From the 1930s to the 1950s, Liberal and Conservative notables and intellectuals embroiled themselves in historiographic disputes aimed at settling old accounts, many of which dated back to the postcolonial period. Political biographies and autobiographies went back and forth in an effort "to unmask," once and for all, the "true" nature of the camps' historic leaders. Perceived by each side as "slanderous," the pertinent claims and counterclaims inevitably turned into convoluted historical refutations.[79] No national authorizing figure could

---

[76] For Somoza García's political view of the world, see Walter, *The Regime of Anastasio Somoza*, 46.

[77] Ibid., 57.

[78] Ibid., 60–1.

[79] Illustrative of the Liberal variant is the biography of the nineteenth century Liberal *caudillo* Máximo Jerez by Sofonías Salvatierra, *Máximo Jerez Inmortal: Comentario Polémico* (Managua: Tipografía Progreso, 1950). For the Conservative treatment of the same *caudillo* (and of his foe, the Conservative *caudillo* Fruto Chamorro), see Pedro Joaquín Chamorro, *Máximo Jerez y sus Contemporáneos* (Managua: Editorial La Prensa, 1937). This bitter historiographic

possibly emerge from this historiographic imbroglio. Nor could the parties to the dispute, unable to tear themselves away from the past, produce any sort of political innovation that might enhance their field of imaginable possibilities.

One important result of all this was that the Liberal Party's rank-and-file increasingly identified with Somoza García, who, after all, not only embraced the Liberal identity but was also in a position to address the Liberals' grievances. Another crucial consequence was the defection of up-and-coming Conservative notables and intellectuals, who, dispirited by the destructive wars of the 1920s, were now looking for novel ideas that their own partisan leaders could not provide. In the early 1930s, future anti-Somoza intellectuals such as Pablo Antonio Cuadra and FSLN sympathizers such as José Coronel Urtecho looked to the civilized nations of the world for possible solutions to their country's recurrent "anarchy." Born into old Granada families, these intellectuals were familiar with the fascist and corporatist ideas then in vogue across much of continental Europe, and entertained their transplantation to the tropics. They even toyed with the possibility of restoring monarchical rule. By the mid-1930s, however, they had settled on a more "realistic" option. They acknowledged Somoza García "as the guarantor of order and progress."[80]

For these young Conservatives, an investigation into the system of neighboring Costa Rica as a possible alternative was not appealing. The intellectual José Coronel Urtecho had already concluded in 1932 that

> ...democratic and liberal ideals, along with democratic institutions, [had] brought about the ruin of Nicaragua in all areas of human activity.[81]

The elder statesman of the Conservative Party, Carlos Cuadra Pasos, on the other hand, was positively intrigued by Nicaragua's neighbors:

> I have traveled throughout Costa Rica...read the history of this Central American oasis...talked to its knowledgeable men, men like Don Ricardo [Jiménez] and Don Teodoro [Picado]....I have been curious about the imponderables that may be at the root of the different effects that similar phenomena produce in our systems....Don Ricardo rejects the tale of ethnic differences [among the conquering Spaniards] as a plausible explanation....I agree. Both peoples descend from the same branch of Spanish conquerors....The same names can be heard in the founding societies of the two countries.... "My own names," said Don Ricardo, "are as Costa Rican as they are Nicaraguan."

But the elder's alternative explanation was as disheartening as it was telling: After intense reflection, he decided that the relevant causal factor might be

---

conflict was a variant of a broader Latin American phenomenon. For an overview of the Argentine variant, see Nicolas Shumway, *The Invention of Argentina* (Berkeley, CA: University of California Press, 1993).

[80] Walter, *The Regime of Anastasio Somoza*, 21.

[81] John D. Heyl, "Patria Libre o Muerte! Death Imagery and the Poetry of Revolt in Nicaragua, 1900–1985," in Ralph Lee Woodward, ed., *Central America: Historical Perspectives on the Contemporary Crises* (New York: Greewood Press, 1988), 153.

traced to Costa Rica's milder temperature, which possibly led to a cooler, more civil rhetorical culture:

The differences in climate...may account for the contrast [in our politics]....This is obvious in the parliamentary oratory of the Costa Ricans....Regardless of how deep their differences may run, the congressmen hardly ever lose their compass. Their speeches proceed serenely within the contours of each speaker's eloquence.[82]

Obviously, it was much more feasible to accept General Somoza García as guarantor of order than to change the country's climatic conditions. In 1937, the general finally assumed the presidency. He continued building his regime, which ultimately would directly control the state bureaucracy, the army, the system of public transportation, the means of communication, the municipal governments, the Congress, and the Liberal Party. He also promulgated the 1939 Constitution, which in typical fashion guaranteed the Nicaraguans' most cherished political right – freedom of expression. But at the same time, the new constitution placed outside the bounds of legal protection anyone who made

...statements contrary to the public order, to the fundamental institutions of the state, to the republican and democratic form of government, to the established social order, to public morality and proper behavior or that cause damage to third parties.[83]

This strict limits placed on political vocality, in combination with the increasing pervasiveness of the regime's political apparatus, created the illusion of spatial confinement in a country that was still far from densely populated in the 1950s. In fact, up to the 1970s, land remained abundant relative to the rapidly growing population. This was the case even along the Pacific Coast, where the majority of Nicaraguans settled down to live and conduct business. And yet a sense of smallness pervaded life because the polity was a constricting arena at the center of which stood a disproportionately large and unworthy judge. As one opposition poet wrote:

> My country is so small
> *that Mr. President*
> *personally settles*
> *even the arguments in the streets.*
>
> My country is so small
> that with the rifles of the Guardia
> any *imbecile* can govern it [emphasis added].[84]

Intellectuals, university students, disillusioned young National Guard officers, and the ascending scions of the aristocracy, such as Pedro Joaquín Chamorro Cardenal, were among the first to form a disloyal opposition to this puissant but

---

[82] Cuadra Pasos, *Obras II*, 211–13.
[83] Walter, *The Regime of Anastasio Somoza*, 93.
[84] Ernesto Gutiérrez, "Mi País es tan Pequeño," 1960. Cited in David Whisnant, *Rascally Signs in Sacred Places: The Politics of Culture in Nicaragua* (Chapel Hill, NC: The University of North Carolina Press, 1995), 160–1.

unfair judge. They launched a rebellion in 1947, which they followed up with a new attempt in 1954. Both were failures that would cost them dearly. Nevertheless, the rebels remained in the grip of their own compelling reasons, which they crafted out of normative grievances and self-seeking interests. Their genuine abhorrence for the injustices committed by the Somoza regime and their hopes of building a political democracy were inextricably entwined with their political ambitions. The rebels' leaders set out simultaneously to remove Somoza García and to secure preeminence for themselves. Each leader, Chamorro Cardenal included, felt best qualified to launch a modernizing developmental agenda that would rely on progressive state intervention and a dynamic private sector.[85]

Members of this armed opposition were partially protected by their social status. Typically, the regime retaliated against them with imprisonment, even torture, but generally refrained from "liquidation." After the 1954 attempt, however, social status was no longer a reliable predictor of a rebel's fate.[86] The assassination of Somoza García in 1956 removed all restraints.[87] Every rebel who was not by then in prison was immediately jailed; those who were still in prison since the 1954 attempt were taken out of confinement to be executed.[88]

With its dynastic links by then firmly established, the regime survived the death of its founder. Between 1956 and 1967, the founding dynast's eldest son, Luís Somoza Debayle, ruled either directly or by proxy. After Luís' death from a massive heart attack in 1967, the regime's leadership passed to his younger brother, Anastasio Somoza Debayle. He, too, ruled either directly or by proxy from 1967 to July 1979. The older brother, Luís, had been careful to continue the broad strategic outlines of his father's regime. Such continuity required, among other things, respect for the clear boundary that divided politics and private business. This was crucial in two ways from the regime's perspective. First, the regime could reach a *modus vivendi* with socioeconomic elites, and thus decrease its dependence on the support of labor unions. (Already in 1946, Somoza García had made sufficient strides in this direction to repress radical factions of the labor movement and sharply curtail labor autonomy.[89])

[85] By the time of the 1954 rebellion, Pablo Antonio Cuadra was a strong opponent of Somoza García and a close ally of Chamorro Cardenal. Chamorro Cardenal's modernizing convictions were clear to his closest allies. Author's interview with Pablo Antonio Cuadra, Managua, June 1995.

[86] Former officers of the National Guard were treated particularly harshly, regardless of social background. Author's interview with Arturo Cruz Porras (a participant in the 1947 and 1954 rebellions), Bethesda, Maryland, 2 July 2002.

[87] Rigoberto López, the assassin, was trained and assisted logistically by the surviving members of the 1947 and 1954 rebellions. He also received support from the avenging male relatives of some of the rebels executed in 1954. Author's interview with Cruz Porras, 2002.

[88] Author's interview with Cruz Porras, 2002.

[89] Richard Stahler-Sholk, "The Dog That Didn't Bark: Labor Autonomy and Economic Adjustment in Nicaragua under the Sandinista and UNO Governments," *Comparative Politics* 28, no. 1 (October 1995): 82.

A clear divide between politics and business was important on a second front: the agrarian countryside. Here, the regime's arbitration of conflict increasingly hinged on the country's sizable agrarian frontier. In the 1950s and 1960s, for example, peasants in the Western zone mounted resistance to the large-scale cotton growers who tried to expel them from their lands. But the regime, by relocating peasants to the interior, was able to favor commercial farmers while precluding intractable class conflicts. Some peasants, to be sure, resented settlement in the new colonies. But others saw it as serendipitous. Lisa Haugaard writes of one settler in Nueva Guinea who recalled: "It was a paradise here. You just had to drop a seed in the ground and it would grow."[90]

The dividing-line strategy, however, was not without flaws. The socioeconomic elites learned to live with the regime, but only so long as the dynastic arbiters kept their implicit commitment not to trespass into the private sector's turf. Any transgression could seriously damage the socioeconomic elites' perception of the fairness of the game. Moreover, socioeconomic elites were also members of extended family clans. They occupied different ranks within the clan structure, which meant that they nursed their own individual grievances and aspirations, particularly in matters of status. Impoverished members of the aristocracy, for example, might simultaneously establish marital links with the rising bourgeoisie and still look upon them as parvenus. The upshot of this complex set of social relations was that the socioeconomic elite, as a class, was far from homogeneous or politically united.[91] And so it was not surprising that from this very class emerged some of the most radical anti-Somoza actors of the 1970s and some of the most ardent Sandinistas in the 1980s.[92]

The dynastic regime of arbitration ran into other problems with time. One such problem concerned the growing imbalance between the urban and rural sectors that resulted from the country's economic modernization from the 1950s to the 1970s. During this period, socioeconomic change was striking but not harmonic. Like the other Central American governments, the Somoza regime made agroexport the lynchpin of the country's economic growth. Agroexport, in turn, hinged on intensive cultivation of grains and cotton in the 1950s and 1960s, and on extensive cattle-raising in the 1960s and 1970s. The expansion of agroexport, however, also shifted landownership and agricultural production from the smallholding and subsistence sectors to the agroexporters. And as this trend became more pronounced, so did rural unemployment and migration to the cities.[93]

---

[90] Haugaard, "In and Out of Power," 161–2.

[91] Shirley Christian, *Nicaragua: Revolution in the Family* (New York: Vintage Books, 1986).

[92] This supports John Booth's claim that "Revolutionary *leaders* have tended to come more from the same social strata as the incumbent elite whom they challenge than from among the ranks of the classes in whose name they make revolution." See John A. Booth, *The End and the Beginning: The Nicaraguan Revolution* (Boulder, CO: Westview Press, 1985), 3.

[93] John Booth, "Socioeconomic and Political Roots of National Revolts in Central America," *LARR* 26, no. 1 (1991): 38.

This dynamic, in itself difficult to manage, was rendered all the more intractable by a demographic explosion, which between 1960 and 1980 doubled the populations of Central American countries. Urban centers reflected in concentrated fashion both the strength and contradictions of the changes under way. On the one hand, advances in education, commerce, light industry, services, and the public sector all contributed to the expansion of an urban middle class. On the other hand, while peasants continued to arrive in the cities seeking employment, Import Substitution Industrialization (ISI) production of consumer goods began to reach its limits, giving rise to additional urban unemployment.[94] As in the case of the Conservative Republic, the dynastic regime's powers of encompassing arbitration lagged the socioeconomic changes it had helped trigger.

Normative Scheming: The Passions and the Interests

In Nicaragua, the most compelling magnet city for internal migrants was the capital. And it was the capital, Managua, that in December 1972 was turned into a pile of rubble by a powerful earthquake. The catastrophe dealt a devastating blow to the city's inhabitants – public employees, small and large merchants, craftsmen, workers, seamstresses, taxi drivers, teachers, and students. The earthquake also demolished the infrastructure that sustained much of the nation's economic life. And yet, in the months following the earthquake, it became increasingly evident that even though the calamity represented an opportunity for the country's ruling dynast to show a degree of benevolence and competent leadership, he took it instead as an opportunity for the violation of the widely accepted informal norms governing state–society relations. Throughout 1973, outrage at this violation began to mount in various quarters.

The first significant expression of condemnation came in March 1974, when the country's broadest association of small, medium, and large businesspeople and farmers – the Consejo Superior de Empresa Privada, or COSEP – openly denounced the regime's unjust use of power. The denunciation, formally articulated in a collective statement, represented a mixture of normative grievances and self-interested concerns. COSEP indicted the regime's thoroughly inadequate reconstruction of low-income housing and sanitation systems. This failure was appalling partly because it unabashedly displayed the regime's utter disregard for basic fairness, partly because it contributed to the city dwellers' shared sense of despair. COSEP also accused the regime of neglecting the reconstruction of the city's commercial center. Here again the resentment was at once rooted in normative sensibilities and self-regard. The old commercial center had housed both businesses and private residences, in which many a kinsman of COSEP members either had been crushed to death or lost their belongings and shelter. (The center was never rebuilt.)

---

[94] Much of this change stemmed from the creation of the Central American Common Market (CACM) in 1960. See Booth, "Socioeconomic and Political Roots," 39.

In addition COSEP accused the regime of according preferential treatment to loyalists in the allocation of business recovery loans. This treatment was inappropriate on two counts. First, it showed the regime's willingness to exploit a public tragedy as an opportunity for expanded profit-seeking activities; that is, it showed the regime's willingness to use its political power – at a moment of generalized weakness – to shift the established boundary between the capitalists' sphere and the regime's own enterprises. Second, by giving a financial advantage to loyalists at this new starting gate in the race for profit, the regime heralded the arrival of unrestrained cronyism. Finally, COSEP protested the regime's levying of high import taxes on nonloyalist businesses. From COSEP's perspective, the taxation policy was akin to adding insult to injury because it essentially forced the private sector to pay for the regime's abuse of power.

Other important actors also condemned the regime's behavior. The Church, particularly the middle and lower echelons of the hierarchy, was appalled at the sheer disregard for human suffering. University students, increasingly radicalized since the 1950s, now had a clear target for their accumulated anger. Labor unions, focused on bread-and-butter issues since the 1930s, enhanced their activism in an effort to provide relief for their distressed constituencies.[95]

Poor and middle-class neighborhoods, the traditional organizing grid for the social life of urban communities, now began to transform themselves into miniature political societies. Even as they continued to rummage through the rubble of their lives, they began to discuss and indict the outright theft of foreign relief assistance by the *guardias* and other state agents.

By mid-1974, the shattered city was transformed into a theater for moral judgment. On stage was a scandalous government; in the audience was a population filled with revulsion. Absent from the drama was the guerrilla movement known as the Frente Sandinista de Liberación Nacional (FSLN). The absence of the FSLN seemed to confirm the general perception that the movement was moribund, if not defunct. But while the FSLN might have missed the political opportunity afforded by the regime's transgressions, the movement was still alive. It was also in trouble.

The movement had been founded in 1959 by Carlos Fonseca Amador and Tomás Borge. At that moment, the Cuban Revolution signaled to them that they too might one day radically alter the course of their country's history. In this transformative process, the virtuous revolutionary – a man of "boundless generosity" – was the indispensable element. For his was the great task at hand:

... to rescue and spread among our people the best qualities and virtues of the revolutionaries who have fought in the ranks of our organization ... to rescue the mystique of the FSLN, that daily attitude of constant sacrifice for our people, of respect for our leaders and comrades, of fraternity, humility and simplicity.[96]

[95] Haugaard, "In and Out of Power," 161.
[96] Donald C. Hodges, *Intellectual Foundations of the Nicaraguan Revolution* (Austin, TX: University of Texas Press, 1986), 257.

The FSLN's founders also looked into the past for an authorizing figure. They found it in Sandino, a leader who remained controversial among Nicaraguans, admired by some and despised by others. In the Nicaragua of 1959, in fact, Fidel Castro held much broader appeal than Sandino. But in 1974, the FSLN was in trouble not because of its choice of authorizing figure. Rather, it was in trouble because neither Castro's liberationist prestige nor the burning memory of Sandino could prevent the bitter internal divisions that began to plague the movement as it expanded to include younger generations of Nicaraguan revolutionaries.[97]

Following the earthquake, the FSLN split into two factions. One was the Maoist faction known as Guerra Popular Prolongada (Prolonged Popular War). This faction, led by Tomás Borge, aimed to establish its *foco* in the mountains through protracted guerrilla warfare. The other faction was the Tendencia Proletaria (Proletarian Current). This faction was led by Jaime Wheelock and Luis Carrión Cruz. They argued for the need to create a workers' party *before* mounting a military apparatus. The differences between these two factions were so pronounced that in 1975, after a turbulent meeting of Sandinista leaders, Wheelock and Carrión Cruz were forced at gunpoint by the rival faction to seek asylum at the Venezuelan embassy in Managua.[98]

Between these two acrimonious factions there emerged a third, led by Humberto Ortega, who lived in Costa Rica. Known interchangeably as Tendencia Insurreccional (Insurrectionalist Current) and the Tendencia Tercerista (Third Current), this faction now envisioned the possibility of a popular insurrection in the near term, in contradistinction to the other two factions, which held on to the belief that a successful revolution required the political maturation of the revolution's leading agent, be it the peasantry or the labor class. Despite these divisions, the FSLN had an undisputed leader: Carlos Fonseca, one of the movement's founders. Like Humberto Ortega, Fonseca had once imagined a scenario in which the FSLN might successfully mobilize a multiclass alliance against the Somoza regime. But Fonseca never could forge such a coalition, and after his death in 1976, a power vacuum began to threaten the FSLN's tenuous coherence.

The best positioned to take advantage of this vacuum was Humberto Ortega, precisely because while Fonseca was still alive, Ortega had proved capable of forging the minimal unity within the movement required to deliver a blow to the Somoza regime. Specifically, Ortega masterminded an operation in which he did not participate but whose success was ultimately attributable to him. In December 1974, an FSLN commando team seized the house of a Somoza

---

[97] For the generational factor, see Irene Agudelo Bulles, "La Política Después de la Política, una Aplicación del Método Generacional de Karl Mannheim as los Sectores Medios de la Militancia Sandinista Nicaraguense" (master's thesis, Facultad Latinoamericana de Ciencias Sociales, Sede México, XI Promoción, 1996–8).

[98] Sergio Ramírez, *Adiós Muchachos: Una Memoria de la Revolución Sandinista* (Merico, D.F.: Tipografía Angélica Alva, 1999), 89–90.

loyalist, and held hostage his dinner guests, including the Nicaraguan ambassador to Washington (Somoza Debayle's brother-in-law). The Somocista dinner host, despite being the father of two Sandinista activists, was shot dead. The other hostages survived. Through the mediation of the archbishop, the commando team received a ransom and safe passage out of the country. The success of the operation, however, did little to alleviate the FSLN's internal rivalries. As late as 1975, Sergio Ramírez recalls, the *comandantes* continued to weave an internal "web of intrigues and conflicts."[99]

Meanwhile, Pedro Joaquín Chamorro Cardenal, now the director of his family's newspaper, *La Prensa*, doggedly investigated and publicized the regime's abuses of power. *La Prensa*'s effectiveness made Chamorro Cardenal a powerful vocal actor. It also put him at risk. In 1975, he began keeping a political diary. In an early entry, he explained why:

I received a visit from [x]. . . . He . . . told me that in the presence of his chief [Somoza Debayle], he heard people talking about how they are going to eliminate me . . . some civilians intend to kidnap me, take me to the air force, and throw me from an airplane into the sea.[100]

In a second entry, Chamorro Cardenal recorded yet another dire warning:

Yesterday [y] came to tell me that he chanced upon [two Guard officers] in a bordello, and that they were drunk. [One of the officers] said that [I] owe my life to the chief [Somoza Debayle] because he [the officer] had asked [the chief] to relieve him from active duty so he could kill me without compromising the chief. But the chief did not grant him his request.[101]

The diary is littered with entries in which the writer seems to be trying to divine whether Somoza Debayle (the regnant arbiter) or himself (the aspirant) would be the first to be snatched by the circling specter of death. In one typical passage, he writes:

Somoza traveled unexpectedly to the United States. It has been confirmed that he suffers from nocturnal attacks of asphyxia.

Yet another entry reads:

Somoza left again yesterday for the U.S. Rumor has it that he is undergoing periodic medical treatment. But no one knows the truth.[102]

Against this background, the Ortega faction launched an offensive of a different kind in 1976. They sent the Jesuit priest Fernando Cardenal, a Sandinista ally, to testify before the U.S. Congress, which at the time was looking into human rights abuses committed by the Somoza regime. Father Cardenal, who rarely wore his vestments, now put them on, as Ortega and the organizers of the trip to Washington had instructed him. Father Cardenal then proceeded to detail

[99] Ibid., 89.
[100] Pedro Joaquín Chamorro, *Diario Político* (Managua: COMPANIC, 1990), 24.
[101] Ibid., 26.
[102] Ibid., 136, 184.

for the Americans a series of gruesome tortures, disappearances, and killings. The outcome of the Washington offensive, whose final objective was to get the United States to cut off military aid to the Somoza regime, was a promising one. By 1977, the determination of a group of liberal Democrats in Congress to delink the United States from the Somoza regime began to pose a counterweight to the support Somoza enjoyed among conservative Democrats and Republicans. This was crucial because the newly elected president, Jimmy Carter, had come to the White House with a human rights policy that seriously called into question American support for Latin American dictators.

The Ortega faction's success in Washington notwithstanding, the FSLN's internal divisions continued unabated. Rival factions accused Ortega and his allies of "adventurism" and stigmatized them as "petty bourgeois."[103] But others outside the FSLN could better appreciate the importance of the priest's testimony. One was the opposition journalist Chamorro Cardenal, who also happened to be Father Cardenal's first cousin. Banned by the regime from leaving the country, Chamorro Cardenal could not travel to Washington. And now he was angry at his Jesuit cousin for ignoring a document that Chamorro Cardenal had prepared for the congressional hearing. In that document, Chamorro Cardenal had argued two central points: First, the history of Somocismo was from the start closely tied to U.S foreign policy; and second, American aid solely benefited the Somoza regime. Chamorro Cardenal's document was designed to trigger a moral response from the United States. In his view, that great power ought to take responsibility for its role in perpetuating the dynasty, and understand before it was too late that continued funding of the regime represented an extension of the United States' prejudicial role.

Chamorro Cardenal was also angry at his cousin because instead of making the sweeping moral argument he had crafted for use at the congressional hearing, Father Cardenal had followed the FSLN's more targeted approach: Make a shocking presentation of human rights abuses, and thus incite revulsion in the chambers of the U.S. Congress and among the American press. This, too, was a moralistic tactic. But in Chamorro Cardenal's view, it suffered from two interrelated flaws. First, some of the allegations made by Father Cardenal were fabricated. Second, everyone in Nicaragua knew this to be the case. Later, Chamorro Cardenal wrote in his diary: "I told Fernando [Cardenal] that one single lie is enough to call into doubt many truths. . . . Besides, with all the real atrocities committed by this regime, there is no need to invent false ones."[104]

The rift between the two cousins deteriorated into mutual resentment. The priest was upset by the rumor that Chamorro Cardenal had characterized his behavior in Washington as "treacherous." This was the most serious charge that one relative could level at another. Chamorro Cardenal denied ever making the accusation, but did admit to his cousin that he was "saddened" by his performance in Washington. Matters got even worse when Chamorro Cardenal learned that his cousin had testified before Congress that he – Chamorro

---

[103] Ramírez, *Adiós Muchachos*, 90–1.
[104] Chamorro, *Diario Político*, 188–92.

Cardenal – like all "rich people," enjoyed special immunity in Nicaragua. An indignant Chamorro Cardenal dashed off a letter to his cousin, "reminding" him of all the prison terms and "processes" (an euphemism for punitive action) he had suffered at the hands of the Somoza regime. Chamorro Cardenal signed the letter sardonically, "Your wealthy cousin." The priest responded with a conciliatory missive, which he signed warmly, "Receive a fraternal embrace from your cousin." This time, Chamorro Cardenal replied in kind, signing off, "Your cousin, who embraces you fondly."[105]

The distinction between wealthy and poor aristocrats was real enough, but so too were the differences between the openly politicized upper class and the country's most powerful capitalist group, the Pellas-Chamorro family clan. Unlike the other groups of the private sector, the Pellas-Chamorro group never took an open political stance. They always preferred quietly to reach a *modus vivendi* with whomever was in the presidency. They had learned to live with all three Somozas; soon they would learn to live with the FSLN; and later still, they would learn to live with the governments that succeeded the FSLN. But in May 1977, the group was worried about the ramifications of Father Cardenal's testimony. Specifically, Alfredo Pellas voiced dissatisfaction with Somoza's rebuttal to the priest's accusations. From Pellas' perspective, Somoza had not acquitted himself well, and as a result, he was partly to blame for the suspension of American aid.

Somoza's failure to manipulate the United States, however, was not the only concern of the Pellas-Chamorro group. They were also nervous about their rather uneven and at times downright mistrustful relationship with the man to whom they were talking, Chamorro Cardenal himself. One problem with Chamorro Cardenal was his independence, which he derived from his control of the widely read *La Prensa*. A second problem was the way in which Chamorro Cardenal used the paper: He not only deployed it as a weapon against the Somoza regime, but also turned it into a platform to advocate progressive socioeconomic programs that did not always square with the group's interests. The conversation thus quickly turned from a discussion about the effects of U.S. foreign policy on Nicaragua to an attempt by the two businessmen both to flatter and restrain Chamorro Cardenal. Pellas began by trying to make Chamorro Cardenal feel like a king maker – a kind of superarbiter who, in a post-Somoza era, could use the power of *La Prensa* to choose and anoint the country's presidents.

Chamorro Cardenal responded with a pointed question: "And if *I* want to be [the president]?" Pellas' reply was direct: "You, too, would win." But Enrique Pereira, Pellas' close ally, also present in the conversation, interjected:

Pereira: No.... You cannot be [the presidential candidate].... The people accept [your endorsement] of others.... But if you propose [to be the president yourself], it's different.[106]

[105] Ibid., 192, 236.
[106] Ibid., 258, 260.

The discussion continued to range between topics pertaining to the interests of individuals and groups and the broader political issues of the day. At one point, however, Chamorro Cardenal addressed the crux of the matter: "We need to do something [against the regime]. What can *you* [the Pellas-Chamorro clan] do?"

Here we can only surmise that Chamorro Cardenal was tacitly asking whether the Pellas-Chamorro group would be willing to provide him with financial assistance to invigorate his political movement, Unión Democrática de Liberación (UDEL). The reply was blunt:

Pellas: Nothing. The private sector does not play a political role... This role belongs to the political parties....

Pereira: ... *You're too much of a moralist. That's your loss, because politics is made with scoundrels; people who are shameless.* Such a pity. The opposition has its best opportunity in forty years, and it cannot do anything because it's divided. Look at UDEL. It now means nothing [because its leaders are fighting]... but I'm sure than in ninety days we will have freedom of the press, and you can take advantage of it to do something.

Pellas: Yes. But let's see how you use it, hombre. Listen, go easy.[107]

The discussion typified the backroom variant of identity positioning. The Pellas-Chamorro group assumed an apolitical posture, but in fact actively maneuvered behind closed doors. This duality allowed group members to pursue their particularistic agenda and still pass judgment both on "shameless" politicians and on "moralists" such as Chamorro Cardenal. The moralist, for his part, framed his own political ambitions in the form of a defiant question – "And what if I want to be the president?" – as if to provoke his interlocutors into an open admission of their distrust for him.

In the end, Chamorro Cardenal "did not go easy." Rather, he intensified his attacks on the regime through *La Prensa*. The regime, in turn, would shut the paper down, then allow it to reopen; or it would censor it, then relax its strictures. Throughout all this, Somoza Debayle complained bitterly about the "slanders" to which he was subjected. Meanwhile, the civil opposition intensified its own efforts. INDE (Instituto Nicaraguense de Desarrollo [Nicaraguan Development Institute]), a broadly representative body of the private sector, demanded a national dialogue with an eye to removing Somoza Debayle, a demand that the Church supported. Chamorro Cardenal's own political movement, UDEL, joined in the call for a dialogue, but also insisted on the FSLN's inclusion in the process.

Manichean Clash

By then, the Ortega faction had established a small political coalition known as the Group of Twelve. The Group included members of the aristocracy and the

---

[107] Chamorro, *Diario Político*, 260–2 (emphasis added).

"high bourgeoisie." Several factors held together their alliance with the FSLN. First, there was a common understanding of political justice. For the non-Sandinista members of the Group of Twelve, the Somoza regime was an affront to the ideal of just government.[108] Second, many of the non-Sandinista members of the Group were either parents or uncles of important Sandinistas. Third, the Ortega brothers committed themselves to a "mixed economy," even though they left undefined the balance of power they envisioned between state and market. Fourth, the members of the Group themselves were either progressive capitalists or impoverished aristocrats with an undisputed anti-Somoza record. (The Group also included two Sandinista members wholly committed to the Ortega leadership. Interestingly enough, they were two of only three Group members who hailed from Somocista families.[109])

The Group of Twelve, which functioned as the FSLN's political envoy in Nicaragua and abroad, was instrumental in securing the FSLN's representation in a new, broad anti-Somoza coalition known as the Frente Amplio Opositor (FAO, the Broad Opposition Front). The FAO sought more than once to find a political solution to the crisis without the FSLN. The Group of Twelve held fast to its position that the crisis called for an armed opposition, and thus for the FSLN's military leadership. By then, the fates were conspiring against Somoza Debayle; they were also smiling upon the FSLN. In Washington, D.C., Carter wavered between allowing the Somoza regime to "reform" itself and pushing his human rights doctrine to its logical conclusion. Carter's indecision allowed Chamorro Cardenal publicly to ridicule the notion of a "self-reforming dictator." As if this were not enough, Anastasio Somoza Debayle suffered a coronary of the kind that years before had killed his brother. Unlike his brother, Anastasio survived and recovered. But in the eyes of the people, he was a wounded beast. The burning question was simply, who would replace him?

This was the recurrent question from which Nicaraguan history could not escape. The answer, once more, arrived drenched in blood. In 1978, Chamorro Cardenal was massacred on his way to work at *La Prensa*'s headquarters. He received twenty bullets in the face, chest, arms, and throat.[110] Who exactly killed him is a riddle that remains unsolved to this day.[111] But at that moment, his family and the Nicaraguan people assigned guilt to Somoza Debayle, even though he had always maintained that it would be irrational for him to eliminate Chamorro Cardenal. Whether genuine or not, the "irrationality" argument

---

[108] Interviews with Group members Felipe Mantica and Arturo Cruz Porras by Christian in *Nicaragua: Revolution in the Family*, 45–6.

[109] The members of the Group of Twelve were Emilio Baltodano, Fernando Cardenal, Ernesto Castillo, Joaquín Cuadra Chamorro, Ricardo Coronel Kautz, Arturo Cruz Porras, Father Miguel Escoto, Carlos Gutiérrez, Felipe Mantica, Sergio Ramírez, Casimiro Sotelo, and Carlos Tunnermann.

[110] Christian, *Nicaragua: Revolution in the Family*, 54.

[111] For example the key assassin, inexplicably escaped from prison after the FSLN came to power, giving rise to the suspicion that the FSLN was the author of the assassination.

proved accurate. Chamorro Cardenal's public burial turned into an immense display of inexorable collective ire.

The funereal upheaval was merely the prelude to greater turmoil. The private sector, in the grip of outrage, mounted a general strike. But the strike was not enough to force Somoza Debayle out. This was a serious defeat because it demonstrated the inadequacy of civil protest, even if massive and well organized. Many in the private sector now turned to the United States and directly asked for it to assume, once again, the role of external arbiter. They asked for the United States to remove "the man." Many others decided that the time had come to throw their support behind the FSLN, which by now began to launch military offensives in minor towns, and soon thereafter undertook systematic agitation among the youth in poor Managua neighborhoods.

But above all, the assassination was a crucial catalyst for the imminent insurrection because it allowed for the brute articulation of the country's Manichean rhetorical frame. Here at last there was a "martyr" of the cause for justice and a defender of the people's right to vocality.[112] *La Prensa* delivered this message at every available opportunity – a message that resonated in the town of Monimbó, where a spontaneous uprising took the form of a collective expression of vengeful wrath and a call to violence.

This reaction was not surprising. Chamorro Cardenal was the political leader who had succeeded best in crafting a moralistic dichotomy that separated Somoza and his associates from "the people." After Chamorro Cardenal's assassination, his successor at UDEL announced that Somoza Debayle simply had to go because one could not ask "Satan to reform Hell."[113]

More than ever, words like "negotiation", "reform", and "agreement" were anathema. The assassination of Chamorro Cardenal, after all, was not just any assassination. Chamorro Cardenal's effective use of popular parlance in articulating the country's moral dichotomy was partly the reason that, by the mid-1970s, nothing could be more degrading in the public's estimation than being a member of the regime's loyal opposition. Chamorro Cardenal labeled the first Conservative faction to take seats in Congress *la puta* (the whore). He labeled the second faction to follow suit, *la putita* (the little whore).[114]

This was more than an invective leveled at the regime; it was a way of separating the reputable opposition from the impure *políticos* who served as deputies. From this, it followed logically that when the FSLN decided to deliver a dramatic blow to the regime, it would target the Congress. In 1978, the *caudillo* Edén Pastora, later to become a Contra leader, led an FSLN commando unit in a raid against the Congress, then in session. Once more, the FSLN received a ransom and safe passage, with the archbishop again acting as mediator between the commando unit and Somoza Debayle.

[112] Jaime Chamorro Cardenal, *La Prensa: The Republic of Paper* (New York: Freedom House, 1988).
[113] Kagan, *A Twilight Struggle*, 44.
[114] Christian, *Nicaragua: Revolution in the Family*, 31.

The regime responded with a series of brutal raids that not only further alienated it from society, but intensified popular approbation of the FSLN's bold move. At last, the movement was gathering significant momentum; at last a variety of groups shared a compelling reason to choose risky involvement over the safety of the sidelines. And momentum bred momentum. If a successful national insurrection was within the realm of the feasible, then the FSLN could postpone its internal fighting to join in a concerted undercover effort to organize, coordinate, and mobilize students, unions, and neighborhood activists. The FSLN could also conduct more frequent and effective guerrilla attacks against National Guard posts.[115]

Through many complicated maneuvers, the FAO had tried to force Somoza Debayle out while working to prevent his replacement by the FSLN. But in the end, the dynamics of Manichean normative scheming trumped the FAO's dual objective. The FAO's own position, especially when addressing the Americans, increasingly narrowed down to an insistent claim: Somoza is intolerable to the FAO. Manichean normative scheming was also behind the formation of the Group of Twelve, which enabled the FSLN simultaneously to remain undercover and confront the regime, face to face, as a righteous opponent of all its evils. Manichean normative scheming even led to the sacrifice of life by upperclass and "obscure" Sandinista fighters alike, as they sought both glory and justice. Finally, the assassination of Chamorro Cardenal – the master practitioner of Manichean rhetoric – increasingly drove everyone, the FAO included, to contribute to the general upheaval.

Nicaraguans undermined the Somoza regime but could not forge a sense of internal unity that might enable them to create an alternative to the FSLN. In retrospect, one could speculate that had Chamorro Cardenal lived, things might have turned out differently. But when Chamorro Cardenal was alive, he trusted no one in the political class, and he was repaid in the same coin. The country's major socioeconomic group did not trust him. The Conservative Party, which he had abandoned, did not trust him. The FSLN did not incorporate him into the Group of Twelve, lest he steal their thunder. And his own political movement, UDEL, was consumed by internal jealousies. Besides, the point is that he died precisely because of the methods that Nicaraguans used to negotiate their way through their rivalries, ambitions, historical memories, and ideals for a better future.

Because the leaders of the non-Sandinista opposition were able to accord Chamorro Cardenal center stage only as a corpse, they now faced the fact that the unimaginable was not only possible, it was reality. A radical movement they had pronounced dead not too long ago, a movement many of them dreaded or even despised, now had managed to mount a massive insurrection with the assistance of a wide array of political actors.[116] The most startling surprise was

---

[115] It did so in key cities such as Managua, León, Estelí, San Carlos, Ocotal, and Masaya.

[116] The Nicaraguan Revolution fits the pattern observed by Booth: "Coalitions among diverse social sectors with different grievances and aspirations have been typical of successful

that the non-Sandinista leadership was included in this insurrectionalist array. By spurning Chamorro Cardenal while he was alive, by insistently demanding that Somoza Debayle leave after Chamorro Cardenal was dead, by mounting strikes that failed to ouster the dynast but succeeded in paralyzing the economy, and by exploiting Chamorro Cardenal's legacy, organizations such as the FAO, UDEL, and private sector associations all had helped to bring the nation to that hot July of 1979. Then, against a backdrop of sporadic popular uprisings in major urban centers, Humberto Ortega – born into a middle-class, devoutly Catholic family – directed the FSLN's military operations from the cooler environs of San José, Costa Rica.

The FSLN's insurgent troops fought a good fight against a daring military officer known as "Bravo." As the revolutionary troops got ever closer to Managua, the Somoza regime, dependent for so long on the support of the United States – even if that support was at times no more than an illusion – collapsed. The final scene was pathetic. At once cowed and unrepentant, the last dynast hurried to the airport, where a few *guardias* guarded his plane as it waited for takeoff in a nerve-wracking delay. The dynast's oldest son, Anastasio Somoza Portocarrero, had yet to be located and brought on board. In the meantime, a peasant soldier bearing a machine gun approached his chief and, subtly pointing the weapon at him, pled "*necesidad*," or dire need. "Don't you have some money to spare, *jefe?*" he inquired. By then it was plain that the Guardia Nacional was being abandoned by the leader it had faithfully served. The *jefe* reached into his pocket and handed the soldier a few pesos.

Normative Scheming: After the Triumph

Well-read in traditional historiography, the FSLN leadership was quite familiar with the Manichean structuration of political conflict and identity formation. The Sandinista leadership, for example, crafted an exigent code of conduct for its militants. Each soldier was expected to display "humility, modesty, honesty, discipline, devotion to duty, and submission to the [FSLN's] National Directorate."[117] The leaders were equally stern when it came to their own code. A true Sandinista leader was supposed to be a man without "vices" – a man free of materialistic concerns and immune to personal ambition.

The Sandinista leadership, moreover, was very much aware of the traditional familial "solution" to disharmony. Nicaraguan revolutionaries were supposed to be "brothers," whereas the Salvadoran guerrillas were "cousins." Internal factions were frowned upon because they violated the "family's" unity.[118] And of course, the FSLN's leaders knew the power of Manichean dichotomization.

---

revolutionary movements; single-class or single-group movements have commonly failed." Booth, *The End and the Beginning*, 3–4.

[117] Roger Miranda and William Ratliff, *The Civil War in Nicaragua: Inside the Sandinistas* (New Brunswick, NJ: Transaction, 1993), 26–7, 45–7.

[118] Ibid., 11.

This is why the induction of the sons and daughters of the upper class into its militant ranks necessitated a special method for them to cross the divide between good and evil.

This method, first used in the early 1970s, was in essence a purification ritual. The young men and women aspiring to join the movement had first to undergo an act of "contrition" and "renounce the world in which they had been raised." After spending months working for the people in one of the city's poorest neighborhoods – under the careful tutelage of a priest – they were finally allowed to join the side of good, from whence they could at last "censure their parents" and everything they stood for.[119] *Comandante* Luís Carrión Cruz summarized the entire procedure when he explained that he had entered the Revolution through a "religious experience."[120]

Carrión Cruz survived the Revolutionary war. But many other young penitents died alongside equally idealistic young men and women from more humble family backgrounds. After the Revolution's triumph, the FSLN leaders once again vowed to enshrine in practice the code of conduct exemplified by these "martyrs." But as Sergio Ramírez would later lament, "that code of conduct was left for the living to interpret; and sainthood was bureaucratized."[121]

As the FSLN guerrillas seized control of Managua in July 1979, the FSLN quickly began to emerge as a political party organized around a vertical structure of command – a political and military hierarchy at the apex of which stood the Sandinista National Directorate, composed of the nine leading *comandantes*. The particular distribution of positions, however, depended increasingly on individual *comandantes'* capacity to take each other by surprise and to exploit to advantage the normative strictures of the movement. The critical importance of normative scheming was particularly evident when the time came to transform the Sandinista guerrilla forces into the Revolution's standing army: the Ejército Popular Sandinista (EPS). In principle, any one of the nine members of the National Directorate was a viable candidate for the position of chief of the army. At the meeting during which the selection was to be made, the nine *comandantes* sitting at the table were all equals. As Ramírez correctly points out, "There was not even a *primus inter pares*, because in order to speak, each had to wait his turn."[122]

This discursive regulation was meant to keep in check displays of eloquence that might sway opinions and destabilize the already precarious relations among the *comandantes*. Borge, a gifted orator, was a particular concern to Humberto Ortega. Who better than Borge to craft a self-abnegating speech designed precisely to earn him the right to the revolutionary virtue of sacrifice and, by extension, garner him a nomination by acclamation? The possible exploitation

---

119 Ramírez, *Adiós Muchachos*, 50–1.
120 Joseph Mulligan, S. J., *The Nicaraguan Church and the Revolution* (Kansas City, MO: Sheed & Ward, 1991), 222.
121 Ramírez, *Adiós Muchachos*, 50–1.
122 Ibid., 110–11.

of the virtuous revolutionary identity generated other anxieties. An individual *comandante*, for example, might not directly propose his own name, but he might well arrange for a proxy nomination.

At any rate, a name was finally thrown on the table. It was the logical one. The name proposed was that of *Comandante* Henry Ruiz, also known by his *nom de guerre*, Modesto, or Modest, in reference to his unassuming character.

Note here that as in the days of the Conservative Republic, actors intuitively understood two things about the environment in which they operated. First, rhetoric was far from inconsequential in politics. Second, in the face of rampant mistrust, character was an important consideration when choosing a leader. Modesto was ideal on both counts. He was a taciturn man, not at all adept or inclined to verbal agitation. Modesto, as his *nom de guerre* implied, was also a self-effacing stoic, even though he had been the commander of a legendary guerrilla column, a role that endowed him with a credible claim to revolutionary prestige and military competence.

But now take note of a different historical replay, this one reminiscent of Zelaya's maneuver during the 1893 meeting that established the revolutionary junta of that year. Upon hearing mention of his name, Modesto kept silent. Ramírez speculates that Modesto's silence might have been due to an excessive display of self-control, or perhaps to an inward calculation that no one would oppose his nomination. Regardless of the motivation, Modesto's reticence allowed Humberto Ortega to behave as if Modesto were refusing the burdensome responsibility of such a high position. In a tone that implied both courage and self-sacrifice, Humberto Ortega proclaimed: "Yo sí acepto." Properly translated, the phrase reveals its contextual connotation, and reads as, "Unlike Modesto, *I* dare to accept."

Although no one had nominated Humberto Ortega, he was now the chief of the EPS. Once in this position, Ortega was able to elevate his brother Daniel to the position of coordinator of the first government junta. Later, Humberto was also able to make Daniel the FSLN's presidential candidate and to anoint him secretary general of the party. But even as the Ortegas assumed these positions, the members of the National Directorate continued to regulate one another's rhetorical displays. This regulation was enforced with special zeal when it came to mass events. The exercise of vocality was carefully distributed, with *comandantes* literally taking turns to address the public at scheduled rallies and revolutionary commemorations.

This incipient form of rhetorical regulation, however, was not compatible with the chosen institutional organization of power. The *comandantes*, for example, were in agreement about the urgent need to create and entrench two commanding vertical structures: the army and the party. They also agreed that rhetorical regulation could prevent capture of either by any one particular *comandante*. But when juxtaposed, the leveling intent of regulation and the hierarchical effect of the leaders' institutional priorities and choices proved worse than incompatible. They created an incentive structure that tempted competing leaders to play to their individual strengths. The Ortega brothers concentrated on gaining and solidifying control of the army and the party, while the more charismatic Borge, for example, tried to establish his predominance by addressing "the masses" from a speaker's platform.

In fairly short order, a regime that featured the worst of both worlds took form. The Ortega brothers established themselves as *primi inter pares* atop a kind of feudal internal structure in which the other *comandantes* established themselves as lords over discrete turfs within the state apparatus, the economy, and the polity.[123] Modesto, for example, seized control of the Ministry of Planning, Jaime Wheelock ruled over the agrarian state sector, Borge directed the security apparatus, and Bayardo Arce led the mass organizations.

This arrangement, though self-serving, also turned into the functional expression of an idealistic transformative vision. As the director of the official FSLN publication *Barricada* explained:

State power was viewed as an instrument of revolutionary change. This meant that *everything* had to be controlled.... There were boundaries, but only to extent that we had a division of labor among the various power holders.[124]

These boundaries became blurred, however, as the politics of territoriality and mistrust gradually blended with genuine policy differences and, as a direct consequence, infested the state's ministerial machinery with corrosive jealousies. Worse yet, as the leadership tried to contain internal dissent by debilitating particular rivals, they embroiled party notables and ministers alike in reputational struggles. A prominent Sandinista minister would later recall "the slanderous accusations" leveled at him by another high-ranking Sandinista. The slanders, as the minister put it, were "perpetually engraved" on his mind. So were the machinations leading to the accusation, which the minister "interpreted as an expression of mistrust." The entire affair made a lasting impression on the aggrieved minister. "Many times, even ten years later," he later wrote, "I would remember this incident."[125]

Conflicts over matters of institutional authority and prerogatives also arose. This was especially the case between the party and the army. Tensions were slow to build, but by 1984 President Daniel Ortega and his brother, General Humberto Ortega, were engaged in a delicate, controlled dispute over institutional ascendance. The top-ranking FSLN officer later chosen by General Ortega to succeed him in the position of army chief recalls:

The Party wanted to meddle in the internal affairs of the Army . . . trying to insert *political commissars* into the ranks of the armed forces. We obviously resisted this attempt.[126]

[123] Miranda and Ratliff, *The Civil War in Nicaragua*, 19–47, 55.

[124] Author's interview with FSLN journalist and *Barricada* director Carlos Fernando Chamorro, Managua, 20 June 1994.

[125] Alejandro Martínez Cuenca, *Nicaragua: Una Década de Retos* (Managua: Editorial Nueva Nicaragua, 1990), 104–5.

[126] Author's interview with *comandante* Joaquín Cuadra Lacayo (selected by General Humberto Ortega to succeed him as chief of the Sandinista army), Managua, June 1995.

The phrase "political commissars," while borrowed from the Soviet lexicon, nevertheless captured the mutual suspicion among Nicaraguan revolutionaries, a suspicion that eventually engulfed even the Ortega brothers. But all these *intramural* struggles would come to light only after the FSLN was defeated at the polls. In the meantime, they rarely spilled into the public arena. An outside observer, in fact, would have been impressed by the neat polarization that, as trumpeted by the regime, seemingly divided the Revolution and its "enemies" into monolithic camps. Political arbitration itself was a polarizing act. And this, the FSLN often admitted by word and deed, was as it should be.

Expanding the Arena of Arbitration: Fomenting and Coping with Keen Contestation

Soon after its assumption of power, the FSLN confiscated all properties belonging to Somoza and his cronies, and it nationalized abandoned and idle assets. Through such measures, the emerging regime gained control of "over 23% of the country's most arable land and a vast assortment of highly-productive agroindustrial firms, ranging from sugar mills to coffee-processing, milk-pasteurizing, and meat-packing plants." Once the regime had assembled all these properties into a collection of state enterprises, known as Area de Propiedad del Pueblo (Area of the People's Property), it became the country's "largest agricultural producer and food processor."[127]

The FSLN also began to deploy a rhetorical strategy aimed at undermining the importance of electoral legitimation. The strategy was in itself interesting because it used the discourse of the vote to bolster the substantive criterion of legitimacy. First, the FSLN argued that the people had already voted by embracing the authorizing figure of Sandino, and by following the leadership of the FSLN in 1978 and 1979. In brief, the act of voting had taken place not at the polls but in historical conflicts in which the people made their preferences known. Second, the *comandantes* also argued that the FSLN derived its claim to supreme authority from the fact that the majority of Nicaraguans *were* Sandinistas. This was an old-fashioned attempt, often used by Latin American leaders, to merge rulers and citizens into an organic whole, with the former acting as the head of the body.[128]

For the head and body to act in concert, however, the regime would have to arbitrate among claims to identity, vocality, and resources. This endeavor began with a rhetorical process aimed at identifying worthy a priori claimants to participation in the Revolution. The regime, for example, proclaimed its "natural allies" to be workers, peasants, and public employees.[129] A second but equally important goal for arbitration was to organize vocality in numbers.

---

[127] Brizio Biondi-Morra, *Hungry Dreams: The Failure of Food Policy in Revolutionary Nicaragua, 1979–1990* (Ithaca, NY: Cornell University Press, 1993), 2.

[128] For striking examples of this rhetorical strategy, see the official *Patria Libre*, no. 4 (May 1980): 22; and no. 13 (April 1981): 3.

[129] Haugaard, "In and Out of Power," 164–5.

In the case of labor, this entailed gathering workers within the bounds of formal unions. In this, the regime met with impressive success: Unionization rose from approximately 11 percent of the salaried work force in 1979 to 56 percent by 1986.[130] A related goal was the establishment of tight institutional links between unions and the FSLN qua political party. As Richard Stahler-Sholk writes:

> The FSLN national directorate appointed the unions' regional and national leadership, which like other mass organizations, were subject to Party discipline. In addition, because these unions were predominant in the state-owned sector – approximately 40% of the economy – they dealt directly with the state. This was another constraining factor on the autonomy of Sandinista unions. The ministry of labor, for example, could approve or reject collective bargaining agreements; and strikes were banned.[131]

The arbitration logic between the regime and organized labor, as in the early years of the Somoza regime, hinged on a crucial exchange. The regime accorded unions resources and legal protection; the unions gave political support.[132] This meant that nonaligned or dissenting labor organizations were at the receiving end of punitive policies:

> Non-Sandinista unions, meanwhile, received discriminatory treatment through a series of policies like closed shops, automatic payroll deductions for union dues, and a "one union per enterprise" rule, all of which favored the Sandinista unions.[133]

This partial approach to labor would come back to haunt the Revolution's leaders. Already, in the agrarian sector, the regime was learning that the body did not always agree with the head. Between 1982 and 1983, a group of former Somoza *guardia* officers funded by the Reagan administration – known in everyday lexicon as the Contra – began attracting substantial peasant support against the regime. The top-level Sandinista officer we met before explains:

> We were facing an extremely difficult situation in the Northern zone. The Contra had appropriated the issue of land distribution as its flag. This was terrible, because *we* were supposed to be the revolutionaries. And the Contras were beating us. In fact, I actually moved to the North to contend with this crisis. Ultimately the way we dealt with it was to accept that we had to distribute land among the peasants and give them a rifle to defend it.[134]

But how had this happened to start with? First, the popular insurrection that had led the FSLN to power had been an urban phenomenon. Peasants thus had no prior bonds of camaraderie or allegiance to the revolutionary leadership. Second, and relatedly,

> ... peasants on the agrarian frontier, where there was little or no state presence, had a legacy of individualism which later made them hostile to what they saw as the

---

[130] Stahler-Sholk, "The Dog That Didn't Bark," 79.
[131] Ibid., 79.
[132] Ibid., 81–2.
[133] Ibid., 79.
[134] Author's interview with Cuadra Lacayo, 22 June 1995.

encroachment of the revolutionary state. Traditional patterns of clientelism, linking peasants to their wealthier neighbors, helped mute the spread of a more radical consciousness.[135]

Moreover, the way in which the regime responded to peasants' claims was deemed inappropriate, even unjust, by a vast segment of those same claimants:

The opportunity to work under better conditions than before on state-owned farms and...later, to join a cooperative was what the new government first offered to the rural population, rather than the individual land reforms that peasants had dreamed about.[136]

Nor were peasant producers accustomed to dealing with a meddling state. They were particularly unhappy with the FSLN's imposition of "state controls over marketing and pricing."[137]

Against this background of unhappiness and with the war raging,

...the draft became the key point of tension between the government and the peasantry. Caught between the draft and the contras, peasants in the country's interior, who might have preferred to remain neutral, often chose the latter.[138]

In its Manichean structuration of identities and politics, the regime committed yet another blunder: It marginalized and even stigmatized the informal sector, which by 1985 included an estimated 60 percent of women and 49 percent of men in the economically active population. These independent-minded urbanites were now instructed from above on how to conduct their business. They also "became objects of official scorn through anti-speculation campaigns which placed the blame on a whole sector for the misdeeds of a few." Worse yet, because sociopolitical stereotyping guided the FSLN's organizational apparatus, the party could recognize the presence and voices of workers and peasants, but failed to understand or accommodate the complex array of social identities that had traditionally pushed the urban economy forward. "For the artisan, market seller, the taxi driver and the baker, there was no place except in the women's and neighborhood associations – the organizations which, as it turned out, proved least capable of mobilizing and advocating for their membership."[139]

The neighborhood associations proved particularly disappointing precisely because they failed to deepen the regime's capacity for legitimate, encompassing arbitration. If anything, they threw grassroots arbitration into a mixture of chaos and polarization. Known as Comités de Defensa Sandinista (Sandinista Defense Committees, [CDSs]), these associations were meant to endow neighborhoods with organized vocality vis-á-vis city government. The ultimate aim

[135] Haugaard, "In and Out of Power," 161–2.
[136] Ibid., 163–4.
[137] Ibid., 164.
[138] Ibid.
[139] Ibid., 164–5.

was for neighborhood committees effectively to lobby authorities on behalf of social projects beneficial to their constituencies. But the committees quickly developed a pronounced "partisan" character, which in turn reinforced the apathy of those citizens who wished to avoid taking "a political stance." The upshot was that these committees turned into petty courts of adjudication, routinely making decisions on who did or did not deserve the resources at their disposal. Yet these little courts depleted rather than built legitimacy. "Accusations of favoritism, of discrimination against non-Sandinista residents dogged the CDSs from their inception. In the late 1980s, as participation plummeted, the CDSs reorganized along less partisan lines and focused more exclusively on concrete community needs."[140]

The lesson that top-heavy arbitration was likely to intensify disputation both at the base and at the apex was lost on the revolutionary leaders when the time came to elaborate the Revolution's Constitution. One of the charter's architects recalls:

The Constitution of 1987 was made especially for the Revolution. I was a member of both the drafting committee and the review commission, and I remember that we consulted with all the Latin American constitutions. We were looking for the strongest justifiable form of presidentialism. In the end,... we gave the president faculties that even in the most powerful presidential systems properly belong to Congress. We did this because, even though we were the majority in the Congress, there was always a lack of trust. And we did not want any more debates.[141]

The Constitution of 1987 was created in the context of the war with the Contras. The war, in fact, was integral to the compelling reason that justified the relevant actors' choice of a superpresidential system. Simply put, the war undermined a regime whose military wherewithal was nearly depleted by the late 1980s:

We were exhausted. We even had to drag into battle *tuertos* [people missing one eye] and *rencos* [the lame]. The Contra had thirty thousand men under arms. The country was destroyed. In the countryside, any boy who could carry a backpack was snatched by whoever got to him first, either us or the Contras.[142]

But the crafting of this compelling reason also involved other elements. In a context of utter military exhaustion and economic deterioration, the informal economy, which the FSLN had previously ignored or vilified, kept expanding rapidly. With the war raging in the countryside, peasants sought refuge and work in the cities only to find that formal jobs were scarce and poorly paid. Meanwhile, the cities' own industrial workers, facing rapid real wage decline, sought better earnings in the informal economy.[143] This growing sector, needless to say, harbored no deep fealty to the regime. Moreover, even Sandinista unions

---

[140] Ibid., 165.
[141] Author's interview with FSLN legal expert Rafael Solís Cerda, Managua, 8 June 1995.
[142] Author's interview with Cuadra Lacayo, 1995.
[143] Haugaard, "In and Out of Power," 164–5.

began to defy party discipline.[144] The government's formal strike ban could not prevent the work stoppages and wildcat strikes by Central Sandinista de Trabajador (CST) affiliates. (Work stoppages were called "active takeovers" because strikes were illegal. In 1987, there were thirty-eight active takeovers.[145])

In other words, like the Somoza dynasty in the late 1970s, the regime found itself at the center of an urban field of normative scheming – a field on which the most intense grievances and contradictory interests came into play in full view of a concentrated population. Should an eruption occur, the leadership needed to be able to take legal measures to contain it. The Constitution of 1987 provided the juridical frame for such a scenario by endowing the regime with the power to contain unrest swiftly. This was key for the regime's top normative schemers; the very last thing the leadership wanted to do was to engage in bloody repression of the popular sectors.[146]

Substantive (De)legitimation

In 1981, Humberto Ortega gave a fiery speech to the EPS troops, arguing that "Sandinismo without Marxist-Leninism could not be revolutionary." Prior to that speech, Ortega had warned in a press interview that in case of a United States invasion, "there would not be enough trees in Nicaragua from which to hang the entire bourgeoisie." The statements made news abroad, especially because Ortega had them published in a pamphlet. After a private censure from the National Directorate, however, he retrieved the pamphlet and issued a new version that deleted the objectionable phrases. The original publication was attributed to a "maneuver by the enemy."[147]

Ortega had gone too far, making statements that imperiled the Revolution's international image as purely nationalist and strategically pursuing a hybrid economic model. But he had also gone too far in making the kind of bid for rhetorical supremacy one might have expected of Borge rather than Ortega. These excesses, however, were a temptation for other members of the Directorate as well. *Comandante* Jaime Wheelock, himself a member of the class slated for hanging, articulated his vision of the private sector's role as follows:

> Their place in the revolution [is that] of those who are called upon to prepare the food at a banquet. But they are not invited [to partake in it]. They merely prepare the food. And we want to keep them hidden away in the kitchen, not to come out.[148]

This statement was problematic for reasons similar to Ortega's. Moreover, the depiction of capitalists as kitchen servants hardly reflected reality. The lack of unity and coherence of the Nicaraguan upper classes in general and the

---

[144] Stahler-Sholk, "The Dog That Didn't Bark," 84.
[145] Ibid., 79.
[146] Author's interview with Cuadra Lacayo, 1995.
[147] Ramírez, *Adiós Muchachos*, 113.
[148] Forrest Colburn, *Managing the Commanding Heights: Nicaragua's State Enterprises* (Berkeley, CA: University of California Press, 1990), 35.

socioeconomic elites in particular actually helped them strike ad hoc deals with the revolutionary regime, especially as the latter confronted the harsh exigencies of making an economy run. As one scholar put it, the regime pursued a strategy of "divide and negotiate."[149] So while there may have been a kitchen, the state and the private sector were cooking not meals but deals.

These deals, however, were unstable. The private sector could not trust the "concessions" made by the regime because they were revocable. The arbiter could change the rules to self-serving advantage depending on how the game played out.[150] The regime, for its part, had to contend with the blunt fact that major producers of cotton and coffee, for example, could opt not to invest or produce, or at least scale down. They held part of the key to the economy's recovery. The upshot of all this was paradoxical. First, a regime whose claim to justifiable power derived from its promise of a better future for the nation's weakest citizens began to spend much time and energy negotiating with the most powerful capitalists. Second, the deals might satisfy short-term economic imperatives on both sides, but the ad hoc and revocable nature of the regime's concessions and the producers' implicit power of blackmail engendered mistrust among the parties to the deals.

Indeed, the parties to these behind-the-scenes negotiations increasingly relied on tactics that simultaneously locked them into an informal alliance and deepened their mutual resentment. The FSLN, by reserving for itself the right to decide who had been a Somocista businessperson or farmer, held in its hand the power to confiscate the property of anyone. Businesspeople and producers, for their part, became more aggressive during negotiations in leveraging their discretionary power over their own investment decisions, whose importance rose dramatically as the failures of the regime's state enterprises became only more glaring.[151]

By 1985, the performance of state enterprises was so dismal that even the government recognized it as a serious problem.[152] In fact, the massive restructuring of the production apparatus – based on a prior judgment in favor of greater equality – was yielding disastrous economic results. Worse yet, the revolutionary regime was more dependent than ever on the cooperation of the very capitalist elites it had once vilified.

Meanwhile, in the explicitly political arena, as in the days of the Somozas, the politicized members of the upper class assumed a variety of positions vis-á-vis the FSLN regime, from supportive to hostile, from sympathetic to cautious.[153] By 1981, virtually every prominent family in the country was beginning to split

---

[149] See Rose J. Spalding, *Capitalists and Revolution in Nicaragua: Opposition and Accommodation 1979–1993* (Chapel Hill, NC: University of North Carolina Press, 1994), 19–30, 128–1, 138–9, 148–55.

[150] Consejo Superior de Empresa Privada (COSEP), *Análisis Sobre la Ejecución del Programa de Gobierno de Reconstrucción Nacional* (Managua: COSEP, 1980).

[151] Biondi-Morra, *Hungry Dreams*, 2.

[152] Ibid., 2–3.

[153] See Spalding, *Capitalists and Revolution*, 123–55.

between Sandinistas and non-Sandinistas. The Chamorro clan and its newspaper *La Prensa* represented only the most visible example of this phenomenon. The immediate reason for the Chamorros' familial division, however, is also particularly instructive, because with control of *La Prensa* at stake, all members were vying to fill the vacuum of preeminence left behind by the martyred *paterfamilias*. Ultimately, the anti-Sandinista faction prevailed, while their pro-FSLN relatives joined the regime's official and semi-official media.[154]

Once in the open, the battle between the FSLN and the Chamorros of *La Prensa* proved remarkably conventional. Each camp aimed to unmask the other. *La Prensa* challenged the *comandantes'* "revolutionary mystique" by highlighting their violations of their own self-abnegating code of conduct – it challenged, in a word, their virtuous identity. FSLN publications, in turn, set out to debunk the notion of the Chamorro clan as an exemplar of self-sacrifice whose deeds were solely aimed at improving the lot of their Nicaraguan "family." Predictably, both perceived the accusations leveled at them as "slander" and "character assassination," and more importantly, as confirmation of the other's perversity.[155]

Other conventional tactics were used. The FSLN, for example, unleashed violent political mobs on its opponents, including those associated with *La Prensa*. By deploying plainclothes groups armed with machetes and stones, the Sandinistas were refining a practice favored by the Somozas.[156] But this kind of violent mobilization, we have seen, goes back even further than the Somoza dynasty. Throughout the transition to independence and most of the nineteenth century, leaders agitated from behind the scenes, encouraging the "crowd" to "demonstrate" their moralist indignation through riots. These were the dramas of inexorable collective ire that at key points in the country's history allowed leaders the degrees of freedom denied to them by the central dictate of obedience – obedience to the Crown, obedience to the constitution, obedience to their chiefs, obedience to their own avowed political tenets.

As the revolutionary regime followed its dual-tack approach – gradual economic accommodation with powerful capitalists such as the Pellas-Chamorro group and increasingly polarized relations with politically powerful groups such as the Chamorros of *La Prensa* – the practice of "unmasking" became central to actors' normative scheming. The large coalition known as United National Opposition (UNO), in particular, was determined to reveal the regime as a band of authoritarian Marxists posing as pluralist builders of a mixed economy.[157] The FSLN, for its part, was bent on showing UNO as a band of retrogrades

---

[154] Chamorro Cardenal's youngest son, Carlos Fernando, became the director of the official FSLN paper *Barricada*, whereas the eldest son joined the Contras. In addition, one of Chamorro Cardenal's brothers founded the pro-Sandinista newspaper *El Nuevo Diario*, while another brother remained at *La Prensa*. See Chamorro Cardenal, *La Prensa: The Republic of Paper*.

[155] Ibid., 5, 20.

[156] Ibid.

[157] See Kagan, *A Twilight Struggle*, 256–61.

who were even afraid to compete at the polls in the 1984 presidential and congressional elections.

These elections, in which Daniel Ortega first ran for president, were a critical turning point precisely because the FSLN now needed to establish its "democratic" credentials, though without risking loss of power, and UNO wanted to deny the FSLN these credentials without risking a defeat of its own at the polls. The entire electoral process came to resemble a poker game between phantoms because on both sides the players merely wanted to appear to be playing the formal game when in fact their intention was to play the game of unmasking.[158]

Intracamp divisions rooted in traditional Manicheanism also afflicted the armed opposition to the FSLN. In the mid-1980s, at the height of the animosity between the FSLN and the Resistance Movement (better known as the Contra), the latter was plagued by bitter internal struggles in which the antagonists perceived themselves as "democrats" and the others as "antidemocrats." But more importantly, beneath these labels were passions and interests that had been at play for a very long time in Nicaraguan politics. These passions and interests, as in the case of the FSLN *comandantes*, had to do with justifiable power conceived as the ability to command authority on the basis of virtuousness. The Contra movement's Manichean confrontation had two fronts: one inside Nicaragua, the other inside itself.[159]

The internal conflicts between former Somoza guard officers and former FSLN allies were undeniably keen. Conflicts between members of the old anti-Somoza civil opposition and members of the old anti-Somoza armed opposition were even keener. Finally, conflicts between those striving for a progressive socioeconomic agenda and those striving for a return to the status quo ante were the keenest. At the rank-and-file level, combatants relied on their military valor and prowess to outdo one another in the battle against the enemy. At the level of the leadership, actors resorted to internal unmasking in competitive bids for the combatants' allegiance. Maneuvering aimed at manipulating their supporters in Washington was also a constant with the Contra leaders.

The result of all this was that Contra elite politics resulted in a high rate of alliance formation and dissolution at the expense of their avowed purpose:

---

[158] In the United States, the Reagan administration was divided between soft-liners, mostly in the State Department, and hard-liners, mostly in the CIA. The latter believed that if the opposition participated in the election, it would be simply legitimating a Leninist dictatorship; the soft-liners preferred to call the FSLN's bluff. The FSLN, for its part, feared that even if it won the presidential election, it might lose seats in the Assembly to the opposition. As the campaign got under way, UNO's presidential candidate, Arturo Cruz Porras, found himself caught between extremes. As a former member of the FSLN government, he was an object of deep mistrust among UNO's hard-liners, especially Enrique Bolaños (elected president in 2002). Bolaños' strategy was to proceed with the electoral campaign up to a point, and then withdraw in protest. Cruz Porras himself wavered between thinking that UNO ought to carry the process to its logical conclusion and feeling that the whole thing was hopeless. Author's interview with Cruz Porras, June 2002.

[159] See Consuelo Cruz Sequeira, "Mistrust and Violence in Nicaragua: Ideology and Politics," *LARR* 30, no. 1 (1995): 223–5.

to articulate the justice of the cause in whose name thirty thousand Contra soldiers were killing and dying. This was just one of many paradoxes. More would follow. As the war dragged on, the Sandinista army increasingly gained autonomy from the party. In fact, because the revolutionary regime's energies were concentrated almost fully on the war effort, the army's voice became the most authoritative. Simply put, through the process of war making, the regime began to lose political control over its organized means of coercion.[160]

Conclusion

The Conservative Republic conciliated to a significant degree the electoral principle and substantive criterion of legitimation. The Republic's collapse, by unhinging the two, reopened the vacuum of legitimate arbitration. The regimes that followed – from the Caesarist and dynastic variants of liberalism exemplified by Zelaya and the Somoza family to the revolutionary FSLN – all sought to fill this vacuum. Both the struggles that brought them to power and those that brought them down were shaped by a system of Manichean normative scheming, on whose field of imaginable possibilities the substantive criterion overpowered but did not eliminate the electoral alternative.

Other changes and continuities came into play. As the national economy modernized, the localities and partisan camps whose conflicting claims had eclipsed all others were themselves gradually overshadowed by new actors and grievances. Dominant economic groups diversified, workers organized, and peasants migrated from countryside to city. But leaders in power continued to claim for themselves the role and prerogatives of grand arbiter; that is, they sought to render and enforce decisions on the validity of public claims and to settle disputes among claimants. Ultimately, their goal eluded them. Indeed, each of these arbiters, in one way or another, injured their people and strengthened the national narrative of fate. By the end of the 1980s, nearly a century after the collapse of the Republic, the nation was once again exhausted by war and economic ruin.

Against this backdrop, and for different reasons, all the relevant actors moved to restore the electoral principle to its original centrality. As we will see next with this restoration came the last critical juncture of the twentieth century. Identities and practices, interests and norms – indeed, reality and realism – all were about to be challenged and reshaped.

---

[160] Author's interview with Cuadra Lacayo, 1995.

8

Transition

Familiar Novelties

> The tradition of all the dead generations weighs like a nightmare on the brain of the living.
>
> –Karl Marx[1]

Had Marx been born in Costa Rica, tradition probably would have been more like a placid dream. Had he been born in Nicaragua, it would have been a nightmare indeed. Of course, had he been presented with these options, he probably would have preferred not to be born at all. In any case, the central point remains: Because our perception of tradition varies across time and place, so does the relationship between legacies and agency. This holds most clearly when political actors are confronted with a tumultuous play of normative dictates and shifting interests. At such moments, we have seen, leaders seek to create and convey compelling reasons that enable and perhaps even embolden them and others to make difficult choices.

By the close of the 1980s, Nicaraguans found themselves at just such a juncture. Political elites shared both a long-standing Manichean historiography – with its concomitant injunctions – and an immediate interest in ending the armed conflict between the FSLN regime and the National Resistance Movement (Contra). This common interest stemmed from a combination of factors: the end of the Cold War, the country's economic devastation and social exhaustion, and a number of foreign governments pressing the relevant domestic actors for pacification.

In this context, the electoral route to peace became an additional point of convergence. The FSLN regime and its domestic opponents managed to agree on an electoral reform that sufficiently enhanced political and civil liberties for credible elections to be held in 1990. This reform, previously deemed unthinkable by leaders across the spectrum, ushered in a generally accepted electoral

---

[1] Karl Marx, *The Eighteenth Brumaire of Louis Bonaparte*, 2nd ed. (New York: International Publishers, 1972), 15.

process that in turn produced stunning results. An uneasy but broad electoral coalition, the Unión Nicaraguense Opositora (UNO), and its candidate, Violeta Barrios de Chamorro, won 54.7 percent of the votes, while the FSLN presidential incumbent, Daniel Ortega, received 40.8 percent of the ballots.[2]

Until the very last moment, polls had shown an increasing lead for the FSLN. Post election analyses would later indicate that even the most seasoned and objective pollsters simply failed to take note of "Nicaraguans' long-standing tradition of concealing their true preferences."[3]

The concealment of preferences at the popular level was but one of several manifestations of the mistrust that, at the elite level, soon would cause previously hidden tensions to degenerate into open splintering both within the UNO coalition and the commanding structures of the FSLN. Before that contentious outcome, however, negotiating the peace remained the most pressing postelectoral goal. After all, a negotiated peace was the primary reason for holding supervised elections in the first place – a reason that was most urgent for President-Elect Chamorro, who simply would not be able to govern absent a modicum of peace.

Early on, Chamorro drew on her newly won electoral legitimacy to bring about the "reconciliation of the national family." The rhetorical strategy of familial harmony, employed so often in the country's history to bypass Manichean obstacles, was once again meant to clear the path for an agreement between opposing camps – an agreement that, from a normative perspective, would be deemed objectionable without the moral suasion presumably implicit in the vision of a national family at peace.

The familial strategy, however, entailed the creation of a political center in a fractious polity. Indeed, success in this endeavor was critical in ways not obvious to those living in the moment. For if the administration managed to create and expand such a center, it could simultaneously attend to its self-seeking and normative goals, building support for its pro-democratic program while legitimating the political ambitions harbored by its leading figures. A legitimate center, in fact, would mark the beginning of a deep transformation in the polity's Manichean system of normative scheming.

This chapter demonstrates that the centering of politics was not necessarily an unrealistic prospect. Important political actors who previously had been engaged in the construction of Manichean historiography and the politics of unmasking[4] were after the elections perplexed and suddenly forced to make

---

[2] Violeta Chamorro is the widow of Pedro Joaquín Chamorro Cardenal, the opposition leader whose assassination triggered the uprising that toppled the Somoza regime. After the FSLN's victory in 1979, she served as a member of the revolutionary junta.

[3] Leslie Anderson, "Elections and Public Opinion in the Development of Nicaraguan Democracy," Mitchell A. Seligson and John Booth, eds., *Elections and Democracy in Central America Revisited* (Chapel Hill, NC: University of North Carolina Press, 1995), 90–3.

[4] Illustrative of the Sandinista variant of Manichean unmasking is Tomás Borge's *The Patient Impatience* (Willimantic, CT: Curbstone Press, 1991). For a more traditional variant, see Jaime Chamorro Cardenal, *La Prensa: The Republic of Paper* (New York: Freedom House, 1988).

sense of a changing reality and their uncertain place in it. As if following the hand of an invisible conductor, they began reshaping their normative realism to regain a relatively firm footing. Even at the highest levels of the FSLN, actors would now argued that "reality" and "justice" dictated that political democracy was an unavoidable precondition for sustainable peace and socioeconomic progress. This emerging normative realism represented a marked departure from the late 1970s and the 1980s, when the FSLN regime subordinated the electoral principle of legitimation to the substantive criterion of socioeconomic transformation.

But the chapter also shows that as actors increasingly framed the transition to democracy as a choice between a dark past and a brighter future, they began to organize their normative scheming in terms drawn from their traditional narrative of fate. That is, they organized their struggles for power and for the greater good according to a Manichean opposition, casting themselves as champions of novelties like democratic moderation and their rivals as the stubborn, living ghosts of intolerance, deceit, and despotism. These struggles, waged by actors themselves convinced and seeking to persuade others that they were in combat with fate, ultimately led even the best to intensify the polarization they sought to transcend. And yet, this was not a foreordained outcome. Rather, it was the result of political-cultural constructs that, after a moment of malleability in the field of imaginable possibilities, increasingly restricted that field.

History, Compelling Reasons, and Transition

Changes in world politics, dramatized by Third Wave democratization and the collapse of the Berlin Wall, gave impetus to the new normative realism emerging among key segments of the FSLN. The first tangible moves appeared as no more than pragmatic accommodation. Most notably, the FSLN leadership – and the Ejército Popular Sandinista (EPS) in particular – was keen to negotiate a settlement with the incoming administration. This became evident during a crucial meeting between Antonio Lacayo, the son-in-law of the president-elect, and three top-ranking Sandinistas: General Humberto Ortega and *comandantes* Joaquín Cuadra and Jaime Wheelock. At this meeting, conducted in the presence of former U.S. President Jimmy Carter, the three FSLN leaders insisted on the demobilization of the Contra, demanded "respect" for the EPS officer corps, and argued that the incoming government ought to recognize the Revolution's agrarian reform as irrevocable and guarantee possession of all expropriated housing.

Chamorro's son-in-law, by then clearly emerging as the president-elect's chief decision maker, would later recall the gist of the discussion:

I told [the FSLN leaders] that [Mrs. Chamorro] wished to be the president of all Nicaraguans and, like Sandino himself, wanted no more than a small national army. This could be accomplished only by respecting and reducing the army that was [already] recognized by the Constitution, that is to say, the EPS, and by demobilizing the other army, the army of the Resistencia Nicaraguense [the Contra]. All this, of course, was premised on the understanding that the constitutional army would respect and support every decision made by the president of Nicaragua, a role soon to be assumed by [Mrs. Chamorro]. Humber to Ortega nodded his head in assent. For me, this was enough.[5]

A month after that meeting, the government-elect turned to the task of dealing with the Contra. To this end, Lacayo traveled to Honduras, where the movement was based. He was accompanied by the cardinal, whose anti-Sandinista credentials and spiritual authority were meant to reassure the Contra *comandantes*. Significantly, the leading Contra interlocutor refused to label the talks a "negotiation" – a term that in Costa Rica connotes open-minded civility but in Nicaragua carries the stigma of "pact making." The Contra leader insisted instead that this was a "dialogue."[6]

The dialogue produced the Toncontín Accord, whereby the new administration and the Contra leadership launched a demobilization process that culminated in the disbanding of approximately twenty-three thousand resistance fighters. The Accord also stipulated that FSLN military forces would be reduced from about ninty-six thousand soldiers at the beginning of January to forty-one thousand by July.[7]

In the hours immediately following the Accord's completion, General Ortega signaled his approval with a single but powerful gesture. That same night, two airplanes left Nicaragua carrying Cuban military personnel back home.[8] From that moment on, the government felt confident that the Accord could serve as the cornerstone of its Transition Protocol.

The Protocol outlined the government's central expectations and commitments. The most salient are worth enumerating. The Contra was to be fully demobilized by April 1990. The EPS, recognized as the constitutional army, was to behave as a professional, apolitical body subject to civilian authority, but in turn, the institutional integrity of the EPS was to be acknowledged and respected, even in such sensitive matters as the appointments and promotion of officers. The government would strive to guarantee the juridical stability of properties assigned by the state to urban and rural beneficiaries prior to February 25, 1990. And lastly, the relevant actors agreed to the orderly transfer of executive authority, and to the preclusion of revanchist agendas.[9]

---

[5] This meeting took place on February 27, 1990, two days after Chamorro's victory at the polls. See Antonio Lacayo, "Introduction" in Violeta Barrios de Chamorro, *Memorias de Mi Gobierno* vol. 1 (Managua: Gobierno de la República de Nicaragua, Dirección de Comunicación Social de la Presidencia, 1996), 21.

[6] Ibid., 22.

[7] Daniel Premo, "The Redirection of the Armed Forces," in Thomas Walker, ed., *Nicaragua without Illusions: Regime Transition and Structural Adjustment in the 1990s* (Wilmington, DE: Scholarly Resources Books, 1997), 68.

[8] Barrios de Chamorro, *Memorias*, 22–3.

[9] Ibid., 72.

At a more profound level, however, the administration's understanding of the transition process took as its point of departure the nation's traditional historiography. For the incoming president, the key historical lesson was inescapable:

Ideological justifications [for authoritarian rule] have been diverse, ranging from Conservatism and Liberalism to Sandinismo. [But] since the days of the Spanish colony, Nicaraguan society has lived under an oligarchic, patriarchical political model.[10]

This was the past that Chamorro, as so many leaders before her, sought to replace with a tabula rasa on which to start anew. And as so many other leaders before her, she held out the structure of the family as the paradigm for the nation's future.[11] From this paradigmatic vision flowed a broad and unconditional amnesty for all past political crimes, as well as a delicate presidential balancing act. On the one hand, Chamorro "ordered" General Ortega "to remain" in the army's leadership position for the duration of the demobilization process. On the other hand, she charged General Ortega with the dual task of reducing the EPS and ensuring its respect for the primacy of civilian authority and the constitutional order.

The EPS leaders were willing to do their part, but they had conditions of their own. As one top-ranking officer later explained:

We are not going to submit to a *mechanical* subordination to civilian authority. Nor are we going to submit to the dictates of an elected or appointed official who is hostile to the army and seeks not its professionalization but its debilitation and displacement.[12]

Chamorro addressed the military's concerns by personally assuming not only the title of supreme commander of the armed forces but also the cabinet position of minister of defense.[13] In so doing, she made plain her determination to insulate the army from revanchist pressures and, by extension, to facilitate the ongoing transition to peace and democracy.

But creating a tabula rasa on which to superimpose the familial model would prove difficult at best and counterproductive at worst. As the new administration set out to implement its austerity and privatization policies, the FSLN's political leaders flexed their protest muscle by mobilizing trade unions in the streets. Meanwhile, alliances were already breaking down inside the administration, where the familial model failed even in the literal sense.[14] The clan-based political arrangements that had provided cohesion during the campaign now generated severe friction. Most notably, the executive and legislative branches – each led by members of two related clans – began to feud for preeminence. By

---

[10] Ibid. 25.

[11] Ibid., 78.

[12] Author's interview with *Comandante* Joaquín Cuadra Lacayo (General Ortega's hand-picked successor, who assumed the role of army chief in 1995), Managua, 22 June 1995.

[13] See Chamorro's inaugural speech. Barrios de Chamorro, *Memorias*, 78–81.

[14] Familial ties had failed to hold the Chamorro clan together as early as the 1980s, right after the triumph of the Revolution. Mrs. Chamorro's own four children were evenly split; two were with the FSLN, two with the opposition.

the end of 1991, President Chamorro and the president of the Congress – recent political/familial allies – had become sworn enemies.[15]

Nor could the administration count on the loyalty of UNO's congressional bloc. If anything, most UNO deputies now considered the administration a unilateral pact maker undeserving of their trust. This meant that the president frequently lacked a legislative majority and had to resort to rule by executive decree. It also meant that the administration could afford alienating the FSLN even less. This is how one high-ranking administration official canvassed the postelection scenario:

We were facing a difficult reality. The FSLN had garnered 40 percent of the votes; it was also belligerent, and quite capable of mobilizing its supporters. *And* it still had an army eighty thousand strong. Recall that in 1990 the FSLN encouraged terribly destructive riots in which even barricades and guns were part of the scene. Trying to govern under those circumstances without finding a way *to moderate* the FSLN would have been a grave mistake. So we took steps in this direction. But what do *they* [the political parties] say? That we, the administration, sold out [emphasis added].[16]

What the administration saw as a realistic attempt at moderation its critics saw as a reassertion of the very patriarchical, oligarchic model that Chamorro disavowed. One disgruntled former cabinet member put it most starkly:

Lacayo had the legality of Mrs. Chamorro's electoral victory. Daniel Ortega had the political leverage of the FSLN's National Directorate. And Humberto Ortega had the means of coercion – the armed forces. The three of them forged a very narrow pact because they were all operating from an oligarchic perspective. The basic agreement they reached was this: The FSLN would stop the riots, and in exchange, the government would give Daniel Ortega and his clientele a slice of the properties slated either for privatization or distribution; the army would keep peace and order, and in exchange, the government would allow General Ortega to remain in his post.

There was no novelty in this framework; no national developmental vision. This was purely an allocation of power and economic quotas.... This was an exclusionary project dating back to the conquest and the colonial regime...*a model that is four centuries old* yet still knows nothing about human dignity.[17]

The idea that state-controlled productive resources could be used to facilitate the transition to peace was intuitively appealing. Land, in particular, could be distributed as compensation to demobilized Contra and EPS combatants. But delays and complications in the formalization of property rights made it impossible for the vast majority of the intended beneficiaries – especially

---

[15] "Letter from Alfredo César, President of the Congress to President Violeta Chamorro," Managua, 8 November 1991. (Cesar was the brother-in-law of Lacayo, President Chamorro's son-in-law and chief decision maker.)

[16] Author's interview with Ernesto Leal (the administration's chief negotiator with Congress), Managua, 21 June 1995.

[17] Author's interviews with Francisco Mayorga (Chamorro's first Central Bank president), Managua, 17 June 1994, and 12 June 1995. By the time of these interviews, Mayorga was out of favor and out of office.

peasant cooperatives and workers – to obtain titles. This lack of titles, in turn, meant that credit was unavailable, and without credit no one could put land to productive use.

The delays and complications stemmed from a variety of sources, including sheer administrative disorder and political arbitrariness. To begin with, immediately after its electoral defeat, the FSLN had rushed through its lame-duck Congress a bundle of laws meant to secure the Revolution's property reform. The laws, for example, granted property rights to occupants of state-owned housing and to agricultural cooperatives. For lack of time, however, the properties at stake could not be registered or titled. This missing step left the beneficiaries vulnerable to future disputations. In addition, a number of FSLN leaders used the laws as a cover for self-dealing, thus rendering the laws themselves vulnerable to political attack and ethical criticism. The new administration also aggravated the problem by making contradictory promises to a multiplicity of claimants, many of whom were still armed.[18]

The lack of effective arbitration powers that the executive demonstrated in handling these disputes further underscored its dependence on the EPS for establishing and maintaining of peace and order. EPS compliance with the transition accord, by definition, required the army to support and enforce executive decisions. But this in turn entailed disencumbering the EPS from its prior commitment to the Revolution and its vanguard party. The leading officers of the EPS recognized this imperative. They also understood the delicate nature of the requisite transformative process. The rhetorical strategy that these officers followed has much to tell us about how highly constrained actors seek to enhance their degrees of freedom. It tells us, most specifically, how actors refashion their normative realism and then proceed to construct compelling reasons for "acting" in ways that deviate from or even contradict their previous positions. In a word, the strategy tells us how actors begin to readjust their normative scheming.

The EPS's leadership made its initial rhetorical move by highlighting its "choice" for peace. All its other claims, in fact, would flow from this choice, which simultaneously distanced the army both from the war and from FSLN politicians. But how did they explain the choice itself? Here, they invoked a new clarity of vision. This is how General Ortega's hand-picked successor for the army's leadership position explained this vision and its distancing consequences:

Prior to 1990, thousands of individuals justified their existence by referencing their FSLN membership. For them, partisan activism was a way of life, and expropriation was a political act. We [the FSLN regime] took away the property of people who were not correctly aligned. The same can be said of the agrarian reform, which we increasingly

---

[18] Many of the farmlands being held in the inventory of the agrarian reform, for example, were distributed at least twice: once to Sandinista cooperatives without title, and in a second round, to demobilized Contra combatants. The upshot was a combustive mix of original owners, invaders, and beneficiaries of the two distribution rounds. Author's interview with Mayorga, 1995, and former FSLN Minister Alejandro Martínez Cuenca, June 1994.

used as a way of managing the war. But then came the shift in the international correlation of forces. At that moment, some of us inside the FSLN gained a degree of *lucidity*. We saw that a return to guerrilla warfare was *not feasible*. We also saw that *we could win even if we lost*, because we could not go on with the war, nor did we want to go on with the war. And besides, a continuation of the war was simply not just. *There was no justice in this for anyone.*[19]

In this rendition, then, changes in world politics lifted a fog, enabling army leaders to see more clearly the reconfigured relationship among constraints, opportunity, and justice. In particular, the army now perceived and seized the opportunity to extricate itself from the role of enforcer of arbitration decisions that were untenable. These decisions, according to the new EPS logic, were untenable on three counts. First, an impoverished and besieged state could not go on providing a livelihood for countless partisan activists. Second, there were limits to the state's use of expropriations as a disciplinary instrument. And third, the time for rational and just armed struggle was over.

By framing "reality" in this way, the EPS admitted to itself and to others that institutional self-redefinition was its one realistic alternative. It began this process of redefinition by recognizing Chamorro's difficult position. EPS officers understood that she had to contend with voices from various quarters calling either for the abolition of the army or, at a minimum, for the dismissal of General Ortega. Moreover, they recognized that she had ruled in favor of the EPS on two occasions already: Not only had she agreed in 1990 to the general's continued role as chief of the army, but in 1991 issued an executive decree endowing the Military Council with the power to dismiss its chief. Indeed, to demonstrate the wisdom of Chamorro's adjudication in such matters, General Ortega crafted an argument designed to prove that the now reduced EPS could in fact be trusted to act as a national – as opposed to a partisan – force.

This argument, cobbled together in increments between 1991 and 1993, hinged on three subsidiary claims. The first was that peace was in the army's self-interest. The second was a stunning acknowledgment: Chamorro's electoral victory, General Ortega asserted, was more likely to lead to rapid pacification than would have been the case if his own brother, Daniel, had been the victor. The third was the general's claim that the army was eager to establish its autonomy from the FSLN party.

But General Ortega's distancing argument, once fully articulated and in the public domain, had unintended consequences. Take the case of demobilized EPS soldiers and Contra combatants. No too long before, these groups had been killing each other. By 1993, however, they had come to share common grievances. The administration's failure to deliver on its promises of land and livelihood, for example, incited in them a shared normative outrage. Invoking "brotherhood," demobilized EPS soldiers and Contra combatants condemned

---

[19] Author's interview with Cuadra Lacayo, 1995.

all political elites, from the FSLN and the administration to the opposition.[20] General Ortega's distancing argument stoked their outrage and precipitated an uprising among demobilized EPS officers and soldiers, who seized by force of arms the town of Estelí.[21]

The EPS top brass responded decisively:

We had to send our best and bravest soldiers to fight their former comrades. It was extremely difficult. But we were determined to show that there could be only one army; that we would not tolerate parallel armies.[22]

The military leadership justified its "extremely difficult" choice to suppress former comrades by grounding it in the dictates of an emerging institutional identity: The army was now a nonpartisan body that claimed to be at the service of the entire nation:

After the election of 1990, our first historic duty was to ensure that we did not fragment into an assortment of miniature armies. This required making the officialdom feel that they were contributing to something higher and greater than their old partisan allegiance.

No foreign or domestic power put a gun to our ribs, or blackmailed us into doing this. It was our own conviction that obliged us to kill forty of our former officers when they rose up in arms. One of them was a captain whom I had personally decorated years before. And now I had to decorate the soldier who put a bullet in his head. This was proof of our commitment to the greater good.[23]

The leadership's compelling reason also suited its self-preserving instincts. Not only could the EPS's top officers not afford the emergence of "parallel armies," they could also not ignore the fact that a new "organic military law" soon would be due for congressional review. Known as the Military Code, the law dealt with several issues pertaining to civil–military relations, but the essential one had to do with the relationship between the chief of the army and the president of the Republic. How much control would the latter exercise over the former?

In its final form, the Code instituted a compromise arrangement for the presidential appointment of army chiefs: The Military Council would provide the president with the names of four officers, and the president in turn could only elect or reject – that is, choose a chief from among those four nominees, or send the entire slate of nominated officers back to the Council for amendment. In essence, the army would set precise parameters for presidential choice making.

---

[20] Howard W. French, "In Nicaragua, No Peace, and Nostalgia for Somoza," *New York Times*, 27 July 1993, A4.

[21] For a sense of the tense political environment, see Howard W. French, "Nicaraguans Say the Army Had a Hand in Attack," *New York Times*, 26 July 1993, A3. See also Douglas Farah, "Dual Hostage Crisis Grips Nicaragua: Chamorro, Opponents Seek Release of 56," *Washington Post*, 22 August 1993, A1.

[22] Author's interview with Cuadra Lacayo, 1995.

[23] Ibid.

Although the law was itself controversial, it is the debate leading up to its approval that is most revealing. Here it is crucial to bear in mind that the law represented an act of mutual accommodation between the two historical contenders for the role of prime arbiter: the executive and the army. But instead of perceiving the law as a triumph of consensus building, the opposition, including prominent FSLN dissidents, saw it as tangible proof of a pacted attempt to combine electoral legality with coercive might for dictatorial purposes. For his part, General Ortega saw the opposition as a nefarious group engaged in "a subversive, terrorist campaign" against the Code.[24] He addressed this group when he declared that the EPS would continue to exist "with or without the law."[25] The declaration, in turn, prompted a rapid-fire sequence of attacks liberally drawn from the country's traditional narrative of fate – a narrative in which Nicaragua appeared as a "semi-savage" land plagued by terror and despotism.[26]

Although explicitly aimed at the Code and General Ortega, these attacks implicitly applied to the Chamorro administration, the Code's cosponsor. Indeed, this implicit attacks were soon made explicit by demobilized Sandinista soldiers who "denounced" before "public and international opinion" the executive's intent to establish a "repressive instrument worse than the [Somoza] National Guard." The former combatants even charged that this "instrument" – the new military law – was designed to help the administration and the army "enthrone" themselves in power through sheer force.[27] The administration responded in kind by leveling a Manichean charge of its own: Opposition to the Code, it declared, was part and parcel of "evil attempts to manipulate the masses."[28]

The administration was ultimately able to gain congressional approval for the law only after Congress itself had gone through a traumatic process of

---

[24] The law's title was Código de Organización, Jurisdicción y Previsión Social Militar. See César Ubeda Bravo, "Ortega Desafía al Poder Civil," *La Prensa* (Managua), 11 June 1994, 1; *La Prensa* 21 June 1994.

[25] Ariel Montoya, "Mayorga Reta a HOS a Debatir el Código Militar"; César Ubeda Bravo, "Pueblo: Habló como Déspota," both in *La Prensa*, 10 June 1994, 1, 14.

[26] From the Movimiento de Acción Renovadora (MAR) came condemnation of General Ortega for "speaking" as a "despot." The president of the Partido Liberal Independiente (PLI) labeled the general "the country's greatest terrorist." A notable from the Partido Nacional Conservador (PNC) declared that Nicaragua was "semi-savage, not yet capable of administering itself," which in turn made it essential to have a "decent army" subordinate to civilian authority. Another PNC leader asserted that the Military Code would "unearth a mummy from the 1970s." The Partido Liberal Constitucional (PLC) derided the law as "unpatriotic." See Ariel Montoya, "Ley EPS Será Puerta de Corrupción," *La Prensa*, 19 June 1994, 1, 12. Former FSLN notable Moisés Hassan publicly stated that the Military Code was a "Trojan horse," which FSLN leaders would use at the opportune time "to seize absolute power," since they "knew that they would likely lose the 1996 elections." See César Ubeda Bravo, "Aprobarán Ley Militar a Toda Prisa; Hassan: Código es Caballo de Troya del FSLN," *La Prensa*, 16 June 1994, 1, 12.

[27] Armando Quintero, "Retirados Actívos Contra Código Militar," *La Prensa*, 21 June 1994, 9.

[28] Antonio Lacayo, *La Tribuna* (Managua), 26 June 1994.

fragmentation and reconfiguration.²⁹ Initially united against the very same administration it had brought to power, the bloc of UNO deputies started to suffer defections in 1991. The defectors, encouraged by the administration, forged a congressional coalition known as the Center Group. In early 1993, the Center Group and the FSLN congressional bench managed to wrest majority control of the Congress from UNO. This defeat outraged a large contingent of UNO deputies, who alleged vote buying by the administration before walking out in protest. Legislative paralysis ensued for an entire year. But something else happened. The FSLN bench remained in Congress, as did several UNO deputies. These remaining representatives also began to establish communication and eventually cooperative links among themselves. By early 1994, they were in a position to elect a new set of congressional leaders, and in September of that year, they even managed to approve the Military Code.

A Shifting Field of Imaginable Possibilities

Much like the EPS leaders, FSLN deputies tied their "realistic" assessment of the future to changes in world politics. Specifically, they perceived a worldwide, inexorable shift away from authoritarian rule and toward representative institutions.³⁰ By the middle of 1994, this perception would reconfigure the boundaries that theretofore had separated friend and foe. The catalyst was the fundamental issue of the 1987 Constitution. Drafted under the FSLN's regime, the charter's fate was now the single most important dispute between the executive and the Congress.

The UNO coalition and its candidate, Chamorro, had run on the platform of constitutional reform. Their argument had been clear throughout the campaign: The 1987 Constitution was by design an enabling extension of the FSLN regime's authoritarian character and goals. Once installed in the executive office, however, Chamorro and her principal minister, Lacayo, no longer viewed the Constitution as intolerable. Thus while the hard-line faction of UNO clamored for a Constituent Assembly and a wholly new constitution, the administration temporized.

The 1987 charter did in fact endow the executive with extraordinary prerogatives at the expense of the legislative branch. Here is a former FSLN notable who in 1987 was a key legal architect of the FSLN regime's charter:

The Constitution of 1987 was tailor-made for the Revolution in power. This is why the president has almost complete authority in matters of fiscal policy and the Congress has nearly none. The executive decides on all issues pertaining to the levy. When we [the

---

²⁹ The Congress has a total of ninety-two deputies. They are formally organized in partisan "benches." In 1994, the UNO bench had fifty-one members; the FSLN bench had thirty-nine. The Military Code was approved in September 1994.

³⁰ Author's interview with FSNL newspaper editor Carlos Fernando Chamorro, Managua, 12 June 1995; with former FSLN leader Sergio Ramírez, 20 June 1995; and with former FSLN legal expert Rafael Solís, 8 June 1995.

FSLN] were in power, the population would wake up on any given morning to learn that a new tax had been imposed the previous night by executive decree. This continued after the 1990 elections.

The 1987 charter also deprives the Congress of the right to approve international treaties and foreign loans. The Constitution even takes away from Congress important faculties in the appointment of justices to the Supreme Court and to the Electoral Tribunal. Court appointees, for example, are chosen from among a list of candidates prepared by the executive. The Congress cannot even reject the list. By constitutional dictate, it has to select one of the names on the list. Meanwhile the executive is entitled to name the president of the Court, and the justices serve at the pleasure of the president because the appointments are not for life.[31]

Between the end of 1993 and the beginning of 1994, the Congress finally revisited the contentious issue of the 1987 Constitution. Once again, UNO hardliners made clear their preference for a constituent assembly and a new charter. The leadership of the FSLN bench, on the other hand, proposed an alternative project: namely, "deep" constitutional reform. They also entered into talks with more flexible UNO deputies.[32] Together they introduced a constitutional reform that aimed to redress the imbalance between presidential and congressional powers, as well as slay what they saw as the "two-headed monster" of executive *continuismo* and clan-based rule. This shared normative goal, combined with their own personal interests in eliminating Chamorro and her son-in-law from the 1996 presidential race, proved a powerful incentive to move fast and in unison. By March 1994, the reform coalition – led by the FSLN bench, the Christian Democrats, and the Conservatives – was ready to conduct informal talks with the administration in hopes of finding common ground. Thirty meetings were held before the talks finally broke down in August 1994.

Other things were falling apart as well. The thirty-nine members of the FSLN bench by then had split between two wings that soon came to be known as *renovadores* (renovators or modernizers) and *ortodóxos* (orthodox), with thirty deputies in the former and nine in the latter. Indeed, these *renovadores* were now in open defiance of their political superiors – that is, Daniel Ortega and the National Directorate. The standard-bearer of the modernizers was Sergio Ramírez, whom we encountered in the previous chapter in his role as the FSLN's leading intellectual and later in his capacity as Daniel Ortega's trusted vice-president.[33]

The early origins of the split could be traced back to the debate on the Military Code, which Ramírez and the FSLN's congressional bench were able to pass by working in close cooperation with General Ortega and the administration and *without* substantial input from the FSLN's National Directorate.

---

[31] Author's interview with Solís, 1995.

[32] The leaders of the Conservative and Christian Democratic benches were instrumental to the project's elaboration and approval in Congress.

[33] Less prominent than Ramírez but nearly as important among the renovadores was *Comandante* Dora María Tellez, one of the guerrilla stars of the FSLN's armed struggle against Somoza.

From the perspective of the party's highest political leaders, this cooporation was inappropriate conduct. One prominent member of the orthodox camp put it this way:

Polarization creates the conditions for dialogue because the nation's history says that without dialogue there will be bloodshed. But dialogue has to have limits, since selfish interests can contaminate arrangements. We began to realize that this triple alliance – Ramírez, [General] Ortega, and the administration [Chamorro's son-in-law, Lacayo] – was seeking its own agenda.[34]

The self-seeking agenda of Ramírez and the others was not the only problem for the orthodox camp. Under Ramírez' leadership, the FSLN bench mustered enough initiative to propose an alternative version of the military law – one that would enhance the choice-making faculty of the president and, by extension, give civilian authority a greater voice in the appointment of the military chief.[35] This initial show of relative independence was but a hint of the radical changes taking place in the bench's perception of its own self-interest, practical competencies, and normative injunctions. This is how one former FSLN notable explained it:

The congressional *renovadores* developed a different mentality. They argued that it was both right and in the interest of the FSLN to deepen democracy. They also viewed themselves differently now that they had a new institutional role. Simply put, they were congressional deputies, and as such they could act with a degree of autonomy from the party.

The discovery of autonomy is a potent experience. I myself learned this at *Barricada* [the FSLN's official newspaper]. The staff and I reached a point where we wanted to choose our own battles. We basically said to the party, "Don't embroil us in all those fights that you organize for your own benefit."[36]

This change was momentous because it signaled a redirection of vocality in the constitutional debates, away from the political apex of the FSLN and toward the FSLN congressional bench. This redirection was no small matter in itself. For the National Directorate, however, it was downright alarming given the *renovadores*' position vis-á-vis the constitutional reform project. The *renovadores* shot down every argument that Daniel Ortega and the Directorate made against the reform. The Directorate argued that protecting the 1987 Constitution was important because the document represented tangible proof that, incredible as it might seem, a revolution of the left had been in power

---

[34] Author's interview with Mónica Baltodano (member of the FSLN's National Directorate and "orthodox" congressional deputy), Managua, October 1998.

[35] At one point, Ramírez even stated publicly that he "would like to see legally established the faculty of the president to ask for a different name than the one proposed by the Military Council." See "A Quemarropa," *La Tribuna*, 23 June 1994, 3A.

[36] Author's interview with Carlos Fernando Chamorro, June 1995. Chamorro had directed the FSLN's official newspaper *Barricada* since its inception; after the split between *renovadores* and *ortodóxos*, he was fired from this position by the party's National Directorate.

for an entire decade.[37] The *renovadores* countered that the 1987 Constitution provided appropriate mechanisms for its own reform, and thus was inherently open to change, which in turn meant that amending it was not a violation of principle.

Faced with this powerful logic, the *ortodóxos* came back with the claim that even if the reform were normatively acceptable, supporting it would be politically imprudent.[38] When pressed to lay out the reasoning behind this prudential claim, Daniel Ortega and other party leaders countered that the reform represented a "concession" to the right, a concession that should not be handed out freely. Rather, they proposed, the reform ought be used as a bargaining tool to extract concessions from both Congress and the administration. To Congress the FSLN would offer support for various pieces of the reform in exchange for legislation that would settle once and for all the property disputes. To the administration the FSLN would offer sacrificing the no-reelection and no-familial succession pieces of the reform in exchange for the property legislature it hoped to extract from Congress.[39]

These conflicting views came to a head at the Special Party Congress of May 1994. At that stormy convention, the *renovadores* tried yet again to persuade the National Directorate to support the reform. The Directorate dug in its heels, maintaining that such support would be premature. The *renovadores*, for their part, adhered to their position that the reform was nonnegotiable. Further, they argued that the reform was the only foundation on which a new order could be built. Only after this foundation was in place, they further argued, could the property disputes be adjudicated.

The party leaders fully understood that the FSLN's rank-and-file strongly approved of the reform against nepotism and *continuismo*. But they also understood that the *renovadores* and their congressional allies were now the protagonists of the reform struggle. In the theater of politics, Daniel Ortega and the Directorate had become at best minor players in the reform drama. The party leaders thus maintained that the reform would have to be negotiated with the administration *outside* Congress:

Daniel Ortega took the position that the debates in the national Congress were no more than a fight between cats and dogs. From his perspective, the only power holders of consequence were the army, the PLC [Partido Liberal Constitucionalista] leadership, and himself. For him, these were the three players that in the future would have to negotiate pacts if they were ever to solve the problems of hunger and unemployment. So, when the FSLN held its special Congress in May, Ortega and the Directorate simply squashed the *renovadores* and proceeded to enforce the party line.[40]

---

[37] Author's interview with "orthodox" deputy Baltodano, 1998. Other pertinent interviews with former editor of *Barricada*, Chamorro; *renovador* leader Ramírez; and FSLN legal expert, Solís, 1995.

[38] Ibid.

[39] Ibid.

[40] Author's interview with Chamorro, 1995.

By imposing internal discipline and insisting on a political negotiation outside Congress, Daniel Ortega sought to shift back vocality to himself and thus reassert his preeminence as FSLN negotiator. This return to the status quo ante, in turn, would allow him to deploy during negotiations his power resources, most notably the Sandinista unions, which were in a position to disrupt farms and factories. The *renovadores* not only resented this attitude, they also saw it as unrealistically outmoded in a democratizing world. When the reform project was presented in Congress, all thirty *renovadores* supported it, while all nine orthodox deputies rejected it. The National Directorate took the *renovadores* support as a worrisome display of "absolute autonomy," and started discussing the dismissal of Ramírez as bench leader.[41] A member of the Directorate outlined the party's concern by alluding to the revolutionary identity and its parameters of the permissible:

During the Revolution we were unable to be true to ourselves. Indeed, we deviated from our purpose. So now we must change, but change for the better. What the *renovadores* have done is simply disconnect themselves from our popular base.[42]

But at the same time, the *ortodóxos'* new normative realism, which dictated that only by engaging in political negotiations with "actors who mattered" could they solve the problems of hunger and unemployment, led them to an ironic choice. Simply put, they chose simultaneously to break with one of the FSLN's most trusted and influential members (Ramírez) and to open up the FSLN to talks with the PLC. This choice was ironic on two counts. First, the upper ranks of the PLC were increasingly filled with the most hard-line opponents of the FSLN. Second, the PLC was controlled by the mayor of Managua, Arnoldo Alemán, a personalistic *caudillo* with presidential ambitions who cultivated his popular support by engaging in severe attacks against pact making between the Chamorro administration and the Ortegas. This is what the PLC leader had to say about the transition process:

The so-called transition was carried out behind the people's back. They call it transition; I call it transaction. And they did it this way because they [the administration] succumbed to the delicacies of dictatorial power. I see flowering [in the administration] attitudes that are as bad or worse than those of the Somozas and the Ortega brothers....

Indeed, the PLC *caudillo* perceived the split within the FSLN as one more stratagem; as a "tactical" move at best, and more likely

...a ploy to lull us democrats into complacency before they [the FSLN] regroup for the 1996 elections. This an enemy that has been trained extremely well. It is smart and cunning.[43]

---

[41] Statement by Baltodano, newly inducted member of the FSLN Directorate. See Felix Navarrate, "FSLN en Encerrona para ver el Caso de Sergio Ramírez," *La Tribuna*, 23 June 1994, 3A.

[42] Author's interview with Baltodano, 1998.

[43] Author's interview with Arnoldo Alemán (leader of the PLC, mayor of Managua, and future president), Managua, 13 June 1995.

The leader of the *renovadores*, Ramírez, was not surprised by such mistrust. This is what he volunteered on the matter:

First I was a member of the Revolution's ruling junta, and after that I was vice-president of the Ortega government. So it's not at all strange that people don't trust me. Polls show that in Managua, León, and Masaya 55 percent of all respondents don't believe that our break with the FSLN is genuine. And even though thirty of our people in Congress have remained steadfast in their support for the reforms, common wisdom has it that we are bound to reunite with the orthodox camp.[44]

Other FSLN dissidents acknowledged that this perception was in fact a problem:

There is deep popular mistrust of the *renovadores*. This is partly due to the considerable sagacity demonstrated in the past by the FSLN. People tend to perceive its leaders as masters of deceit. The *renovadores* suffer by association. They are suspected of theatricality. . . .

Popular suspicion of the *renovadores*, in fact, was marked enough to feed the inclination of *renovadores* and *ortodóxos* alike to differentiate themselves in polarizing ways. In other words, the politics of identity formation at the elite level were driven by its own internal Manichean logic but were also closely connected to elite perceptions of popular sentiment:

The more virulent the attacks that go back and forth between the *ortodóxos* and the *renovadores*, the more people are willing to believe in the authenticity of the rift. And the rift *is* real. It is also deep. It stems from divergent visions of the future. Of course, there is also a clash of interests. But underlying the struggle for power are the conflicting convictions of the two sides.[45]

Ramírez, in fact, foreclosed the possibility of reunification with the *ortodóxos* as "ethically unacceptable,"[46] and continued to engage with the *ortodóxos* in public rhetorical battles. Meanwhile, the PLC *caudillo* Alemán directed his sharpest attacks at the administration:

Lacayo is capricious, dictatorial, and stubborn. . . . He divided UNO through his brother-in-law, who was president of Congress during the first years of the administration. Together with the FSLN deputies, [Lacayo and his brother-in-law] accomplished their *malevolent* goals. UNO went from having fifty-one deputies to a mere twenty-eight or twenty-nine. They deprived the reform of the requisite majority. UNO regained the necessary fifty-seven deputies only after the FSLN split.[47]

The *caudillo* failed to note the contradiction between his view of the FSLN split as "tactical" and the undisputable fact that it was precisely that split that had made the reform project viable in Congress, something that Alemán himself acknowledged. Further, he failed to note that while he vilified the administration for "pacting" with the FSLN, he and the PLC had eventually supported

44 Author's interview with Ramírez, 1995.
45 Author's interview with Chamorro, 1995.
46 Author's interview with Ramírez, 1995.
47 Author's interview with Alemán, 1995.

the *renovadores'* reform project in Congress, even though he doubted their authenticity all along:

After the FSLN split, ... we the Liberals joined [the *renovadores*] because we were seeking the lesser of two evils. We had always demanded a totally new constitution, but once we were left to choose between the purely Sandinista charter of 1987 and the current reform project, we had to go with the latter.[48]

Choosing the lesser of two evils was an option the PLC leader reserved for himself alone. This double standard, in turn, was rooted in Alemán's exclusive claim to the "democratic" identity. But other crucial actors were making special claims as well.[49] Here is, Ramírez, the leader of the *renovadores*:

We the *renovadores* are the only ones truly trying to forge a center. ... The traditional leaders of the FSLN may deny it all they want, but their deepest ambition is to return to the old authoritarian framework. The administration, too, has gone back to the historical curse of familial succession. This is due to the conviction that says "I must remain in office because I am doing what is best for the country."

The great *leitmotif* in our history has been "without me, the country will be ruined." The 1987 Constitution is the enabling instrument of this *caudillismo* and its authoritarian vision – a vision shared by the left and the right.[50]

But as we have seen, the leaders of "traditional" Sandinismo also acknowledged that the country's bloody history demanded compromise if it was not to repeat itself. They disagreed, however, on the kind of compromise. They certainly disapproved of the compromise forged by the "self-seeking" *renovadores*, who had managed nothing more than to "detach" themselves from the FSLN's constituencies. The differences between *ortodóxos* and *renovadores* became so profound, in fact, that they could no longer recognize one another as "genuine" Sandinistas.[51]

Their claims and counterclaims, moreover, steadily eroded the credibility of centrist agendas. One labor leader put it most succinctly when he publicly cautioned that no serious centrist movements should use the term "center" because it had become "discredited and questionable."[52] Still, the fight for the center continued. For as we are about to see, the administration not only claimed the centrist position on an exclusive basis, it actually argued that others were not yet capable of trust and dialogue.

[48] Ibid.
[49] The administration and its allies accused Ramírez of applying a double standard. Fernando Zelaya, a notable of the Conservative Party, a congressional deputy, and an ally of President Chamorro, asked rhetorically, "Was not Ramírez determined to reelect Daniel Ortega and himself under the FSLN regime?" Author's interview with Zelaya, Managua, 9 June 1995.
[50] Author's interview with Ramírez, 1995.
[51] "Bitter Feud Is Dividing Sandinistas," *New York Times*, 28 November 1994, A9.
[52] Statement by José Espinosa, leader of the Confederación de Unificación Sindical (CUS), quoted in César Ubeda Ravo, "Acomodan candidatura de Antonio Lacayo," *La Prensa*, 21 June 1994, 12.

The Center Cannot Hold

The administration's resistance to the reform project reflected its determination to avoid a clash with the FSLN, and it partly reflected its interest in retaining the prerogatives that the 1987 Constitution concentrated in the executive. But the administration also tried to appease the FSLN and to retain its prerogatives because it believed that if it succeeded at both, it could better perform what it considered to be its heroic task of national salvation. The former editor of the FSLN newspaper *Barricada* – and interestingly enough, the president's youngest son – explained it this way:

They [Chamorro and her son-in-law, Lacayo] have a political project that verges on the messianic. They say: *We* are the only alternative. *We* stopped the pendulum that oscillated between the right and the left. If *we* leave, anarchy will return. *We* are the only ones who can sustain the incipient center.[53]

The essence of the administration's position can be partially gleaned from a private conversation between the leader of the Christian Democratic Party, who by 1995 was also the president of the Congress, and Lacayo. Here is what the presidential minister purportedly said to the congressional leader:

What do we want reform for? *We are honest people, you and I.* Suppose we forge an alliance in the next government [looking forward to 1996]. As honest people, why would *we* need constitutional controls? Such controls are meant for individuals like Alemán [the Liberal *caudillo*, who was favored in opinion polls to win the 1996 election]; controls which he can circumvent anyway. If he wins the presidential elections, all he has to do is bribe certain members of Congress to render the controls useless. From whichever angle you look at it, the constitutional reform is an exercise in futility [emphasis added].[54]

Whether this argument was in fact made or not in private, the administration's public reasoning was a more sophisticated elaboration of its logic. In Nicaragua, the administration's public reasoning went, a strong political center could be constituted only by honest elements capable of depolarizing the polity while at the same time implementing a national developmental program. From this perspective, moreover, the construction of that honest center ought to precede the process of constitutional reform. As one high-ranking administration official argued:

The reform ought to be the result of a prior political consensus. But consensus building is extremely difficult because Nicaraguans are unaccustomed to dialogue, and need to learn to communicate in order to avoid polarization. There is excessive mistrust in our country. The people do not trust the political class. And the politicians don't trust one another.[55]

53 Author's interview with Chamorro, 1995.
54 Author's interview with Luís Humberto Guzmán (Christian Democratic leader and president of Congress), Managua, 13 June 1995.
55 Author's interview with Leal, 1995.

Implicit in this argument was the administration's view of itself as a political tutor whose historic duties included the instruction of others in the art of dialogue and consensus building. This task was difficult enough, and it was rendered only more so by a series of urgent socioeconomic and political problems whose solutions could not be postponed.[56] The constitutional reform, from the administration's vantage point, simply had to wait. But the administration also made another key argument: When the appropriate time for a discussion of the reform had finally arrived, the reform's own proponents had sabotaged the very process that could have led to a consensual solution:

UNO's internal fragmentation did not begin with the elections. It began when Mrs. Chamorro was designated as the coalition's candidate. Every political party had wanted its own candidate. And as the campaign got under way, old jealousies deepened. By the time of the presidential inauguration, the mistrust within UNO had been accumulating steadily.

The administration's reason for delaying the constitutional reform was so compelling in its own estimation that the proper line of action was utterly clear:

The proposed reforms...would take us to a system that is virtually parliamentary. But parliamentary systems have never succeeded in Latin America. What we need is equilibrium between the branches. And equilibrium can be achieved *only* through a political arrangement, because *mistrust* makes every political party want to have one of its own sitting on the electoral tribunal, for example, in order to guarantee electoral transparency [in the 1996 round].[57]

The FSLN shared the administration's conviction that a political agreement was absolutely essential prior to a legislative process of reform. Indeed, while these two crucial actors managed to craft similar compelling reasons to reject significant pieces of the constitutional reform when Congress approved it (in February 1995), other key actors managed to craft similar compelling reasons to press ahead with the reform project. Thus few were surprised when the executive and Congress reached an impasse over Article 150, which aimed to preclude familial *continuismo*.

After the impasse came escalation. The president of the Congress proceeded to publish the newly approved reform in three different newspapers. This act, in essence a promulgation of the reform, incensed the executive. It also bifurcated the polity, with some political groups adhering to the 1987 Constitution and others to the 1995 amended version, which the president now refused to ratify.

With two different constitutions in effect, the polity lost its overall institutional coherence and was dispossessed of encompassing powers of arbitration – a situation that grew only more alarming. Not only did the crisis swiftly embroil the Supreme Court, but as the Court reviewed the dispute between the executive and legislative branches the contending camps launched waves of

---

[56] Ibid.
[57] Ibid.

rhetorical campaigns aimed at drawing popular support for their respective positions.

These campaigns ignited passions because they extracted and amplified key themes from the traditional narrative of fate. Here is a typical rendition:

Our country has been burdened by a profound moral crisis *since the conquest*.... [This crisis]... reached its most acute point, first under Ortega and then under Chamorro.... [We now live in a country where] keeping one's commitments is seen as an unforgivable stupidity [emphasis added].[58]

As the Supreme Court came closer to a ruling, pro-reform groups' mistrust of the Court itself deepened. So too did their willingness to imperil the democratic institutions in whose name they struggled. Deputies signed petitions for the removal of the Court's president.[59] The leader of the PLC issued veiled warnings of another civil war.[60] The president of the Congress openly admitted that he could not discard the option of a referendum.[61]

The actual ruling, when it finally arrived, prompted further threats. The ruling was as follows: Although the reform was constitutional, its publication by the president of the Congress was not. The Court also directed the executive to promulgate the reform, but failed to provide a deadline.[62] The president of the Congress immediately expressed his suspicions, characterizing the ruling as "inspired" by the executive.[63] Others launched a more frontal attack on the sitting justices. One former FSLN leader denigrated the ruling as a "juridical aberration," and ventured that in preparing it the Court had merely obeyed "instructions" from Daniel Ortega and the administration. Similarly, a leading member of the *renovadores* charged that the justices were "politically aligned" with the administration and denied the validity of their decision. And a notable from UNO went so far as to dismiss the ruling as an "absurdity" that in no way could "obligate the congress to anything."[64]

---

[58] Moisés Hassan (former FSLN notable and member of the Revolution's governing junta), *La Prensa*, 28 April 1995.

[59] César Ubeda Bravo, "5 Diputados Piden Destituir a Trejos," *La Prensa*, 5 May 1995, 2.

[60] Roger Suárez, "Alemán: Elecciones de 1996, en Peligro," *La Prensa*, 6 May 1995, 1.

[61] Claudia Chamorro G., "Guzmán: Asamblea no Descarta Referéndum," *La Tribuna*, 7 May 1995, 4A.

[62] The Court ruled on May 8, 1995.

[63] In addition, sixteen political parties represented in Congress warned that if they should win in the 1996 elections, they would not honor any of the administration's international treaties unless the administration accepted the reformed Constitution. A wide range of parties also agreed not to ratify the executive's privatization proposals. See Claudia Chamorro G., "Fallo Aborta la Democracia," *La Tribuna*, 9 May 1995, 2A–5A.

[64] The leading *renovador* critic in this instance was Dora María Tellez (Movimiento de Renovación Sandinista (MRS). Members of the Partido Acción Nacional Conservadora (PANC) and Unión Demócrata Cristiana also dismissed the ruling. See Oliver Bodán, "Diputados Rechazan Sentencia de CSJ," *La Tribuna*, 10 May 1995, 2A.

As if all this were not enough, the PLC and other political parties targeted the administration with renewed intensity, urging the population to apply "civic pressure" on the president to approve the reforms. At the same time, the FSLN urged the people to mobilize "combatively" against the administration's economic policies. And in the Congress, pro-reform deputies registered their displeasure by refusing even to discuss the administration's proposed privatization of the national telephone company.[65]

As the political system moved to the brink of disaster, the *renovador* Ramírez suggested capitulating to the administration on one point: removing the constitutional ban that would prohibit relatives of the incumbent – in this case, the presidential minister, Lacayo – from participating in successive presidential races. Opposition to this concession, however, quickly mounted. Conservatives, Liberals and several other parties argued against any alteration to the reform.[66] Leading deputies assumed an unyielding stance. From the Alianza Popular Conservadora (APC) came the following:

> The country has been submerged for more than a hundred years in a crisis caused by personal caprice and ambitions. The time has come to eliminate these causes, once and for all.[67]

A former Sandinista leader, now with the Movimiento Unidad Revolucionaria (MUR), was equally unyielding. "The reform," he asserted, "is nonnegotiable."[68]

While advocates of the reforms set out to solidify pro-reform public opinion through incessant reference to the national nightmare, the FSLN leadership took the position that the "*políticos*" were bent on "reducing" the country's crisis to an "institutional conflict" – a conflict, they argued, that marginalized popular demands. For the FSLN and supporting economic groups, the true crisis was socioeconomic; they added that the people were more concerned with the effects of the structural adjustment program than with the dispute raging between the branches of government.[69]

The reformist camp raised the ante by making the case that an even broader issue was at stake. As one leader saw it, the country's "morality" was "bankrupt" and had to be "restored."[70] Indeed, for reformers, the

---

[65] Ariel Montoya, "Políticos Presionan a Presidenta Chamorro, Piden Promulgación de Reformas," *La Prensa*, 11 May 1995, 2; César Ubeda Bravo, "Ramírez Desestima Plazo Pereira," *La Prensa*, 12 May 1995, 3.

[66] Roger Suárez, "Hassan Expresa Sospecha de Acuerdo Sobre Inhibiciones," *La Prensa*, 22 May 1995, 14.

[67] Ibid.

[68] Statement by Hassan. See Oliver Bodán, "Ramírez Sugiere Suspender Inhibiciones," *La Tribuna*, 20 May 1995, 2A.

[69] Antonio Chávez, "Al Diálogo Debemos Ir Con Propuestas," and Xavier Rayo Valle, "Diálogo: Requisito *Sine qua Non*," both in *Barricada* (Managua), 22 May 1995, 5.

[70] Statement by Noel Vidaurre (pre-candidate of the PNC). See César Ubedo Bravo, "Vidaurre con los Convencionales de Managua," *La Prensa*, 22 May 1995, 2.

future of the nation hung in the balance. The president of the Congress put it this way:

[Because Lacayo] has a profoundly authoritarian vocation...it would be extremely dangerous to leave in place the strong presidential powers accorded by the 1987 Constitution....[71]

Restricting the Field of Imaginable Possibilities

By 1995, all sorts of previously unimaginable possibilities had become historical facts. The FSLN regime acceded to transparent elections, which it lost. The opposition's electoral coalition came to view its victorious candidate as an enemy. Demobilized combatants who had been mortal foes for a decade developed a shared sense of aggrievement vis-á-vis political elites. The EPS (now, Ejército Nacional, or EN) employed its coercive powers against its own former officers and soldiers. UNO lost its majority in Congress. The FSLN party lost control over its congressional representatives, who then mounted a political revolt against the leadership. And last but not least, Congress itself became the institutional stage for a strong alliance between reformers from the FSLN and UNO.

This astonishing chain of events notwithstanding, the rhetorical strategies of the pertinent actors ultimately reorganized the polity's "reality" according to old, easily recognizable parameters. To begin with, key leaders continued to challenge the capacity of rivals to transcend authoritarian predilections. The president of the Congress, for one, could appreciate the army's changed behavior but would not accord the administration even the benefit of the doubt:

[Lacayo] has been unable to squelch the reforms simply because the army refuses to shut down the Congress. The army is bent on gaining recognition as an impartial, apolitical entity. So the one person I don't trust is [Lacayo]. On one occasion, he even lamented that it was "unfortunate" that the administration could not simply dispatch the army to close down the Congress.[72]

Army leaders did indeed refuse embroilment. But they also reasserted the primacy of monopolistic coercive power while relegating the basic formal rules of any democratic regime of arbitration – the Constitution – to a secondary place:

A crisis that leads to two constitutions is obviously not good. But in this country we can have two of everything; what there can never be is two armies. For as long as there is a single army, things will work out in the end. This does not mean that the army can opine on juridical matters. We are not jurists. Plenty of politicians have tried to embroil us in this dispute to no avail. Our principal objective is to keep the army organized and united.[73]

[71] Author's interview with Guzmán, 1995.
[72] Ibid.
[73] Author's interview with Cuadra Lacayo, 1995.

Army leaders also recognized politicians' attempts to bring the army into the fray as both normal and dangerous:

In some quarters there is even a clamor for the army to send quarreling politicians home.... This is normal...that they would say to us: "only you can set things right in this country that needs order, discipline, and a purging of personal ambitions."

But we in the army see this argument as a *trap*.... The one thing we can never tolerate is a repetition of the armed rebellions of 1993 and 1994; we will not tolerate any group that seizes a piece of the national territory by force of arms. If this last scenario should come to pass, we have made it plain, we will repress unequivocally.[74]

This fear of traps was not exclusive to the army. The Church hierarchy, one of the most influential political actors in the country, characterized the army's new image as illusory:

Some say that the army has become professionalized. We [the Church] believe that a person cannot change overnight.... Ideology is permanent. During the past decade, a certain ideology was inculcated in the army. Besides, they have the power.[75]

The fear of ploys and traps, a recurring theme in the country's history, was once again salient. The president of the Congress had this to say:

Everywhere [Lacayo] sees nothing but *traps* designed to hurt him in the future, when he becomes president....[76]

The PLC caudillo, Alemán, cast himself as the intended victim of a far-reaching trap:

There are persons and political parties who are interested in preventing the 1996 election from taking place...because the polls indicate that while 20 percent of the voters would cast their ballot for Daniel Ortega, 4 percent for Ramirez, and 3 percent for Lacayo, 39 percent would vote for me.[77]

In the end, neither ploys nor traps brought these rivals to the negotiation table. Rather, they were brought to the table by external financial donors such as the Nordic countries and the United States. Simply put, the donors used their leverage to demand an agreement. As one high-level Church official explained:

...international organizations and outside powers have pressed for a solution to the institutional crisis. The executive and the Congress may deny it, but they are being told by foreigners to put their house in order.[78]

Indeed, once the talks were ongoing, it was the cardinal who assumed the role of umpire, one moment proscribing mutual recriminations, the next forcing

[74] Ibid.
[75] Author's interview with Cardinal Obando y Bravo's chief aid, vicar general of the Archdiocese of Managua, Monsignor Edie Montenegro, Managua, 13 June 1995.
[76] Author's interview with Guzmán, 1995.
[77] Author's interview with Alemán, 1995.
[78] Author's interview with Monsignor Montenegro, 1995.

opposite numbers to focus on a compromise agenda. With 75 percent of all congressional deputies claiming that the reform was already promulgated, and under the persistent pressure of the cardinal and outside governments, the negotiation finally devolved into a debate about how to put in place a "framework" for the reform's implementation.

As the talks proceeded, reform advocates continued to conjure historical specters in the theater of public politics. The alternatives, as they saw them, were dire. On one side loomed the possibility of convening a constituent assembly to draft a new charter. This option was depicted as a "fatal" invitation for a resumption of "the old cycle of constituent assemblies, coups, and dictatorships."[79] On the other side loomed the possibility of conceding the struggle to the administration. This was depicted as equally dangerous. Here is a representative opinion:

No other ruler in our history has harbored as much ambition as Lacayo....It is this ambition that blocks the nation's democratic development....[He is] an aspiring dictator whose unabashed pact with the Sandinistas proves him an implacable foe of democracy.[80]

Editorializing along these lines was not hard to find. One opinion maker had this to say:

First Anastasio Somoza, then Daniel Ortega, now Antonio Lacayo....It seems we are condemned to a sad legacy of subjugation. Every day new dictators are born.[81]

Pro-reform opinion makers also set out to bolster the cardinal's authority, especially after the cardinal himself warned the negotiating camps that he was departing for Rome within days and that his participation in the talks would per force come to an end at that point. Another vocal opinion maker put it simply: "Only the cardinal's moral suasion can bring to their senses those individuals who place their own ambitions above all else."[82]

The *renovadores*, too, placed their best hopes on the cardinal:

The cardinal is the maximum moral authority and therefore the greatest political authority. The cardinal compelled the administration to sign the agreement....What would happen if the cardinal did not exist?[83]

Two days before the cardinal's departure, an agreement was finally reached. Congress allowed the executive to keep her relatives in their official positions until the end of her term, and allowed the executive branch the role of colegislator. In exchange, the administration committed itself to the reform's promulgation.

---

[79] Statement by the Liberal jurist Iván Escobar. See "El Político Invitado," *La Tribuna*, 11 June 1995, 2A.
[80] Hugo Ramón García, "La Ambición Tiene un Nombre," op-ed., *La Prensa*, 11 June 1995, 6.
[81] Juan Navarro, "Hagamos un Alto: No Más Dictadores," op-ed, *La Tribuna*, 11 June 1995, 6A.
[82] Luis Sánchez, "Reformas son para Aplicarse Ya," *La Tribuna*, 13 June 1995, 6A.
[83] Author's interview with Ramírez, 1995.

All that remained at that point was for the legislature to approve the implementation framework. At that point, too, the FSLN's orthodox union leader spearheaded a labor invasion of the Congress, threatening to remain on the premises until property titles were handed to the Frente Nacional de Trabajadores (FNT) and demobilized EPS soldiers.[84] The ensuing turmoil was further complicated by the involvement of orthodox deputies in the takeover – an involvement that in turn prompted reform deputies to demand the impeachment of all orthodox deputies.[85] For the *renovadores*, there was no doubt that the orthodox wing of the FSLN was both the agitator and the beneficiary:

There is a very simple scheme at work here. The most radical elements burn tires and set up barricades. Daniel Ortega then steps in and placates them. This is his role.[86]

As the crisis came to a resolution, however, fundamental questions about justifiable power arose. One editorial stated it bluntly: "There can be no rule of law when the executive allocates rewards and punishments in arbitrary fashion."[87] The Church hierarchy, too, raised the issue of justice, although in a more complicated fashion, acknowledging the electoral process as an instrument of popular justice while simultaneously suggesting that the substantive outcomes of electoral democracy can be deleterious:

The people used the vote [in 1990] to punish those who had trampled upon them.... But the Structural Adjustment programs have been catastrophic. Unemployment is eroding democracy; and those who voted for something different are disillusioned.[88]

But it was Ramírez, whose history of Nicaragua as hell on earth had prior to the Revolution set the stage for Sandino's emergence as national savior and authorizing figure, who now recast history in a sweeping and familiar way:

History repeats itself. External pressure is the only force that can sway the administration to negotiate. The Swedish government is an important donor to Nicaragua; it also exercises influence over other benefactors like Switzerland, Norway, and Holland. They have told the administration either to negotiate or forego economic aid. The United States government, too, has favored the reforms. And finally, there is the cardinal, who does not like the administration.[89]

The externally oriented Manicheanism that had been incipient in Ramírez' old historical narrative was now erased completely. Indeed, foreign actors, including the United States, were now assigned a positive role. Furthermore,

---

[84] "Comentario de la Redacción: La Toma de la Asamblea," *La Prensa*, 16 June 1995, 10.
[85] The takeover began on June 15. In less than a week, the leader of the *Renovadores'* bench, together with deputies from Partido Acción Nacional (PAN) and Unión Demócrata Cristiana (UDC), demanded impeachment. *La Tribuna*, 21 June 1995, 2A.
[86] Author's interview with Ramírez, 1995.
[87] Editorial, "Ley Marco y Estado de Derecho," *La Tribuna*, 23 June 1995, 6A.
[88] Author's interview with Monsignor Montenegro, 1995.
[89] Author's interview with Ramírez, 1995.

retrograde domestic actors now played their nefarious parts not as imperial lackeys but as stubborn creatures of historical habit. Yet, as in the old narrative, hope was embodied in the persona of a single leader: the cardinal.

As if to supply the closing sentence to this newly adapted rendition of history, the chief of the army offered an assessment and a prediction:

> In the final analysis, the army has shown a better understanding of democracy than certain sectors of civil and political society.... The army will remain the ultimate point of reference in this country.[90]

Conclusion

The establishment of an electoral democracy in Nicaragua brought a new government to the highest position of authority and opened the way for the pacification of a country riven by civil war. The polity, however, remained without a deep and broad consensus on the proper construction, deployment, and enforcement of justifiable power. The electoral mechanism survived, but its central function became quite specific and narrow: to select the chief negotiator of ad hoc arrangements that allow for the distribution of power quotas and public graft.

In the 1996 election, the dominant Liberal *caudillo* emerged victorious to preside over an administration rife with corruption – an administration whose scandals, in fact, continued to play themselves out even after the *caudillo* had left office. Most ironically, or perhaps predictably, this implacable foe of pacts, who had ferociously attacked his predecessor for negotiating with the FSLN, ruled supported by a pact with that same FSLN. And of course, the FSLN, too, fell into this ironic pattern, as it continued to argue for broad socioeconomic solutions while settling for narrow agreements.[91] Thus, the PLC *caudillo* and the head of the FSLN

> ...submerged deep-seated personal and ideological animosities to collaborate in a pact that maintains democratic forms but diminishes democratic content in key institutions.... [T]en years after the fall of the revolution, Nicaragua appears trapped in a vicious cycle. In this cycle, politics is dominated by *caudillos* who benefit from the public treasury while institutions fail to curb the impunity of the powerful.[92]

This description is accurate. But it is just that: a description of a formal democracy that arbitrates through self-dealing and mutual accommodation between foes. Underlying this regime of arbitration is a complex dynamic driven by a

---

90 Author's interview with Cuadra Lacayo, 1995.

91 See, for example, Adolfo Acevedo, "La Necesidad de Una Alternativa Económica y Social," *Barricada*, 4 April 1995, 5. Also, until the last moment, the FSLN derided the reform process as an act of "pragmatism" that ushered in an "illegal" and "absurd" legal framework. See Carlos García Castillo, "Pragmatismo Político Domina Absurda Ley," *Barricada*, 4 July, 1995, 2.

92 Stephen Kinzer, "Country without Heroes," review of David R. Dye et al., *Patchwork Democracy: Nicaraguan Politics Ten Years after the Fall*, *New York Review of Books*, 48, no. 12 (19 July 2001): 31–3.

historically shaped Manichean *lingua franca* that translates actors' self-interests into vicious reincarnations of an awful past. But like political actors everywhere, Nicaraguans simultaneously harbor self-seeking agendas and pursue their visions of the greater good. The paradox is that the more intense their quest for the greater good becomes, the more they are forced to hide their own ambitions; and the more they hide these ambitions, the more they serve only that which they hide.

Conclusion

> For an emerging people to be capable of appreciating the sound maxims of politics and to follow the fundamental rules of statecraft, the effect would have to become the cause. The social spirit which ought to be the work of that institution, would have to preside over the institution itself. And men would be, prior to the advent of laws, what they ought to become by means of laws.[1]
>
> —Jean-Jacques Rousseau

Rousseau's dilemma has vexed theorists and political actors alike. Ultimately, Rousseau settled for the *deus ex machina* of the "lawgiver." So too have many powerful leaders who have made themselves the arbiters of their peoples' conflicting claims to status, wealth, and justice. We have seen, however, that postcolonial Costa Ricans solved this dilemma differently. They forged a national identity that conceived of "the people" not as a republican abstraction but as a historically grounded group whose defining narrative trumpets its high normative worth and the practical attributes associated with its collective virtues.

Such practical attributes, it should be noted, included not only the competencies but also the vulnerabilities that attached to their defining virtues. Furthermore, both in Costa Rica and Nicaragua, the narratives themselves were not reducible to a shared identity that hinged merely on a common "sense of belonging" either to a "distinctive culture" or "to a polity."[2] Rather, the narratives flowed from "belonging" to a system of normative scheming that enabled actors to make political and institutional choices they could claim to be both realistic and appropriate.

---

[1] For quote and discussion, see Bonnie Honig's *Democracy and the Foreigner* (Princeton, NJ: Princeton University Press, 2001), 18–21.

[2] See Arash Abizadeh, "Does Liberal Democracy Presuppose a Cultural Nation? Four Arguments," *APSR* 96, no. 3 (September 2002): 495–509.

At the dawn of independence, the Costa Rican narrative of collective virtue advanced two claims. Put in Rousseau's terms, the first stated that the people of Costa Rica were, prior to the advent of laws, what others ought to become by means of laws. The second qualified the first: The people of Costa Rica could remain in their virtuous natural state only with the advent of laws.

At the level of competition and struggle, these two claims emerged early on as a compelling reason for normative schemers to choose pragmatic gradualism while at the same time proposing competing programs aimed at preserving their exemplary people from the alien dangers of jealousy and anarchy. From the continuities and ruptures engendered by this dynamic emerged an arbitration regime that by 1950s had settled on the principle of election while rededicating itself to the promotion and distribution of socioeconomic prosperity.

Postcolonial Nicaraguans, in contrast, declared their group tyrannical, anarchic, *arriviste*, and untrustworthy. This is the identity-based narrative that shaped the relationship between culture and polity, both at the micro level of normative scheming and at the macro level of regimes of arbitration. On the one hand, postcolonial leaders sought to arbitrate power struggles through electoral procedures. On the other, they interpreted electoral outcomes in Manichean terms. Compelling reasons were thus increasingly crafted to persuade citizens not in favor of particular programs, but rather in favor of particular leaders and camps. The result was that substantive agendas were thrown into irrelevance, as rivals dedicated themselves to the politics of unmasking and purification.

The ensuing bloodshed and destruction created a generalized craving for order. Yet by mid-nineteenth century, newspapers, pamphlets, and broadsides had proliferated rapidly, as debates over how best to establish order reached new levels of animosity. Content analysis of these polemical publications reveals a field of imaginable possibilities in which "paternal" and "fraternal" governments emerged as the two competing solutions to the problems of "anarchy" and "despotism."

More than metaphorical, the familial image turned out to be the trigger mechanism for a new civil war and, subsequently, the disastrous Walker episode. And yet, a new, postwar impasse led elites into a process of political-cultural innovation and institutional adaptation that ushered in the Conservative Republic, which in turn began to alter the logic of Manicheanism in ways that diminished its potency. This was no small feat. For approximately three decades, the Republic managed to uphold and expand both the electoral and substantive criteria of legitimacy. The Republic, in brief, was able to create an effective regime of encompassing arbitration. But in the end, the Republic also failed to uproot the Manichean system that was to shape the country's political, institutional, and economic development in the twentieth century.

The contrasting experiences of our two archetypical cases points us in the direction of political culture as a causal force in the development of nations. Values like trust, once emphasized by Gabriel Almond and Sydney Verba and later rediscovered by Robert Putnam and others, do shape the chances and performance of democratic arbitration.[3] Such values, however, cannot be expected necessarily to flow from what Dankwart Rustow called the "habituation phase," by which he meant the process of democratic acculturation that presumably takes place once the formal institutions of democracy are installed.[4] Nor are values the essence of political culture. In the abstract, both the Nicaraguan and Costa Rican citizenries valorize extensive participation and inclusive political rights.[5] But political values, as this book has argued, are merely one construct of political culture. Collective narratives that tell a group who they are vis-á-vis themselves and the world are a more fundamental and powerful force.

This last claim runs counter to the argument, elaborated most clearly by Adam Pzreworski, that the veneration of democracy leads to democratic stability because it simultaneously prompts the "policing" of democracy's potential desecrators and evokes the committed defense of democracy itself.[6] This argument is plausible only if we assume that a critical mass of actors have a decent chance at establishing an undisputed democratic identity and, by extension, can credibly claim to be the sentries of democracy. Stated differently, keen disputation over the authenticity of democratic identities is likely to remain endemic when actors operate within a set of intersubjective relations that, embedded in a negative collective self-image, predisposes them to take a dim view of their rivals' claims to democratic allegiance.

Defining the "people" in historically grounded terms and assigning them high worth – that is, anchoring the play of politics in a collective identity that is "credibly" declared as entwined with a complex of virtues, competencies, and vulnerabilities that make political agents worthy of trust – can provide a "focal solution" to the "coordination dilemma" that Barry Weingast sees as implicit in democratic self-reinforcement. Weingast argues that such a dilemma arises because, when assessing different policy issues, "individuals have different understandings of legitimacy." One possible focal solution, also proposed by Weingast, would be an elite pact that establishes the "general principle of limits on state power."[7] But this kind of "limiting pact" may provide an adequate solution to coordination dilemmas associated with discrete policy differences and still leave unresolved the broad and often intractable legitimacy contestation that typically accompanies the politics of polarization and mistrust. For

3 Gabriel Almond and Sydney Verba, *The Civic Culture, Political Attitudes and Democracy in Five Nations* (Princeton, NJ: Princeton University Press, 1963), 257.
4 Dankwart A. Rustow, "Transitions to Democracy: Toward a Dynamic Model," *Comparative Politics* 2 (April 1970): 360. See also Lisa Anderson, "Transitions to Democracy: A Special Issue in Memory of Dankwart A. Rustow," *Comparative Politics* 29 (April 1997): 254–6.
5 John Booth and Mitchell Seligson, "Paths to Democracy and the Political Culture of Costa Rica, Mexico, and Nicaragua," in Larry Diamond, ed., *Political Culture and Democracy in Developing Countries* (Boulder, CO: Lynne Rienner, 1994): 99–130.
6 Cited in Barry Weingast, "The Political Foundations of Democracy and the Rule of Law," *APSR* 91, no. 2 (June 1997): 262.
7 Ibid., 246.

this reason, limiting pacts ultimately run up against their own limitations, as the examples of Venezuela and Colombia illustrate only too well.

A high-worth collective identity, on the other hand, provides a generally applicable presumption of good intent that allows rivals, as normative schemers, not only to tackle policy differences but also to minimize the danger of embroilment in destructive struggles that place undue stress on democratic institutions. A high-worth collective identity, moreover, improves the chances of citizenship enhancement through encompassing arbitration. For as we have seen in our two cases, if trust allows both for risk taking and for coping with the freedoms of others,[8] then trust in the "people" will make it more likely that elites will submit to arbitration outcomes that may run counter to their own short-term interests. This is key because, as Thomas Janoski points out, citizenship has at its core some "specified level of equality," and although equality is never complete, "it most often entails an increase in subordinates' rights *vis á vis* social elites."[9]

Consider this last claim in the light of some of this book's central empirical findings. Costa Rican coffee elites, we saw, have benefited greatly from the moderating sociopolitical effects that flow from the fact that small and medium size agrarian producers, urban workers, and the middle class share their brand of exceptionalism. Indeed, recent polls show a remarkably high level of system support among Costa Ricans across the socioeconomic spectrum.[10] But we also saw that while elites benefit from this broadly shared exceptionalism, this same exceptionalism also diminishes elites' capacity to block or ignore subaltern classes' bids for greater political and social equality. Indeed, the concomitant dictates of exceptionalism have actually forced competitive elites to embrace inclusionary reformism.

Partly for this reason, by the 1960s Costa Rica easily fit the view held by many scholars that an early historical precedent of a "partial, elite democracy" contributes to the ultimate development of "full democracy."[11] On this view, the Latin American oligarchic democracies of the nineteenth century, by allowing for peaceful power contestation among elites, made state building possible. For as this view further posits, where oligarchic democracies emerged, elites gained "experience" in democratic competition and, by connection, elite factions

---

[8] N. Luhmann, cited in John Dunn, "Trust and Political Agency," in Diego Gambetta, ed., *Trust: Making and Breaking Cooperative Relations* (Cambridge, MA: Basil Blackwell, 1988), 80.

[9] Thomas Janoski, *Citizenship and Civil Society* (New York: Cambridge University Press, 1998), 9–10.

[10] Mitchell Seligson has demonstrated that Costa Rica's domestic tolerance indicators are quite stable because they are rooted in the citizenry's approbation of the polity in which they operate. Mitchell A. Seligson, "Political Culture and Democratization in Latin America," in Roderic Ai Camp, ed., *Democracy in Latin America: Patterns and Cycles* (Wilmington, DE: Scholarly Resources Book, 1996), 81–2.

[11] Larry Diamond and Juan J. Linz, "Introduction: Politics, Society, and Development in Latin America," in Diamond, Linz, and Seymour Martin Lipset, eds., *Democracy in Developing Countries: Latin America*, vol. 4 (Boulder, CO: Lynne Rienner, 1989), 8.

developed mutual trust. And just as importantly, oligarchic democracies enabled elites to regulate the gradual incorporation of subordinate social groups into the political arena (without threatening their own economic interests).[12]

The Costa Rican and Nicaraguan cases, however, suggest three important qualifications. First, the construction of nineteenth century oligarchic democracies was itself an extremely challenging task that required prior political-cultural adaptations of postcolonial rhetorical strategies and patterns of identity formation. Second, oligarchic democratic institutions worked only as long as they were supportive of the political-cultural adaptations that made them possible to begin with. Third, and finally, while institutions are crucial to the future of democratic and economic development, even positive and long-lived institutional legacies, as with the Regime of the Thirty Years, can be lost because political actors in general, and elites in particular, remember and learn from past experience in the context of historiographic contestations and settlements.

Indeed, we have seen that these contestations and settlements matter greatly to political and economic development because they help shape actors' fields of imaginable possibilities. Recall that the rhetorical eclipse of Nicaragua's Republic from memory formation contributed mightily to the emergence of a normative realism that recommended dictatorial arbitration. Recall further that the rhetorical struggles and victories associated with the Costa Rican Revolution of 1948 entrenched a normative realism whose basic tenet is that the country's "inherent conditions" demand a democratic regime of arbitration based both on substantive and procedural principles.

The long-term ramifications of the Costa Rican settlement are worth considering. If prior to 1948 electoral processes and institutions were not the primary source of legitimation in Costa Rica, by the mid-1950s such processes and institutions were indispensable to the creation and exercise of justifiable power. They remain so to this day. The Supreme Electoral Tribunal (Tribunal Supremo de Elecciones) is empowered by the 1949 Constitution to supervise elections and prevent or punish fraud. The Tribunal's extensive prerogatives merit enumeration:

> The Tribunal administers the Civil Registry and public campaign finance, monitors executive neutrality in the elections, reviews political advertisements, and even takes control temporarily of the civil and rural guard to "defend the freedom to vote" should it become necessary. The tribunal is also in charge of ensuring compliance with electoral laws, scrutinizing and validating election results and investigating charges of partiality.[13]

The upshot is that elections in Costa Rica are "essentially uncontroversial events."[14] If anything, criticism is directed mostly at the Tribunal's censorship of the content of political advertisement, which excludes from debate "religion

---

[12] Ibid., 8.

[13] Cynthia H. Chalker, "Elections and Democracy in Costa Rica," in Mitchell Seligson and John Booth, eds., *Elections and Democracy in Central America Revisited* (Chapel Hill, NC: University of North Carolina, 1995), 106.

[14] Chalker, "Elections and Democracy," 106.

and the sexual habits of candidates."[15] Political debate, however, is vigorous and supple enough to negotiate and settle the differences of opinion that naturally arise both in normal competition and in the face of difficult choices. Debate, in fact, has been at the core of partisan identity transformation and related changes in policy. Prior to the economic downturn of the 1980s, for example, the Partido Liberación Nacional (PLN) was a statist, welfarist party. Today, it accommodates a wide range of tendencies, including a neoliberal wing.[16]

This expansion was no easy matter. Statist intervention, after all, was a hallmark of the PLN's social democratic identity. Indeed, prior to the 1980s, stalist intervention was an essential factor differentiating Costa Rica from the rest of Latin America in general and Nicaragua in particular.[17]

However, in the 1950s and 1960s, the different arbitration policies examined in this book – pursued in one country by an increasingly consolidated social democracy and in the other by a dynastic authoritarian regime – began to insert a significant wedge between the countries' patterns of socioeconomic development. We saw that while Costa Rican elites constructed an increasingly broad welfare state that ameliorated the social dislocations wrought by economic modernization, in Nicaragua the Somoza dynasty failed to do the same.[18]

We also saw that in Costa Rica the extension of a welfare net, together with the expansion of wealth, became a source of national pride. For scholars of political and economic development, this sort of accomplishment is evidence that democracies that perform well in the socioeconomic sphere are more likely to survive.[19] But the ways in which Costa Ricans achieved socioeconomic development also point to the need for the exercise of analytical care in establishing causality. Recall, for example, that Costa Ricans first argued for land reform and for state distribution and enforcement of property rights as early as 1825 and 1830 – nearly two decades before the coffee boom, and more than a century before their first truly democratic elections. Recall further that at the time, the property rights argument was grounded in the notion of preemptive adjudication. That is, the goal was to prevent the disputes over land that the leaders anticipated before they actually arose. Finally, recall that this prescient move was motivated by the urgent need that Costa Rican leaders felt to avoid internal discord and thus insulate the country from the alien disorders of the region.[20]

---

[15] Ibid.

[16] Ibid., 111.

[17] The countries' socioeconomic structures were not radically different. See Frederick Stirton Weaver, *Inside the Volcano: The History and Political Economy of Central America* (Boulder, CO: Westview Press, 1994), 163, 203, 211.

[18] As in the earlier displacements associated with the introduction of coffee at the end of the nineteenth century, in the 1950s peasants moved on to uncultivated lands, much of which had been traditionally "owned" by the state, either de facto or by constitutional fiat.

[19] See, for example, Adam Przeworski et al., *Sustainable Democracy* (New York: Cambridge University Press, 1995).

[20] The case of Nicaragua also underscores the need for analytical precision in establishing causality. With the fastest growing economy in Latin America between the 1950s and 1960s, Nicaragua's per capita income rose impressively, surpassing all but Costa Rica's at various points in the 1960s and 1970s. See Stirton Weaver, *Inside the Volcano*, 163, 203, 211.

All this sets Costa Rica apart not only from Nicaragua but also from those established democracies that, while adhering to the procedural norms of fair electoral competition and constitutional rule, nevertheless have failed to develop the institutions and policies necessary for substantial gains in both economic performance and social welfare. In this regard, Costa Rica seems to support the observation that "what seems to matter for economic performance and social welfare is not just democracy in general but specific democratic institutions and policies."[21]

This last observation, however, invites inquiry into the origins and development of the pertinent institutions and policies. This book has shown, for example, that in Costa Rica their origins and development have been entwined with an identity-based repudiation of "extremes." This was the case immediately after independence, when elites argued that broadly assigned and firmly guaranteed property rights were indispensable to the prevention of strife among their peaceful and industrious people. And this was the case with INDECAFE. Created in 1933 by the state as a semi-autonomous body, INDECAFE soon came to understand its central function as the balancing of the "reasonable" demands of small and medium-size coffee producers, on one hand, and the coffee elites' overall dominance, on the other. Indeed, with time, INDECAFE turned into an arbitration arena whose effective workings made possible the implementation of promotional policies and mediating mechanisms for the entire coffee economy.

These two examples show that Costa Rican elites have recognized at key points in time the fundamental importance of "credible commitment" to a market economy.[22] But they also show that elites have been able to act effectively on this recognition by framing it in the *lingua franca* of national exceptionalism. Moreover, this finding refutes the argument that Costa Rica's developmental pattern began only in the mid-nineteenth century with the advent of Liberal state building and reformism. In so doing, this finding also helps us better specify the complexities in the timing and sequencing of political-cultural, institutional, and economic development – a central concern to students of comparative politics in general and comparative development in particular.

This book also has argued that in the twentieth century, as in the nineteenth, institutional design – a crucial piece of established views of political development – cannot wholly account for divergences in regime types between the two neighboring countries. For instance, Costa Rica in the 1950s developed a strong and autonomous electoral tribunal that was simply unparalleled in Nicaragua; and while Costa Rica eliminated its standing army, Nicaragua relied heavily on the military to maintain the regime at critical moments. But Costa Rica's institutional innovations were a central outcome of both the political-cultural struggles associated with 1948 and the political-cultural renovation that subsequently allowed for democratic consolidation. In short, the changes

---

[21] Adam Przeworski, "The Neoliberal Fallacy," *Journal of Democracy* 3, no. 3 (July 1992): 54.
[22] Douglas C. North, "The Evolution of Efficient Markets in History," in J. A. James and M. Thomas, eds., *Capitalism in Context* (Chicago: University of Chicago Press, 1994), 259.

in Costa Rica's institutional structure, like the continuities that characterized authoritarian Nicaragua, are not the explanation but rather part and parcel of the outcomes in need of explanation.

In addressing these puzzles, this book concludes that a regime of democratic arbitration, like any other regime type, is enduringly successful if it justifies its own power by devising encompassing settlements to disputes over vocality, resources, and authority as they arise in the public realm. The book also concludes that we can understand the strengths and weaknesses of arbitration regimes only if we grapple effectively with the politics of identity formation. Seymour Martin Lipset once argued:

> ...economic development, producing increased income, greater economic security, and widespread higher education, largely determines the form of the "class struggle," by permitting those in the lower strata to develop longer time perspectives and more complex and gradualist views of politics. A belief in secular reformist gradualism can be the ideology of only a relatively well-to-do lower class.[23]

The Costa Rican experience in the nineteenth and early twentieth century turns this argument on its head: Economic development and its beneficial ramifications were shaped by identity-formation processes that, at critical junctures, helped normative schemers privilege reformist gradualism. Moreover, as the politics of the 1940s suggest, the appropriate pace and scope of reformist gradualism can be a point of such intense contention that normative schemers may well put at risk the very reformist gradualism they espouse.

This dilemma is, of course, inherent in reformism itself: If reformers accelerate and expand reformist gradualism, they risk careening out of control; if they decelerate and limit its reach, they risk inertia, perhaps even reversal. Costa Rican elites have met this challenge by engaging in reformist struggles at precisely those junctures that they perceived as moments of danger for the nation's collective identity. For it is at those moments that rivals have been able to deploy the binary opposition between domestic virtues and external threat to craft compelling reasons in favor of alternative reformist strategies. Although the 1948 juncture represents the most dramatic illustration of this dynamic, other more subtle remnants can still be detected. The vast majority of Costa Ricans, for example, not only support their political system but also continue to show defensive anxiety about foreign threats to their system, perceived or real.[24] In addition, the successful "preservation" of their national virtues has led Costa Rica's political leaders to harbor great confidence in the arbitration regime's reformist capacities and in their own democratic competence. In 1988, with the FSLN still in power in neighboring Nicaragua, President Oscar Arias

---

[23] Seymour Martin Lipset, *Political Man: The Social Bases of Politics* (Baltimore, MD: Johns Hopkins University Press, 1981), 45.

[24] The citizens' approbation of the polity in which they operate, for example, was accompanied in the late 1980s by a broad perception of the Nicaraguan regime as a "danger" to Costa Rica (88.5 percent of respondents in a 1987 poll). See Seligson, "Political Culture and Democratization in Latin America," 81–2.

articulated for his nation a seemingly fluid vision of a brilliant future based on an equally brilliant past.

Costa Rican democracy, Arias argued, could look forward to a process of constant perfecting because it was clear, yet again, that the nation possessed the necessary means to pursue this goal; that is, it possessed the capacity for "dialogue." On this view, politics qua civic exchange was bound to facilitate the rediscovery and reaffirmation of the nation's "traditional values" – most notably "freedom and peace." Indeed, Arias declared that these values were an "eternal" treasure "inherited" from generations past.[25] And it was precisely this felicitous combination of political agency and normative legacies that, the logic held, would render the perpetual improvement of democracy more than a possibility – it would make it destiny.[26] Given its "exceptional political culture," Arias concluded, Costa Rica could even hope to transform representative democracy into its participatory variant.[27]

This vision of expanded possibilities is by no means assured. Between 1950 and 1980, the regime amply demonstrated the necessary political-institutional capacity to allocate effective vocality and political-organizational resources to the citizenry by creating agricultural cooperatives, neighborhood associations, and a complex of governmental agencies designed to carry out developmental programs. But the rhetorical strategies used by leaders to legitimate the Revolution of 1948, for example, also delegitimated communism as an "alien" ideology, and set the development of organized labor on a bifurcated path.[28] The state and public sector not only tolerated unionism but allowed it to thrive; as the welfare-entrepreneurial state grew, state and public sector syndicates proliferated. But in the private sector, entrepreneurs and governments alike persistently assumed a hostile stance vis-á-vis syndicates. Partly for this reason, unionization in the private sector remained extremely low, hovering until the late 1990s between 5–7 percent of the labor force.[29] Moreover, the privatization of public services tends to erode labor's organizational strength, which has

---

[25] Oscar Arias, "Palabras del Dr. Oscar Arias, Presidente de la República," in Jorge Mario Salazar, ed., *Democracia y Cultura Política* (San José: Ministerio de Cultura, Universidad de Costa Rica, 1990), 18.

[26] Ibid., 19, 22.

[27] Ibid., 19.

[28] The Revolution dismantled the Confederación de Trabajadores de Costa Rica (CTCR) because of its close ties to the Communist Party during the critical decade of the 1940s. The Revolution, moreover, married the Confederación Costarricense de Trabajadores Rerum Novarum (CCTRN), created under the auspices of the Catholic Church, to the ascendant Liberación Party. See Deborah Yashar, *Demanding Democracy: Reform and Reaction in Costa Rica and Guatemala, 1870's–1950's* (Stanford: Stanford University Press, 1997).

[29] Some of the most prominent syndicates were: the Federación de Empleados Bancarios (FEB), the Asociación de Empleados del Consejo Nacional de la Producción (CNP), the Unión de Empleados del Ministerio de Agricultura, la Unión de Empleados de la Caja Costarricense de Seguro Social (UNDECA), la Asociación de Empleados Públicos (ANEP), and the Federación Nacional de Trabajoderes de la Administración Pública (FENATRAP). In the educational system, teachers formed the Sindicato de Educadores Costarricenses (SEC), while university students organized under the Federación de Estudiantes de la Universidad de Costa Rica (FEUCR). Vladimir de la

been historically tied to the state sector, where in the late 1990s 55 percent of workers were unionized.[30] Labor's diminishing organizational strength, in turn, impinges on the configuration of the political spectrum. Voting for the left, for example, peaked in 1982 at the height of the economic crisis, and by 1986 had fallen to its lowest point since 1970.[31]

The end of the economic crisis, of course, helps account for the left's diminished electoral strength. But the overall electoral picture still shows one disturbing sign – namely, the moderately rising levels of voter abstention that began in the 1990s. This trend is especially noteworthy given the fact that abstention dramatically declined between the early 1950s and 1990.[32] This pattern reversal may well be linked to voter dissatisfaction with the options offered by the major political parties. The emergence of a powerful third contender in the 2002 elections, which culminated in the first second-round vote to take place under the 1949 Constitution, seems to suggest that this may be the case. The prospect of a second round raised concerns among the political class. Would Costa Rican democracy be able to negotiate this unexpected turn? It was. But talk of an accelerated and expanded process of "democratic perfecting" by the regime's visionaries may be premature.

What is indisputable is that organized labor has demonstrated considerable capacity to act effectively within reformist bounds. This is partly so because syndicates, like other key political actors in Costa Rica, tend to eschew fundamental challenges to the socioeconomic system, demanding instead improvements in salary and working conditions. This self-limiting aspect of Costa Rican unions, in fact, is considered a hallmark of the "peaceful coexistence" said to reign between organized labor and the state.[33] Moreover, the effectiveness of organized labor within the strictures of peaceful coexistence is due to the general perception of dissent and argument as part and parcel of normal politics. Normal politics, in turn, is ultimately regarded as a vehicle for compromise.[34]

Cruz, "Características y Rasgos Históricos del Movimiento Sindical en Costa Rica," in Jorge Nowalski, ed., El Sindicalismo Frente al Cambio; Entre la Pasividad y el Protagonismo (San José: Editorial Departamento Ecuménico de Investigaciones, 1997), 26–9.

[30] Nowalski, "El Sindicalismo: Actor Pasivo en el Proceso de Desarrollo de Costa Rica," in Nowalski, ed., *El Sindicalismo Frente al Cambio*, 45–8, 51.

[31] Chalker, "Elections and Democracy," 116.

[32] In the late 1990s, Costa Ricans became concerned about the fact that while voting is compulsory, the turnout rate had declined to 65 percent. Experts believed that this low turnout was due to citizens' "reluctance to register to vote any place other than where they originally registered when they reached the age of eighteen." In response, the Costa Rican government began seriously to consider holding the 2002 elections entirely on the Internet. See Jeri Clausing, "Costa Rica to Try Online Elections," Cybertimes 22 October 1997 (http://www.nytimes.com/library/cyber/week/102297costarica.html).

[33] Between 1943 and 1978, labor's grievances were virtually confined to issues of remuneration and working conditions. See de la Cruz, "Características y Rasgos," 37.

[34] Leslie Anderson, "Mixed Blessings: Peasant Unions in Costa Rica," *LARR* 26, no. 1 (1991): 111, 139, 143.

Conceived in this way, compromise is quite compatible with Costa Rica's exceptionalist identity. The economic crisis of the 1980s and the state's neoliberal response, for example, showed that peasant and public sector unions are prepared to protest the deterioration in social services that result from structural adjustment programs. They are even prepared to take their grievances to court, something they did in the 1980s successfully, often winning wage concessions despite strong executive opposition. And as seen with unprecedented frequency between 1980 and 1988, unions do participate in strikes.[35] At the same time, however, the traditional capacity of unions and other pressure groups to "work with the state" remains undiminished, and helps account for the country's emergence from the economic crisis of the 1980s and the attendant structural adjustment programs with restored output growth, and price stability but no significant increase in inequality.

So when all is said and done, the Costa Rican regime continues to outperform dramatically the other long-lived Latin American democracies, Venezuela and Colombia. The former is plagued by coup attempts, polarized mass mobilization, the evisceration of the political party system, and acute uncertainty. The latter is tethered to a state whose capacity to exercise executive, judicial, and military authority over the national territory is daily called into question by antisystem challengers.

Democracy's Discourse: Elections and Strife

Variations in political and civic culture, as conventionally understood, are in themselves inadequate explanations for developmental divergences between cases and for discontinuities within cases. The "cultural-ideological" climate, Guillermo O'Donnell argues, crucially affects political actors' disposition to experiment politically and institutionally. This argument goes as follows. In the "traditional climate" of Latin American politics, intellectual leaders, both of the right and the left, proved hostile to democratic experiments; and political parties, from one end of the ideological spectrum to the other, were ambiguous in their valorization of political democracy. But as the cultural-ideological climate improved in the 1970s and 1980s with the emergence of "democracy-oriented" discourses, so too did the conditions for democratic development in cases where, as in Robert Dahl's model of successful democratization, antagonistic forces had learned that the cost of zero-sum politics is higher than the cost of mutual tolerance. In such cases of utilitarian enlightenment, the emergence of new "modes of thinking" (discourses) that uphold the virtues of institutionalized pluralism can contribute mightily to the establishment of a new political order.[36]

---

[35] Chalker, "Elections and Democracy," 115.
[36] Guillermo O'Donnell, *Transitions from Authoritarian Rule: Prospects for Democracy*, Section 2 (Baltimore, MD: Johns Hopkins University Press, 1986), 15–16.

And yet, authentic democratic discourses can themselves be the source of destructive conflict when mixed with the identities and practices – including the rhetorical strategies – of a prior game that is incompatible with the democratic ethos. This is so because, as discussed at the beginning of this book, ideologies are ultimately processed and held internally, and as a consequence, actors cannot ascertain that the new democratic discourse embraced by others is indeed a reflection of an inner ideological transformation. Thus democratic discourse itself is often used to organize and deploy rhetorical dichotomies between "true" and "false" advocates of democracy. Recall Jorge Domínguez' observation that in the Latin America of the 1990s, "many still believe[d] that...democracy's worst enemies are the politicians who speak in its name."[37]

A high worth collective identity can provide a bridge of faith that allows competing actors to make the transition from a nondemocratic to a democratic regime of arbitration. In other words, rivals can at least trust one another's genuine commitment to what they collectively deem to be an identity-based imperative. After 1948, for example, Costa Ricans transited to social democracy under the auspices of a revolutionary junta that was not legitimated by democratic procedure, but was nonetheless bound by its public precommitment to "restore" the polity to its "natural" condition. Indeed, although endowed with dictatorial powers, the junta defined itself as a temporary arbiter whose principal task was to identify and build a "modern" but suitable political-institutional structure for the country's "traditional" values. This is why the Constitution of 1949 is the formal expression of a social democratic regime of arbitration grounded in the seemingly veridical narrative of an exceptional national character.

Nicaragua's 1995 reform of the 1987 Constitution, on the other hand, is the formal expression of an electoral regime of arbitration grounded in the seemingly veridical narrative of a fated community. The politics of fate, in fact, help explain why since the historic elections of 1990, subsequent electoral contests have come be seen as calendric markers in an endless cycle of abuse. In the late 1990s, this is how one Nicaraguan political leader made sense of present and future in light of a collective identity that appears immutable:

The two major political blocs are involved in a dirty project. The PLC, led by [President] Alemán, and the FSLN, led by Daniel [Ortega], have sliced up the country and taken their respective shares. They are also determined to keep the small political parties out; and in fact, we are about to be destroyed.

This is the state of affairs because Nicaraguans are warriors, absolutists, and *caudillistas*. This is why in this country every family had six corpses to show at the end of the Civil War [between the FSLN and the Contras] – three who fought on one side and three who fought on the other. These families don't want any more deaths, so they put up with

---

[37] Jorge Domínguez, "Latin America's Crisis of Representation," *Foreign Affairs* 76, no. 1 (January/February 1997): 101.

pacts. As for the pacts' architects, their idea is to get rich in five years because if they don't, the others will anyway.[38]

This vision of self-dealing would-be despots and a betrayed citizenry resigned to its fate is part and parcel of the country's defining narrative. As such, it is deserving of careful study. The experience of democratization teaches that regular, even transparent elections do not necessarily make a robust democracy. Most Latin American democracies, in fact, leave so much to be desired that some scholars have concluded that they ought to be seen as hybrids that display "elements typical of electoral competitive regimes and elements that corrode the components of democratic citizenship."[39] The possibility that these corrosive elements are political-cultural cannot be dismissed.

Nor can we hope that the material determinants of democracy one day will do the work of politics and culture, at least not in our two cases. Their histories strongly endorse the claim that neither democratic nor authoritarian regimes can be directly linked to stages of socioeconomic development or to a particular distribution of socioeconomic resources.[40]

Thus this book has sought to identify the political-cultural dynamics underlying stories of success and failure broadly conceived. These dynamics, in fact, are themselves stories that actors continue to tell, and that affect the strategies of rivals and the transformation and consolidation of regimes. An FSLN hard-liner such as *Comandante* Tomás Borge, for example, was able to transform himself into a soft-liner by putting a twist on an old Manichean strategy of persuasion. The problem he faced was stark: He had vowed that his party would never negotiate with its mortal enemy, the Contras. Before he would consent to such negotiations, he had promised, "the stars in the sky would cease to shine, and the rivers on earth would reverse their course." The negotiations, however, not only took place, but *Comandante* Borge accepted them. This is how he explained the turnaround:

At that moment, I truly believed [that negotiations would never happen] because I was intolerant; because I was possessed by Death; because *I thought I was the owner of the truths of The Malevolent One* [emphasis added].[41]

This sort of reasoning would seem more appropriate for the mid- and late nineteenth century, when the forces of "enlightenment" and "obscurantism" waged battle. And yet, it was in the mid- and late nineteenth century that the

[38] Author's interview with Enrique Sánchez (president of the PLN, as well as the party's congressman from León), Managua, October 1998.
[39] Felipe Aguero and Jeffrey Stark, "Conclusion," in Aguero and Stark, eds., *Fault Lines of Democracy in Post-Transition Latin America* (Coral Gables, FL: North-South Center Press, University of Miami, 1998), 373.
[40] Karen Remmer, *Military Rule in Latin America* (Boston: Unwin Hyman, 1989), 8.
[41] Statement made by *Comandante* Borge in 1996 at the Central American Parliament. See "Ahora Tomás Borge Abjura del Socialismo y Admite Haber Sido Poseído por el Demonio," *Diario Las Américas*, 1 April 1996, 6-A.

Republic successfully regulated the destructive use of this kind of binary opposition. The result was an increasingly national sense of viability, pride, and competence among Nicaraguan elites – a new emerging field of imaginable possibilities that was ultimately undermined by the tenuous nature and exigent expectations of the regime's own regulatory code.

Identity formation, then, does not proceed along a straight line, just as the passions and the interests do not live in segregation. The discourses of democracy and its rivals do not necessarily repel each other; rather, they interact in the hands of actors. Historiography and myth are not distinctive constructs; the one borrows from the other as rhetorical strategies are crafted and employed. For all these reasons, in fact, hybrid regimes abound in the world.

Are we forever caught in the complexities of these hybrids? Moments of discontinuity in our two cases have shown us that while political-cultural change is not easy, it can actually occur in a relatively brief span of time. Still, some will say that giving political culture as much weight as I have is tantamount to imparting despair among those too deeply immersed in polarizing systems of normative scheming. Central to this book, however, is the argument that enhanced agency and power can be attained through political-cultural strategies, tactics, and techniques. After all, it was agency and power derived in precisely this way that led Costa Ricans to put at peril their virtuous cycle, and brought Nicaraguans so close to breaking their vicious alternative.

Indeed, these two cases suggest that as political actors we begin to seize our transformative potential when we first grasp the link between institutions and political culture. The cases further suggest that grasping that link is a difficult challenge because it calls on us to reflect, and to reflect not so much on how we understand the world but on how we arrived at that understanding. Perhaps this is why to assert that Rome was not built in a day is more than a plea for patience; it is also a recognition that even the most awe-inspiring architectonic expression of power and wealth stands as proof that what we make of time depends greatly on how we read the marks that time has left on us.

Index